Vancouver & Victoria For Dummies®, 1st Edition

Cheat Sheet

Downtown Vancouver Transit

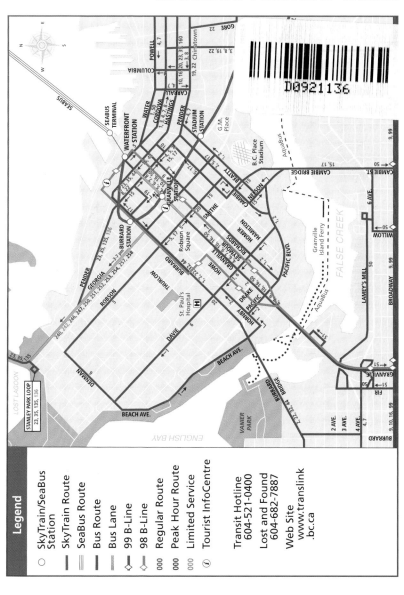

D0921136

Legend

- ○ SkyTrain/SeaBus Station
- SkyTrain Route
- SeaBus Route
- Bus Route
- Bus Lane
- ◇ 99 B-Line
- ◇ 98 B-Line
- 000 Regular Route
- 000 Peak Hour Route
- 000 Limited Service
- ⓘ Tourist InfoCentre

Transit Hotline
604-521-0400

Lost and Found
604-682-7887

Web Site
www.translink
.bc.ca

For Dummies: Bestselling Book Series for Beginners

Vancouver & Victoria For Dummies, 1st Edition

Cheat Sheet

Downtown Victoria Parking

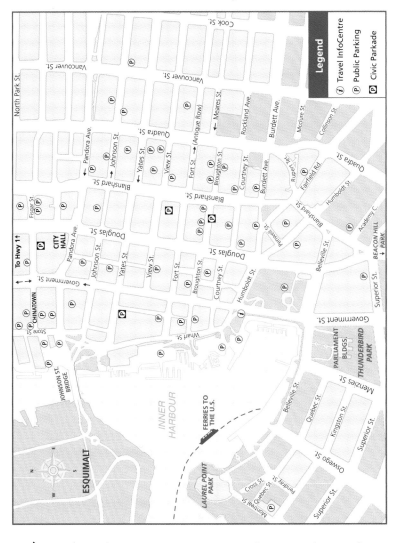

Legend
- ℹ Travel InfoCentre
- Ⓟ Public Parking
- 🄿 Civic Parkade

For Dummies: Bestselling Book Series for Beginners

Vancouver & Victoria

FOR

DUMMIES®

1ST EDITION

by Paul Karr

Hungry Minds™

Best-Selling Books • Digital Downloads • e-Books • Answer Networks
e-Newsletters • Branded Web Sites • e-Learning

New York, NY ◆ Cleveland, OH ◆ Indianapolis, IN

Vancouver & Victoria For Dummies® 1st Edition™

Published by:
Hungry Minds, Inc.
909 Third Avenue
New York, NY 10022
www.hungryminds.com
www.dummies.com

Library of Congress Control Number: 2001091993

ISBN: 0-7645-5383-6

ISSN: 1534-9187

Printed in the United States of America

10 9 8 7 6 5 4 3 2 1

1B/QS/QY/QR/IN

Distributed in the United States by Hungry Minds, Inc.

Distributed by CDG Books Canada Inc. for Canada; by Transworld Publishers Limited in the United Kingdom; by IDG Norge Books for Norway; by IDG Sweden Books for Sweden; by IDG Books Australia Publishing Corporation Pty. Ltd. for Australia and New Zealand; by TransQuest Publishers Pte Ltd. for Singapore, Malaysia, Thailand, Indonesia, and Hong Kong; by Gotop Information Inc. for Taiwan; by ICG Muse, Inc. for Japan; by Intersoft for South Africa; by Eyrolles for France; by International Thomson Publishing for Germany, Austria and Switzerland; by Distribuidora Cuspide for Argentina; by LR International for Brazil; by Galileo Libros for Chile; by Ediciones ZETA S.C.R. Ltda. for Peru; by WS Computer Publishing Corporation, Inc., for the Philippines; by Contemporanea de Ediciones for Venezuela; by Express Computer Distributors for the Caribbean and West Indies; by Micronesia Media Distributor, Inc. for Micronesia; by Chips Computadoras S.A. de C.V. for Mexico; by Editorial Norma de Panama S.A. for Panama; by American Bookshops for Finland.

For general information on Hungry Minds' products and services please contact our Customer Care department; within the U.S. at 800-762-2974, outside the U.S. at 317-572-3993 or fax 317-572-4002.

For sales inquiries and resellers information, including discounts, premium and bulk quantity sales and foreign language translations please contact our Customer Care department at 800-434-3422, fax 317-572-4002 or write to Hungry Minds, Inc., Attn: Customer Care department, 10475 Crosspoint Boulevard, Indianapolis, IN 46256.

For information on licensing foreign or domestic rights, please contact our Sub-Rights Customer Care department at 212-884-5000.

For information on using Hungry Minds' products and services in the classroom or for ordering examination copies, please contact our Educational Sales department at 800-434-2086 or fax 317-572-4005.

Please contact our Public Relations department at 212-884-5174 for press review copies or 212-884-5000 for author interviews and other publicity information or fax 212-884-5400.

For authorization to photocopy items for corporate, personal, or educational use, please contact Copyright Clearance Center, 222 Rosewood Drive, Danvers, MA 01923, or fax 978-750-4470.

Hungry Minds is a trademark of Hungry Minds, Inc.

About the Author

Paul Karr (atomev@aol.com) is a prize-winning journalist and the author of more than a dozen travel books. While making a career of writing about people and places, he has divided his time among the U.S., Canada, and Europe, but still maintains that British Columbia is one of the most wonderful and powerful places he's seen on Earth to date; he vows to continue returning time and again. His other interests include screenwriting, songwriting, hiking, and golf.

Martha Coombs, who assisted in the research for this book, is a singer, writer, cook, and translator. An expert in obscure '70s and '80s music trivia, she says her favorite thing about Vancouver and Victoria is their natural beauty, which recalls her roots in Maine and Sweden.

Author's Acknowledgments

First, I owe a large debt of thanks to Martha Coombs, an all-around wonderful person, who assisted in the research for this book.

Kind thanks also to everyone who pitched in, but especially to those mentioned here. Aaron Naiman shared his insights into local culture and some very kind hospitality. Asifa Lalji and Laura Serena of Tourism Vancouver and Heather Leary of Victoria Tourism, among others in those fine organizations, patiently answered many questions and supplied useful information at every turn. Malcolm Andrews and Benoit Simoneau of VIA Rail in Montréal were enormously helpful with travel arrangements and information. Mike Ablitt, Moni Murray, and Dwight Elliott helped introduce the wonders of British Columbia at various stages.

Finally, this book would not have happened without the support and vision of Suzanne Jannetta and Alexis Lipsitz, and the extremely fine editing of Lisa Torrance, all at Hungry Minds.

Publisher's Acknowledgments

We're proud of this book; please send us your comments through our Online Registration Form located at www.dummies.com.

Some of the people who helped bring this book to market include the following:

Editorial

Editors: Allyson Grove, Lisa Torrance

Copy Editor: Corey Dalton

Cartographer: John Decamillis

Editorial Manager: Jennifer Ehrlich

Editorial Assistant: Jennifer Young

Senior Photo Editor: Richard Fox

Assistant Photo Editor: Michael Ross

Front Cover Photo: The Stock Market, © D. Trask

Back Cover Photo: Accent Alaska, © Jim Corwin

Production

Project Coordinator: Nancee Reeves

Layout and Graphics: Amy Adrian, LeAndra Johnson, Julie Trippetti

Proofreaders: Laura Albert, Andy Hollandbeck, Dwight Ramsey, Marianne Santy, TECHBOOKS Production Services

Indexer: TECHBOOKS Production Services

General and Administrative

Hungry Minds, Inc.: John Kilcullen, CEO; Bill Barry, President and COO; John Ball, Executive VP, Operations & Administration; John Harris, CFO

Hungry Minds Consumer Reference Group

Business: Kathleen Nebenhaus, Vice President and Publisher; Kevin Thornton, Acquisitions Manager

Cooking/Gardening: Jennifer Feldman, Associate Vice President and Publisher; Anne Ficklen, Executive Editor; Kristi Hart, Managing Editor

Education/Reference: Diane Graves Steele, Vice President and Publisher

Lifestyles: Kathleen Nebenhaus, Vice President and Publisher; Tracy Boggier, Managing Editor

Pets: Dominique De Vito, Associate Vice President and Publisher; Tracy Boggier, Managing Editor

Travel: Michael Spring, Vice President and Publisher; Brice Gosnell, Publishing Director; Suzanne Jannetta, Editorial Director

Hungry Minds Consumer Editorial Services: Kathleen Nebenhaus, Vice President and Publisher; Kristin A. Cocks, Editorial Director; Cindy Kitchel, Editorial Director

Hungry Minds Consumer Production: Debbie Stailey, Production Director

◆

The publisher would like to give special thanks to Patrick J. McGovern, without whom this book would not have been possible.

◆

Contents at a Glance

Cartoons at a Glance

By Rich Tennant

"Yes sir, our backcountry orientation programs are held at the Footblister Visitor Center, the Lostwallet Ranger Station, or the Centreadacompass Information Pavilion."

page 7

"The closest hotel room I could get you to the Inner Harbour for that amount of money is in Seattle."

page 41

WHALE WATCHING IN VANCOUVER

"Would you like to watch the whale a little longer, sir, or should I ask him to leave?"

page 303

"We saw that girl from MTV, ran into Jason Priestley and toured locations from the X-Files. I'm not sure why, but I feel like just going back to the hotel and watching TV."

page 81

RALPH AND ELMA VISIT THUNDERBIRD PARK, VICTORIA, BC

"...which reminds me— is your cousin's family still planning to visit us this summer?"

page 221

Cartoon Information:
Fax: 978-546-7747
E-Mail: richtennant@the5thwave.com
World Wide Web: www.the5thwave.com

Maps at a Glance

Table of Contents

Introduction

● ●

*V*ancouver, city of many personalities.

To some visitors, Vancouver is Seattle North or (as locals are fond of calling it) Lotus Land — a decadent hippie hangout where you can laze on the beaches, munch organic breads, and just generally bliss out in a no-hassle existence. This view is partly true. To others, it's an international city with top-class hotels, restaurants, shopping, and sightseeing, or a spicy taste of the Far East without ever leaving the mainland. And in pockets these views holds true. Or maybe it's a Honolulu or a Hong Kong — the sort of place where you can scale enormous mountains in the morning, sail a boat in the afternoon, and lie your head down amidst spectacular scenery at night. No argument there.

Victoria comes with a different reputation. Here you find better weather than Vancouver, great English beer, double-decker buses, and gardens. In addition, the city hosts a thriving arts community, an Asian community, and a profusion of Native Canadian art and craftwork.

To some extent the two cities can be whatever you want them to be. Vancouver is big enough to offer something — a neighborhood, a brewpub, a sushi bar, a beach — for everyone's taste. And although a lot smaller, Victoria provides tremendous variety that's easily accessible. History buffs are in heaven here, but so are beer nuts and antiques collectors.

I wrote this book because I enjoy these two cities more than just about any others I know — and I do know them well from repeated visits over the years. They're both extremely welcoming, refreshingly un-stuffy, and vibrant with a mixture of immigrant cultures. Plus, the climate is just beautiful during most summers. And — maybe this is really why I'm so fond of them — you are never out of sight of water and woods here. Nature is still a looming presence in these cities, whether you're staring at the Lions (mountains to the north), puffing up the Grouse Grind (the most difficult trail up Grouse Mountain), or just sitting in a ferry heading across Victoria's Outer Harbour.

So kick back, set those sails for western Canada, and let's make a little deal. I promise to be as handy a guide as I can be if you promise to keep your eyes open for the wonderful and the unexpected — and to smile when you see it.

About This Book

Vancouver and Victoria For Dummies, 1st Edition, is a reference guide, not a comprehensive, this-is-everything-you-can-do guidebook weighing a hundred pounds in your suitcase. Although the chapters are organized in a logical sequence, I have written each chapter so that you can read it separately. That means you can read as many or as few of these chapters as you like, according to what you feel you need to know, and just skip the rest. You can read the book back to front, front to back, inside out — it doesn't matter. It's built for you.

I have even separated Vancouver and Victoria into different sections. If you're only going to hit one of these two cities instead of both of them, voilà! Just dip into the section that applies. To figure out exactly where to start reading, just use the index in the back of the book — or look through the table of contents preceding this introduction.

Although you don't need to read every page of *Vancouver and Victoria For Dummies,* you will find some pretty interesting stuff tucked within its pages. I cover everything you want to know: good eats, cool bars, hot hotels, stunning sights, decadent day-trips, and much more. I packed a lot in so you won't need to buy a pile of other guidebooks to make sure you have the inside skinny you need.

Conventions Used in This Book

Vancouver and Victoria For Dummies uses a few conventions so that you can get the information you need quickly and easily.

All prices in this book are shown in both Canadian and U.S. dollars. I use "C" and "US" to let you know exactly which currency I'm quoting.

In the hotel section, the prices I list are the *rack rates* (the official rates published by the hotel in question) for one night for a double room. You may find significant differences in this rate depending on time of year, demand, discounts accepted, and other factors. Parking charges are also calculated per night.

In the restaurant section, the prices I list reflect the range of main course prices on each restaurant's dinner menu. Drinks, tips, and appetizers are not included in this calculation. If the restaurant doesn't serve dinner, the price range applies to main courses at lunch, brunch, or breakfast, as appropriate to that particular eatery.

Dollar sign symbols ($) precede the listings of each hotel and restaurant. These symbols give you an approximate idea of the price range for a night's stay or a meal at a given place — at hotels, one night's rack rate; at restaurants, the price of one dinner including drinks and tip. For exact price ranges, see the tables in Chapters 10 and 17 for hotels and Chapters 11 and 18 for restaurants.

Please keep in mind that travel information is subject to change at any time, and that this fact is especially true of prices. I suggest that you write or call ahead for confirmations when making your travel plans.

I also use credit card abbreviations in the hotel and dining listings that correspond to the following:

- AE   American Express
- CB   Carte Blanche
- DC   Diner's Club
- DISC   Discover
- JCB   Japan Credit Bureau
- MC   MasterCard
- V   Visa

I divide the hotels into two categories — my personal favorites and those that don't quite make my preferred list but still get my hearty seal of approval. Don't be shy about considering these "runner up" hotels if you can't get a room at one of my favorites or if your preferences differ from mine — the amenities that the runner ups offer and the services that each provides make all these accommodations good choices to consider as you determine where to rest your head at night.

The Canadians use the term "First Nations" to refer to the various indigenous peoples that U.S. residents call "Native Americans." To avoid any confusion, I use the term "Native Canadians" in this book — but expect to see First Nations when in Vancouver. Canadians also use the correct term "Inuit" to designate those far northern people that some in the United States call "Eskimos."

Foolish Assumptions

I work with a couple assumptions in this book; stop me if this isn't you, okay?

- One. You've never been to Vancouver or Victoria before — or you've been here briefly, and have wanted to get back ever since. My thoughts? They are two of the most wonderful places on the continent. I want to help you enjoy 'em.

- Two. You don't have a lot of time to spend planning this trip, and you're looking to me to do all the legwork so that you don't have to. You trust that I won't lead you astray. I am a professional traveler (it's harder than it looks!) and I promise to do my best to be a good guide.

✔ Three. You don't want to wade through a ton of information and brain-numbing history. Neither do I. Maybe next time.

✔ Four. You've had a frustrating experience using other guidebooks. Some were too boring, some were inaccurate, some weren't opinionated enough, and some were just plain useless.

Well, I can give you a gold-minted promise that you won't find this book useless, boring, or unopinionated. The text is as accurate as possible (although a few things may change between the time I write this and the time you buy the book).

How This Book Is Organized

Vancouver and Victoria For Dummies is both a trip-planning guide and a reference guide to all the key information you need to know before ever setting foot here. The basic idea is to prepare you well enough that you won't end up stumbling around town, nose buried in a map, looking like an obvious tourist, and too busy getting oriented to notice anything around you.

Here's how the book is organized:

Part I: Getting Started

This section introduces you to Vancouver and Victoria, giving you a very basic overview and helping you start to think about when to visit — I discuss the weather and some fun annual events, for instance. I give you some guidance on making a realistic budget for your trip, and point out ways to cut unnecessary costs. I also discuss how to carry money around the city, including the various merits of traveler's checks, cash, credit cards, and ATM cards. Finally I discuss the various resources you may need if you're a traveler with special considerations such as a family, a senior citizen, a physically challenged traveler, or a gay or lesbian traveler.

Part II: Ironing Out the Details

In this section, I help you plan the trip and buy tickets. These chapters cover the pros and cons of booking a trip through a travel agent; whether using package tour companies is a good idea or not; how to get the best airfare; and other potential ways of getting here from the United States and elsewhere. I show you some insider's tricks for getting the best rate on your hotel room, tell you what to expect for your money, discuss hotel booking Web sites, and discuss all those other nagging details you need to attend to — passports, paperwork, how to pack for Vancouver, how to book a car rental in advance (and whether you should or not), currency exchange, health and travel insurance, and which events and restaurants advise making advance (for you, that's pre-trip) reservations.

Part III: Exploring Vancouver

This section focuses on Vancouver, first orienting you to the city and then diving in to what makes it unique. This is where you find my exclusive listing of the city's top hotels, restaurants, and attractions. I tell you all about the various guided tours of the city as well as the shopping districts, bars, music halls, dance clubs, and performing arts venues. I provide a couple sample itineraries for people with special tastes and interests in case you don't have time to draw up your own plan. Finally, I lay out some fun day-trip options that get you out of the city to experience the wonderful islands, mountains, and beaches that make living in the Vancouver area such a pleasure.

Part IV: Exploring Victoria

Just like Vancouver, Victoria has its own special feeling. These chapters introduce you to this unique city and its offerings. I give you my top picks for where to stay and dine, and tell you all you need to know about Victoria's top sights. I describe guided tours to the city and sur-rounding area, as well as the best shopping streets, pubs, dance clubs, and Shakespearean theater performances. Finally, I offer a sample itin-erary for those who want to discover the city's English roots.

Part V: The Part of Tens

Here's where I get to have some real fun. This last section is my chance to share a little bit more about the cities I love, using a Top Ten format. I tell you what you can't possibly come to Vancouver and Victoria with-out bringing (often with my tongue planted firmly in my cheek).

Icons Used in This Book

To help save you time — something no one has enough of — the *For Dummies* series has created a series of icons that serve as road signs to a quick read of the book. Being a visually oriented person, I really like icons; you can think of them as the "Dummies Guide to Dummies Guides." Here are the ones I sprinkle liberally throughout this book:

Yes, it's true: kids can have a great time in Vancouver and Victoria without simultaneously driving their parents crazy. This icon alerts you to attractions, restaurants, and hotels that are especially geared to young ones.

This icon simply alerts you to the inside skinny on something I've learned — where to stand in line, when to grab a bite, or how to bribe a ticket-writer (no, just kidding).

Bargains are easy to find in a big Canadian city, and Vancouver is no exception; in Victoria, it takes a little more work, but you can still shave expenses in places without compromising the experience of visiting. I use this icon to highlight some of my tricks and tips for saving a buck in these two cities.

Sad to say it, but even in ultra-polite Vancouver and Victoria, a few folks out there are going to try to separate you from your money. I use this icon to stop you in your tracks and take notice of something — a scam, a bad deal, something — where you need to look before you leap.

Finally, some facets of visiting Vancouver and Victoria should be experienced simply because they convey what is unique — whatever that is — about this part of the world. I use this icon to helpfully point the way to foods, museums, and other only-in-this-corner-of-British-Columbia stuff.

Where to Go from Here?

Now you're primed. You're as ready to go to Vancouver and Victoria as you're ever going to be. So: What do you do next?

Dive into this book — tonight. Read a few chapters, whatever strikes your fancy, to start getting the flavor (only they spell it "flavour;" might as well get used to it now) of these two cities. I suggest reading the hotel and restaurant sections if you want to start learning about what people eat, and the kinds of places where you may be staying.

That should get you sufficiently excited to take a minute at lunch tomorrow to contact a travel agent, package operator, or online ticket broker to price your tickets — maybe even buy them. When you get home tomorrow night, or the next, you may actually start practice-packing a suitcase. You may notice what's too bulky, and think about leaving it. You may notice what's missing, and make a note to shop for it.

See? You're already halfway there.

Part I
Getting Started

The 5th Wave   By Rich Tennant

"Yes sir, our backcountry orientation programs are held at the Footblister Visitor Center, the Lostwallet Ranger Station, or the Cantreadacompass Information Pavilion."

In this part . . .

Planning a trip to Vancouver and Victoria may seem daunting, especially if you've never done it before, but let me assure you that it's not. Both cities are easy to navigate and friendly, so it won't take long for you to figure out which way is which. Of course, the more you discover about these destinations, the more confident you'll feel about your plans. This part of the book tells you about the top attractions and events, addresses, budgeting and general costs, and provides info for travelers with special needs.

Chapter 1

Discovering the Best of Vancouver and Victoria

. . . .

In This Chapter

▶ Delighting in Vancouver's ethnic mosaic, natural attributes, and cultural offerings

▶ Becoming civilized: Victoria's British heritage and gardens

▶ Brushing up on the area's history and lingo

. . . .

*T*here's a buzz in the air in British Columbia lately, a buzz that's not just from the shade-grown organic coffee you can get anywhere in downtown Vancouver.

No, the populations of Vancouver and Victoria keep growing because they are, quite simply, two fabulous cities in which to live and work. Everyone from expatriate Brits to stressed-out Toronto lawyers to Japanese students, Chinese businessmen, and even Hollywood types decide Vancouver is *the place* to raise a family. Victoria, too, is experiencing its own renaissance as longtime Vancouver residents relocate there in search of that perfect combination of small town and big city that Vancouver once was.

So don't mistake these cousins for each other. Vancouver and Victoria are two quite different cities: different from each other, and different from just about anyplace else in North America. I won't tell you everything to do in these destinations just yet — that's what the rest of this book is for. But this chapter provides a quick taste of each city.

For those of you who want a jumpstart on your "don't-miss" list, let me tell you what to pencil in at the top right now. In Vancouver, visit the spacious, scenic grounds of the **University of British Columbia** and world-class **Museum of Anthropology** (see Chapter 12); check out the shops and markets of **Granville Island,** reached if possible by mini-ferry (see Chapter 13); walk through **Chinatown** (see Chapter 12); and hike or take a cable-car ride up **Grouse Mountain** (see Chapter 12). In Victoria, visit the waterfront for fish and chips (see Chapter 18), take tea in **The Empress** hotel (see Chapter 17), and sample locally brewed beer in one of several brewpubs (see Chapter 21). Catch a play (see Chapter 21) and make sure to drive out to **Butchart Gardens** (see Chapter 19).

Exploring the Mosaic

Where the United States describes itself as a melting pot, Canada likes to describe itself as a mosaic — a place where all the different immigrant cultures retain unique identities while, at the same time, forming a cohesive nation. That idea's nowhere more apparent than in Vancouver.

Indeed, a short drive through town does give you the sense that more is here than meets the eye — that this is a place where many different kinds of cultures have decided to settle. Painfully yuppie in certain parts, the city possesses surprising diversity in others, everything from the obvious **Chinatown** district — where you can sample Asian cuisine rivaling that of San Francisco — to less obvious **Japanese** and **Indian** enclaves. For dining and attractions in Vancouver's ethnic neighborhoods, see Chapters 11 and 12, respectively.

Finding the Nature of the Business

First and foremost, you come to Vancouver for city amenities amidst a breathtaking setting. Name another major city in the world, after all, surrounded by sparkling ocean beaches and rocks, huge mountains constantly creating their own weather, and green, green parks; there are very few.

You undoubtedly want to experience the city's natural treasures by land, water, or even air. Hiking **Stanley Park** within sight of the city skyscrapers, ascending a gondola to the top of **Grouse Mountain** that overlooks the city, walking along **Wreck Beach,** or cruising the harbor while tasting the salt air on your tongue, you begin to understand why everyone here seems so relaxed. (For more on these attractions, see Chapter 12.)

Roaming Green Acres

You also soon notice an abundance of "green" shops and lifestyles in Vancouver. Local residents are among the continent's most health-conscious and socially active people, downing fresh-squeezed juice at **Capers** or organic coffee at **Joe's Café** or vegetarian spring rolls at **The Naam,** and then heading out on cycles to work or to the beach. (See Chapter 11 for more on these places.) Recycling is all but mandatory. Birkenstocks only appear to be.

Vancouver history 101

Long a series of small native salmon fishing settlements — including one in present-day Stanley Park — the Greater Vancouver area was but a quiet (if beautiful) backwater for thousands of years. That all changed late in the 18th century, however, when Spanish and English navigators looking for water routes between Asia and Europe stumbled across the network of tidal inlets, rivers, islands, and sounds.

After a bit of sparring between the two nations, Captain George Vancouver staked a British claim in 1792. Lumbering, fishing, trapping, and trading interest slowly began to build in the Empire, and the Hudson's Bay Company soon established a post here. The discovery of gold in the backcountry to the north of Vancouver brought hundreds to the area in several waves during the middle of the century, solidifying Vancouver's future as a port of call.

The gold veins soon played out, but people still came; when Canadian Pacific Railroad surveyors showed up to lay out a terminal station for a new trans-continental railroad line, things would never be the same again. The trains began rolling in from the East Coast in 1887, and Vancouver — after a disastrous citywide fire nearly stopped the entire project in its tracks — grew exponentially.

Going Native

The huge, ornately carved totem pole in Stanley Park is symbolic of the peace that Vancouver has made with its past: They call native residents "First Nation" citizens, and they are treated with respect. As a result, this is one of the best places on the continent to experience Native American culture (and buy native crafts, if that's what you're looking for). You can find native arts and crafts at **Hill's Native Art** (see Chapter 13) and food at **Liliget Feast House** (see Chapter 11).

Feeding Culture Vultures

Vancouver's cultural scene is going great guns. The musical offerings run the gamut from ponytailed, strumming folkies to serious jazz players to alternative rockers to a top-flight orchestra, **Vancouver Symphony Orchestra** (see Chapter 14). And the **Vancouver Art Gallery,** along with other galleries and museums, provides an intriguing visual-arts scene (see Chapter 12). You also find nightlife aplenty in several different areas including a thriving — even surging — **coffeehouse and dining scene** (see Chapter 11).

Victoria history 101

Victoria, once a small *Salish* (native) fishing and farming village, was established as a British city in 1843 after one James Douglas, a representative of the Hudson Bay Company, landed in the harbor, looked around, began using words like "Eden," and sent word back to London. The Hudson's Bay Company went on to build a fur-trading post and fort here, and the British Navy — realizing at once the strategic advantages of the island port over Vancouver's harbor — also soon moored its own fleet of ships here. It was only a matter of time before gold-panners and fishermen arrived, stayed, and banded together to formally charter a city.

Victoria was named capital of the province of British Columbia in 1866 and remains the province's top tourist draw today.

Learning Modern English

In comparison to Vancouver, Victoria, located at the southern tip of Vancouver Island — a huge island sitting just offshore the Canadian mainland, not far from Vancouver but an island nevertheless — is much smaller than Vancouver, more intimate, and probably more civil as well. That's because Victoria is intensely British, right down to the rose gardens and fish-and-chip shops. (It was named, after all, for the Queen Mother.) You come to Victoria to see boats, sip tea, drink ale, admire gardens, and perhaps do some leisurely shopping. And you must try the tea: You can take afternoon or high tea in many restaurants and tearooms. I recommend **The Empress** hotel's tea lounge (see Chapter 17).

Walking About

Victoria is heavier on historical sights — a terrific little museum, plus a number of old houses, hotels, and maritime attractions — than high-rise-dominated Vancouver, and as a bonus the city is refreshingly compact and walkable. From **The Empress** hotel to the scenic **Dallas Beach Road** or other sights is only a few minutes' stroll. Despite a population of more than half a million, the city does not have traffic jams. You can even step from downtown right onto a boat that will whisk you to Vancouver or Washington state — the city is closer to the U.S. mainland than to that of Canada. (See Chapter 19 for more on touring Victoria.)

Strolling through Gardens

Victoria is world-renowned for its **Butchart Gardens.** Carved out of an abandoned quarry, the gardens represent the dream of a single person, Jenny Butchart, who sought to reclaim a wasteland. She did it, and today thousands of visitors marvel at the great variety of flowers here and their artful arrangements. These aren't even the only gardens in town — this is, after all, the land of gardeners. You can view numerous other gardens, parks, and conservatories, such as the nearby **Victoria Butterfly Gardens** and **The Empress Hotel and Rose Gardens.** (See Chapter 19 for more on Victoria's gardens.)

Tasting the Suds

Quite simply, Vancouver and Victoria are at the epicenter of the North American beer universe. Forget what you may have heard about a micro-brewing renaissance centered around California, Oregon, Maine, or anywhere else. This is where the return of craft brewing first took root on the continent, and the best examples of the form are still made here at places such as **Spinnakers** and **Swans** in Victoria (see Chapter 21) and **Yaletown Brewing Company** in Vancouver (see Chapter 14).

Speaking the lingo

Despite the close proximity of the United States — the border is less than an hour's drive away — Vancouver and Victoria are closer, culturally speaking, to London than they are to Seattle. As a result, you find more than your share of fish-'n'-chip shops, afternoon high teas, umbrellas, golf courses . . . and polite expressions that you may not quite understand. Herewith, a (very) short primer on what the locals mean when they say something you've never quite heard before:

boot	trunk of a car
chip	French fry
cheque	check
chippie	fish-and-fries shop
dear	expensive
lorry	truck
loonie	one-dollar Canadian coin
lovely	good
parkade	parking lot
twoonie	two-dollar Canadian coin

Tucking in Early

The only truly critical word that you ever hear about Vancouver and Victoria is that, well, they're a bit . . . how shall I put this? . . . *dull.* Local youths and artsy types try hard to create a "scene" — they're the ones hanging around looking disaffected in the streets after nine o'clock; in fact, they're the *only* ones out at night after nine o'clock — but the truth is that most locals are in bed by then.

Face it. Most of the nightlife was created for tourists. Ah, well, what price paradise?

Chapter 2

Deciding When to Go

In This Chapter

▶ Facing the rain

▶ Finding out about the seasons

▶ Flipping through Vancouver's and Victoria's event calendars

*V*ancouver and Victoria are fine any time of year — this part of the world never gets very hot or cold — but, given a choice, I'd come in late summer or fall. Why? Oceanside Vancouver has a maritime climate, characterized by beautiful summers and falls, and cool, damp winters with strong storms blowing in off the Pacific and springs of variable, though relatively mild, weather.

Summer is by far the busiest season for Vancouver and Victoria tourism. Book accommodations (see Chapters 10 for Vancouver accommodations, Chapter 17 for Victoria accommodations) as far in advance in possible if you plan to visit during July, August, or September.

Rain, Rain Go Away

No travel plans to Vancouver and Victoria can begin without discussing the weather. Yes, it will probably rain while you're here, but you probably won't get too wet — the rain tends to be a (sometimes steady) drizzle, rarely a downpour.

More interestingly, however, *where* you stay can make a big difference in the amount of precipitation that you see. Facing the open Strait of Georgia, Vancouver has little protection from storms moving west to east, and so tends to get the coastal rains that have also made Seattle famous.

But Victoria, set on the easternmost spit of land on Vancouver Island, is a little different. A high range of coastal mountains to the east guards the city from the rains. This *rain shadow* effect means that a bit less rain falls here each year than on its neighbor, Vancouver, across the strait.

The mainland area just northwest of Vancouver — beginning at Gibsons Inlet — is so well guarded by the same sorts of mountains that the region calls itself "The Sunshine Coast." That name's a bit euphemistic, perhaps, but meteorological records do bear out the boast: This coastal area receives less rain than the city.

 In fall and winter, rain becomes sleet and snow at higher altitudes. And as you drive up Route 99 toward Whistler, you gradually ascend into honest-to-goodness high mountains. That means that a rainy or even merely overcast day in Vancouver can become a bad snowstorm, without warning, by the time that you reach the ski resorts. (Why do you think they're located there?) To keep accidents to a minimum, the provincial government sometimes closes the Sea-to-Sky highway when heavy snows are possible.

The Secret of the Seasons

Vancouver is green and beautiful anytime of year, but certain times are better than others. Most locals do their heavy-duty enjoyment of the outdoors in summer and fall, when the weather is mild and sunshine actually makes regular appearances.

This section takes a look at the pros and cons of each season. For information on average temperature and rainfall, see Table 2-1.

Spring

The season's pros include:

- ✔ Crowds are still thin.
- ✔ Vancouver's and, especially, Victoria's gardens are in full bloom.
- ✔ Days are long with up to 16 hours of sunlight.

But, spring can have its drawbacks, such as:

- ✔ The weather is still a crapshoot — mighty fine one year and rain, rain, rain the next.
- ✔ The temperature is not warm enough yet to sunbathe or skinny-dip.

Summer

Summer's a great time to visit because:

- ✔ This is Vancouver's sunniest season, and that means hiking trails aren't muddy. Some days you can actually leave your umbrella in the hotel room.
- ✔ The beach water is as close to warm and swimmable as it's ever going to get.
- ✔ Many attractions stay open longer.

Keep the following in mind, however:

- ✔ An army of tourists descends on the area.
- ✔ As this is high season, air fares to Vancouver shoot sky high.

Fall

Some reasons to plan a fall trip to the area include:

- ✔ The weather remains wonderful; a Vancouver fall can be brighter and drier than the summer.
- ✔ Salmon run in the rivers.
- ✔ The leaves turn in Stanley and Pacific Spirit Parks.
- ✔ The number of tourists thins noticeably.
- ✔ Airfares drop from their summertime highs.

But, remember these pitfalls to the fall season:

- ✔ Conventions, business trade shows, and international conferences kick into high gear come September, so finding a hotel room — at a nice price — can be surprisingly difficult.
- ✔ Daylight hours become shorter.

Winter

Vancouver and Victoria can be a winter wonderland for the following reasons:

- ✔ The tourists disappear, eliminating lines at museums and other popular attractions.
- ✔ Airlines and tour operators often offer exceptionally good deals on flights and packages.
- ✔ Hotel prices drop; expect considerable discounts.
- ✔ The skiing at Whistler and Grouse is exceptional; snow is guaranteed.

However, winter does have its downsides:

✔ Rain falls anytime from November through February, sometimes drizzling for weeks on end.

✔ Though the temperature stays above freezing, the gray skies bring bone-chilling dampness; bring a thick sweater.

✔ Daylight hours are short.

Table 2-1	Vancouver's temperature and precipitation	
Month	**Daily mean temperature**	**Total monthly precipitation (inches)**
January	38.0	5.9
February	41.2	4.9
March	44.6	4.3
April	39.6	3.0
May	46.2	2.4
June	62.4	1.8
July	66.4	1.4
August	66.6	1.5
September	60.6	2.5
October	42.0	4.5
November	48.0	6.7
December	39.0	7.0

Vancouver's Calendar of Events

Vancouver's calendar becomes most crowded during the pleasant summer. Spring and fall also bring various events and festivals to the city, while winter is trade show and exhibition time.

January

The **Annual Polar Bear Swim** brings out hardy locals who don't mind freezing their extremities off as they welcome the new year in English Bay. Definitely a spectator sport. January 1. For information, call ☎ 604-665-3424.

The big, colorful **Chinese New Year Festival** at BC Place Stadium (777 Pacific Boulevard) culminates in the annual dragon parade followed by fireworks. Late January or early February. For information, call ☎ **604-415-6322** or visit www.bcchinese.com/newyear.

March

The **International Wine Festival,** at the Vancouver Convention and Exhibition Center (200–999 Canada Place), is North America's biggest wine-tasting soirée, with fine snacks to match. Late March or early April. Call ☎ **604-873-3311** or visit www.winefest.bc.sympatico.ca for information.

June

Colorful teams compete in races right on the water in the **Alcan Dragon Boat Festival,** a unique and eye-catching celebration of the city's vital Chinese community. Takes place at the Plaza of Nations on False Creek (750 Pacific Boulevard) during the third week in June. For information, call ☎ **604-688-2382.**

One of best jazz festivals going, the popular **du Maurier International Jazz Festival Vancouver** features some of the world's top jazz acts performing on a combination of open-air (often free) stages and indoor venues. Late June or early July. Call ☎ **604-872-5200** or visit www.jazzvancouver.com for information.

July

Ceremonial gunshots kick off **Canada Day,** Canada's national holiday, celebrated in several locations around the city. July 1. Call ☎ **604-666-8477** for information.

One of North America's best folk festivals, the **Vancouver Folk Music Festival** takes over a variety of venues around town — especially pretty Jericho Beach Park. Special musical programs and face-painting booths help occupy children. Second or third weekend in July. For information, call ☎ **604-602-9798** or ☎ **604-280-4444** or visit www.thefestival.bc.ca.

Summer's climax is the citywide marine **Sea Festival,** which culminates in the two-week **Symphony of Fire,** a nightly fireworks display over English Bay; special cruises and tour boats provide waterside views. Late July through early August. Call ☎ **604-738-4304** for information.

August

Air Canada Championship, Canada's only stop on the PGA tour, brings professional golfers to Northview Country Club in Surrey. Canadian Mike Weir thrilled the home crowd with a victory in 1999. Late August through early September. For information, call ☎ **604-647-3909** or visit www.aircanadachampionship.com.

An annual Vancouver tradition since 1910, **Fair of the Century** features livestock shows, craft exhibits, and carnival rides, and takes place at the Pacific National Exhibition at Hastings Park. Mid-August through early September. For information, call ☎ **604-253-2511** or visit www.pne.bc.ca.

September

Vancouver International Film Festival, the last pearl in Canada's string of three fall film festivals (try saying *that* five times fast), takes place at dozens of theaters around the city over a two-week period, drawing more than 100,000 connoisseurs. Late September through early October. For information, call ☎ **604-685-0260.**

Victoria's Calendar of Events

Victoria is also festival-happy on a year-round basis, celebrating everything from beer to Shakespeare. Summer is busiest, when *buskers* (street performers) fill the parks and squares as event after event marches through the downtown area, but fall also brings a number of harvest and fishing festivals to surrounding Vancouver Island communities.

February

Astonishingly, enough flowers bloom at this time of year to count them during **Flower Count,** a citywide festival. Late February. For information, call ☎ **250-383-7191.**

April

Despite the silly name, **TerrifVic Dixieland Jazz Party** brings top jazz acts to Victoria for four straight days at venues all over the city. Second week in April. For information, ☎ **250-953-2011.**

May

A 10-day series of events highlighting Victoria's marine heritage, **Harbour Festival,** held in the downtown district, culminates in a weekend of yacht races. Last week of May. Call ☎ **250-953-2033** for information.

July

All day long for more than a week, folkies and other musical acts take over the harbor for the much-appreciated **Folkfest.** The main venues are Inner Harbour and Market Square. Late June or early July. For information, call ☎ **250-388-5322.**

August

First People's Festival, a celebration of Canada's native cultures at the Royal British Columbia Museum, includes sacred dances, totem pole carving, food, and exhibits. Second week in August. Call ☎ **250-387-2134** for information.

September

Modeled after Edinburgh's summer festival, the **Fringe Festival** — a mix of avant-garde comedy, music, dance, and performance art, among other things — is rapidly becoming a Canadian institution. Early September. For information, call ☎ **250-383-2663.** (Another very good version of this festival also happens in Vancouver during this month. For information call ☎ **604-257-0350.**)

November

Don't miss the **Great Canadian Beer Festival,** an all-under-one-roof beer tasting of the province's best microbrewery. This event is held at the Victoria Conference Centre during the second week in November. For information, call ☎ **250-952-0360.**

Chapter 3

Money Matters

In This Chapter

▶ Preparing your budget

▶ Uncovering hidden costs

▶ Cutting corners to save bucks

▶ Deciding on a form of payment

▶ Dealing with emergencies

*V*ancouver and Victoria have so many great parks, restaurants, and other attractions that not immersing yourself in the experience is foolish; on the other hand, the illusory pleasures of a good exchange rate can turn sour when your credit card bill shows up later, indulgences — and Canadian taxes — spelled out in black and white. Believe me, I've seen many a tourist come to these cities vowing to hold to a budget, only to overspend on totem poles, horse-drawn tours, native art, gifts of smoked salmon, teacups, tartans, and all the rest.

But don't despair. After you have a strategy, you can have a blast without sinking your bottom line.

 I give the prices in this guide in both Canadian and U.S. dollars, with all U.S. dollar amounts more than $5 rounded to the nearest dollar. The good news is that, thanks to a very favorable exchange rate, most everything costs less in Vancouver and Victoria than in a comparable U.S. city.

 At press time, C$1 was roughly equal to US$.67. To quickly figure the U.S. equivalent of what you're paying, figure two-thirds of the Canadian dollar: In other words, a C$30 meal really costs US$20, a C$4.50 beer costs US$3, and that C$2,000 totem pole . . . well, never mind.

Planning a Budget

A well-constructed budget is like a tricky jigsaw puzzle and making it work can be as satisfying as dropping that 1,000th piece into place. By running through several expense categories, this section helps you begin to pull your budget together. For the next step in the process, turn to the chapters mentioned later for exact prices, and use the budget worksheet at the end of this book.

Lodging

Without question, lodging will be your biggest expense, but the amount really depends on where you choose to stay. In the downtown or West End of Vancouver, or the Victoria waterfront, figure at least C$150 (US$101) a night in high summer season — more (C$300–$500 [US$201–$335]) for a swankier place, less (but not much less) for a bland chain, family-style hotel. Bed-and-breakfasts may cost less, as little as C$75 (US$50), or more, especially in Victoria where you can easily drop C$300 (US$201) a night on a really nice B&B — but at least one of those Bs stands for "breakfast." See Chapters 10 and 17 for exact hotel prices in each city.

Transportation

You don't need a rental car in Vancouver or Victoria, but getting one is a good idea if you want to explore the parks, gardens, and beaches on the outskirts. A rental car costs about C$30 to C$50 (US$20–$34) per day — higher on summer weekends, but watch for deals and promotions — plus about C$12 to C$15 (US$8–$10) a day for insurance, which you can hopefully waive thanks to your own coverage. (See Chapter 8 for more about renting a car.)

Gas in Canada is expensive — not as expensive as in Europe, maybe, but still pretty costly. At this writing, Canadian newspapers and television are abuzz with the news that gas prices have *dropped* to the equivalent of C$3.20 a gallon! Even when converted to U.S. dollars, that's a hefty US$2.25 a gallon. Clearly, any sort of extended driving tour — even in the city, where the miles eat up gas much more quickly — will add significantly to your budget.

Other transportation costs to keep in mind include:

- ✔ **Ferry transport.** If you plan on visiting islands in your car, you'll have to pay to transport the car on the ferry in addition to the fee for yourself and others travelling with you. Transport for a car varies, according to ferry and distance, from C$6 to C$25 (US$4–$17) per one-way hop from within British Columbia, more from the United States.

- ✔ **Parking fees.** Metered parking in downtown Vancouver can be difficult to find. When this happens, you'll want to use one of the downtown's many garages, which charge between C$2.50 to C$3.00 (US$1.68–$2) per hour or approximately C$12 to C$15 (US$8–$10) a day. If you park early, you may receive a discount for the whole day.

What things cost in Vancouver and Victoria

Taxi from the airport to downtown Vancouver	C$25 (US$17)
Taxi from ferry in Swartz Bay to downtown Victoria	C$45 (US$30)
SeaBus to Lonsdale Quay	C$2.50 (US$1.68)
Local telephone call	C$0.25 (US$0.17)
Double room at Ogden Point Bed & Breakfast, Vancouver	C$160–C$180 (US$107–US$121)
Double room at Granville Island Hotel and Marina, Vancouver	C$240 (US$161)
Double room at Stratchona Hotel, Victoria	C$104 CDN (US$70)
Double room at Abigail's Hotel, Victoria	C$260 CDN (US$174)
Dinner for one (without alcohol) at Gyoza King, Vancouver	C$8.00 (US$5)
Dinner for one (without alcohol) at Spinnakers Brewpub, Victoria	C$15 (US$10)
Dinner for one (without alcohol) at CinCin, Vancouver	C$35 (US$23)
Pint of microbrewed beer	C$3.65–C$6 (US$2.46–US$4)
Double cappuccino	C$2.95–C$3.50 (US$1.98–US$2.35)
Adult admission to the Vancouver Art Gallery	C$10 (US$7)
Adult admission to the Royal British Columbia Museum, Victoria	C$10.65 (US$7)
Movie ticket	C$6.00–C$9.75 (US$4–US$7)

My advice on transportation? Hoof it around central Vancouver or use the good public transit system or taxicabs to get from point to point. The cost per day for a transit pass or one downtown cab ride is a bargain at C$7 (US$5). If you do rent a car, restrict its usage to longer trips and stay in a hotel and/or B&B that provides complimentary guest parking.

Restaurants

When eating out, you can save or splurge — the choice is really up to you. I usually recommend dining out at fine restaurants for lunch, then eating at more family-oriented places for dinner, to cut costs. That way, you can splurge on lunch — which ranges from C$5 (US$3.35) per person in a Chinatown eatery to no more than C$20 (US$13) per person at the very finest restaurants — then trim the fat at dinner, which costs from C$5 to C$10 (US$3.35–$7) per person at a chain restaurant, C$10 to C$20 (US$7–$13) per person at most local restaurants, and C$25 to C$100 (US$17–$66) per person at the *really* exclusive places. See Chapters 11 and 18 for exact meal prices in each city.

Attractions

For most major attractions, the cost is somewhere around C$24 (US$16) per couple, but prices vary wildly and can escalate to as much as C$50 (US$34) for a couple to visit, say, Butchart Gardens in Victoria. Or, prices can drop to as little as C$10 to C$15 (US$7–$10) for two adults to visit an attraction, such as a small museum. Always figure about half as much for teens, and attractions are normally free for children under the age of 6. Figure two to three of these attractions per day in your calculations. See Chapters 12 and 19 for exact prices in each city.

Shopping

Souvenirs cost anywhere from two bucks in Chinatown to several thousand dollars for a piece of Native Canadian art; shops on Robson Street and similar areas are definitely going to put a dent in your wallet. Still, I'd personally figure no more than C$100 per day (and that's a hefty amount), but you'll have to determine the final amount yourself.

Nightlife

The cost of stepping out to a bar or club varies according to how much you drink — and where. Clubs rarely charge covers — well, the ones that think they're important do — and drink prices vary from the C$2 (US$1.34) well drink at happy hour to the C$6 (US$4.02) microbrew to the C$15 (US$10) watered-down drink at a gentleman's club. For the culturally minded, theater and opera tickets start at C$10 (US$7) per person and swiftly climb to as much as C$75 (US$50) per person for a major, say, orchestral performance. Usually, though, you can enjoy a performance for C$10 to C$25 (US$7–$17) per person. For more guidance on nightlife prices, see Chapters 14 and 21.

Keeping a Lid on Hidden Expenses

No matter how diligently you plan, an item-by-item budget can take you only so far, because last-minute temptations will test your willpower. More importantly, any number of "invisible" expenditures and nasty surprises can spell disaster if you're traveling on a tight budget. This section includes a few below-the-radar expenses to keep in mind.

Taking taxes into account

Canada's high quality of life doesn't come cheaply: You pay two, and often three, taxes on everything you buy in Vancouver and Victoria.

First, a 7% *General Sales Tax* (known as the GST) applies to every purchase except liquor, to which a special 10% tax is added. Next, another 7% *Provincial Sales Tax* (PST) is applied. Every hotel tacks on an additional 10% lodging tax (which is composed of an 8% provincial hotel tax and a 2% tourism tax.)

The good news is that the GST is refundable for non-Canadian residents if it adds up to more than C$14 in tax (or C$200 in hotel bills). Of course, you have to fill out some impressive government paperwork to get it — and part with your original receipts forever when you send them. The necessary forms are available at border customs offices or, more conveniently, at some hotels and merchants.

If you want the GST refund while in Canada, you can bring your hotel receipts, two forms of photo identification, and a return plane ticket to a company called **Maple Leaf Tax Refunds** (☎ 800-993-4313 or 604-893-8478) for an instant refund. But be aware that this private company keeps 18% of each refund for its services. Maple Leaf has offices in Vancouver in the lower lobby of Hotel Vancouver (☎ **604-893-8478**) and in a kiosk in Pacific Centre Mall (☎ **604-685-4538**). **National Tax Refund Services** (☎ **250-389-2228**) offers a similar service in Victoria from its office in Eaton Centre. To get a refund here, which is also subject to a fee, visitors need to bring in all purchased items, credit card, picture ID showing home address, and a departure ticket for proof of exiting Canada. Or to receive your refund for next to nothing, you can write to the **Visitor Rebate Program,** Summerside Tax Centre, Revenue Canada, Summerside, PE, C1N 6C6, Canada.

Gauging gratuities

The average tip for most service providers, such as waiters and cab drivers, is 15%, rising to 20% for particularly good service. A 10 to 15% tip is sufficient if you just drink at a bar. Bellhops get C$1 or C$2 a bag, hotel housekeepers should receive at least C$1 per person per day, and valet parking and coat-check attendants expect C$1 to C$2 for their services.

If your server was really good enough to merit a 40% tip, perhaps you ought to think about skipping the meal next time and just chatting with him or her. Remember to check your restaurant bill carefully before laying down a tip on the table. Some pricier establishments may have included the cost of service as an automatic 15% tip in the bill, although this practice isn't as widespread in Vancouver as it is in many other tourist towns.

Tips for Cutting Costs

So you want to save a few dollars, but not skimp on your vacation fun? No problem. What follows are cost-saving tips that you can use for any vacation, as well as some specific tips for Vancouver and Victoria:

- ✔ **Go in the off-season.** If you can travel at nonpeak times (November through May, for example), you find hotel prices that are as much as half the cost of peak months.

- ✔ **Travel midweek.** If you can travel on a Tuesday, Wednesday, or Thursday, you may find cheaper flights to your destination. When you inquire about airfares, ask if you can get a cheaper rate by flying on a different day.

- ✔ **Try a package tour.** For many destinations, you can book airfare, hotel, ground transportation, and even some sightseeing just by making one call to a travel agent or packager, for a lot less than if you tried to put the trip together yourself. (See Chapter 5 for more on package tours.)

- ✔ **Reserve a room with a kitchen.** Doing your own cooking and dishes may not be your idea of a vacation, but you save a lot of money by not eating in restaurants three times a day. Even if you make only breakfast and pack an occasional bag lunch, you save in the long run. And you'll never be shocked by a hefty room service bill.

- ✔ **Always ask for discount rates.** Membership in AAA, frequent flyer plans, trade unions, AARP, or other groups may qualify you for savings on car rentals, plane tickets, hotel rooms, even meals. Ask about everything; you may be pleasantly surprised.

- ✔ **Ask if your kids can stay in the room with you.** A room with two double beds usually doesn't cost any more than one with a queen-size bed. And many hotels won't charge you the additional person rate if the additional person is pint-sized and related to you. Even if you have to pay $10 or $15 extra for a rollaway bed, you'll save hundreds by not taking two rooms.

✔ **Think twice about upgrading your rental car.** Because of the tremendous volume of package-tour traffic that comes through Vancouver, some of Vancouver's central-city car rental companies deal almost exclusively in minivans. Sure, you may end up getting a van for the price of a midsize, but do you really want the hassle of driving and parking it, not to mention the increased cost of gas that poor-gas-mileage vehicle entails?

✔ **Take island ferries.** Ferries are by far the most scenic — and sometimes most efficient — way to get around the area, and to get from Vancouver to Victoria they're the *only* way (save a mighty expensive commuter flight). But they do cost money, because the positions of the docks (10 miles north and south of Vancouver, 15 miles north of Victoria) almost demand that you rent a car to drive to and from the docks.

✔ **Put away that U.S. money.** Resist the temptation to whip out your wallet full of U.S. cash for small purchases when you don't have the time to hit an ATM or change bureau. That US$20 bill you just used to buy a C$20 Canadian souvenir is actually worth C$30 — you just overpaid by 50%. Any club, bar, shop, or hotel that takes U.S. money is not doing you a favor — they're taking advantage of you.

✔ **Avoid exchange bureaus.** I cannot stress enough that change bureaus are no longer a necessary evil; if you have an ATM card, you can get Canadian cash at your bank's rates, guaranteed to be much much better than any currency exchange bureau's. The only time that you need a change office is when:

- You can't find an ATM (unlikely in downtown Vancouver or Victoria)
- You have lost your ATM card, or it suddenly won't work.

In either case, be prepared to pay an exchange bureau a commission or fee that will deduct perhaps 10% from the value of what you get back in return.

Paying Up

How do you pay for that 10-foot totem pole? Today's travelers have several options from cold cash to virtual money — virtual, that is, until the bill arrives. This section helps you decide which form of currency is right for you.

Going with greenbacks

If your preference is for good, old-fashioned hard currency, you won't have any trouble exchanging your money to Canadian dollars. Tourists from all over the world visit this corner of British Columbia, and every major bank offers some sort of currency exchange services. **Royal Bank** ☎ **604-665-0855** operates exchange desks at Vancouver International Airport from 5:30 a.m. to 9:30 p.m. daily.

In addition, several private exchange companies operate in downtown Vancouver and in Victoria. See "Fast Facts: Vancouver" and "Fast Facts: Victoria" in the Appendix for the addresses of some of them.

Before you decide to exchange your money, however, consider using an ATM machine, which almost always provides a better exchange rate. For more on this, see my warning in the previous section and the information on ATMs in the next section.

Opting for ATMs

These days, most cities have 24-hour ATMs linked to a national network that almost always includes your bank at home. **Cirrus** (☎ **800-424-7787**; Internet: www.mastercard.com/atm) and **Plus** (☎ **800-843-7587**; Internet: www.visa.com/atms) are the two most popular networks; check the back of your ATM card to see which network your bank belongs to. (A third Canadian card network known as **Interac** is universally accepted in these cities, but unfortunately U.S. banks don't offer it as an option.) The 800 numbers and Web sites give you specific locations of ATMs where you can withdraw money while on vacation. You can withdraw only as much cash as you need every couple of days, which eliminates the insecurity (and the pickpocketing threat) of carrying around a wad of cash.

All major banks in Vancouver and Victoria maintain ATMs that dole out Canadian currency and automatically deduct the converted amount — at favorable rates — from your home bank. You do pay fees for some of these transactions, depending on the bank and your card. But take heart: Canadian teller machines are much more forgiving with regard to user fees than is common in the United States, and you're likely to pay a fee only at your own bank for going outside of its network.

The major banks in Vancouver and Victoria, and the bank card systems they honor, are as follows:

- ✔ Bank of Montreal: Cirrus
- ✔ Bank of Nova Scotia (Scotia Bank): Plus
- ✔ Canada Trust: Cirrus and Plus
- ✔ CIBC: Plus
- ✔ Hong Kong Bank of Canada: Cirrus
- ✔ Royal Bank of Canada: Cirrus and Plus
- ✔ Toronto Dominion (TD): Plus

For exact locations of ATMs, see "Fast Facts: Vancouver" and "Fast Facts: Victoria" in the Appendix.

 Popping up around Vancouver and Victoria are several ATM machines not affiliated with any bank, and these charge the highest fees in exchange for the convenience of their locations in supermarkets, pharmacies, corner stores, and the like. Fees can be $2.50 or more for a single withdrawal at these little monsters. Avoid them if at all possible.

Dealing with debit cards

Many U.S. banks now issue a type of ATM card called a debit card that has a Visa or MasterCard logo and can be used exactly like a credit card. These cards are really convenient, but should be used with extreme caution in the event of theft. Unlike with a credit card, the amount is automatically deducted from your checking account as soon as you make the purchase or withdraw cash. These cards, which do not incur interest charges, are popular in Canada.

Choosing credit cards

Credit cards are invaluable when traveling — a safe way to carry money and a convenient record of all your travel expenses when you arrive home. Plus, you can get cash advances from your credit card at any bank, and you don't even need to go to a teller; you can get a cash advance at the ATM if you know your PIN number. If you've forgotten your PIN number or didn't even know you had one, call the phone number on the back of your credit card and ask the bank to send it to you. It usually takes 5 to 7 business days, though some banks will do it over the phone if you tell them your mother's maiden name or some other security clearance.

 Before you get that cash advance, keep in mind that interest rates for cash advances are often significantly higher than rates for credit card purchases. More importantly, you start paying interest on the advance the moment you receive the cash. On an airline-affiliated credit card, a cash advance does not earn frequent flyer miles.

Trying traveler's checks

Traveler's checks are something of an anachronism from the days when people wrote personal checks instead of going to an ATM. Because traveler's checks could be replaced if lost or stolen, they were a sound alternative to filling your wallet with cash at the beginning of a trip. Some people, maybe out of habit, still prefer to use them. As long as vendors still accept traveler's checks — and they do just about everywhere in Vancouver and Victoria — these people have no need to change their habits.

To guarantee a fair rate of exchange, convert your U.S. dollars into traveler's checks in Canadian dollars before you leave the United States. You can make this exchange at most U.S. banks and travel clubs such as AAA. Be aware, though, that you may have to pay a commission fee if you use a bank where you do not hold an account. If this is the case, you may want to rethink using an ATM card while in Canada, because the card may give you a more favorable rate of exchange.

If for whatever reason you choose to bring traveler's checks in U.S. dollars to Canada, you can find places to spend them. Retailers in Vancouver and Victoria are accustomed to cashing U.S. traveler's checks in U.S. dollars and will happily calculate the exchange rate — although the rate may not be very good.

If you prefer the security of traveler's checks, you can get them at almost any bank. **American Express** offers checks in denominations of C$10, C$20, C$50, C$100, and C$1,000. You pay a service charge ranging from 1 to 4%, although AAA members can obtain checks without a fee at most AAA offices. You can also get American Express traveler's checks over the phone by calling ☎ **800-221-7282;** American Express gold and platinum cardholders who call this number are exempt from the 1% fee. For the locations of the American Express and AAA offices in Vancouver and Victoria, see the Appendix.

Coping with Emergencies

Almost every credit card company has an emergency toll-free-number that you can call if your wallet or purse gets stolen. The company may be able to wire you a cash advance from your credit card immediately; in many places, the company can get you an emergency credit card within a day or two. The issuing bank's toll-free-number is usually on the back of the credit card, but that won't help you much if the card was stolen. Write down the number on the back of your card before you leave, and keep it in a safe place just in case. The Canadian toll-free, emergency numbers for the major credit cards are: **American Express** ☎ **800-268-9824,** **Diners Club** ☎ **800-363-3333,** **MasterCard** ☎ **800-826-2181,** and **Visa** ☎ **800-336-8472.**

If you opt to carry traveler's checks, be sure to keep a record of their serial numbers so that you can handle just such an emergency.

Odds are that if your wallet is gone, you've seen the last of it, and the police aren't likely to recover it for you. However, after you realize that it's gone and you cancel your credit cards, call to inform the police. You may need the police report number for credit card or insurance purposes later.

Chapter 4

Tips for Travelers with Special Needs

- -

In This Chapter

▶ Traveling with the family

▶ Making the most of being gray

▶ Moving beyond disabilities

▶ Finding gay and lesbian resources

- -

*A*mazingly welcoming, Vancouver and Victoria are prime vacation spots for just about anyone — and that includes families with kids, older folks, disabled travelers, and gay or lesbian travelers.

Advice for Families

Safe, clean, and filled with kids, dogs, festivals, and open spaces, Vancouver is extremely family-friendly. Victoria has an older population, so it's not as geared toward youngsters, but you still can bring the kids to this smaller city with little trouble.

What follows are my tips for getting the most out of your family trip:

✔ **Involve the kids in planning.** Before you travel, let the kids help you plan the trip — send away for brochures that you can view together or click onto the Web sites of family-friendly destinations you're likely to visit.

You can also surf the Web sites of **Monday Magazine** (www.monday.com) or **Tourism Victoria** (www.tourismvictoria.com) for information on special children's events and exhibits.

If you come in May, one happening you should not miss is the big **Vancouver International Children's Festival** (☎ 604-280-4444) in Vanier Park, an event with storytellers, mimes, clowns, music, and other events geared to kids of all ages — even teens.

✔ **Locate kid-friendly attractions.** Throughout this book, I use the kid-friendly icon to designate hotels (see Chapters 10 and 17), restaurants (see Chapters 11 and 18), and attractions (see Chapters 12 and 19) that are particularly welcoming to youngsters.

For more recommentations, you can contact **kid friendly!** (☎ 604-625-6063), a non-profit organization that reviews local businesses for their family friendliness and accredits those offering useful programs for kids and families. Or get a hold of *Just Kidding!,* a reference guide to area happenings for kids, available in most local bookstores for C$13.95 (US$9).

✔ **Contact a travel agent.** If you don't have much time to plan, turn to **Infinity Travel Concepts** (☎ 800-661-7176 or 888-986-2262; Internet: www.trvlconcepts.com), which creates specialized family-oriented vacations in the Vancouver area.

✔ **Rent kid-friendly wheels.** If you're bringing a large family, know that several of Vancouver's downtown car rental agencies stock a good supply of passenger vans. The spacious vehicles are convenient for accommodating families and all their gear. Try **National** (☎ 604-609-7150), centrally located at 1130 West Georgia Street, for starters.

✔ **Pack kid-friendly diversions.** Keep children entertained while traveling by carrying travel games, books, or puzzles.

✔ **Pick up a kid-oriented guide.** On arrival in Vancouver, the very first thing you should do is drop by the Vancouver **TouristInfo Centre,** 200 Burrard Street (☎ 604-683-2000; Internet: www.tourism-vancouver.org), and stock up on reading material. Be sure to pick up a free copy of the city's kid-oriented guide, *Good Contacts and Useful Information Kids' Guide to Vancouver,* published by *Where Vancouver Magazine* (☎ 604-331-8771), which includes coupons, information, and a local map. Just ask for the Kids' Guide at the visitor's center, and they'll know what you mean.

You may adore your kiddies, but sometimes you want to leave them behind — under careful, trustworthy supervision, of course. Several baby-sitting and child-care services, accredited by the tourist office, are located in Vancouver's downtown business area. **Kids Included** (☎ 604-803-3337), one of them, provides childcare for children aged 3 to 12. For more recommended agencies, see "Fast Facts: Vancouver" and "Fast Facts: Victoria," in the Appendix.

Advice for Seniors

People over the age of 60 are traveling more than ever before. And why not? Being a senior citizen entitles you to some terrific travel bargains. If you're not a member of **AARP** (American Association of Retired

Persons), 601 E St. NW, Washington, DC 20049 (☎ **800-424-3410** or 202-434-AARP; Internet: www.aarp.org), do yourself a favor and join. You'll get discounts on car rentals and hotels.

Mature Outlook, P.O. Box 9390, Des Moines, IA 50322 (☎ **800-336-6330**), is a similar organization, offering discounts on car rentals and hotel stays at many Holiday Inns, Howard Johnson's, and Best Westerns. The $19.95 annual membership fee also gets you $200 in Sears coupons and a bi-monthly magazine. Membership is open to all Sears customers 18 and over, but the organization's primary focus is on the 50-and-over market.

In addition, most of the major domestic airlines, including American, United, Continental, US Airways, and TWA offer discount programs for senior travelers, so be sure to ask whenever you book a flight. In most cities, people over the age of 60 get reduced admission at theaters, museums, and other attractions, and they can often get discount fares on public transportation. Carrying identification with proof of age can pay off in all these situations.

The Mature Traveler, a monthly newsletter on senior citizen travel is a valuable resource. It is available by subscription ($30 a year); for a free sample send a postcard with your name and address to GEM Publishing Group, Box 50400, Reno, NV 89513. Or, you can also send an e-mail request to maturetrav@aol.com. GEM also publishes *The Book of Deals,* a collection of more than 1,000 senior discounts on airlines, lodging, tours, and attractions around the country; it's available for $9.95 by calling ☎ **800-460-6676.**

Another helpful publication is *101 Tips for the Mature Traveler,* available from **Grand Circle Travel,** 347 Congress St., Suite 3A, Boston, MA 02210 (☎ **800-221-2610;** Internet: www.gct.com). Grand Circle Travel is one of the literally hundreds of travel agencies that specialize in vacations for seniors. But beware: Many of these tours are of the tour-bus variety, with free trips thrown in for those who organize groups of 20 travelers or more.

Seniors seeking more independent travel should consult a regular travel agent. **SAGA International Holidays,** 222 Berkeley St., Boston, MA 02116 (☎ **800-343-0273**), offers inclusive tours and cruises for those 50 and older.

To get the skinny on the latest Vancouver seniors' activities, consult the **Seniors' Services Directory,** online at www.seniorsservingseniors.bc.ca, a kind of community resource handbook listing everything from government and community services to events and gathering places.

Advice for Travelers with Disabilities

A disability shouldn't stop anybody from traveling. More options and resources exist now than ever before.

Worldwide resources

A World of Options, a 658-page book of resources for disabled travelers, covers everything from biking trips to scuba outfitters. It costs $35 and is available from **Mobility International USA,** P.O. Box 10767, Eugene, OR, 97440 (☎ **541-343-1284,** voice and TTY; Internet: www.miusa.org).

Another important resource is **Access-Able Travel Source** (Internet: www.access-able.com), a comprehensive database of travel agents who specialize in disabled travel, as well as a clearinghouse for information about accessible destinations around the world.

Vision-impaired travelers should contact the **American Foundation for the Blind,** 11 Penn Plaza, Suite 300, New York, NY 10001 (☎ **800-232-5463**), for information on traveling with Seeing-Eye dogs.

Many of the major car rental companies now offer hand-controlled cars for disabled drivers. **Avis** can provide such a vehicle at any of its locations in the United States with 48-hour advance notice; **Hertz** requires between 24 and 72 hours of advance reservation at most of its locations. (See the Appendix for the toll-free numbers for these companies.) **Wheelchair Getaways** (☎ **800-536-5518** or 606-873-4973; Internet: www.wheelchair-getaways.com) rents specialized vans with wheelchair lifts and other features for the disabled. Their closest office to Vancouver is in Seattle, Washington.

Travelers with disabilities may also want to consider joining a tour that caters specifically to them. One of the best operators is **Flying Wheels Travel,** P.O. Box 382, Owatonna, MN 55060 (☎ **800-535-6790;** Fax: 507-451-1685). It offers various escorted tours and cruises, as well as private tours in minivans with lifts. Another good company is **FEDCAP Rehabilitation Services,** 211 W. 14th St., New York, NY 10011 (☎ **212-727-4200;** Fax: 212-727-4373).

Vancouver resources and information

Vancouver itself has the reputation of being one of the most specially-abled cities in the world. Everything from its public transit and airport counters to crosswalks and public bathrooms has been designed with disabled travelers in mind.

For those who want someone else to worry about their travel plans, **Pacific Coach Lines** (☎ **604-662-7575**) runs handicapped-accessible bus trips between Vancouver and Victoria.

At the airport

Vancouver International Airport, your most likely arrival point, is very handicapped-accessible. The ticket and service counters have amplified hand-sets; flight departure and arrival information boards are mounted low and printed with high-contrast typefaces to facilitate easy reading; the airport maintains visual paging monitors and public address systems displayed in written form; and the information kiosks are equipped with closed-captioned decoders. There are tactile guidance maps of the terminal building for the visually impaired, and fully accessible public telephones and services for the deaf or hard of hearing. If you need to know more, call the airport's operations department at ☎ **604-207-7070.**

A special service, the **Airporter** (☎ **800-668-3141** or 604-273-8436), arranges transit from the city airport for disabled visitors. Call to arrange a ride, which costs C$10 (US$7). Handicapped-accessible taxis and a handicapped-accessible bus shuttle are available at the arrivals terminal; call ☎ **604-521-0400** for schedule information.

At your hotel

Hotels are visited and rated on their senior- and handicapped-accessibility by a group called **Access Canada** (☎ **604-731-2197**), and then grouped into four categories:

✔ A1: Suitable for active seniors and people with minor disabilities.

✔ A2: Suitable for seniors and people with moderate disabilities.

✔ A3: Suitable for people with advanced ability, hearing, mobility, and vision disabilities, and independent wheelchair users.

✔ A4: Suitable for people with severe disabilities.

You can call the organization to check the handicapped accessibility of certain Vancouver and Victoria hotels.

In transit

In Vancouver, most local buses are now handicapped-accessible. Handicapped-accessible buses and bus stops are identified by a wheelchair symbol. Or look for the letter "L" next to a route on a bus timetable.

The **SkyTrains** are also wheelchair-accessible, with help buttons and elevators at all but those stations in the Granville neighborhood (where you find a free shuttle to the next stop). Specially-abled travelers should board the trains through the doors with wheelchair symbols.

BC Ferries are fully equipped with elevators, bathrooms, and decks that can accommodate handicapped travelers; be sure to ask the ticket seller for a parking spot near the elevator. SeaBus terminals and boats are also wheelchair accessible.

For a handicapped-accessible taxi in Vancouver, contact **Vancouver Taxi** (☎ 604-255-5111 or 604-871-1111). To rent a lift-equipped van, call the **BC Paraplegic Association** (☎ 604-324-3611).

Even walking or wheeling around Vancouver is a snap: Thousands of sidewalk ramps exist for wheelchairs, and the "Walk/Don't Walk" cross-walk signs downtown beep or chirp when they change.

Victoria resources and information

Compared to Vancouver, Victoria has fewer amenities for handicapped visitors. Many city buses now include wheelchair lifts or other design considerations to allow disabled access. Call ☎ 205-382-6161 for transit information. Handy **DART** (☎ 205-727-7811) vans are also available for those who can't find an accessible bus. The downtown area also has beeping crosswalk signs.

Other Canadian resources

The following groups, agencies, and offices provide information for disabled travelers to the area:

- ✔ **BC Paraplegic Association** (☎ 604-324-3611)
- ✔ **Canadian National Institute for the Blind** (☎ 604-431-2121)
- ✔ **Coalition of People with Disabilities** (☎ 604-875-0188, TTY 604-875-8835; Fax: 604-875-9227)
- ✔ **Office for Disability Issues** (☎ 205-387-3813, TTY 205-387-3555; Fax: 205-387-3114)
- ✔ **UBC Disability Resource Centre** (☎ 604-822-5844, TTY 604-822-9049)
- ✔ **We're Accessible Quarterly**, a newsletter (☎ 604-576-5075)
- ✔ **Western Institute for the Deaf and Hard of Hearing** (☎ 604-736-7391, TTY 604-736-2527)

Handicapped-accessible attractions

Many Vancouver and Victoria attractions are handicapped-accessible. The following list is just a small sampling; call ☎ 604-576-5075 (in Vancouver) or visit any tourism office in Victoria for fuller details, listings, and information.

✔ You can take a free wheelchair-accessible trolley ride around **Stanley Park.** Call ☎ **604-801-5515** for information.

✔ All **horse-drawn carriage tours** of Stanley Park are wheelchair-accessible. These depart from the Coal Harbour parking lot next to the information booth on Park Drive, east of the Rowing Club.

✔ Grouse Mountain's blue **Skyride** gondola is handicapped-accessible with 24 hours' notice. Call ☎ **604-984-0661** for information.

✔ The provincial parks system's **Disabled Access Pass** gives free camping space to the disabled in parks. For information, call ☎ **205-356-8794.**

✔ The **BC Sport and Fitness Council for the Disabled** (☎ **604-737-3039**) runs a hosts of competitive events and recreational outings, including (but not necessarily limited to) skiing, horseback riding, sailing, sledge hockey, and track and field.

✔ Handicapped-accessible sailing and other outdoor activities are offered by the **Mobility Opportunities Society** (☎ **604-688-6464**).

Advice for Gay and Lesbian Travelers

About as gay-friendly as a North American city can be, Vancouver has an exceptionally tolerant attitude, a concentrated population of activist gays and lesbians, and a network of services, such as bookstores, clubs, and other organizations. Victoria's scene is less developed. Despite its more straight-laced attitude in comparison to Vancouver, however, a tolerant attitude and plenty of resources exist here.

Ground zero for the gay/lesbian scene in Vancouver is probably the stretch of Davie Street that runs between Burrard and Jervis Streets: Cafés, restaurants, and stores with a gay tilt are thick in this territory. A secondary stretch, a bit more upscale, runs along Denman Street from Davie to Robson Streets; this area isn't exclusively gay, but gay travelers certainly feel comfortable here with the many gay-friendly eating, shopping, and beach options. What gay nightlife exists in Victoria is probably centered on **Hush** (☎ **250-385-0566**), a bar at 1325 Government Street.

Gay and lesbian resources

The main nerve center for gay and lesbian activity in Vancouver is, named appropriately enough, **The Centre,** 1170 Bute Street (Internet: www.vanpride.org), in the heart of the West End. The group hosts discussion groups; maintains a library; and runs health, legal, and youth clinics. It also runs the **Prideline** (☎ **604-684-6869**), a free telephone hotline with volunteer operators working nights from 7 to 10 p.m., Monday through Saturday.

In Vancouver, you should make a point of picking up **Xtra West** (☎ 604-684-9696), a free biweekly gay/lesbian newspaper with community news, event listings, and the latest report on the bar scene. You can find it — and other gay and lesbian resources — at **Little Sister's,** 1238 Davie (☎ 604-669-1753), a bookstore that maintains a bulletin board and sells tickets to gay and lesbian events. In Victoria, look for the publication known as the **Pink Pages.**

Gay and lesbian events

Several annual events are worth catching. The **Pride Festival,** hosted by the **Vancouver Pride Society** (☎ 604-687-0955) during the first weekend of each August, is a series of parties, dances, cruises, and other events; a Sunday parade beginning at Denman Street and live concerts in the park beside Sunset Beach cap off the festivities. Happening at almost the same time is the annual **Out on Screen Queer Film and Video Festival** (Internet: www.outonscreen.com), which also takes place at the beginning of August.

Lesbian Week (☎ 604-688-9378 ext. 2149) is a similar, though much smaller, event held around the middle of each November.

Where to eat, stay, and play

Gay bars, clubs, and restaurants are easiest to find on Davie and Denman Streets. Some of the most popular night haunts of the moment include **Numbers** (1098 Davie Street; ☎ 604-685-4077), **Odyssey** (1251 Howe Street; ☎ 604-689-5256), **Denman Station** (860 Denman Street; ☎ 604-669-3448), and the **Royal Hotel** (1025 Granville Street; ☎ 604-685-5535). The **MoonBeans Cafe** (1262 Davie Street; ☎ 604-632-0032) and **Delany's** (1105 Denman Street; ☎ 604-662-3344) are quieter spots with heavily gay clientele. Finally, **Hamburger Mary's** (1202 Davie Street; ☎ 604-687-1293) is a diner popular with straights, gays, and lesbians alike. For more gay-friendly bars, see Chapters 14 and 21.

Most any accommodation in Vancouver is suitably gay-friendly, but those especially friendly include the **Royal Hotel** (1025 Granville Street; ☎ 604-685-5535), the **Colibri Bed and Breakfast** (1101 Thurlow Street; ☎ 604-689-5100), the **Sylvia Hotel** (see Chapter 10 for full details), and the **Nelson House** (977 Broughton Street; ☎ 604-684-9793). In Victoria, try the **Prior House B&B** (see Chapter 17 for full details) or the **Oak Bay Guest House** (1052 Newport; ☎ 250-598-3212).

Part II
Ironing Out the Details

The 5th Wave   By Rich Tennant

"The closest hotel room I could get you to the Inner Harbour for that amount of money is in Seattle."

In this part . . .

Although the more laid-back among you may want to show up in this corner of Canada without any planning, the truth is that a little bit of advance work goes a long way to saving you money and ensuring an enjoyable trip. This part helps you through the stickier details of how to get there and where to stay. I also tackle some of the least exciting (but actually critical) matters — customs, travel insurance, health care, car rentals, activity reservations, and packing — in what I hope is a straightforward enough way to keep your eyes from glazing over.

Chapter 5

Getting to Vancouver and Victoria

In This Chapter

▶ Using a travel agent or buying a packaged tour

▶ Planning the trip on your own

▶ Getting to Vancouver and Victoria by train, ferry, or car

▶ Traveling between the two cities

*I*f the details of trip planning start to bog you down, you may begin to suspect that the *longest* distance between two points is a straight line. You don't have to feel that way. This chapter outlines your options, from hands off to hands on, for flying, driving, or boating to Vancouver and Victoria. Plus, I tell you the best way to travel between the two.

Consulting a Travel Agent: A Good Idea?

A good travel agent is like a good mechanic or good plumber: Hard to find, but invaluable when you locate the right one. The best way to find a good travel agent is the same way that you find a good plumber or mechanic or doctor — word-of-mouth.

To get the most out of your travel agent, do a little homework. Read up on your destination (you've already made a sound decision by buying this book) and pick out some accommodations and attractions that appeal to you. If you have access to the Internet, check prices on the Web yourself (see the section, "Making Your Own Arrangements" later in this chapter for ideas) to get a sense of ballpark figures. Then take your guidebook and Web information to your travel agent and ask him or her to make the arrangements for you. Because travel agents can access more resources than even the most complete travel Web site, they generally can get you better prices than you can get by yourself.

And they can issue your tickets and vouchers right in the agency. In addition, your travel agent can recommend an alternative if he or she can't get you into the hotel of your choice.

Travel agents work on commissions. The good news is that *you* don't pay the commissions — the airlines, accommodations, and tour companies do. The bad news is that unscrupulous travel agents may try to persuade you to book the vacation that nabs them the most money in commissions. Over the past few years, however, some airlines and resorts have begun to limit or eliminate these commissions altogether. The immediate result has been that travel agents don't bother booking certain services unless the customer specifically requests them. Additionally, some travel agents have started charging customers for their services.

Considering Package and Escorted Tours

Say the words *escorted tour* or *package tour* and you may automatically feel as though you're being forced to choose: Your money or your lifestyle. Think again, my friends. Times — and tours — have changed.

An **escorted tour** does, in fact, involve an escort, but that doesn't mean it has to be dull — or even tame. Escorted tours range from cushy bus trips, where you sit back and let the driver worry about the traffic, to adventures that include running Canada's Indian Arm or Lynn River Canyon gorge in a kayak. You do, however, travel with a group, which may be just the thing for you if you're single and want company. In general, your expenses are taken care of after you arrive at your destination, but you still need to cover your airfare.

Which brings me to **package tours.** Unlike escorted tours, these generally "package" costs rather than people. Some tour companies bundle every aspect of your trip, including tours to various sights. However, most tour companies deal just with selected aspects of your trip, allowing you to get good deals by combining airfare and hotel costs, for example. A package tends to leave you a lot of leeway, while saving you a lot of money.

How do you find these deals? Well, I suggest some strategies in the next two sections, but keep in mind that every city is different. The tour operators that I mention may not offer deals convenient to your departure city. If that's the case, check with your local travel agent: They generally know the most options close to home and how best to put together things such as escorted tours and airline packages.

Joining an escorted tour

You may be one of the many people who loves escorted tours. The tour company takes care of all the details and tells you what to expect at each leg of your journey. You know your costs up-front, and, in the case of the tamer ones, there aren't many surprises. Escorted tours can take you to the maximum number of sights in the minimum amount of time with the least amount of hassle.

If you decide to go with an escorted tour, I strongly recommend purchasing travel insurance, especially if the tour operator asks to you pay up-front. But don't buy insurance from the tour operator! If the tour operators don't fulfill their obligation to provide you with the vacation you paid for, you have no reason to think they'll fulfill their insurance obligations either. Get travel insurance through an independent agency. (I give you more about the ins and outs of travel insurance in Chapter 8.)

When choosing an escorted tour, along with finding out whether you need to put down a deposit and when final payment is due, ask a few simple questions before you buy, such as:

- **What is the cancellation policy?** How late can you cancel if you can't go? Do you get a refund if you cancel? If *they* cancel?

- **How jam-packed is the schedule?** Does the tour schedule try to fit 25 hours into a 24-hour day, or does it give you ample time to relax by the pool or shop? If getting up at 7 a.m. every day and not returning to your hotel until 6 or 7 p.m. sounds like a grind, certain escorted tours may not be for you.

- **How big is the group?** The smaller the group, the less time you spend waiting for people to get on and off the bus. Tour operators may be evasive about this, because they may not know the exact size of the group until everybody has made their reservations, but they should be able to give you a rough estimate.

- **Does the tour require a minimum group size?** Some tour operators exact a minimum group size and may cancel the tour if they don't book enough people. If a quota exists, find out what it is and how close they are to reaching it. Again, tour operators may be evasive in their answers, but the information may help you select a tour that's sure to happen.

- **What exactly is included?** Don't assume anything. You may be required to get yourself to and from the airports at your own expense. A box lunch may be included in an excursion, but drinks may be extra. Beer may be included, but not wine. How much flexibility does the tour offer? Can you opt out of certain activities or does the bus leave once a day, with no exceptions? Are all your meals planned in advance? Can you choose your entree at dinner or does everybody get the same chicken cutlet?

Picking a peck of package tours

For Vancouver and Victoria, package tours can be a smart way to go. In many cases, packages that include airfare, hotel, and transportation to and from the airport cost less than if you book the individual elements yourself. That's because packages are sold in bulk to tour operators, who resell them to the public. The process is kind of like buying your vacation at a buy-in-bulk store — except the tour operator is the one who buys the 1,000-count box of garbage bags and then resells them, 10 at a time, at a cost that undercuts the local supermarket.

The cost of package tours can vary. Ask a lot of questions when you book your trip. Prices vary according to departure city, hotel, and extras, such as car rental and optional tours. Timing is as important as other options in determining price. Adjusting your travel dates by a week (or even a day) can yield substantial savings.

Tips for choosing a Vancouver and Victoria package

Loads of package-tour operators — big and small — offer tours of Vancouver and Victoria. Unfortunately, that means you have to do a lot of weeding out to separate the wheat from the chaff. When grabbing the weed-whacker, keep these points in mind:

✔ Most of the all-inclusive packages to Vancouver and Victoria actually encompass a wider swath of Western Canada. They typically last about 10 days, and spend only a day or two in each of these cities; the rest of the time is spent in other beautiful places — Alaska, Banff, Seattle, Calgary, usually on a train or cruise ship — but *not* in Vancouver or Victoria. Be aware that any tour with "British Columbia" or "Canadian Rockies" in its title is probably of this variety.

✔ Small, under-the-radar tour operators know the cities better and give you a more local flavor than the big names can ever hope to capture. On the other hand, however, these tour companies also tend to go out of business more frequently than established firms. Check into trip-cancellation provisions when inquiring about bookings, and remember — nothing they tell you is technically true until it's in writing.

✔ Because flying into Seattle from a U.S. departure point is usually cheaper than flying into Vancouver, I recommend looking into a package tour that begins in Seattle. (Package tours do not typically include air travel; you have to get there yourself.)

How to find a packager serving Vancouver and Victoria

If you decide to investigate these package options further, your next task is to find the package that fits your needs. A great place to look is online at www.vacationpackager.com — just type in "Vancouver" or "Victoria" and dozens of options appear alongside contact information.

You can also check ads in the travel section of your Sunday newspaper or in national magazines such as *Arthur Frommer's Budget Travel, Travel & Leisure,* and *Condé Nast Traveler.*

Your best bet, however, is to peruse my recommendations later in this chapter. I include two types of packages: Those created by airlines, which offer land-air packages with air tickets and ground transportation between all points, and the rest, which offer land-only deals for which you must buy your own airline ticket.

Because this industry changes constantly, any one of the tours that I describe may be dropped from an operator's schedule by the time you read this book. Plus, some prices, which are always subject to change, do not include hidden expenses such as airport departure fees and taxes — make sure to ask about these when you call.

Without further delay, here are my picks, in alphabetical order:

- ✔ **Air Canada Vacations** (☎ 800-254-1000; Internet: www.aircanada vacations.com) is the single largest carrier flying into Vancouver. Contact them directly to find out about their many package options.

- ✔ **Alaska Airlines** (☎ 800-252-7522; Internet: www.alaskaair.com) and its busy shuttle service **Horizon Air** (☎ 888-766-9754; Internet: www.horizonair.com) offer a selection of tours of both places, mostly from Western U.S. cities. The airline offers air-hotel-sightseeing packages including tours of Vancouver harbor, Butchart Gardens, and Craigdarroch Castle or cruises with sunset dinners, whale-watching, and even seal or sea lion viewing. The cost of a 4-day tour is a flat C$725 (US$486), which includes sightseeing, air, and hotel; for a sunset dinner cruise, add C$25 (US$17) per person.

- ✔ **Collette** (☎ 800-340-5158, Internet: www.collettetours.com) offers two tours including Vancouver and/or Victoria. The Islands of the Pacific Northwest folds Seattle, Victoria, Vancouver, Washington State's San Juan Islands, and whale-watching in U.S. waters into an 8-day package costing C$1,450 to C$1,880 (US$972–US$1260) per person. The Canadian Rockies tour combines time in Banff and Jasper with visits to Vancouver and Victoria for C$1,100 to C$3,300 (US$737–US$2211) per person.

- ✔ **Globus** (no telephone; Internet: www.globusandcosmos.com) is the budget-travel half of an operator offering 10-day tours of Western Canada ending in Victoria and Vancouver. After seeing Calgary, the Rockies, and Whistler, you get about 1½ days in Victoria (including Butchart Gardens) and then from 1½ to nearly 3 days in Vancouver, mostly at your leisure. Prices vary. **Cosmos** (same Web site), the upscale half of the same operation, offers 5- and 11-day tours of British Columbia, including time in Vancouver, for about C$600 to C$2,100 (US$402–US$1407) per person.

✔ **Gray Line of Seattle** (☎ **800-426-7505** or 206-624-5077, Internet: `www.graylineofseattle.com`) operates several Vancouver and Victoria tours out of Seattle, a good way to sample all three cities. The 4-day, 3-night Vancouver-Victoria Excursion, offered from May through September, includes an Amtrak trip to Vancouver, bus tours of the city, the ferry ride to Victoria, a tour of Butchart Gardens, ferry to Seattle, and a city tour. You spend one night in each city. The cost is from US$525 per person (double occupancy). The 3-day, 2-night Discover Vancouver tour, which cuts out the Victoria leg, costs from US$320 per person (double occupancy) high season and from US$270 per person (double occupancy) off-season.

✔ **Mayflower Tours** (☎ **800-323-7604**; Internet: `www.mayflower tours.com`) books through your local travel agent or the company's Web site, not by phone. The Canadian Rockies Featuring Vancouver tour lasts 8 days and kicks off with a day and 2 nights of Vancouver sightseeing — highlighting Gastown, Stanley Park, English Bay, and Robson Street — before moving through the Canadian Rockies and ending in Calgary; an *open-jaws* air ticket into Vancouver and out of Calgary would be a good idea, though expensive. Cost of the tour is approximately C$1,600 to C$2,120 (US$1072–US$1420) per person.

Finally, lots of local operators put together escorted day tours of both cities. See Chapters 12 and 19 for more information on these.

Making Your Own Arrangements

You may want to be totally independent, whether because you're a control freak and can't stand even a single detail being out of your hands; because you're into spontaneity and hate to have anything prearranged outside of what's absolutely essential (like, say, your flight); or because you just like to do your own thang. Whatever your reason, I'm happy to supply some basic transportation data.

Finding out who flies where

Vancouver International Airport, which serves as a major hub to Asia, Australia, and New Zealand, is well connected to most U.S. flight routes. Although the airport's major players are Air Canada and United, a number of airlines fly directly to Vancouver from Chicago, San Francisco, Los Angeles, and New York, as well as from all major Canadian cities. For a complete list of the airlines flying into Vancouver, see the Appendix.

All passengers departing from Vancouver International Airport must pay (in cash or credit card) an Airport Improvement Fee — C$10 (US$7) if you're returning to North America (including Mexico and Hawaii), C$15 (US$10) if you're flying outside North America. You actually have to pay this danged thing right before boarding to get your boarding pass. At least they take both cash and credit cards.

Victoria International Airport (abbreviation: CYYJ; ☎ **250-953-7500**) is about a 30-minute drive or bus ride north of Victoria, 5 miles outside Sidney on the Saanich Peninsula. More than 50 flights a day connect it with Vancouver International Airport, Seattle-Tacoma Airport, and several other airports in Canada and the United States. For a list of airports serving Victoria, see the Appendix.

Count the number of passengers in the cabin the next time you fly. You may just have counted the number of different fares, too. *Yield management* — making each flight as full and as profitable as possible — can be harsh, but it can also work to your advantage.

Snagging the best airfare

If you need flexibility, be ready to pay for it. The full fare usually applies to last-minute bookings, sudden itinerary changes, and round trips that get you home before the weekend. On most flights, even the shortest routes, a full fare can approach US$1,000.

 You pay far less than full fare if you book well in advance, can stay over Saturday night, or can travel on Tuesday, Wednesday, or Thursday. A ticket bought as little as 7 or 14 days in advance costs only 20 to 30% of the full fare. If you can travel with just a couple days' notice, you may also get a deal (usually on a weekend fare that you book through an airline's Web site — see the section, "Getting away on the weekend," later in this chapter, for more).

 Airlines periodically lower prices on their most popular routes. Restrictions abound, but the sales translate into savings. For instance, a cross-country flight may cost as little as US$400. You may also score a deal when an airline introduces a new route or increases service on an existing one.

Watch newspaper and television ads and airline Web sites (see the Appendix for Web addresses and phone numbers), and when you see a good price, grab it. These sales usually run during slow seasons — for Vancouver and Victoria, from mid-October through May. Sales rarely coincide with peak travel times such as summer vacation and the winter holidays, when people must fly, regardless of price.

Cutting ticket costs by using consolidators

Consolidators, also known as bucket shops, are good places to find low fares. Consolidators buy seats in bulk and resell them at prices that undercut the airlines' discounted rates. Be aware that tickets bought this way usually are nonrefundable or carry stiff (as much as 75% of the ticket price) cancellation penalties. **Important:** Before you pay, ask the consolidator for a confirmation number, and then call the airline to confirm your seat. Be prepared to book your ticket through a different consolidator if the airline can't confirm your reservation.

Consolidators' small ads usually appear in major newspapers' Sunday travel sections at the bottom of the page. **Council Travel** (☎ 800-226-8624; Internet: www.counciltravel.com) and **STA Travel** (☎ 800-781-4040; Internet: www.statravel.com) cater to young travelers, but offer bargain prices to people of all ages. **Travel Bargains** (☎ 800-247-3273; Internet: www.1800airfare.com) offers deep discounts with a 4-day advance purchase. Other reliable consolidators include **1-800-FLY-CHEAP** (☎ 800-359-2432; Internet: www.1800flycheap.com); **TFI Tours International** (☎ 800-745-8000 or 212-736-1140), which serves as a clearinghouse for unused seats; and *rebaters* such as **Travel Avenue** (☎ 800-333-3335 or 312-876-1116; Internet: www.travelavenue.com), which rebates part of its commissions to you.

Snaring a deal on the Web

Use the Internet to search for deals on airfare, hotels, and (if you insist) car rentals. Among the leading sites are **Arthur Frommer's Budget Travel Online** (www.frommers.com), **Travelocity** (www.travelocity.com), **Lowestfare** (www.lowestfare.com), **Microsoft Expedia** (www.expedia.com), **The Trip** (www.thetrip.com), **Smarter Living** (www.smarterliving.com), and **Yahoo!** (http://travel.yahoo.com).

Each site provides roughly the same service, with variations you may find useful or useless. Enter your travel dates and route, and the computer searches for the lowest fares. Several other features are standard, and periodic bell-and-whistle updates make occasional visits worthwhile. You can check flights at different times or on different dates in hopes of finding a lower price, sign up for e-mail alerts that tell you when the fare on a route you specify drops below a certain level, and gain access to databases that advertise cheap packages and fares for those who can get away at a moment's notice.

Remember that you don't have to book online; you can ask your flesh-and-blood travel agent to match or beat the best price you find.

Getting away on the weekend

The airlines make great last-minute deals available through their Web sites once a week, usually on Wednesday. Flights generally leave on Friday or Saturday (that is, only 2 or 3 days later) and return the following Sunday, Monday, or Tuesday. Some carriers offer hotel and car bargains at the same time.

You can sign up for e-mail alerts through individual Web sites or all at once through **Smarter Living** (www.smarterliving.com). If you already know what airline you want to fly, consider staying up late on Tuesday and checking the site until the bargains for the coming weekend appear. Book right away and avoid losing out on the limited number of seats.

Arriving by Other Means

Sometimes flying just won't do. Maybe you have mobility issues, you're on a big road-trip vacation, or every flight is booked. Maybe you can't fly, and driving holds no appeal. Here's the scoop on traveling by train, ferry, and car.

By train across Canada

VIA Rail (☎ **888-842-7245**; Internet: www.viarail.ca), Canada's national passenger rail network, offers a rather romantic and luxurious way to get to Vancouver from the East Coast while seeing the spectacular countryside that lies between — if you have the time it takes, that is. The cross-country train service known as the Canadian runs three times a week, departing Toronto on Tuesday, Thursday, and Saturday mornings and passing through Winnipeg, Saskatoon, Edmonton, and Jasper before arriving in Vancouver three mornings later. Costs vary depending on how far you go and whether or not you get a sleeping compartment and/or meal package.

The summer cross-country trains are especially popular and require booking weeks, even months, ahead to ensure a seat.

By train from Seattle

Amtrak (☎ **800-872-7245**; Internet: www.amtrak.com) offers a much shorter rail journey from Seattle. It runs a slow, once-daily service at a cost of US$22 in each direction. The train leaves Seattle at 7:45 a.m. and rolls into Vancouver about 4 hours later; the return trip leaves Vancouver each night at 6 p.m. and arrives just before 10 p.m.

By ferry from Washington state

Taking a conventional car ferry or fast-moving catamaran (passengers only) from Washington state to Victoria is convenient and probably less expensive than you'd expect. On a clear, summer day the ride can even be delightful — you pass pretty islands, towering mountains, and possibly seals and whales. The companies providing this service include:

- ✓ **Black Ball Transport** (☎ 360-457-4491 [information only] or 250-386-2202 [reservations and information]), a cruise-ship-sized ferry, departs from Port Angeles, Washington, on the Olympic Peninsula west of Seattle. The ferry takes about 90 minutes and runs four times daily from May to October; twice daily in May, October, and November; and just once daily during the winter months. The ferry costs US$7.50 per person, children under 11 ride free. This is the only ferry that carries cars; the cost is US$29.50 per car one-way.

  If you don't have a reservation, call for sailing times — then arrive an hour early for summer departures.

- ✓ **Victoria Clipper** (☎ 800-888-2535, 206-448-5000 in Seattle, or 250-382-8100 in Victoria) carries passengers from Pier 69 on the Seattle waterfront. A boat departs four times a day in summer and once a day in winter. The trip can take anywhere from a shade under 2 hours to more than 5 hours depending on ocean and wave conditions and the route. Depending on the time of year and week, summer weekends being the most expensive, the round-trip cost is US$99 to US$125 for adults, US$89 to US$115 for seniors over 65, and US$62.50 for children ages 1 to 11 (children under 1 are free).

  In summer, the first sailing of the day at 7:30 a.m. stops at other islands along the way, greatly slowing the ride. If you have the time, the trip is wonderful. Otherwise, take the high-speed, direct ferry — at 8:30 a.m. — which costs an extra US$16 round-trip per adult.

- ✓ **Victoria Express** (☎ 800-633-1589 from the United States, 250-361-9144 from Canada) carries foot passengers and runs only during the summer. The speedy boat departs from Port Angeles, Washington, twice daily, and takes 1 hour to cross to Victoria's harbor. The cost is US$20 round-trip per adult, US$18 for seniors, US$10 for children under age 18; bicycles cost an extra US$3.

Other ferry lines from the United States to Vancouver Island include **Victoria-San Juan Cruises** (☎ 800-443-4552), which goes from Bellingham, Washington, to Victoria in 3 hours during the summer only; and **Washington State Ferries** (☎ 206-464-6400), which makes 3-hour trips from Anacortes, Washington, to the Sidney docks about 20 miles north of Victoria.

Bear in mind that summertime lineups for these ferries can be very long. You may even be bumped from one sailing to the next if the first boat sells out. Also, you will be inspected by a customs or immigration officer on the Victoria docks; have your driver's license and any declaration forms at the ready, and don't joke around with the inspectors. Just answer their questions patiently and truthfully.

By car from Seattle

Another attractive option, especially given recently expensive airfares from the United States to Canada, is to fly to Seattle, rent a car at the airport, and drive the 140 miles north to Vancouver. Most of the major rental agencies are at Seattle-Tacoma International Airport (see the Appendix for the agencies' toll-free numbers.)

The route to Vancouver is relatively straightforward. From the airport, follow signs to Interstate 5, and simply proceed north; at the border, the route number changes to Highway 99. It eventually crosses a series of bridges and becomes a two-way road, at which point the going slows considerably. Remember to make a left at 70th Avenue and proceed a few blocks west to Granville Street, then make a right onto Granville, and continue straight downtown.

As you get closer to Vancouver, Route 99 tends to become clogged at its bridges after 3 or 4 p.m. in the afternoon. If possible, try to leave Seattle early in the day to avoid this problem.

Under normal conditions this drive should take about 2 or 2½ hours. On summer weekends, or when the border post is understaffed, the backup of cars and resulting wait can seem interminable. Also, Vancouver's rush-hour traffic can be heavy; Friday and Sunday afternoons are especially congested. So what's the moral? Allow an extra hour for the border congestion and possible city traffic.

Traveling between Vancouver and Victoria

Though separated by water, Vancouver and Victoria are connected by several modes of transportation: plane, helicopter, and ferry.

By plane

The following commercial airlines fly between Vancouver and Victoria:

- ✔ **Air B.C. Connector (☎ 800-776-3000** from the United States, 800-663-3721 from Canada), a subsidiary of Air Canada, runs more than a dozen daily flights linking Vancouver, Victoria, and Seattle.

- ✔ **Canadian Regional shuttle (☎ 800-363-7530** or 250-382-6111), a subsidiary of Canadian Airlines, flies more than a dozen daily trips between Vancouver and Victoria, with about 10 flights daily on weekends.

- ✔ **Horizon Air (☎ 800-547-9308)**, a subsidiary of Alaskan Airlines, operates six to seven flights daily between Seattle and Victoria, some landing in Washington state for customs business en route.

- ✔ **WestJet Airlines (☎ 800-538-5696)** operates two to three flights per day between Victoria and other Western Canadian airports.

Two seaplane (also known as a floatplane) shuttles operate between British Columbia's two major cities. This is the hippest, quickest, and most scenic way to get from Vancouver to Victoria or vice-versa; however, the half-hour flight doesn't come cheaply.

- ✔ **Harbour Air (☎ 800-665-0212)** flies between the city harbors (and also to Vancouver Airport) eight to ten times daily on weekdays, three to four times daily on weekends. The cost is about C$100 (US$67) each way. In Vancouver, planes land at Coal Harbour near Stanley Park and the West End; in Victoria, in the Inner Harbour.

- ✔ **West Coast Air (☎ 800-347-2222,** 604-606-6888, or 250-388-4521) flies the exact same routes as Harbour Air up to 30 times daily in summer, and as long as daylight lasts the rest of the year, for C$100 (US$67), including tax, each way.

By helicopter

Helijet (☎ 800-665-4354, 604-273-1414 in Vancouver, 250-382-6222 in Victoria) flies helicopters to Victoria's Ogden Point on the Inner Harbour from Vancouver's waterfront Canada Place (22 times daily on weekdays, 5 times daily on weekends), Vancouver International Airport (5 times daily), and Seattle's Boeing Field (2 to 3 times daily). The cost is about C$160 (US$197) round-trip from Vancouver to Victoria and vice versa, or US$270 per person round-trip from Seattle to Victoria; one-way trips cost half as much.

By ferry (and car)

Traveling between the cities by ferry isn't the quickest option, but it is the most popular. **BC Ferries (☎ 888-223-3779;** Internet: www. bcferries.bc.ca) sails once every hour (on the hour) from 7 a.m. to

10 p.m. in summer, every 2 hours (usually on the odd hours) from 7 a.m. to 9 p.m. the rest of the year. The ride takes about 90 minutes. Boats depart from the BC Ferry terminals, each located about a 30-minute drive outside of Vancouver and Victoria. The Tsawwassen dock is south of Vancouver on Highway 17 and the Swartz Bay dock lies to the north of Victoria on Highway 1. Fares and schedules fluctuate, so make sure to call or check the Web site for updated information.

To travel to the terminals, you can take a bus or drive a rental car. By bus to Swartz Bay from Victoria, take city bus #70 from downtown. To Tsawwassen from Vancouver, take city bus # 601 from Howe Street (downtown) or West 4th Avenue and Granville Street (in Kitsilano) to Ladner, where you need to change to bus #640, which continues to the ferry terminal.

Remember to make reservations in summer for ferries traveling between Vancouver and Vancouver Island: Lines are long.

Chapter 6

Deciding Where to Stay

● ●

In This Chapter

▶ Reviewing your hotel options

▶ Getting to know the neighborhoods

▶ Finding out what your dollar buys

● ●

*W*ith a million and one options to pick from, you don't need to worry about supply-versus-demand issues here — Vancouver and Victoria both possess plenty of beds, even in high season. Vancouver has such a glut right now, in fact, that construction of new hotels has basically come to a standstill.

You still have to do a little legwork, however, and this chapter tells you everything you need to know.

Finding the Place That's Right for You

No two travelers are exactly alike, and no two recommended hotels will appeal to everyone reading this book. To help you zero in on the kind of place that's right for you, what follows is a rundown on what you can expect to find in Vancouver and Victoria.

Independent hotels

Vancouver and Victoria each offer particularly strong concentrations of independent hotels, both downtown and elsewhere. In fact, the overwhelming majority of my recommendations are independently owned and operated. Rooms in these hotels tend to possess more character than chain hotels do; prices, however, may be higher.

Bed-and-breakfasts

The strongly English heritage of Vancouver and, especially, Victoria means plenty of bed-and-breakfasts in each city, more than the usual number — some in quiet locations, others on side streets right in the heart of the city. These people understand the need for a fluffy pillow, a full breakfast, and friendly tips on where to go and what to see. You may even get a serving of free afternoon tea, who knows?

Chain hotels

Giant chain hotels tend to be well appointed, centrally located, and somewhat boring. But don't reflexively dismiss them — the benefits of size include a larger supply of rooms and a wider range of prices. The listings in Chapters 10 and 17 include some agreeable choices, and the area boasts plenty of other reliable options. See the Appendix for a list of the major chains' toll-free numbers and Web sites.

Location, Location, Location

The old saying really is true — location does mean everything, and that's certainly true when talking about accommodations in Vancouver and Victoria. You want to bunk down near the action if at all possible, in good-value accommodations in a safe neighborhood.

For more information on the neighborhoods, see Chapters 9 and 16.

Vancouver's neighborhoods

Vancouver will spoil you with its many hotel choices. Before you go running off to phone your travel agent or cruise the Web for the hottest hotel deals, however, remember that not every location is a good one. For starters, toss out any place with an address that you don't recognize. These places are in the suburbs, connected to downtown only by slow drives or bus rides. Forget that.

What you want is the ability to get to the important spots on your own two feet if at all possible. That means, for all practical purposes, either stay on the small peninsula that contains downtown and the West End, or hunker down on one of the English Bay's two shores, North Shore and West Side, that face the peninsula.

With the field narrowed to these central areas, you next have to select the sort of neighborhood in which you want to stay. Vancouver is full of rooms with water views, but some of them are in urban neighborhoods while others feel almost as quiet as mid-coast Maine. Some are full of pierced and tattooed young people — who may actually be Web designers or film technicians — and others are full of the sort of middle-aged folkies who spend most of their time sipping organic-roast shade-grown coffees and discussing the pitfalls of NAFTA and tuna fishing. Still others are strictly for the business-travel set. Whatever your preference, you'll probably find it here.

Downtown

This is the most central place to most attractions and shopping. The area is also reasonably safe, filled with bland high-rises, and *very* touristy — especially along the waterfront area near Canada Place, where corporate types and package tourists pack the malls and streets. Hotel options abound.

In a nutshell:

✔ You can't get more central.

✔ Restaurant choices are virtually unlimited, and the nightlife choices are thickest here, too.

But . . .

✔ You pay extra for the privilege of being right downtown, not only in your hotel room but in cafés, bars, and restaurants, as well.

✔ In the early morning and late at night, the area is noisier than other Vancouver neighborhoods described in this chapter.

West End

One of the most pleasant places to sleep in the city, West End offers quiet nights, thanks to light traffic and a notable lack of crime, and a friendly and diverse feel thanks to local residents. As a bonus, nearly all the available hotel options are located within a block or two of English Bay or green Stanley Park.

In a nutshell:

✔ Famous visitors stay here, so you may actually glimpse a celebrity.

✔ Good restaurants abound.

✔ Just a short walk away is Stanley Park in one direction and downtown in the other.

But . . .

✔ It's expensive.

✔ Availability can be limited at times — whenever a film or TV show is shooting in town, for example.

West Side

This area stretches west a long way beginning approximately at
Granville Island — just across the Granville bridge from downtown —
and extending several miles through the section known as Kitsilano (or,
locally, as Kits) out to the tip called Point Grey. Head a few blocks
south and you can also toss the Broadway and South Granville neighborhoods in this pile, too.

Almost completely residential, West Side contains a mix of ridiculously
puffed-up mansions on the water and bungalow-style small homes on
the many side streets. The district stays very quiet — almost dull — at
night, except along various stretches of West 4th Avenue and
Broadway.

In a nutshell:

✔ This is one of the best places to meet interesting locals.

✔ Many of the city's best restaurants, known only to locals, are
located here along West 4th Avenue and Broadway.

✔ The large green campus of the University of British Columbia, and
its excellent Museum of Anthropology (see Chapter 12), are here
in Kitsilano.

✔ Several excellent beaches ring the peninsula.

But . . .

✔ The region is pretty far from downtown.

✔ Accommodations are limited.

North Shore (North Vancouver, West Vancouver)

Looking for lodging on the North Shore can be confusing thanks to the
series of local names that have evolved for various neighborhoods and
municipalities. You may think everyone's caught up in a contest over
who can seem farthest west. The North Shore consists of a string of
three or four communities strung out along the northern bank of the
Burrard Inlet; none is particularly attractive in an architectural sense,
but each offers relative peace and quiet compared with downtown
hotels. And they're just a quick ride over the Lions Gate Bridge — or
across the Inlet by AquaBus — from both Gastown's sightseeing and
Downtown's shopping and eating.

For the purposes of this guide, I ignore any town in this region without
the word "Vancouver" in it. But don't worry. You're not missing a thing.
These places are all too far away anyway.

In a nutshell:

🖙 The North Shore is a local's, not a tourist's, kind of place.

🖙 This shore is higher in elevation than the city and the West Side, so views of the city and nearby islands are splendid.

🖙 A number of parks and gorges are nearby.

🖙 The ferry boat to Nanaimo, Vancouver Island, leaves from Horseshoe Bay, just a few miles west of here.

🖙 You save a good 20 minutes or more on drives to popular northern places, such as Whistler (see Chapter 15 for more on this mountain town).

🖙 An especially large number of rustic bed-and-breakfasts are in this area.

🖙 You're close to downtown by car, and a ferry makes it even possible to visit the city without one.

But . . .

🖙 The hotels tend to be simpler here, so if you're looking to be pampered in high style, look elsewhere.

🖙 You can't walk to much of anything except, if you stay near Lonsdale Quay, the public market and the AquaBus dock.

🖙 Except for the SeaBus, public transit is spotty here.

Victoria's neighborhoods

In Victoria, the picture's a bit different. This city grew up around its harbor and an old fort (now demolished) on the water, and nearly all the places you should stay are located within a surprisingly compact radius. This is, by far, a quieter and safer city than Vancouver, and somewhat more conservative; lodging options reflect this, with more B&Bs per square mile than just about any city that isn't in the British Isles and a host of buttoned-down old hotels as well.

Inner Harbour

It all happens here: Ferries come and go, boats sail, the sun sets, and The Empress hotel looms. Everyone makes it to the Inner Harbour sooner or later, so why not stay here? Well, it costs an arm and a leg — but it *is* the most interesting part of town. Note that many of the accommodations and restaurants are not at the head of the harbor, close to The Empress and the tourism office, but rather out on a peninsula.

In a nutshell:

✓ Here you find Victoria's best restaurants, hotels, and views.

✓ Light traffic makes the streets walkable.

But . . .

✓ Hotel rates are the most expensive in town.

✓ Cars outnumber the available parking spaces.

✓ You have to walk some distance to get to the downtown district.

Downtown and the Old Town

Downtown — the commercial center of town — begins near The Empress hotel and extends away from the water and north; most of the practical services such as banks and stores are located here. Old Town, the oldest and most historic part of town (a fort once stood here), is where you find the most attractive architecture, shopping areas such as Market and Bastion squares, and plenty of restaurants, bars, and cafés.

In a nutshell:

✓ Here you find Victoria's best shopping and nightlife.

✓ Good people-watching provides cheap entertainment.

But . . .

✓ You won't be alone.

✓ The area has fewer "sights" than you may hope or expect to find.

Esquimalt and Songhees

Once an industrial area, this part of town — across the Johnson Street Bridge, on the northern edge of the Inner Harbour — has transformed itself into a fairly chic part of Victoria, with resorts, brewpubs, and other diversions.

In a nutshell:

✓ Hotels are on the water, with good views.

✓ Just across the bridge is shopping, drinking, and dining.

✓ You can catch a ferry to other parts of the downtown area.

But . . .

✓ You're not right in the center of things.

✓ The accommodation choices are limited.

James Bay, Oak Bay, Lower Cook Street Village, Fairfield, and Rockland

These residential neighborhoods have quieter, more attractive streets and, for the most part, better ocean views than the commercial districts listed earlier in the chapter. But accommodations aren't easy to find, and the majority of them are B&Bs — which is fine if that's what you're after. (In Chapter 17 I let you know about the best accommodation options here.)

In a nutshell:

✔ These areas are quiet and have little traffic.

✔ Locals, rather than tourists, tend to come here.

✔ The ocean is close.

But . . .

✔ Sometimes these areas are *too* quiet.

✔ You need to drive, take a cab, or walk at least a mile to get to the central shopping, dining, and attractions.

✔ Accommodations and restaurants aren't thick on the ground.

✔ Most of what you find are bed-and-breakfasts and pubs.

Defining My Criteria for Recommending Hotels

When I recommend a place, I think about comfort, accessibility to the sights, warmth of welcome, and value — and that's it. In Chapters 10 and 17, I tell you what makes each place unique.

I rated accommodations in this guidebook from one to four dollar signs, depending on the price per night. (For the exact price ranges, see Chapters 10 and 17.) Here's what you can expect in each category:

$. These accommodations are relatively simple and inexpensive. Rooms will likely be small, and televisions are not necessarily provided. Parking is not provided but rather catch-as-you-can on the street.

$$. A bit classier, these mid-range accommodations offer more room and more extras (such as irons, hair dryers, or a microwave) than the previous category. If they don't, they offer closer access to the key sights.

$$$. Higher-class still, these accommodations begin to look plush. Think chocolates on your pillow, a classy restaurant, underground parking garages, maybe even expansive views of the water.

$$$$. These top-rated accommodations come with luxury amenities such as valet parking, on-premise spas, and in-room hot tubs and CD players — but you pay through the nose for 'em.

Chapter 7

Booking Your Room

● ●

In This Chapter

▶ Finding out about rack rates

▶ Getting the best room at the best rate

▶ Booking rooms online or at the last minute

● ●

*S*ome people book a room by calling a hotel, asking for a reservation, and paying whatever price the clerk quotes. These people
also pay sticker price for their cars. That won't be you, though,
because after reading this chapter, you'll know how to find the best
hotel rates.

The Truth about Rack Rates

The *rack rate* is the standard amount that a hotel charges for a room. If
you walk in off the street and ask for a room for the night, you'd pay
the rack rate. You sometimes see this rate printed on the emergency
exit diagrams on the back of your hotel room door.

You don't have to pay the rack rate. Hardly anybody does. Perhaps the
best way to avoid paying it is surprisingly simple: Ask for a cheaper or
discounted rate.

In all but the smallest accommodations, room rates depend on many
factors, not the least of which is how you make your reservation. For
example, a travel agent may be able to negotiate a better deal with certain hotels than you can get by yourself. (That's because hotels sometimes give agents discounts in exchange for steering business their way.)

Prices also fluctuate with the seasons and the occupancy rate. If a
hotel is nearly full, it's less likely to offer you a discount. If it's nearly
empty, the reservations staff may be willing to negotiate. These circum-
stances can change from day to day, so if you're willing to be flexible,
say so. Business hotels often offer special weekend rates and packages.
Lodgings in vacation areas may extend midweek discounts, especially
during the off-season.

Vancouver and Victoria's high season extends from May until the end of September, sometimes even into October. Reservations are a must at this time. During the off-season, be sure to ask about discounts, packages, and weekend specials, particularly for Victoria. (Christmas and New Year's are two notable exceptions to this rule; everyone in Western Canada seemingly converges upon the cities to shop and celebrate.)

Getting the Best Room at the Best Rate

Finding the best rate may require some digging. For example, reserving through the hotel's toll-free number may result in a lower rate than if you call the reservations desk directly. On the other hand, the central reservations number may not know about discounts at specific locations. For example, local franchises may offer a special group rate for a wedding or family reunion, but may neglect to tell the central booking line. Your best bet is to call both the local number and the central number and see which one offers you a better deal.

Be sure to mention your membership in AAA, AARP, frequent flyer programs, and any other corporate rewards program you belong to when you make your reservation. You never know when a membership may be worth a few dollars off your room rate.

Both Vancouver and Victoria levy heavy taxes on room rates. Hotels automatically add a 7% GST (Canadian federal tax) followed by a 10% lodging tax. The good news is that the GST is refundable for non-Canadian residents if it adds up to more than C$200 in hotel bills (up to C$14 for other purchases). (See Chapter 3 for information on how to get the refund.) When you make your reservation, be sure to ask whether the quoted rate includes taxes.

After you know where you're staying, asking a few more questions can help you land the best possible room. Ask for a corner room. They're usually larger, quieter, and brighter, and may cost a bit more. Request a room on a high floor. Upper floors may contain "club" or "concierge" level rooms; if you don't want to pay for extra features, ask for the highest standard floor. Ask if the hotel is renovating; if it is, request a room away from the renovation work, and ask again when you check in. Inquire about the location of restaurants, bars, and meeting facilities, which can be noisy. And if you aren't happy with your room when you arrive, return to the front desk right away. If another room is available, the staff should be able to accommodate you, within reason.

If you need a room where you can smoke, be sure to request one when you reserve. If you can't bear the lingering smell of smoke, tell everyone who handles your reservation that you need a smoke-free room.

Surfing the Web for Hotel Deals

Many Web sites allow you to gather information about Vancouver-area hotels. The Internet is an invaluable resource, allowing you to compare various properties' features and to see hotels before you book. Reserving online can save not just time but also money — Internet-only deals can represent substantial savings.

 Subpar travel arrangements can cost you time and money. Choosing the wrong hotel based on incomplete information can drag down your whole trip. If you are not satisfied with the information you gather via the Internet, pick up the phone and call the hotel directly. The extra time that you spend on a single phone call may help you confirm that the hotel meets your expectations.

You may want to start at a general travel site (see Chapter 5 for more details); at the site of a hotel chain you know and trust (see the Appendix for a list of major chains' toll-free numbers and Web sites); or at a locally oriented site.

The Web site **www.tourism-vancouver.org** has a searchable database and secure online reservations. Don't book through the site until you do enough comparison shopping to know when you find a competitive price.

Reservation bureaus can be a good option if you're not up for negotiating on your own. These bureaus reserve blocks of rooms, a practice that allows them to offer rooms in sold-out hotels. Do remember that the deep discounts they tout generally calculate savings off the rack rate — which you probably wouldn't pay anyway. Among the reputable sites listing Vancouver and Victoria hotels and bed-and-breakfasts are the following:

- ✔ Although the name **All Hotels on the Web** (www.all-hotels.com) is something of a misnomer, the site does have tens of thousands of listings throughout the world. Bear in mind that each hotel has paid a small fee (of $25 and up) to be listed, so the list is less like an objective list and more like a book of online brochures.

- ✔ **hoteldiscount.com** (☎ 800-96-HOTEL; www.180096hotel.com) lists bargain room rates at hotels in more than 50 U.S. and international cities. Select a city, input your dates, and you get a list of best prices for a selection of hotels. This site is notable for delivering deep discounts in cities where hotel rooms are expensive. Call the toll-free number if you want more options than are listed online.

- ✔ **InnSite** (www.innsite.com) has B&B listings in more than 50 countries around the globe. Find an inn at your destination, see pictures of the rooms, and check prices and availability. This extensive directory of bed-and-breakfasts includes a listing only if the proprietor submitted one (it's free to get an inn listed). The innkeepers write the descriptions; and many listings link to the inn's own Web sites. If you're interested in bed-and-breakfasts, see also the **Bed-and-Breakfast Channel** (www.bedandbreakfast.com).

✔ **TravelWeb** (www.travelweb.com) lists more than 26,000 hotels in 170 countries, focusing on chains such as Hyatt and Hilton, and you can book almost 90% of these online. TravelWeb's Click-It Weekends, updated each Monday, offers weekend deals at many leading hotel chains.

Use the Web to do some sleuthing. Suppose a hotel description says "overlooking the water" (or the park, or some other desirable neighbor), but its photos don't show the building in relation to the water. Download a map from another source that shows the eight-lane highway between the hotel and the beach.

Arriving without a Reservation

The local tourist office can usually fix you up with a bed from one of its members in a jiffy, unless things are exceptionally tight. Here's who to contact for this free service:

✔ In Vancouver, call **Travel InfoCentre** (☎ **800-663-6000** or 604-683-2000; Internet: www.tourism-vancouver.org), located near Canada Place on the Plaza Level in the Waterfront Centre at 200 Burrard Street. They're open daily in summer from 8 a.m. to 6 p.m. During the rest of the year, hours are Monday through Friday from 8:30 a.m. to 5 p.m. and Saturday from 9 a.m. to 5 p.m.

They also operate a desk at Vancouver International Airport (☎ **604-207-7077**) at the arrivals area on level two. Hours are daily 6:30 a.m. to 11:30 p.m

✔ In Victoria, a **Travel InfoCentre** (☎ **250-953-2033**) is located at 812 Wharf Street near the Empress Hotel, open Monday through Friday 9 a.m. to 5 p.m.

✔ Also in Victoria, **Tourism Victoria** (☎ **800-663-3883** or 250-953-2022) can probably find you a room in one of their member bed-and-breakfast accommodations, though these aren't always inexpensive.

Within normal working hours, you can also consult one of these four Vancouver-based bed-and-breakfast agencies, all of which handle booking in both cities:

✔ **Beachside Bed & Breakfast** (☎ **800-563-3311** or 604-922-7773)

✔ **Born Free Bed & Breakfast** (☎ **800-488-1941** or 604-298-8815; Internet: www.vancouverbandb.bc.ca)

✔ **Canada-West Accommodations** (☎ **800-561-3223** or 604-990-6730; Internet: www.b-b.com)

Chapter 8

Last-Minute Details to Keep in Mind

In This Chapter

▶ Crossing borders: passports and customs

▶ Ensuring peace of mind: travel insurance and health care

▶ Renting a car: Everything you need to know

▶ Making reservations and getting tickets in advance

▶ Packing your suitcase

*W*hat's worse than the nagging feeling that you forgot something, but you don't know what it is? I'd nominate the sensation of remembering it just as your plane leaves the ground.

This chapter attempts to relieve that sense of impending doom (or at least inconvenience) with a roundup of topics that can simplify your final trip planning. How do you get a passport? Do you need insurance? What if you get sick? What's the story with rental cars? How far ahead can you schedule a fancy dinner and a night at the theater? Perhaps most important, what should you pack?

For all information related to money matters — budgeting, cost cutting, choosing a legal tender, and more — turn to Chapter 3.

Crossing the Border

Canada is known as an exceptionally welcoming country, but immigrations officers are still likely to question you on the length and purpose of your trip. Technically, for entry to Canada U.S. citizens are supposed to show a birth certificate, baptismal certificate, or voter registration card *and* a passport or some other form of photo ID — but in practice you'll probably never be asked to produce any of these documents. A driver's license isn't considered proof of citizenship, but may help in a tight spot. These officers may also, in rare cases, ask for proof that you carry enough cash to support yourself during your stay; exchanging some money beforehand isn't a bad idea. All other foreign visitors need, at the very least, a valid passport. Residents of many countries will also need the appropriate entry visa.

For information on how to get a U.S. passport, check the **U.S. State Department's** travel-related Web site (http://travel.state.gov) or call the **National Passport Information Center** (☎ **900-225-7778;** US35¢ a minute for automated service; US$1.05 a minute to speak with an operator).

If you travel with a passport, keep it with you at all times — securely in your money belt. The only times to give it up are at the bank for them to photocopy when they change your traveler's checks or at the border for guards to peruse. If you lose your passport while in Canada, go directly to the nearest U.S. embassy or consulate, or that of your own country. (See the Appendix for consulate and embassy locations.)

Passing through Customs

You can take it with you or bring it back — up to a point. Technically, there are no limits on how much loot you can take to Canada, but the customs authority does put limits on how much you can transfer for free (this is mainly for taxation purposes, to separate tourists with souvenirs from importers).

Going into Canada

If you're bringing something into Canada besides clothing or personal effects, you're supposed to fill out a declarations form. Here's the limit of what you can bring: 50 cigars, 200 cigarettes, and 200 grams (8 ounces) of tobacco, and either 1.14 liters (40 oz) of liquor or wine or 8.5 liters/288 ounces (one case of 12 ounce bottles) of beer. Revolvers, pistols, and fully automatic firearms — not that you were thinking about it — are definitely *not* allowed, and, needless to say, neither are narcotics. Hunting rifles and shotguns are allowed, though they must be declared. A customs official may, in rare cases, ask to search your car or person. I don't recommend cracking jokes about a stash of drugs or whatnot.

For more information on Canadian customs regulations, contact **Revenue Canada's Customs and Excise Department** (☎ **604-666-0545**), which maintains offices in downtown Vancouver and at Vancouver International Airport.

Returning to your home

If you're a citizen of the United States, you may bring home US$400 worth of goods duty-free, providing you've been out of the country at least 48 hours and haven't used the exemption in the past 30 days. This includes one liter of an alcoholic beverage, 200 cigarettes, and 100 cigars. Anything you mail home from abroad is exempt from the US$400 limit. You may mail up to US$200 worth of goods to yourself (marked "for personal use") and up to US$100 to others (marked "unsolicited gift") once each day, so long as the package does not include alcohol or tobacco products. Anything over these limits, you'll have to pay an import duty on.

If you have further questions, or for a list of specific items that you cannot bring into the United States, look in your phone book (under U.S. Government, Department of the Treasury, U.S. Customs Service) to find the nearest customs office, or check out **Customs Service** Web site (www.customs.ustreas.gov/travel/travel.htm).

Citizens of the United Kingdom, Australia, and New Zealand may contact the following agencies for information on returning to their countries:

- ✔ **HM Customs & Excise** (for the United Kingdom), ☎ **0181-910-3744.**
- ✔ **Australian Customs Services,** ☎ **02-9213-2000.**
- ✔ **New Zealand Customs,** ☎ **09-359-6655.**

Buying Travel and Medical Insurance

Buying insurance is kind of like carrying around an umbrella; if you carry it, you won't need it. Insurance, however, can be expensive. So, should you or shouldn't you? To decide, you first must know about the three primary kinds of travel insurance — trip cancellation, medical, and lost luggage.

Trip-cancellation insurance comes in two forms. One type is for when the trip gets cancelled. This insurance makes sense if you've paid a large portion of your vacation expenses up-front (say, by purchasing a cruise or a package tour). The other type is for when you have to cancel because of illness or a death in the family. Trip-cancellation insurance costs roughly 6% to 8% of the total value of your trip.

Medical and **lost luggage insurance** don't make sense for most travelers. Your existing health insurance should cover you if you get sick while on vacation (though if you belong to an HMO, check to see whether you are fully covered when away from home). Homeowner's insurance should cover stolen luggage if it includes off-premises theft. Check your existing policies before you buy additional coverage. The airlines are responsible for US$2,500 on domestic flights (and US$9.07 per pound, up to US$640, on international flights) if they lose your luggage; if you plan to carry anything more valuable than that, keep it in your carry-on bag.

Among the reputable issuers of all three kinds of travel insurance are the following:

- ✓ **Access America,** 6600 W. Broad St., Richmond, VA 23230 (☎ **800-284-8300;** Fax: 800-346-9265; Internet: www.accessamerica.com)

- ✓ **Travelex Insurance Services,** 11717 Burt St., Ste. 202, Omaha, NE 68154 (☎ **800-228-9792;** Internet: www.travelex-insurance.com)

- ✓ **Travel Guard International,** 1145 Clark St., Stevens Point, WI 54481 (☎ **800-826-1300;** Internet: www.travel-guard.com)

- ✓ **Travel Insured International, Inc.,** P.O. Box 280568, 52-S Oakland Ave., East Hartford, CT 06128-0568 (☎ **800-243-3174;** Internet: www.travelinsured.com)

Dealing with Sickness Away from Home

Medical issues that arise when you're out of town can be tough to resolve. The following tips can help you cope with some of the most common situations:

- ✓ If you are covered by health insurance, be sure to carry your identification card in your wallet. Note the emergency number that you need to call if your provider requires pre-treatment authorization. If you don't think your existing policy is sufficient, consider buying medical travel insurance.

- ✓ Don't forget to pack your medications (in your carry-on, never in checked luggage), as well as a prescription for each one if you think you may run out.

- ✓ Pack an extra pair of contact lenses or glasses in case you lose them.

- ✓ Remember over-the-counter remedies for common travelers' ailments, such as upset stomach and diarrhea.

- ✓ If you suffer from a chronic illness, discuss your trip with your doctor. For conditions such as epilepsy, diabetes, severe allergies, or heart ailments, wear a MedicAlert identification tag. This tag immediately alerts doctors to your condition and gives them access to your medical records through a 24-hour hotline. Membership costs US$35, plus a US$15 annual fee. Contact the **MedicAlert Foundation,** 2323 Colorado Ave., Turlock, CA 95382 (☎ **800-ID-ALERT;** Internet: www.medicalert.org).

If you need a doctor, ask your hotel's concierge or front desk. Most large hotels can recommend someone at any hour. This recommendation may be more reliable than what you'd receive from a national consortium of doctors available through an 800 number.

If you can't get a doctor to help you right away, try a walk-in clinic. You may not get immediate attention, but you won't pay the high price of an emergency room visit. Vancouver has a number of clinics that stay open late hours. Fees generally range from C$40 to C$50, compared to a minimum of C$300 for most emergency room visits.

For the locations of hospitals, doctors, and dentists in Vancouver and Victoria, see the Appendix.

Debating the Car Question

Renting a car and driving it in Vancouver or Victoria is an extremely easy undertaking. If you plan on spending most of your trip in the downtown core with some journeys to other parts of the metropolitan area, I suggest you take advantage of the excellent public transportation network in the city. If your trip includes likely journeys to Whistler or Vancouver Island, however, consider renting a car for the duration of your stay.

When trying to decide whether or not to rent a car, keep this in mind: Gasoline costs a lot more in Canada than in the United States. At this writing, Canadian gas prices were about C$3.20 (US$2.25) a gallon.

Several rental car companies are located in Vancouver and Victoria. At the Vancouver International Airport, you'll find the car rental desks on Parkade Level B. At Victoria International Airport, they're located just inside the entrance to the arrivals area. See the Appendix for a list of rental car companies and their toll-free numbers and Web sites.

Ensuring the best deal for yourself

Car rental rates vary even more than airline fares. The price depends on the size of the car, the length of time you keep it, where and when you pick it up and drop it off, where you take it, and a host of other factors.

The following is a list of things to keep in mind to get the best deal:

- ✔ **Weekend rates may be lower than weekday rates.** If you keep the car 5 or more days, a weekly rate may be cheaper than the daily rate. Ask if the rate is the same for pickup Friday morning as it is for Thursday night.

- ✔ **Do not rent your car at the airport.** If possible, try to rent your car from a location away from the airport to avoid paying the airport concession recovery fee, which adds 10.5% to your bill.

✔ **Rent a car with unlimited kilometers.** Always opt for this kind of deal because planning how far you'll drive when you're on vacation is hard. Even if the daily rate is slightly higher, you'll probably come out ahead because the charge for each kilometer over your limit can be anywhere from 10 to 25¢ (and remember that kilometers are shorter than miles).

✔ **Avoid over-upgrades.** Some of Vancouver's car rental companies deal almost exclusively in minivans, which can be a hassle to park, not to mention gas-guzzling — and gas here ain't cheap. Make sure to ask about this when you call.

✔ **If you see an advertised price in your local newspaper, be sure to ask for that specific rate.** If not, you may be charged the standard (higher) rate. Don't forget to mention membership in AAA, AARP, and trade unions. These memberships usually entitle you to discounts ranging from 5% to 30%.

✔ **Check your frequent flyer accounts.** Not only are your favorite (or at least most-used) airlines likely to send you discount coupons, but most car rentals add at least 500 miles to your account.

✔ **Use the Internet to comparison shop for a car rental.** All the major booking sites — **Travelocity** (www.travelocity.com), **Expedia** (www.expedia.com), **Yahoo!Travel** (www.travel.yahoo.com), and **Cheap Tickets** (www.cheaptickets.com), as examples — utilize search engines that can dig up discounted car rental rates. Just enter the size of the car you want, the pickup and return dates and location, and the server returns a price. You can even make the reservation through any of these sites.

Identifying the additional charges

In addition to the standard rental prices (about C$30 to C$50 a day in Vancouver and Victoria), other optional charges apply to most car rentals. You encounter some of these charges wherever you rent a car; others are specific to this corner of Canada.

General charges

Many credit card companies cover the **Collision Damage Waiver (CDW),** which requires you to pay for damage to the car in a collision. Check with your credit card company before you go to avoid paying this hefty fee (as much as US$15 a day).

The car rental companies also offer additional **liability insurance** (if you harm others in an accident), **personal accident insurance** (if you harm yourself or your passengers), and **personal effects insurance** (if your luggage is stolen from your car). Your insurance policy on your car at home probably covers most of these unlikely occurrences. If your own insurance doesn't cover you for rentals or if you don't have auto insurance, however, definitely consider the additional coverage. Unless you're toting around the Hope diamond — and you don't want to leave that in your car trunk, anyway — you can probably skip the personal effects insurance. Driving around without liability or personal accident coverage, however, is never a good idea; even if you're a good driver, other people may not be, and liability claims can be complicated.

Some companies also offer **refueling packages,** in which you pay for your initial full tank of gas up-front and return the car with an empty gas tank. The prices can be competitive with local gas prices, but you don't get credit for any gas remaining in the tank. If you reject this option, you pay only for the gas you use, but you need to return your rental car with a full tank or face charges (usually at a per liter rate twice that of Canadian gas stations) for the shortfall. So, I usually forego the refueling package and allow plenty of time for refueling en route to the car rental return. However, if you usually run late and a refueling stop may make you miss your plane, you're a perfect candidate for the fuel-purchase option.

If you refuse the refueling option and you're traveling south of Vancouver, consider making a detour to Blaine or Point Roberts, Washington, to refuel. This short hop over the border can translate into big savings at the pump.

Vancouver and Victoria charges

A 7% General Sales Tax (known as the GST) and another 7% Provincial Sales Tax (PST) will also be added to your rental car bill. If you rent your car from an airport location, you can add another 10.5% for an airport recovery fee. Finally, a small environmental tax of C$1.50 (US$1) is also applied.

For more information on putting together a transportation budget, including the rundown on gas, parking, and ferry-transport fees, see Chapter 3.

Knowing additional tips for car rentals

Many car firms offer cars with CD or tape players. Remember to pack a few of your favorite CDs or tapes if you intend on cruising around a lot. (Just remember to eject them when you return the car.) As a safety precaution, make sure your rental car has a secure trunk; be wary of hatchback cars, in which all your belongings are in plain view. And, of course, remove all valuables from the car. Parking in garages may seem safe, but all those parked cars are a temptation to thieves, and even in relatively safe Vancouver and Victoria break-ins do happen.

Making Reservations and Getting Tickets in Advance

Vancouver's a big, internationally connected city with professional sports teams, plenty of trade shows, and all the rest. As such, advance reservations are always recommended for popular events, hot night-clubs, and, especially, trendy fine dining spots around the city. This is true, to a lesser extent, with smaller Victoria, where lines aren't as long, but lots of tourists descend in high summer season.

Finding out what's happening

The Internet is often your best bet for finding out what's happening in Vancouver or Victoria. All the major local newspapers and magazines have Web sites that can link you to upcoming cultural events, museum exhibitions, and sporting events — and tell you how to get tickets.

By far the best general source for tickets for Vancouver and Victoria is **Ticketmaster** (☎ **617-931-2000**; Internet: www.ticketmaster.com).

Here are my favorite sites with the scoop on Vancouver:

- ✔ **Georgia Straight** (www.straight.com), a free entertainment weekly, should be your first stop; it's the best source for event listings.

- ✔ **Vancouver Sun** (www.vancouversun.com), another reliable option, comes out daily and contains a weekly entertainment insert every Thursday.

- ✔ **Vancouver Magazine** (www.vanmag.com) comes out 10 times a year and, although slickly packaged, has a surprisingly hip and youthful feel. It really has its finger on the pulse of the city, and its restaurant reviews are especially well-informed.

- ✔ **Where Vancouver Magazine** (www.wherevancouver.com), a more mainstream (and advertising-heavy) publication, can guide you to general interest events.

- ✔ **myBC.com** (www.myBC.com) has information on sports, clubs, and city events.

A few good sources exist for the computer-challenged — or those who simply like to hear a human voice. A 24-hour **Arts Hotline** (☎ **604-684-2787**; Internet: www.allianceforarts.com) lists Vancouver's latest cultural and entertainment information. Jazz aficionados can call the **Jazz Hotline** (☎ **604-682-0706**) for upcoming performances. For events managed by the City of Vancouver at venues including the Queen Elizabeth Theatre, the Orpheum, and the Vancouver Playhouse, dial up **Talking Yellow Pages** (☎ 604-299-9000). Sports buffs can call ☎ 604-899-7444 for information on events and ☎ 604-280-4444 to purchase tickets.

For Victoria, look to the daily **Times Colonist** for news and the current weather. **Monday Magazine** (www.monday.com) is the city's free weekly entertainment paper, with superior listings. Because there are no events hotlines, you have to contact theaters or city tourism offices directly to find out more. For contact numbers, see Chapter 21 for theaters and Chapter 16 for tourism offices.

Reserving a table for dinner or tea

In the listings in Chapters 11 and 18, I tell you which restaurants require reservations. Keep in mind that dining between 5 and 6 p.m. or after 9 p.m. can help you get a seat faster.

British high tea is one British Columbia experience that you may want to reserve in advance; most top-end hotels in Vancouver and Victoria offer this service. My favorites include **The Empress hotel's tea lounge** and **James Bay Tearoom** both in Victoria (see Chapter 18) and **Sutton Place Hotel** in Vancouver (see Chapter 10). In summer, make reservations a week or two in advance — even for hotel guests. Cancellations occur, but you can't depend on them. Most places offer five daily seatings for high tea.

The **Pacific Starlight Dinner Train** chugs along the narrow tracks that hug the Sea-to-Sky Highway from North Vancouver to Whistler from June to October, and it's very likely that many of your dining companions will be locals. Make reservations one or two weeks in advance, or as far ahead as possible for summer and early fall trains. (See Chapter 12 for more on the train.)

Packing Tips

Start by assembling enough clothing and accessories to get you through the trip and piling it all onto the bed. Now put half of it into your suitcase and return the other half to your dresser.

Pack light, not because you can't take everything you want on the plane — you can, with some limits — but because spraining your back in an attempt to lift your whole wardrobe is no way to start a vacation.

What not to bring

Unless you plan on attending a board meeting, a funeral, or one of the city's finest restaurants, you probably won't need a suit or a fancy dress. You'll get more use out of a pair of jeans or khakis and a comfortable sweater.

What to bring

Most airlines allow each passenger two pieces of carry-on luggage, some just one. The dimensions for these bags vary, but the strictest airlines say carry-ons must measure no more than 22 x 14 x 9 inches, including wheels and handles, and weigh no more than 40 pounds. Airlines enforce the limit strictly, especially on crowded flights.

In a carry-on bag that you know will get through, pack valuables, prescription drugs, vital documents, return tickets, and other irreplaceable items. Add a book or magazine, anything breakable, and a snack. Leave room for the sweater or light jacket that you pull off after a few minutes of hauling bags through the overheated terminal.

Here are some packing specifics:

- Start with comfortable, broken-in walking shoes, and make sure they're fit for Vancouver and Victoria — rain falls here frequently, so don't wear anything that water can ruin. On the flip side, these are casual towns — sandals are fine for most functions.

- Although Vancouver and Victoria are casual, the upscale restaurants are full of people decked out in up-to-the-second fashions. If you want to sparkle like your dining companions, bring something elegant yet comfortable.

- Of course, you should also bring an umbrella and rain gear, such as a raincoat, rubber overshoes, and rain pants (Gore-Tex is advisable). Polar Fleese overshirts, headbands, gloves or mittens, and neck warmers work well in damp and cold winter weather or if you plan on hiking or whale watching on the open ocean, even in spring, summer, and fall. These clothing items are lightweight to pack and comfortable to wear. Thermal leggings and undershirts are also a good idea in case you catch a spell of cool, rainy weather.

Getting tickets to the big game

Information about Vancouver's professional and semi-professional sports teams can be found in Chapter 12. The following list includes whom to contact to reserve tickets for the following teams:

- **Vancouver Canucks** (NHL hockey) shoot the puck at **GM Place** (☎ **604-899-4667**; Internet: www.canucks.com).

- **BC Lions** (CFL Football) chuck it around **BC Place Stadium** (☎ **604-589-7627**; Internet: www.bclions.com).

- **Vancouver 86ers** (pro soccer) get their kicks at **Swangard Stadium** (☎ **604-589-7627**; Internet: www.86ers.com).

- **Vancouver Canadians** (minor league baseball) play the old ballgame at **Nat Bailey Stadium** (☎ **604-872-5232**; Internet: www.canadians baseball.com), next to Queen Elizabeth Park.

Pro golf fans will enjoy the Air Canada Championship, a prestigious event that swings into town the last weekend of August at the **Northview Country Club** (☎ **604-576-4653**; Internet: www.aircanadachampionship.com) in Surrey.

Part III
Exploring Vancouver

The 5th Wave · By Rich Tennant

"We saw that girl from MTV, ran into Jason Priestley and toured locations from the X-Files. I'm not sure why, but I feel like just going back to the hotel and watching TV."

In this part . . .

Welcome to the lovely Northwest! In this part I guide you through Vancouver's many highlights, including the best hotels, restaurants, attractions, and nightlife. For those who don't want to plan their own time, I also include a couple itineraries. I begin, however, with a chapter orienting you to the city so you can easily get your bearings. I then finish with a few recommended day trips, just in case you're hungry for more.

Chapter 9

Orienting Yourself in Vancouver

. . . .

In This Chapter

▶ Getting your bearings

▶ Finding information

▶ Transporting yourself around the city

. . . .

*V*ancouver stretches out on all sides, but the central area is fairly compact. After I help you figure out how to get from the airport or highway to where you're staying, I show you where to pick up bagfuls of tourist information. Navigating around the city to sights, restaurants, and all the rest doesn't have to be a hassle, either; Vancouver's public transit is actually clean and efficient, and in this chapter I take you through the nuts and bolts of it.

Arriving in Vancouver

Upon arrival in Canada, you first have to pass through Customs and Immigration. See Chapter 8 for what you can expect at this time.

Flying into the airport

Vancouver International Airport (abbreviation: YVR) is big and busy, with daily flights to every continent except Antarctica. Located on Sea Island, in the middle of the Fraser River about 8 miles south of Vancouver, this major facility is uncrowded, easy to navigate, and clean.

The airport has two terminals: an older one, exclusively for Canadian departures and arrivals, and a slick, newer one for international travel. You'll probably arrive at the newer one, which has customs and immigration checkpoints, an ATM, currency exchange facilities, and car rental agencies. All these facilities are easy to find and handicapped accessible.

The international terminal also hosts the **Tourist InfoCentre** (☎ 604-276-6101), open daily from 6:30 a.m. to 11:30 p.m., located on level two. The facility sells bus and shuttle tickets, calls cabs and limousines, and can put you on the right bus to Victoria or Whistler if you're heading there first. Staff can also book accommodations for any night (at no extra fee only if you walk in). You can also call some downtown hotels for free on special phones. Plenty of baggage carts, skycaps, and "Green Coat" travel assistants are available to answer questions about the airport, the city, and Canada.

Getting from the airport to your hotel

You have plenty of options for getting into town from Vancouver International Airport: taxi and limousine services, the Airporter shuttle, and a wide choice of rental cars.

Taxis and limousines, the easiest option and quite affordable for two or more travelers arriving together, can be hailed curbside in front of the airport's two terminals. The ride into the central downtown area takes about 25 minutes. Taxis should cost no more than C$25 to C$30 (US$17–US$20). The more comfortable limousine service runs a flat C$30 (US$20) — a good deal. An appropriate tip for the taxi or limousine driver is 15%.

The next easiest option, and a less expensive one for a single traveler, is the green shuttle bus, **Airporter** (☎ 800-668-3141 or 604-946-8866). Beginning at 6:15 a.m., the shuttle runs every 15 minutes from a spot right outside the international arrivals terminals (the first stop is the domestic arrivals terminal), dropping off at a number of central downtown hotels about 30 or 40 minutes later. One-way fares are C$10 (US$7) for adults, C$9 (US$6) for seniors, and C$5 (US$3.35) for children; buy tickets either inside or outside the terminal.

Rental car facilities are located on the ground floor of the new parking deck beside the international arrivals terminal, just a short shuttle ride from the domestic arrivals terminal. (For information about car rentals and agencies, see Chapter 8.) To get downtown from the airport, drive out of the parking lot and follow Great McConachie Way over the Arthur Laing Bridge. Turn onto SW Marine Drive and continue along West 72nd Avenue to Granville Street. Turn right and follow Granville several miles north to the foot of the Granville Bridge, where you need to make a decision, depending on where you plan to stay. For directions after the Granville Bridge, see the next section, "Driving into town."

Driving into town

If you drive north from Seattle to Vancouver, take Route 99 (it becomes Granville Street) right to the foot of the Granville Bridge. Your next move depends on where you plan to stay.

To reach **Gastown,** continue all the way to the end of the street and turn right. To reach **Stanley Park,** make the second exit off the bridge (to Pacific Street), then turn right on Pacific and drive west to the beach. To reach **Kitsilano,** you need to exit and head west out 4th Avenue. If you're staying in **North Vancouver,** you make an even more spectacular approach; drive through Stanley Park and right onto the Lion's Gate Bridge, which deposits you in North Vancouver.

Riding the rails

If you take the train from Canada or Seattle, you'll arrive at **Pacific Central Station,** which has vendors, an ATM, and ticket windows open daily from 9:30 a.m. to 6 p.m., a bit earlier and later on Tuesdays, Fridays, and Sundays. Exit the front of the station. If you're staying downtown or in the West End, hail a cab right there — it's the most convenient way to travel with luggage, and the ride shouldn't set you back more than C$8 (US$5).

To reach North Vancouver, cross the street and climb to the SkyTrain platform, buy a ticket from the machine (C$1.75; US$1.17), and take the SkyTrain to Waterfront station. Walk across the covered walkway to the SeaBus terminal, buy another ticket for the SeaBus ferry, take the ferry to Lonsdale Quay, then walk or hail a cab, depending on the location of your hotel.

Finding Information after You Arrive

The city of Vancouver maintains a handy network of four information booths known as **Tourist InfoCentres.** You find them at the airport in the international terminal (☎ **604-207-7077** answered 24 hours) between customs and immigration checkpoints and the rest of the terminal, and in the domestic terminal (☎ **604-303-3602**) on arrivals level two. Both offices are open daily from 7 a.m. (international terminal) or 8 a.m. (domestic terminal) until midnight.

The main **Tourist InfoCentre** (☎ **800-663-6000** or 604-683-2000) is on the harbor at 200 Burrard Street, in the Waterfront Centre near Canada Place. This large office is open daily in summer, 8 a.m. to 6 p.m.; in winter, Monday through Friday 8:30 a.m. to 5 p.m. and Saturday 9 a.m. to 5 p.m.

The fourth **Tourist InfoCentre** (☎ 604-666-5784), in the middle of Granville Island at 1398 Cartwright Street, tends to focus on island attractions but is still useful. This branch is open daily 9 a.m. to 6 p.m.

Greater Vancouver

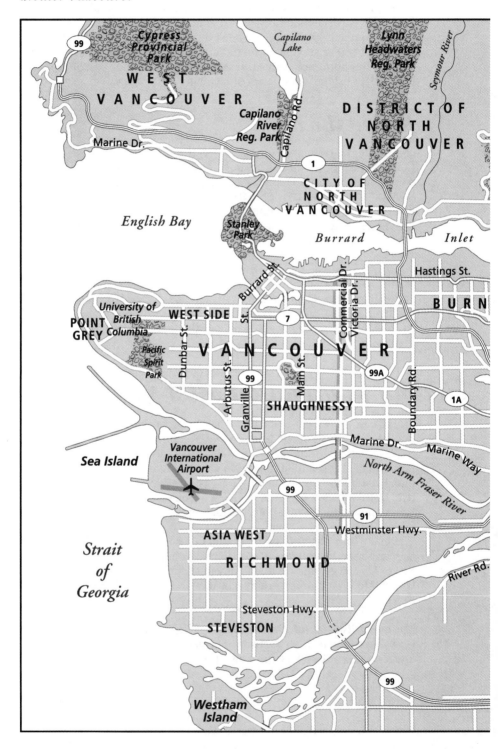

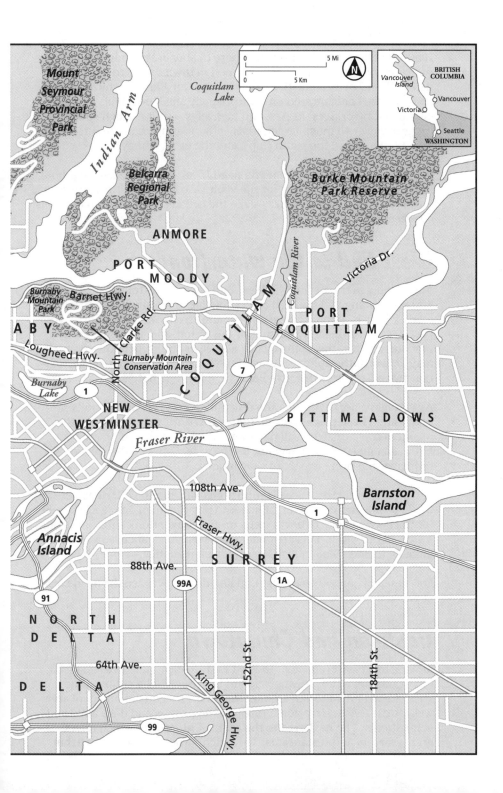

Mount Seymour Provincial Park

Coquitlam Lake

5 Mi

0

0   5 Km

N

BRITISH COLUMBIA

Vancouver Island

Vancouver

Victoria

Seattle

WASHINGTON

Indian Arm

Belcarra Regional Park

Burke Mountain Park Reserve

ANMORE

PORT MOODY

Coquitlam River

Victoria Dr.

Burnaby Mountain Park

Barnet Hwy.

PORT COQUITLAM

C O Q U I T L A M

Lougheed Hwy.

Burnaby Mountain Conservation Area

North Clarke Rd.

7

Burnaby Lake

1

NEW WESTMINSTER

PITT MEADOWS

Fraser River

108th Ave.

Barnston Island

Annacis Island

Fraser Hwy.

1

SURREY

88th Ave.

99A

1A

91

N O R T H

D E L T A

64th Ave.

152nd St.

184th St.

D E L T A

King George Hwy.

99

Vancouver by Neighborhood

Half the battle when figuring out where to stay in Vancouver is figuring out where you are; every neighborhood in town seems to sport the name "West," even some that aren't west at all. Plus, downtown sights and eats are concentrated on a surprisingly small peninsula, which is connected by bridges, ferries, and highways — but no high-speed expressway — to much larger areas with differing characters to the north (suburban), the south (hip), and the east (grungy).

In this section, I tell you what you need to know about each neighborhood that offers something for the visitor. To figure out their exact location — west or otherwise — see the Greater Vancouver map in this chapter.

West End to the waterfront

Any lodging in the residential **West End** is very central to Robson Street shopping and Denman Street café life and a small beach. Even Stanley Park is at most an easy 15-minute stroll away. West End is your best bet for staying in the center of the action, and although prices obviously reflect this convenience as well as the stupendous views, it may be worth the splurge. Some of the hotels are high-rise monstrosities, but others are attractive B&Bs or suite-style hotels.

As you move north through the **downtown** area, business hotels predominate. These places jack up their rates during weekdays for the business travelers who will pay them. Weekends should be cheaper, but in summertime this may not be the case. Expect either blandness or luxury, but don't expect to save money.

Finally, the **waterfront** area is tourist central, and the offerings here are huge, bland, and convenient. Expect to pay too much, once again, just for the convenience of being steps from a convention center or having a view of the water. This area books out well in advance, so you're unlikely to find a bed in high season on short notice.

For a map of Vancouver's West End and downtown, see the inside front cover of this book.

Gastown and Chinatown

Moving from west (adjacent to West End) to east, this district starts out in **Gastown,** the oldest section of Vancouver. The cobblestone streets and late Victorian architecture make this quaint and cool area well worth a visit. Here you find interesting shops and delis amid souvenir stands. The next area to the east is **Chinatown,** which offers great markets and restaurants. The neighborhood may be small, but the bustling atmosphere is intense. Although you should walk through both Gastown and Chinatown, I don't recommend staying in them, as the offerings tend to be shabby.

Kitsilano and West Side

Perhaps the quietest and most attractive location, this area is largely residential, free of heavy traffic, and blessed with both parks and even better weather than downtown Vancouver. In short, it's ideal. You're also close to many of the city's top restaurants. However, you face a half-hour bus ride or 10- to 20-minute drive to reach most of the central attractions such as Robson Street, Vancouver Art Gallery, or the waterfront.

Commercial Drive

Once the center of Vancouver's Portuguese and Italian immigrant population, **Commercial Drive** is heavy on coffee shops and has a funky vibe with clothing stores, health food restaurants, and alternative music clubs. What it *isn't* heavy on are accommodations, although this is slowly changing; it also isn't especially quiet, because all the commercial activity tends to draw lots of traffic.

North Vancouver

North Vancouver — usually referred to by locals as simply "North Van" — is an area that actually includes two suburban cities that are administratively separate from Vancouver: North Vancouver and West Vancouver. Go figure. Anyway, all you need to know is that North Van is a quiet lodging choice — if a little far from the action, requiring a SeaBus ride or a commute over the steep, narrow Lion's Gate Bridge to get to the downtown peninsula.

Getting around Vancouver

When friends ask my advice, I always recommend using public transit or walking if at all humanly possible while visiting Vancouver. After all, this city has all the traffic and parking headaches you'd expect at home but wish to avoid on vacation.

By public transportation

Vancouver planned its public transit well. The transit authority, **TransLink** (☎ **604-521-0400;** Internet: www.translink.bc.ca), operates a smoothly integrated network of buses, elevated trains, and ferries, which is pleasant, clean, and punctual. (Privately operated, short-hop ferries also supplement the system quite usefully along with a commuter-train service that can transport you even farther afield.) TransLink claims that the system covers some 700 square miles, which probably includes just about everywhere you'll want to go. (See Chapter 4 for information on public transportation for the disabled.)

Getting a ticket and figuring out routes and schedules can be a bit of a hassle, especially if you just arrived and are still getting used to Canadian money — or if you're like me and you spend those first hours looking around google-eyed at all the new sights.

To use public transit, you need either a ticket (for all boat and train rides) or exact change (for all bus rides). Then you must validate (punch) each ticket at a machine before boarding the bus, SkyTrain, or SeaBus. You keep the ticket and show it to a transit officer if one requests to see it. (They do occasionally check, and the fine isn't cheap — about C$40 [US$27].)

The TransLink network is seamlessly integrated. Buy a ticket for the bus, say, and the transfer you get from the driver will get you onto other parts of the system.

You have only 90 minutes after the moment you stamp that first ticket to use a transfer, however; after that, it turns into a pumpkin and you have to start over again.

The entire transit system runs all day, but only parts of it run in the evening. (I give you exact schedules later in this chapter where I discuss buses, trains, and ferries individually.) Timetables are essential if time is tight. Sources to consult include the comprehensive **BC Transit Guide** and the flyer **Discover Vancouver on Transit,** both available free of charge at the Tourist InfoCentre at 200 Burrard Street. You can pick up free bus schedules at the Tourist InfoCentre, from a FareDealer (see "Where and how to buy tickets," later in this chapter), or at the main city library (350 West Georgia Street) or a branch library.

The city maintains a **lost-and-found office** (☎ 604-682-7887) specifically for items found on city buses, trains, and ferries. Located at the SkyTrain's Stadium station, it's open weekdays only, from 8:30 a.m. until 5 p.m.

For answers to any questions you may have about how to use Vancouver's public transportation, call the city's **Transit Hotline** ☎ 604-521-0400 from 6:30 a.m. until 11 p.m. daily. Operators are *extremely* helpful. You can also log onto the agency's somewhat helpful Web site at www.translink.bc.ca.

The fare deal

Fares are the same for all Vancouver buses and elevated trains and some of the ferries, though they do vary according to time of day, distance traveled, and age of the traveler. Here's a quick guide.

✔ Greater Vancouver is divided into three fare zones. Zone one includes all central areas, including the downtown peninsula and the Point Grey peninsula; it ends at the line known as Boundary Road (same as the Second Narrows Bridge). Zone two includes airport, North Van, West Van, and suburbs out to Port Moody in the east and the Fraser River in the south. Zone three is everything else — Horseshoe Bay, Bowen Island, Tsawwassen, and more.

✔ To travel within one zone any time of the week costs C$1.75 for adults and C$1.25 for seniors and children.

✔ To travel from one zone to another costs C$2.50 for adults and C$1.75 for seniors and children during weekdays until 6:30 p.m. The price drops to C$1.75 for adults weekdays after 6:30 p.m. or on weekends, and down to C$1.25 for seniors and children weekdays after 6:30 p.m. or on weekends.

✔ To travel among all three zones costs C$3.50 for adults and C$2.50 for seniors and children — but, again, the rate drops all the way down to C$1.75 (adults) and C$1.25 (seniors or children) weekdays after 6:30 p.m. and on weekends.

Fares for children (ages 5 to 13) and seniors (over 65) represent a savings of 35% to 40% off the adult fares. Children under age 4 ride free.

Where and how to buy tickets

Transit tickets are dispensed singly, in books of ten, called FareSavers, or as a DayPass. You can buy them at fare machines inside SkyTrain stations or from a **FareDealer,** designated by a FareDealer decal placed prominently on a door or window. FareDealers are in all major malls and at convenience and grocery stores such as 7-11, Safeway, or Save-On Foods.

Fare machines give change and accept C$10 bills, C$5 bills, C$2 coins (called *twoonies*), and C$1 coins (*loonies*). Remember these terms when using fare machines:

✔ **Regular fare** is for an adult during weekday hours.

✔ **Discount fare** applies on weekends and after 6:30 p.m. on weekdays.

✔ **Concession fare** is only for senior citizens or children ages 5 to 13.

You can save money on transit costs by buying books of tickets called **FareSavers**. They come in booklets of 10 tickets each. They cost

C$16.00 (US$11) for one-zone travel (children and seniors pay C$12.50 [US$8]), C$22.75 (US$15) for two-zone travel, and C$32.50 (US$22) for three-zone travel.

If you plan on doing a lot of riding in a single day, the **DayPass** is the best deal both in terms of cost savings and the avoided hassle of standing in lines buying ticket after ticket. A DayPass costs C$7.00 (US$5) per day of unlimited SeaBus, SkyTrain, and city-bus travel; seniors and children pay C$5.00 (US$3.35). The days of the week are preprinted on the ticket; you must cross off the present day so that the conductor can see when you started using the pass.

You can't begin using a DayPass until after 9:30 a.m. on a weekday. Officially, the pass is good until midnight; however, if you're riding past midnight, the pass is still valid — you won't get kicked off the bus or have to pay extra.

Buses

Buses travel the widest network of routes through the city and beyond, and for that reason you may end up riding one at some point or another. City buses in Vancouver run from 4 a.m. until 3:30 a.m. weekdays and from 5 a.m. until 1 a.m. weekends — certainly long enough to get all but the busiest night owls home before bedtime. Some late-night routes run even later, until 4:20 a.m. to and from the suburbs.

Remember that you will need exact change to ride a Vancouver city bus — the drivers don't carry any. Also, figuring out routes and stops can be a hassle, as bus lines fan out in all directions in a complicated, changing pattern. The best way to decipher the system is to pick up a map at a Tourist InfoCentre, SeaBus terminal, SkyTrain stations, or libraries.

SkyTrain

Look up! It's a bird! It's a plane! It's a train! No, actually, it's an elevated light-rail system driven by computers and magnetic levitation, better known as SkyTrain. This relentlessly efficient system will get you from Main Street station or Chinatown to the waterfront in a jiffy — no more than about 6 minutes.

The advantages of SkyTrain — the closest thing Vancouver has to a subway system — are its speed (50 miles per hour) and its ease of use (no ticket takers or gates). And, as is so often true in Canada, the cleanliness is beyond reproach, shocking perhaps to New Yorkers.

On the downside, only one train line carries the SkyTrain, and even that only skirts the downtown peninsula. So its usefulness is limited. The bottom line? Check a map before making plans to SkyTrain around town. If you need to get to Kitsilano or even the West End, forget it except in combination with other transit methods. (For example, from the SkyTrain Waterfront Station, you can catch bus #1 to English Bay

[West End], bus #2 or #22 to Kitsilano, bus #5 up Robson Street, and bus #23 or #35 to Stanley Park.)

The line runs west to east from distant suburbs to the city's waterfront, leaving every 3 to 5 minutes from about 5:30 a.m. until about 1 a.m. There are 20 SkyTrain stations in all, but for practical purposes you can forget about all but the easternmost six or so. These stations are, in order, **Broadway Station** (you can transfer to downtown or Kitsilano buses here), **Main Street** (near Chinatown, where the cross-country VIA Rail train arrives and close to Science World), **Stadium** (the stop for BC Place Stadium, the lost-and-found office of the bus company, and — with a hike — Chinatown), **Granville** (close to several shopping areas), **Burrard** (beside the Hyatt Regency hotel), and **Waterfront** (connected to the Canada Place center, the ferry to North Vancouver, and close to Gastown). Most stations connect with handy bus routes, but bear in mind that none, with the exception of Waterfront, is really located in what's considered the central downtown area of Vancouver.

Buy tickets at any station (you don't need exact change) before boarding. You ride on the honor system, though inspectors occasionally show up to check your honesty. (They claim to make some three-quarters of a million spot checks each month — that's 24,000 a *day* — and although I'm not sure about that number, buying a real ticket rather than risking your luck is still a good idea.)

SeaBus ferry

To shuttle you quickly between Vancouver and North Vancouver — where a few attractions and accommodations await you — the city has taken full advantage of its waterside position with something called SeaBus, a very scenic way to get across Burrard Inlet in a hurry.

I recommend riding the SeaBus for a quick first introduction to the local scenery — few of the big-bucks cruise boats can offer better views than these do.

The two catamaran SeaBus ferries, known as the *Burrard Beaver* and the *Burrard Otter,* dock two to four times per hour and carry up to 400 passengers each. They take about 12 minutes to cross the sometimes placid, sometimes roiling surface of the inlet; doors open and close automatically to let you in and out, and views are splendid. As a bonus, this service can get you where you're going even when bad weather has closed down the buses, bridges, and roads.

SeaBus has two terminals: one on the Vancouver waterfront and the other at North Vancouver's Lonsdale Quay. The boats sail from Vancouver every 15 minutes from about 6:15 a.m. to the approximately 6:45 p.m., then every half-hour afterward until about 12:45 a.m.; from North Vancouver, they begin around 6 a.m. and sail every 15 minutes until 6:30 p.m., then every half-hour until about 12:30 a.m. Saturday boats sail roughly at the same times, although less frequently during the early-morning hours. Sundays and holidays, the boats sail half-hourly from around 8 a.m. until around 11 p.m. (Note that during the summer — defined here as early June to Labor Day — SeaBuses sail more frequently on Sundays and holidays, departing every 15 minutes during most of the day.)

Fares are the same as those for city buses and SkyTrains. But note that the trip across Burrard Inlet takes you from one "fare zone" to another, which increases the cost — figure an extra C75 ¢ each way. (See "The fare deal" section earlier in this chapter for more on prices.)

Bringing a bike on the SeaBus? During peak hours (early morning until 6:30 p.m., Monday through Friday), you must buy a second ticket for it. The rest of the time it rides free.

AquaBus ferry

Not to be confused with the city's SeaBus (and that's easy to do), the privately run **AquaBus** (☎ **604-689-5858;** Internet: www.aquabus.bc. ca), a system of a dozen tugboat-like ferries, is *not* part of the official city transit system. But AquaBus is very handy for getting to Granville Island and some other places, and you'll likely catch a ride on one at some point. This is definitely the most enjoyable transit option in the city, though the price you pay for such a short ride is higher than you'd expect — and for a family it can add up fast. Tickets cost C$1.75 to C$3 for short downtown hops, C$6 for longer tours of the waterfront.

The ferries leave from the southern end of Hornby Street (almost beneath the Granville Bridge) and arrive right at the island market; the several-minute ride across False Creek is pleasant and festive with anticipation. Other routes run up the Creek and to English Bay.

By foot

The first thing you need to know about getting around Vancouver is that you can see many of the best sights on foot. Assuming that you're staying in a downtown or West End hotel — the two most central areas — you can walk without much trouble to Stanley Park (20 minutes at most), Robson Street (10 minutes), Gastown (10–20 minutes), and Chinatown (15–30 minutes). Granville Island is a longer hike, but certainly doable if you have plenty of time.

Walking in Stanley Park is wonderfully scenic. Notice all the locals who make it part of their daily routine. Some merely walk to the nearest point — the seawall at English Bay — and hang out, maybe eating an ice cream, while others make the full circuit, a trip easier done by bicycle (see the "By bicycle" section later in this chapter for details).

Gastown and Robson Street are best explored on foot, simply poking from shop to shop, and stopping where you like. The same is true of

Chinatown, although you have to walk farther to get here. If you *don't* like wandering at will, a number of companies and individuals offer walking tours of city neighborhoods and attractions. See Chapter 12 for my recommendations.

By bicycle

Vancouver is one of the most cycle-friendly cities in the world — and local cycle activists fight a two-wheeled fight to keep it that way. The city even runs a **Bicycle Hotline** (☎ **604-871-6070**) to keep its cyclists apprised of bike lane changes, construction projects, events, and so forth.

If walking or running isn't your speed, and you want to fully experience Stanley Park (and you do, believe me), I recommend renting a bicycle for at least half a day during your Vancouver visit. The park is so big and beautiful that you should cover it in detail, and the active sightseer will find two wheels better than two feet.

The best places to find rentals are Robson Street, Granville Island, and Stanley Park. I recommend **Alley Cat Rentals**, 1779 Robson Street (☎ **604-684-5117**); **Bayshore Bicycle** (also known as Stanley Park Rentals), 745 Denman Street (☎ **604-688-2453**) in the Westin Bayshore Hotel and 1601 West Georgia Street (☎ **604-682-3377**); and **Spokes,** 1798 West Georgia Street (☎ **604-688-5141**). Rates vary, but don't expect to pay more than C$20 (US$13) a day for a regular bike.

For bike repairs go to **Alley Cat Rentals** (see previous paragraph); **Cyclepath** — love that name — 1421 West Broadway, Kitsilano (☎ **604-737-2344**); and **Reckless the Bike Store,** 110 Davie Street (☎ **604-648-2600**) and 1810 Fir Street, South Granville (☎ **604-731-2420**).

For the latest on what's happening in the Vancouver cycling scene, contact **Cycling BC,** 1367 West Broadway, Kitsilano (☎ **604-737-3034**).

For information on bicycle tours of Vancouver, see Chapter 12.

Biking and walking: Not always best

My favorite ways to see Vancouver are by foot or bicycle. Two factors, however, sometimes cause me to rethink my plans. First is the sometimes-drippy Vancouver weather. Lots of rain doesn't make a walk or a bike ride much fun. Second, although most sights are nearby, others — such as those in Kitsilano or North Vancouver — are simply too far to reach by foot or bike, particularly if your time is limited. When these situations arise, consider public transportation.

By taxi

Vancouver cabs are reasonably clean and punctual; maybe that's because the drivers are trained by something called the TaxiHost Centre, under the auspices of the Justice Institute of British Columbia, and operations are tightly regulated by the city.

Find a cab by heading for any taxi stand or by flagging down one with its light on in the street. Cabs also linger outside or cruise past the major downtown hotels, the convention center, Granville Island, Robson Street, and other areas frequented by visitors. Cabs cost C$2.10 to start the meter, then an additional C$1.18 per kilometer, and $24/hour (the regular hourly rate) to sit and wait at stoplights or outside your swanky hotel. An appropriate tip is 15%.

The two largest cab companies are **Black Top & Checker Cabs** (☎ **604-731-1111**) and **Yellow Cabs** (☎ **604-681-1111**). If you leave something in a taxi, call their lost-and-found departments at ☎ **604-681-3201** for Black Top & Checker Cabs or ☎ **604-258-4702** for Yellow Cab. Another company is **Vancouver Taxi** (☎ **800-871-8294** or 604-255-5111), which has wheelchair-accessible cabs.

By car

Drivers here are exceedingly polite; road rage simply isn't a factor. (**Note:** This doesn't mean that you have a free pass to do your best Mario Andretti impression. Do unto others.) In fact, the mechanics, traffic cops, parking enforcement officers — and just about anyone else car-related you may meet — are also polite. Really.

Figuring out the basics

Traffic rules are mostly the same as they are in the United States: You drive on the right and stop at red lights. Plus, you can turn right on a red light if no traffic is coming. Blinking green arrows, however, can be confusing: They mean "proceed with caution," *not* "go ahead . . . turn left, I dare ya.") Headlights must be on at all times, although on Canadian rental cars this happens automatically, and seat belts are always required.

Don't run red lights or stop signs here. Vancouver was one of the first cities in North America to test out "camera cops" — basically, camcorders that record the plates of traffic offenders — and you never know when you're being watched. Even in a rented car, you can bet your bippy you'll be caught; the rental company will just tack the fines onto your credit card bill.

Traffic jams can be a problem during rush hour — in Vancouver, that's roughly from 7:30 to 9:00 a.m. and again from 3:30 to 6:00 p.m. The biggest trouble spots are the Burrard, Lions Gate, and Granville Bridges; any stretch of Granville Street; and the Trans-Canada (Highway 1). Other parts of town can be jammed anytime of day, depending on construction, local events, sudden weather, road closures and detours, and a number of other factors. The Lions Gate Bridge occasionally closes entirely for short periods of time for renovations.

Parking the car

Parking is a hassle in downtown Vancouver — what with all the off-limits neighborhood streets and rush-hour restrictions — and not cheap, even when the exchange rate is considered. Plenty of **garages and lots** are available, however. For example, you can find several lots on Thurlow Street, another facility at The Bay on Richards Street, one near the public library, and a huge garage underground at the Pacific Centre. After working hours, a number of private lots open up to the general public. These lots are usually cheap, though sporting or other special events can jack up the all-night rate on occasion.

Metered parking can be convenient and cheap, but it does have its downsides. First, it can be difficult to find anytime of year, but especially during summer. Second, parking meter attendants vigilantly scrutinize the meters and will mark the tire of your car with chalk to discourage you from "feeding the meter." Finally, many of downtown's metered parking spots disappear at 3 p.m., not to reappear for several hours later. The city does this to free up extra lanes for rush hour — and if you park a moment past 3 p.m., you'll surely get towed. Check street signs carefully when parking in the afternoon.

In the West End of Vancouver, **on-street parking** is for residents with permits only; you will be towed and ticketed. If ticketed, the ticket will automatically be sent to the car rental company who will, in turn, charge your credit card for the amount of the ticket and then some, maybe.

For more information on parking by-laws, fines, and penalties, visit Vancouver's official Web site at www.city.vancouver.bc.ca.

Chapter 10

Vancouver's Best Hotels

. . . .

In This Chapter

▶ Vancouver's best hotels

▶ More options in case your top picks are full

▶ At-a-glance lists arranged by location and price

. . . .

*T*he hotels in this chapter are my favorites. They're the ones I suggest when friends call to ask for recommendations. Although I list my top picks, by no means are these lodgings the only acceptable choices. Near the end of this chapter, I also include options that can be helpful if you find your top choices booked. If you're still having difficulty finding a room, see Chapter 7 for my suggestions on how to find something at the last minute.

Each listing in this chapter includes a $ symbol that indicates the price range of the hotel's rack rates. (Remember: You should never pay the rack rate — always ask about discounts.) Prices are for a standard double room for one night, not including taxes. (For all-suites hotels, the price represents a standard suite rate for night, not including taxes.) The $ signs correspond with the following ranges (for more information about these symbols and ranges, see Chapter 7):

$	less than C$100 (US$67)
$$	C$100–C$200 (US$67–US$134)
$$$	C$200–C$300 (US$134–US$201)
$$$$	more than C$300 (US$201)

Also remember that the $ symbols are guidelines. A great off-season rate or package deal can knock a hotel down a category or two, and a huge citywide event can drive up prices even at modest establishments. (See Chapter 7 for pointers on getting the best rates.)

Vancouver Accommodations

Best Western Vancouver
  Downtown **14**
Blue Horizon Hotel **9**
Buchan Hotel **5**
Century Plaza Hotel and Spa **18**
Coast Plaza Suite Hotel
  at Stanley Park **2**
Crowne Plaza Hotel Georgia **25**
Delta Vancouver Suites **31**
English Bay Inn **3**
Four Seasons **26**
Georgian Court Hotel **32**
Granville Island
  Hotel and Marina **13**
Holiday Inn
  Vancouver Centre **34**
Holiday Inn
  Vancouver Downtown **15**
Hotel Dakota **17**
Hotel Vancouver **24**
Hyatt Regency Vancouver **23**
Kenya Court Guest House **12**
La Grande Residence **20**
Metropolitan Hotel **27**
"O" Canada House **19**
Ogden Point B&B **11**
Pan Pacific Hotel **29**
Parkhill Hotel **10**
Pillow 'n Porridge
  Guest Suites **35**
Rosellen Suites **4**
Shaughnessy Village **33**
Sheraton Suites Le Soleil **28**
Sheraton Wall Centre Hotel **16**
Sutton Place Hotel **21**
Sylvia Hotel **1**
Times Square Suites **6**
Waterfront Centre Hotel **30**
Wedgewood Hotel **22**
West End Guest House **8**
Westin Bayshore Resort **7**

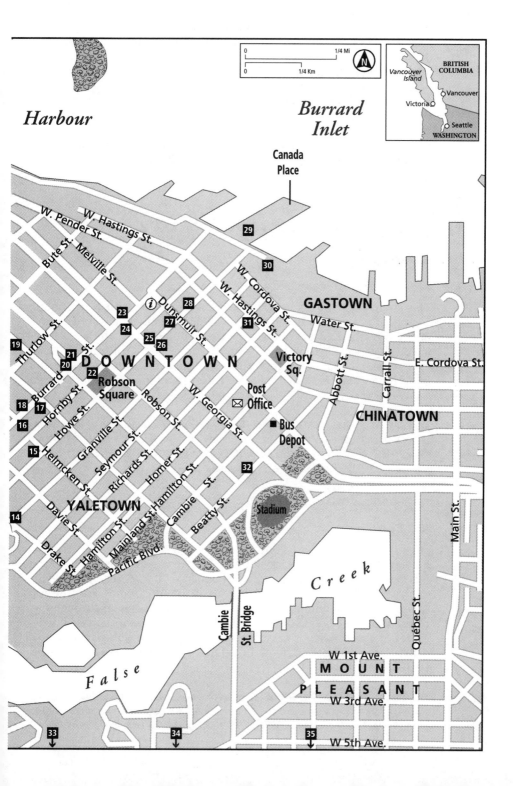

This icon indicates hotels that are especially family friendly. Many of these accommodations have swimming pools, some offer family packages (usually on weekends), and all offer their all-ages clientele plenty of patience and good advice. A listing without this symbol does not necessarily mean "kid unfriendly." Keep in mind, though, that most B&Bs in Vancouver (though not all) explicitly state that they don't take children under the age of around 12 — make sure to ask about this when you call.

See the Vancouver accommodations map in this chapter for the locations of all hotels, except those on the North Shore (North Vancouver and West Vancouver).

Vancouver Hotels from A to Z

Beachside B&B

$$–$$$ **West Vancouver**

This swanky B&B puts you in super-scenic West Van on the North Shore, right next to a private beach that's available to guests. It serves up four nicely furnished guest rooms; two are equipped with whirlpool tubs, making it especially romantic. The guest rooms contain no phones, however — which could be a good thing. Guests can watch movies on the VCR, though smokers will have to puff elsewhere: Smoking is not allowed on the premises.

4208 Evergreen Ave. (from downtown, take Trans-Canada Hwy. 1 to exit 10 and continue 4 miles west on Marine Dr. to Ferndale Ave.; turn south on Evergreen Ave.). ☎ ***604-922-7773.*** *Fax: 604-926-8073. Rack rates: C$120–C$250 (US$80–US$168) double, C$200–C$250 (US$134–US$168) suites. MC, V.*

Best Western Vancouver Downtown

$$ **Downtown**

Sure, it's a chain property, but a pretty decent one. Opened in 1997, this hotel really goes out of its way for both long-term guests on business and independent travelers who value flexibility — it features 31 efficiency units with full kitchens in addition to standard hotel rooms. For true star treatment, the penthouse suites are very comfortable (at through-the-roof prices). The hotel's near the hip Yaletown neighborhood, so finding a spot to dine or shop is easy. You can also opt for a whirlpool room for a little extra dough. The hotel thoughtfully provides a free shuttle service to downtown.

718 Drake St. ☎ ***888-669-9888*** *or 604-669-9888. Fax: 604-669-3440. Internet:* www.bestwesterndowntown.com. *Parking: Valet parking in underground garage (fee). Rack rates: C$99–C$219 (US$66–US$147) double, C$200–C$350*

(US$134–US$235) penthouse suites. AE, DISC, JCB, MC, V. Some wheelchair-accessible rooms.

Blue Horizon Hotel

$$–$$$ West End

This high-rise on the upper end of Robson Street near Stanley Park has the advantage of offering all corner rooms with private balconies that are more spacious than at a typical hotel. Rooms come in a variety of configurations, the most plush (and expensive) being the suites with one or two beds on the top 15 floors: Each comes with two bathrooms, a living room, two televisions, and other amenities. The bottom 12 floors have smaller rooms but require shorter elevator rides. Bonus points for this: It's a *green* hotel (despite the name), meaning that management employs energy-saving practices such as super-efficient lighting, low-flow shower heads, and recycling bins in all the rooms.

1225 Robson St. ☎ 800-663-1333 or 604-688-1411. Fax: 604-688-4461. Internet: www.bluehorizonhotel.com. *Parking: Underground garage, C$8 (US$5). Rack rates: C$109—C$265 (US$73–US$178) double. AE, DISC, MC, V. Wheelchair-accessible.*

Buchan Hotel

$–$$ West End

An older hotel by Vancouver standards, the Buchan (say "buckin'") isn't for everyone — especially those who dislike sharing bathrooms. It *is* an affordable alternative to big-bucks digs on a quiet residential street with views of the park. It's European-style, from the antique photos throughout the place to the size of the rooms: rather small, unless you request one of the four executive corner rooms, which do have their own private baths. In keeping with its backpacker-like clientele, the hotel offers bike, ski, and luggage storage as well as on-site coin laundry.

1906 Haro St. ☎ 800-668-6654 or 604-685-5354. Fax: 604-685-5367. Internet: www.buchanhotel.com. *Parking: Free on street 6 p.m. to 11 a.m., otherwise none. Rack rates: C$50–C$135 (US$34–US$90) double. AE, DISC, MC, V.*

Century Plaza Hotel and Spa

$$ Downtown

The best reason to stay at the sumptuous Century Plaza is its famous spa, but paradoxically the spa is difficult to get into — unless you're a stressed-out celeb, of course. Rooms all have kitchen facilities with handsome dining tables; bedrooms come with big, comfortable beds. The 30th floor penthouse suite looks like something out of *House Beautiful;* it's got a spacious living room with sectional couches and then a separate bedroom with a customized king bed. There's also a Honeymoon Suite where you're offered hand-dipped chocolate strawberries and private room service. The hotel graciously allows you to check out as late as 3 p.m. — just remember to hang that "Privacy Please" sign on the door.

1015 Burrard St. ☎ 800-663-1818 or 604-687-0575. Fax: 604-682-5790. Internet: www.century-plaza.com. Parking: Garage, C$6.50 (US$4.36). Rack rates: C$159–C$189 (US$107–US$127) double, C$209–C$427 (US$140–US$286) suites. AE, DISC, MC, V.

Coast Plaza Suite Hotel at Stanley Park

$$ West End

A fave with both Hollywood film crews and their families, this former apartment building is perfectly located just off Denman Street, one of the city's best dining areas; yet most of the suites here have kitchens if you feel overwhelmed by the dining choices. In addition, Stanley Park is literally a few minutes' walk away. Make sure to ask for a room with a view.

1763 Comox St., ☎ 800-663-1144 or 604-688-7711. Fax: 604-688-5934. Internet: www.coasthotels.com. Parking: C$8 (US$5). Rack rates: C$130–C$200 (US$87–US$134) double, C$160–C$300 (US$107–US$201) suites. AE, DC, DISC, JCB, MC, V. Wheelchair-accessible rooms.

Crowne Plaza Hotel Georgia

$$$–$$$$ Downtown

This grand hotel, polished up and prettified in 1998, offers a stunning array of amenities plus great views of the Francis Rattenbury–designed Vancouver Art Gallery. All furnishings here show off a snazzy, 1920s Art Deco look; standard guest rooms feature king, queen, or double (but full-sized) beds, and two-line phones, while king suites add a spacious sitting area. Executive Club Floor rooms include such extras as bathrobes and evening turndown service, CD players, speaker phones, and breakfast. The hip Chameleon Urban Lounge (see Chapter 14) is right downstairs. Traffic noise can be a problem on the gallery side, however.

801 West Georgia St. ☎ 800-663-1111 or 604-682-5566. Fax: 604-642-5579. Internet: www.hotelgeorgia.bc.ca. Parking: Valet parking, C$18 (US$12). Rack rates: C$240–C$350 (US$161–US$235) double. AE, DC, DISC, JCB, MC, V. Wheelchair-accessible.

Delta Vancouver Suites

$$–$$$ Downtown

Smack in the middle of Vancouver's bustling financial district, this all-suite business hotel is almost like home — except, surprisingly, there are no kitchenette facilities, possibly to lure guests downstairs to the trendy restaurant on the ground floor. All units have spacious work areas with movable (even expandable) desks, CEO-type chairs, speaker phones, and high-speed Internet access, and most of the bedrooms are separated from work areas by a door. Other personal touches here include bathrobes, Nintendo games for children, and irons and ironing boards. To get more Vancouver views for your buck, ask about "king corner suites" with windows on two sides.

*550 West Hastings St. ☎ **800-268-1133** or 604-689-8188. Fax: 604-605-8881. Internet: www.deltahotels.com. Parking: Valet parking in underground garage, C$15 (US$10). Rack rates: C$160–C$215 (US$107–US$144) suites. AE, DC, DISC, JCB, MC, V. Wheelchair-accessible.*

English Bay Inn

$$ West End

This hideaway in the cozy West End is romantic and well-located, close to Stanley Park and the beach at English Bay. The inn has five guest rooms in all, each decked out in period antiques; two overlook a nice garden out in back. The upstairs suite, more luxurious, comes with its own fireplace and costs about C$100 (US$67) extra. All guests receive comfy bathrobes and are treated to a complimentary evening aperitif.

*1968 Comox St. ☎ **604-683-8002**. Internet: www.englishbayinnvancouver. com. Parking: Free. Rack rates: C$175 (US$117) double, C$295 (US$198) suites. AE, MC, V.*

Four Seasons

$$$$ Downtown

One of the city's very best (and most expensive) hotels, the Four Seasons shows its caring side by going out of its way to attract both families with children and travelers who can't go anywhere without man's best friend. Kids feel right at home as they slip into mini bathrobes, munch freshly baked cookies, and hop up onto the stool thoughtfully placed in bathrooms to help them reach the sink; there's also a teddy bear provided to help the kids drop off to sleep. Adults seem to like the place too: Rooms are huge and beyond plush, while the staff is attentive. Even dogs are given the royal treatment here: Special water bowls, designer dog biscuits, and dog beds mean Rover won't ever want to leave. The Pacific Centre, just beneath the hotel, has a good restaurant, **Chartwell** (see Chapter 11).

*791 West Georgia St. ☎ **800-332-3442** or 604-689-9333. Fax: 604-684-4555. Internet: www.fourseasons.com. Parking: Valet parking in underground garage, C$16 (US$11). Rack rates: C$315–C$480 (US$211–US$322). AE, DC, DISC, JCB, MC, V. Wheelchair-accessible rooms.*

Georgian Court Hotel

$$–$$$ Downtown

This place, a member of the Golden Tulip family, is something of a find — as good as some much higher-priced hotels, and right in the city's currently hippest district. (It's also well located for sports fans, not far from B.C. Place and GM Place stadiums.) Lots of mahogany, brass, beveled glass, and even a grandfather clock in the lobby set the tone. The handsomely appointed rooms have been designed with business travelers in mind: Think spacious work areas and multi-line telephones. You're steps from plenty of clubs and bars. Perhaps the most compelling reason to stay, though, is the popular and excellent **William Tell Restaurant** (see Chapter 11) right in the hotel, with its hearty Swiss cuisine.

773 Beatty St. ☎ *800-663-1155 or 604-682-5555. Fax: 604-682-8830. Internet:* www.georgiancourt.com. *Parking: Underground garage, C$12.50 (US$8). Rack rates: C$115–C$260 (US$77–US$174) double. AE, DC, JCB, MC, V.*

Granville Island Hotel and Marina

$$–$$$ Granville Island

Right next to the Granville Island Public Market and all the island's other hotspots, this is quite simply a fun place to stay — and the views are fantastic, too. Little touches such as in-room microwaves, a free morning newspaper delivered to your door, and the on-site microbrewery make up for the sometimes raucous atmosphere in the halls. The crowd here tends to be young and restless, and a discotheque in the hotel cranks up on weekend nights, so think twice if you're a light sleeper. You can find room to relax, though, in the rooftop health club (it has great views). Or you can rent a canoe or ocean kayak from the hotel marina. Yes, a kayak. Now I ask you: Is that quintessentially Vancouver, or what?

1253 Johnson St. ☎ *800-663-1840 or 604-683-7373. Fax: 604-683-3061. Internet:* www.granvilleislandhotel.com. *Parking: Garage, C$6 (US$4). Rack rates: C$139–C$219 (US$93–US$147) double. AE, DC, JCB, MC, V.*

Hotel Dakota

$–$$ Downtown

An older hotel that was recently completely renovated to reflect a new attitude in this neighborhood, this small hotel serves an in-between crowd: Those who don't want to spend a fortune on a swanky place, but don't want to head for a youth hostel, either. The smallish rooms are tasteful enough, with beds covered in thick duvets and modern artwork gracing the walls. Smoking is forbidden on entire floors, and no — no bathrooms are shared. You also get continental breakfast with your room and a ride to the airport if need be. Good nightclubs such as **Babalu and Fred's** (see Chapter 14) are close at hand, and hotel staff can put you at the top of the waiting list.

645 Nelson St. ☎ 888-605-5333 or 604-605-4333. Fax: 604-605-4334. Internet: www.hoteldakota.com. *Parking: None on-site; lot next door, C$8.50 (US$6) per 24 hours. Rack rates: C$79–C$169 (US$53–US$113) double. Rates include continental breakfast. AE, DC, JCB, MC, V.*

Hotel Vancouver

$$$ Downtown

The bland name doesn't begin to describe the luxury inside. Part of the venerable Canadian Pacific Hotel Chain (which includes the Empress in Victoria), the hotel's big and comfortable rooms come in dozens of configurations. Courtyard Suites offer more privacy, space, and televisions, while the Entrée Gold floor is super-exclusive and includes dedicated staff and your own private lounge. The Premier Rooms are more like suites designed for longer stays, with full kitchens, dining rooms, entertainment areas, and extra beds — plus sweeping views of the city. Two good restaurants are on the premises, **900 West** (see Chapter 11) and **Griffins.**

900 West Georgia St. ☎ 800-441-1414 or 604-684-3131. Fax: 604-662-1907. Internet: www.cphotels.ca. *Parking: Valet parking in underground garage, C$19 (US$13). Rack rates: C$199–C$299 (US$133–US$200). AE, DC, JCB, MC, V. Wheelchair-accessible rooms.*

Hyatt Regency Vancouver

$$$ Downtown

Shoppers and tour groups flock to the Hyatt, whose cookie-cutter rooms offer loads of space and terrific views. (This spot is also quite popular with conventioneers, making weekday rates rather high, although weekend rates can be lower.) The rooms are bigger than at most any other downtown hotel, and you can request rooms with all the comforts of home: VCRs, microwaves, refrigerators, and telephones with two lines. As with all of downtown's big-name hotels, there's even a special category of stay where — for big bucks — you receive a private elevator, personal concierge, afternoon snacks, and access to a private lounge complete with stereo and big-screen television.

655 Burrard St. ☎ 800-532-1496 or 604-683-1234. Fax: 604-689-3707. Internet: www.vancouver.hyatt.com. *Parking: Valet parking C$19 (US$13). Rack rates: C$265 (US$178) double. AE, DC, DISC, JCB, MC, V. Wheelchair-accessible rooms.*

Kenya Court Guest House

$$ Kitsilano

This three-story apartment building out in Kitsilano has been completely renovated to provide short-term suite accommodations just a few paces from Kits Beach and the good collection of restaurants lining Corneal Avenue. Each room is a suite, and has a living room, separate bedroom, fully equipped kitchen, and bathroom.

2230 Cornwall Ave. (from downtown, follow Burrard St. across Burrard Bridge).
☎ *604-738-7085. Parking: Free on street. Rack rates: C$135–C$155 (US$90–US$104)*
double. Rates include full breakfast. Credit cards not accepted.

La Grande Residence

$$ Downtown

Associated with the Sutton Place Hotel (see its listing later in this chapter), one of the top hotels in Vancouver, La Grande Residence is for those folks who are planning to be temporary residents of the city — hence the name, get it? That means people in town on a film shoot, and maybe you if you can afford these top-quality digs. Rooms are basically one- and two-bedroom apartments with kitchens, dining rooms, living rooms, and balconies. However, you can't stay fewer than 7 nights. It's a good deal if you know you'll be in the city for a week and need to be independent. For extra dough, you also get access to Sutton Place's health club. On site are business services and the popular **Fleuri** restaurant (see Chapter 11).

845 Burrard St. ☎ *800-961-7555 or 604-682-5511. Fax: 604-682-5513. Parking: Underground garage, C$17 (US$11). Rack rates: C$169 (US$113) suites (C$1,183 [US$793] per week). AE, DC, DISC, E, JCB, MC, V.*

Lonsdale Quay Hotel

$$–$$$ North Shore

Located right inside the Lonsdale Quay Public Market complex (where the SeaBus from Vancouver lands), this modern and unpretentious hotel has unbeatable views of the city, plus well-appointed, affordable rooms. You're well-positioned for treks on this side of the Burrard Inlet to the Lynn Canyon Bridge and the Seymour Demonstration Forest. Plenty of restaurant stalls, gourmet foods shops, and produce markets are inside the market complex, though it closes rather early at night. Just don't expect the same sorts of do-everything service (turndown, valets and the like) that the big names across the inlet offer; you won't find them here.

123 Carrie Cates Court, North Vancouver (attached to SeaBus terminal). ☎ *800-836-6111 or 604-986-8782. Fax: 604-986-8782. Internet:* www.lonsdalequayhotel.bc.ca. *Parking: C$7 (US$4.69) (free weekends/holidays). Rack rates: C$140–C$225 (US$93–US$151) double, C$250–C$350 (US$168–US$235) suites. AE, CB, DISC, DC, MC, V.*

Metropolitan Hotel

$$$–$$$$ Downtown

One of the most stylish hotels in all Vancouver, rooms here have almost a modern B&B look, rather than the typical hotel blah room you often find in the city. For example, rooms include fresh flowers, a retro-looking bedstand lamp, lively red throw pillows, and homey duvets on the beds, and floor plants rather than sterile empty spaces. The hotel lists 18 luxury suites, 3 containing whirlpools, but every room in the place features large bathrooms, fluffy down comforters, voice mail, and (almost always) a private balcony or two. The business center is especially good, with everything from laser printers, fax machines, and speakerphones to limousines and secretarial services on call, while the health club includes squash courts (a rarity), along with a heated indoor pool, sauna rooms with built-in televisions, and massage service. Finally, the hotel restaurant, **Diva at the Met** (see Chapter 11), is one the city's very finest.

645 Howe St. ☎ 800-667-2300 or 604-687-7267. Fax: 604-643-7267. Internet: www.metropolitan.com. *Parking: Valet parking in underground garage, C$18 (US$12). Rack rates: C$285–C$395 (US$191–US$265) double. AE, DC, DISC, JCB, MC, V. Wheelchair-accessible rooms.*

"O" Canada House

$$–$$$ West End

A gracious Victorian home a little more than a century old, this B&B offers a quiet space and proximity to downtown. All six guest rooms are big enough to accommodate a separate sitting area, and all have modern bathrooms, televisions, VCRs, refrigerators, and telephone — you don't usually find *those* in a B&B. Opt for the Penthouse Suite and you add more space and a decent view of downtown; there's also a small cottage with gas fireplace and an outdoor patio. Evenings, the inn serves a complimentary aperitif in the nicely furnished common area or (in good weather) outside on the porch. The name? Why, this is the very place where the Canadian national anthem was written — the one you hear before every hockey game.

1114 Barclay St. ☎ 604-688-0555. Fax: 604-488-0556. Internet: www.vancouver-bc. com/OCanadaHouse/. *Parking: Free behind inn. Rack rates: C$125–C$225 (US$84–US$151). MC, V.*

Ogden Point B&B

$$ Kitsilano

An older home built during the early 20th century, this waterfront place is affordable — although bathrooms especially reflect the era in which the house was constructed; they're not terribly modern. Still, the B&B overlooks English Bay, and the North Shore mountains loom in the distance. The home has three guest rooms: one with queen bed and private bathroom, the other two — one a double, one with two twins — sharing a bathroom. The common area has a small refrigerator and coffee and tea service. You're right in the heart of the Kitsilano action, though, including proximity to Kits Beach, Vanier Park and its museums, and Granville Island.

1982 Ogden Ave. (from downtown, follow Burrard St. across Burrard Bridge, make an immediate right onto Chestnut St. and follow to water). ☎ *604-736-4336. Parking: Free on street. Rack rates: C$110–C$180 (US$74–US$121). Rates include continental breakfast. Credit cards not accepted.*

Pan Pacific Hotel

$$$$ Downtown

The Pan Pacific is one of the city's most luxurious hotels, with fantastic views, meticulous service, and sky-high prices to match. Rooms are modern and well-appointed, but really more notable for their size and views than any unusual decorative touches; the corner suites, with more of an eyeful of the outdoors, cost an extra C$100. Health club access, including the racquetball court and whirlpool rooms, also costs extra. A favorite of conventioneers and Japanese tourists, the hotel is located right in Canada Place, Vancouver's most visually interesting building (it's topped by white Teflon "sails") and home of the gourmet **Five Sails** restaurant (see Chapter 11)

999 Canada Place. ☎ *800-937-1515 from the U.S., 800-663-1515 from Canada or 604-662-8111. Fax: 604-685-8690. Internet:* www.panpacific-hotel.com. *Parking: Underground garage, C$25 (US$17). Rack rates: C$390 (US$261) double, C$590 (US$395) suites. AE, DC, JCB, MC, V. Wheelchair-accessible rooms.*

Parkhill Hotel

$ West End

Right in the heart of trendy Davie Street, this 24-story high-rise has live-in amenities such as hairdryers, ironing boards, balconies, and more; the bottom 21 floors are a real steal, at less than C$100 (US$67) per night, though they're pretty plain. Deluxe suites on the upper three floors add bathrobes, slippers, fluffy duvets — and a stuffed duck emblazoned with the hotel's logo, for some reason. For even more elegance, you can book the large top-floor Penthouse Suite. It's not an architectural award-winner by any means, but does give you another suite-hotel option in the West End. Two restaurants and a cappuccino bar are on the ground floor.

1160 Davie St. ☎ *800-663-1525 or 604-685-1311. Fax: 604-681-0208. Internet:* www.parkhillhotel.com. *Parking: Underground garage, C$7 (US$4.69). Rack rates: C$89 (US$60) double, C$200–C$400 (US$134–US$268) suites. AE, DC, DISC, MC, V.*

Rosellen Suites

$$–$$$ West End

A secluded, all-suite, bungalow-type of place on a quiet street very near Stanley Park, the Rosellen is one of Vancouver's suite deals. It's an older property and has been known to house celebrity types (Katharine Hepburn loved it), though the prices for the smaller suites won't break your bank. A good arrangement for families, each suite is completely furnished with kitchens, one or two bedrooms, and a living/dining area; some even have in-room dishwashers and laundry facilities. You even get your very own telephone number with voice mail during your stay. Two warnings, however: a 3-night minimum exists and the manager is only on duty during business hours (9 a.m. to 5 p.m.). Keep the latter in mind when making plans to arrive.

2030 Barclay St. ☎ *888-317-6648 or 604-689-4807. Fax: 604-684-3327. Internet:* www.rosellensuites.com. *Parking: Free but limited behind hotel. Rack rates: C$110–C$280 (US$74–US$188) apartments, C$300–C$375 (US$201–US$251) penthouse. AE, DC, MC, V. Wheelchair-accessible rooms.*

Sheraton Suites Le Soleil

$$$–$$$$ Downtown

For a taste of the high life, Sheraton Suites doesn't disappoint. Its fashionable design, ripped from the pages of upscale interior design magazines, can seem a bit overdone; but the services and little touches definitely make you feel pampered. For example, not-tested-on-animals Aveda cosmetics are in the bathrooms, and yummy Godiva chocolates wait on pillows. Rooms aren't enormous, but some suites do have big balconies to give the illusion of more space. Other amenities include the usual business-set perks — speakerphones, dataports, a business center. You also find 'round-the-clock room service and one of Vancouver's hottest new restaurants, **Oritalia.** Although the hotel has no on-site health club, you can use fitness equipment at the nearby YWCA.

567 Hornby St. ☎ *877-632-3030 or 604-632-3000. Fax: 604-632-3030. Internet:* www.lesoleilhotel.com. *Parking: Valet parking in underground garage, C$20 (US$13). Rack rates: C$250–C$350 (US$168–US$235) double, C$300–C$400 (US$201–US$268) suites, C$460–C$560 (US$308–US$375) penthouse. AE, DC, MC, V. Wheelchair-accessible rooms.*

Sheraton Wall Centre Hotel

$$$ Downtown

This Sheraton wins the height prize in Vancouver for tallest manmade structure, and it's fairly opulent; the higher you go, the more opulent rooms become. the Crystal Club rooms allow guests access to the suave Crystal Club lounge, where they can savor breakfast, snacks, and drinks and gaze out windows at the too-close-to-believe mountains to the north. The hotel doesn't shortchange on rooms, either; expect comfortable linens, fluffy duvets, heated bathroom floor tiles, and exquisite room furnishings. You can carry on six telephone conversations at once with the three two-line phones in the room, or leave in a hurry using the express video-checkout system. A beauty salon and restaurant are on premises as well.

1088 Burrard St. ☎ 800-663-9255 or 604-331-1000. Fax: 604-331-1001. Internet: www.sheratonvancouver.com. *Parking: Underground garage, C$19 (US$13). Rack rates: C$240 (US$161) double, C$400 (US$268) suites. AE, DC, JCB, MC, V. Wheelchair-accessible rooms.*

Sutton Place Hotel

$$–$$$ Downtown

Downtown Vancouver certainly doesn't lack for luxury hotels, but most folks agree this one tops them all. Whether it's in-room fresh flowers or an in-room ice dispenser you need, Sutton has you covered. The hotel also provides bathrobes, business-hotel niceties such as computer dataports and multi-line phones, king-sized beds in every room, complimentary umbrellas and shoe shines. Fleuri (see Chapter 11) is Sutton's contribution to the vibrant Vancouver dining scene. Nonsmokers are thankful for 11 floors here that forbid all forms of tobacco, while wheelchair users are grateful for extra-spacious rooms. It wouldn't be a top hotel without a great spa, and free esthetics services are available to all guests. Even pets are well taken care of, with gourmet room service, designer dog dish water(!), and massage services — maybe this is taking luxury a little *too* far. Ah, what the heck. Sip that cognac in the Gérard Lounge and check out the crowd for celebs. You're not going anywhere.

845 Burrard St. ☎ 800-961-7555 or 604-682-5511. Fax: 604-642-2926. Internet: www.suttonplace.com. *Parking: Underground garage, C$17 (US$11). Rack rates: C$179–C$269 (US$120–US$180) double, C$279–C$429 (US$187–US$287) suites. AE, CB, DC, DISC, JCB, MC, V. Wheelchair-accessible rooms.*

Sylvia Hotel

$ West End

Despite its obviously well-loved rooms (some would say *too* well loved), the Sylvia steadfastly remains one of the most popular budget hotels in the city, mainly for its prime location next to English Bay Beach and Stanley Park — and the great service provided by an attentive and unharried staff. Too bad its rooms are fairly threadbare, and furniture is an afterthought at best; consider this place only if you want to rough it for a night. The hotel actually consists of two buildings, a vine-covered structure built in the early 20th century and a second, newer building. The advantage to the older property is the top floor, where views are spectacular; rooms in the newer building have better heating and less-worn rugs. The older building also has some suites with full kitchens, good for a family or small group. The hotel's lounge (see Chapter 14) is legendary among locals. For this hotel, plan on making reservations several months in advance.

1154 Gilford St. ☎ 604-681-9321. Fax: 604-682-3551. Parking: C$8 (US$5). Rack rates: C$65–C$105 (US$44–US$70) double, C$105–C$140 (US$70–US$94) suites with kitchen. AE, DC, MC, V.

Times Square Suites

$$ West End

A home-away-from-home is what these spacious suites offer. The 42 units are tucked away in a new building designed in Victorian style; each offers fully-equipped kitchens that include a dishwasher and a microwave, a washer and dryer, expanded cable TV, VCRs, and CD stereo systems. Housekeeping comes by twice a week, and you can grill your salmon (or whatever else that's grillable) on the rooftop barbecue. The location is ace, too: Denman Street is just around the corner, and Stanley Park is only a few more minutes away.

1821 Robson St. ☎ **_604-684-2223_**_. Internet:_ www.timessquaresuites.com. _Parking: Free, in underground garage. Rack rates: C$150 (US$101) suites. AE, MC, V._

Waterfront Centre Hotel

$$$$ Downtown

Most guests stay at this very expensive hotel for one of two reasons: stellar views from most of the unusually spacious rooms, and the fact that the hotel has a link to an Alaska cruise ship terminal. Either way, you find this modern hotel quite comfortable, and it takes its location on the West Coast of Canada very seriously by displaying interesting local art in the lobby. It's also one of a handful of Vancouver hotels that is beginning to employ practices that reflect a concern for energy conservation: installing low-flow toilets, encouraging guests to re-use towels, and thoughtfully placing recycling bins in the rooms. On-site for dining is **Herons,** which features West Coast cuisine (the chef keeps a garden on the third floor from which he plucks menu items).

900 Canada Place Way. ☎ **_800-441-1414_** _or 604-691-1991. Fax: 604-691-1999. Internet:_ www.fairmont.com. _Parking: Valet parking in underground garage, C$22 (US$15). Rack rates: C$360–C$460 (US$241–US$308) double, C$375–C$1,700 (US$251–US$1,139) suites. AE, DC, MC, V. Wheelchair-accessible rooms._

Wedgewood Hotel

$$$–$$$$ Downtown

A small, exquisite boutique hotel catering to different types of guests depending on the day of the week, this is perhaps the city's most intriguing upscale option. During the week, businesspeople line up to book this place for its proximity to the heart of the city's financial district and plentiful amenities such as in-room ice dispensers and around-the-clock room service. Weekends, couples arrive to cozy up in the sumptuous rooms filled with elegant antiques, toasting each other in the hotel's highly touted restaurant **Bacchus** (see Chapter 11) or just gazing out at the city lights from their flower-decked balconies. As you may guess, this hotel goes all out to provide amenities such as turndown service and bathrobes, and a personality gradually emerges here — something well worth the cost, given the number of other equally luxurious, but *far* blander, business hotels in Vancouver's city center.

845 Hornby St. ☎ *800-663-0666 or 604-689-7777. Fax: 604-688-3074. Internet:* www.wedgewoodhotel.com. *Parking: Valet parking in underground garage, C$15 (US$10). Rack rates: C$220–C$680 (US$147–US$456) double. AE, CB, DC, MC, V. Wheelchair-accessible rooms.*

West End Guest House

$$–$$$ West End

Guests appreciate the quiet West End residential neighborhood in which this small, eight-room inn is located — not to mention the personal attention lavished on them by the inn's hardworking owner. You can splurge on the spacious top-floor suite with a queen-sized brass bed, gas fireplace, and huge bathroom with an antique clawfoot bathtub. Or choose smaller rooms featuring queen or double beds; it doesn't matter. All the accommodations retain a cozy, Victorian feel thanks to lots of antiques and duvets, and a dose of modern conveniences such as televisions and phones. Hot breakfast and complimentary refreshments are included with the price of your stay, and you're also allowed to help yourself to snacks in the kitchen throughout the day. Still not convinced? Free bicycles will get you to Stanley Park in a jiffy, parking is free, and there's no smoking on the premises. Ask about the resident ghost.

1362 Haro St. ☎ *604-681-2889. Fax: 604-688-8812. Internet:* www.westendguest house.com. *Parking: Valet parking, free. Rack rates: C$120–C$235 (US$80–US$157) double. Rates include full breakfast. AE, MC, V.*

Westin Bayshore Resort

$$$–$$$$ West End

One of the best-located of Vancouver's upscale accommodations, the Westin Bayshore is the only true resort anywhere near downtown, and thus it's a serious splurge (except for the jet-set) — at least it teeters right at the entrance to glorious Stanley Park. A hit among vacationing families, the hotel provides *very* comfortably furnished rooms, each and every one of them with unhindered water and mountain views. There's a marina where guests can moor their own boats or pick up a charter, and a helpful information desk that arranges all sorts of sightseeing excursions and expeditions. Other amenities include child-sitting, business and concierge services, as well as bicycle rentals. The resort underwent major renovations in 2000, and everything is now better than ever.

1601 West Georgia St. (from downtown, follow West Georgia St. toward Stanley Park; hotel is on right, just before park entrance). ☎ *800-228-3000 or 604-682-3377. Fax: 604-687-3102. Internet:* www.westin.com. *Parking: Valet parking in underground garage, C$18.50. Rack rates: C$200–C$332 (US$134–US$222) double, C$210–C$382 (US$141–US$256) suites. AE, DC, DISC, JCB, MC, V. Wheelchair-accessible rooms.*

Runner-up Hotels

Holiday Inn Vancouver Centre

$$–$$$ West Side

You know exactly what you're getting at this well-known chain. The hotel's Web site often runs special rates. 711 West Broadway. ☎ ***604-879-0511.*** *Fax: 604-872-7520. Internet:* www.holidayinnvancouver.com.

Holiday Inn Vancouver Downtown

$$ Downtown

Yes, another chain, but if you have kids, this is a good, centrally located pick thanks to its play area for children and kitchenettes in some units. 1110 Howe St. ☎ ***800-663-9151*** *or 604-684-2151. Fax: 604-684-4736. Internet:* www.hi-vancouver.bc.ca.

Park Royal Hotel

$$ North Shore

This spot's close to downtown and Stanley Park via the Lions Gate Bridge. Rooms range from plush to unremarkable; ask for one facing the river. 540 Clyde Ave. ☎ ***604-926-5511.*** *Fax: 604-926-6082. Internet:* www.parkroyalhotel.com.

Pillow 'n Porridge Guest Suites

$–$$ West Side

You get the best of both worlds at this place: beautiful and residential surroundings, plus many of the amenities of downtown suite hotels without the parking or traffic hassles. 2859 Manitoba St. ☎ ***604-879-8977.*** *Fax: 604-879-8966. Internet:* www.pillow.net.

Shaughnessy Village

$ West Side

A bargain hunter's dream, if you don't mind the oddly tiny rooms, this high-rise has all the facilities of a full-service hotel without the price tags or attitude. 1125 West 12th Ave. ☎ ***604-736-5511.*** *Fax: 604-737-1321. Internet:* www.shaughnessyvillage.com.

Index of Accommodations by Neighborhood

Downtown

Best Western Vancouver Downtown ($$)
Century Plaza Hotel and Spa ($$)
Crowne Plaza Hotel Georgia ($$$–$$$$)
Delta Vancouver Suites ($$–$$$)
Four Seasons ($$$$)
Georgian Court Hotel ($$–$$$)
Holiday Inn Vancouver Downtown ($$)
Hotel Dakota ($–$$)
Hotel Vancouver ($$$)
Hyatt Regency Vancouver ($$$)
La Grande Residence ($$)
Metropolitan Hotel ($$$–$$$$)
Pan Pacific Hotel ($$$$)
Sheraton Suites Le Soleil ($$$–$$$$)
Sheraton Wall Centre Hotel ($$$)
Sutton Place Hotel ($$–$$$)
Waterfront Centre Hotel ($$$$)
Wedgewood Hotel ($$$–$$$$)

North Shore (North Vancouver and West Vancouver)

Beachside B&B ($$–$$$)
Lonsdale Quay Hotel ($$–$$$)
Park Royal Hotel ($$)

West End

Blue Horizon Hotel ($$–$$$)
Buchan Hotel ($–$$)
Coast Plaza Suite Hotel at Stanley
  Park ($$)
English Bay Inn ($$)
"O" Canada House ($$–$$$)
Parkhill Hotel ($)
Rosellen Suites ($$–$$$)
Sylvia Hotel ($)
Times Square Suites ($$)
West End Guest House ($$–$$$)
Westin Bayshore Resort ($$$–$$$$)

West Side (Granville Island, Kitsilano, Point Grey, South Granville, Shaughnessy)

Granville Island Hotel and Marina ($$–$$$)
Holiday Inn Vancouver Centre ($$–$$$)
Kenya Court Guest House ($$)
Ogden Point B&B ($$)
Pillow 'n Porridge Guest Suites ($–$$)
Shaughnessy Village ($)

Index of Accommodations by Price

$$$$

Crowne Plaza Hotel Georgia (Downtown)
Four Seasons (Downtown)
Metropolitan Hotel (Downtown)
Pan Pacific Hotel (Downtown)
Sheraton Suites Le Soleil (Downtown)
Waterfront Centre Hotel (Downtown)
Wedgewood Hotel (Downtown)
Westin Bayshore Resort (West End)

$$$

Beachside B&B (North Shore)
Blue Horizon Hotel (West End)

Delta Vancouver Suites (Downtown)
Georgian Court Hotel (Downtown)
Granville Island Hotel and Marina
  (West Side)
Holiday Inn Vancouver Centre (West Side)
Hotel Vancouver (Downtown)
Hyatt Regency Vancouver (Downtown)
Lonsdale Quay Hotel (North Shore)
"O" Canada House (West End)
Rosellen Suites (West End)
Sheraton Wall Centre Hotel (Downtown)
Sutton Place Hotel (Downtown)
West End Guest House (West End)

$$

Best Western Vancouver Downtown
   (Downtown)
Buchan Hotel (West End)
Century Plaza Hotel and Spa (Downtown)
Coast Plaza Suite Hotel at Stanley Park
   (West End)
English Bay Inn (West End)
Holiday Inn Vancouver Downtown
   (Downtown)
Hotel Dakota (Downtown)
Kenya Court Guest House (West Side)
La Grande Residence (Downtown)
Ogden Point B&B (West Side)
Park Royal Hotel (North Shore)
Pillow 'n Porridge Guest Suites (West Side)
Times Square Suites (West End)

$

Parkhill Hotel (West End)
Shaughnessy Village (West Side)
Sylvia Hotel (West End)

Chapter 11

Dining and Snacking in Vancouver

• •

In This Chapter

▶ Getting the lowdown on the local dining scene

▶ Finding Vancouver's best restaurants

▶ Seeking out the best snack spots

• •

*Y*ou can sample more kinds of cuisine here, probably, then almost anywhere else on the continent. Malaysian? Hawaiian? You can find it here. And it's all healthy — the organic farms in the area help supply fresh ingredients. Even vegetarians are exceptionally well taken care of in this city, whose chefs, cooks, and menu-planners keep the options fresh and stylish.

In this chapter I give you the rundown on what's happening in the city's dining scene, followed by my recommendations for the best places to eat and snack. For the locations of the majority of these spots, see the Vancouver Dining and Snacking map in this chapter.

What's Hot Now

First things first: Asian cuisine is still strong. Vancouverites love their sushi, and there's been no appreciable slowdown in the move toward *nouvelle* Japanese cuisine that began in the '80s. You can get authentic fish soup; raw fish that may have spent the morning in Japan. On a completely different note, the Yaletown and Commercial districts are the two hot dining spots of the moment, with growing concentrations of microbreweries and bistros. (For descriptions of the places mentioned in this section, see "Vancouver's Best Restaurants" later in this chapter).

Vancouver Dining and Snacking

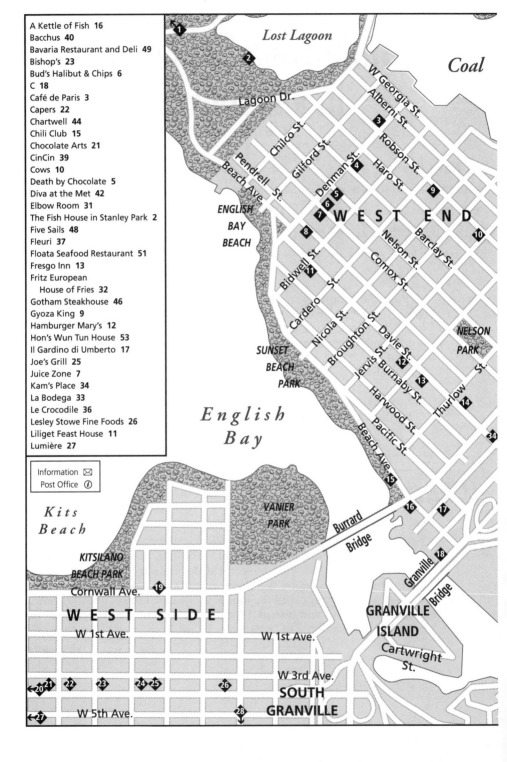

A Kettle of Fish **16**
Bacchus **40**
Bavaria Restaurant and Deli **49**
Bishop's **23**
Bud's Halibut & Chips **6**
C **18**
Café de Paris **3**
Capers **22**
Chartwell **44**
Chili Club **15**
Chocolate Arts **21**
CinCin **39**
Cows **10**
Death by Chocolate **5**
Diva at the Met **42**
Elbow Room **31**
The Fish House in Stanley Park **2**
Five Sails **48**
Fleuri **37**
Floata Seafood Restaurant **51**
Fresgo Inn **13**
Fritz European
  House of Fries **32**
Gotham Steakhouse **46**
Gyoza King **9**
Hamburger Mary's **12**
Hon's Wun Tun House **53**
Il Gardino di Umberto **17**
Joe's Grill **25**
Juice Zone **7**
Kam's Place **34**
La Bodega **33**
Le Crocodile **36**
Lesley Stowe Fine Foods **26**
Liliget Feast House **11**
Lumière **27**

Information ✉
Post Office ⓘ

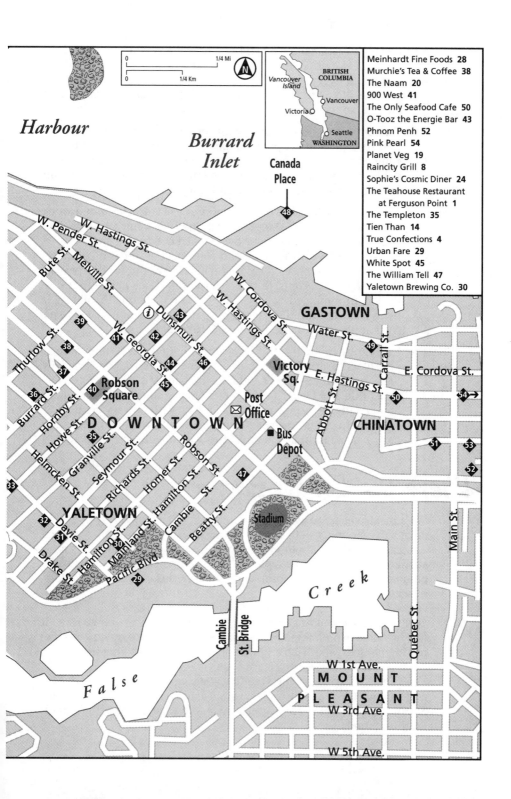

Meinhardt Fine Foods **28**
Murchie's Tea & Coffee **38**
The Naam **20**
900 West **41**
The Only Seafood Cafe **50**
O-Tooz the Energie Bar **43**
Phnom Penh **52**
Pink Pearl **54**
Planet Veg **19**
Raincity Grill **8**
Sophie's Cosmic Diner **24**
The Teahouse Restaurant
  at Ferguson Point **1**
The Templeton **35**
Tien Than **14**
True Confections **4**
Urban Fare **29**
White Spot **45**
The William Tell **47**
Yaletown Brewing Co. **30**

BRITISH COLUMBIA

Vancouver Island

Vancouver

Victoria

Seattle

WASHINGTON

Harbour

Burrard Inlet

Canada Place

GASTOWN

Water St.

E. Cordova St.

CHINATOWN

W. Pender St.
W. Hastings St.
Bute St.
Melville St.
W. Cordova St.
W. Hastings St.
Dunsmuir St.
W. Georgia St.
Thurlow St.
Victory Sq.
E. Hastings St.
Carrall St.
Robson Square
Abbott St.
Post Office
Bus Depot
Burrard St.
Hornby St.
Howe St.
Granville St.
Seymour St.
Richards St.
Homer St.
Hamilton St.
Cambie St.
Beatty St.
Robson St.
Helmcken St.
Stadium
Main St.
YALETOWN
Davie St.
Hamilton St.
Mainland St.
Pacific Blvd.
Drake St.
Cambie
St. Bridge
Québec St.

Creek

W 1st Ave.
MOUNT PLEASANT
W 3rd Ave.
W 5th Ave.

False

Other trends happening now:

✔ Locally caught salmon is still — and will probably always be — a perennial favorite amongst West Coasters, and can be found on just about every menu in town either raw (as sushi), grilled, or smoked. No matter how you eat it, it's been fresh caught, not farmed, somewhere in the province and undoubtably delicious.

✔ Vancouver's tapas-ed out! Not all good things come in small, *dim sum* style packages; Spanish tapas-style restaurants have blossomed in the city, a bonus for those who like to nibble on such delicacies as grilled Japanese eggplant, deep-fried calamari, and other treats at places such as **La Bodega.**

✔ Also red-hot (literally) on the dining scene is the hot pot. Not the handy heating device so popular in the 1980s, but a scheme by which you pay to cook your own meal. Each table comes equipped with a little stove, and you select a broth and fillings. The menu is Chinese or Japanese; most folks opt for live prawns (basically, big shrimp) or *geoduck* (jumbo clams native to the Pacific, pronounced "gooey-duck"). Then you dunk the fillings in the hot broth until they don't move anymore, and it's time to eat. A great place for this is **Landmark Hot Pot House.**

✔ Everybody thought rich, classic French food was a thing of the past when *nouvelle* French hit in the health-conscious early '80s. Well, guess what? What's old is new again. At such places as **Le Crocodile** and **Fleuri's,** Vancouverites are enjoying traditional French cuisine — mega-calories and all, with buttery cream sauces, cheese for dessert (Camembert, chèvre, and brie), and meat carved right at the table. Bring on the cherries jubilee!

Where the Locals Eat

Most locals seems to agree that eating "local" in Vancouver doesn't mean any one thing — in fact, it can mean just about anything. "Locals" are made up of just about every ethnic group on the planet, so eating sushi or biryani is just as typically Vancouver as noshing on fish 'n' chips. See "Vancouver's Ethnic Eats" later in this chapter for my top picks in that category.

Still, I try to stick to Anglo favorites here. That means, you guessed it, fish 'n' chips, which remains one of the city's favorite quick bites. For my top choices, see "Fish and pub grub," later in this chapter.

You can also partake of high tea (basically, tea with sweets, scones, and sandwiches) in many hotel restaurants around town such as the **Sutton Place Hotel** or the **Hotel Vancouver.** (See Chapter 10 for more on these hotels.)

Most local foods associated with Vancouver come from the sea. Beyond fried fish, try alder-grilled salmon at the **Liliget Feasthouse** or the hot-smoked fish known as "Indian Candy." Dungeness Crab, geoduck, rock cod, and West Coast oysters all grace the menus of hotspots such as **C**. Trendy locals — or stars in town shooting movies and pretending to be locals — also prefer the upscale ambiance of **CinCin,** where you have to be up on the latest clothing and music to even *think* of eating. (See "Vancouver's Best Restaurants," later in this chapter, for details on the places mentioned here.)

Burgers remain enduringly popular here as well, both at chains (such as the beloved **White Spot**) and a host of drive-ins and diners. See "Burgers and fried" later in this chapter for my recommendations.

But just as there's a yin for every yang, vegetarians also make up a huge part of the population — especially in the Kitsilano district — and are well served by places such as **The Naam** on West 4th Avenue (see "Vancouver's Best Restaurants" later in the chapter). For more vegetarian options, see "Restaurant rescue for vegetarians" later in this chapter.

Money-Saving Tips

Here are some of my favorite insider's tips for dining inexpensively while in Vancouver:

- ✔ **Picnic.** Vancouver's mild year-round weather makes picnicking a possibility anytime of year; inquire if a restaurant provides a take-out service (sometimes even an expensive restaurant will do this). Picknicking eliminates the pressure to tip, order appetizers, dessert, or beverages. See "Urban guerrilla power picnicking," later in this chapter, for my recommendations on where to pick up great picnic fare.

- ✔ **Do as Europeans do and eat your big meal at lunch rather than dinner.** Often you can get more for your money this way, because many mid-range restaurants offer the same items on their lunch menu as they do on a more expensive dinner menu.

- ✔ **Take advantage of club memberships.** Use your membership in an automobile club such as AAA to receive discounts (usually around 10–15% of your bill) at restaurants that accept the card.

- ✔ **Double up.** Take advantage of two-for-one specials often advertised in the free weekly *Georgia Strait* newspaper or the daily *Vancouver Sun*. Or inquire at the Tourist InfoCentre for other coupons.

- ✔ **Share.** Either split an entree with your partner or, if eating alone, ask for a half-order. You may have to pay a little extra for the additional plate, but the vast majority of Vancouver's mid- or budget-priced restaurants seem to have no problem with the practice. (I wouldn't try this in a fancy place.)

✔ **Pay one price for an unlimited meal.** At all-you-can-eat buffets, you eat more than your fill — and you probably won't have to tip, either. Many East Indian and other Asian restaurants in the city offer these buffets at lunchtime and on the weekends.

✔ **Go lowbrow.** Despite its glitzy new profile, Vancouver still has lots of cheap diners where real people eat plain meals at low prices — you just need to get away from the main tourist areas to find them. The food is hearty and ridiculously inexpensive, cooked breakfast being the biggest bargain. Factor in the favorable exchange rate, and you're practically eating for free.

✔ **Eat in.** Some suite-style hotels provide in-room refrigerators, microwaves, or both, and you can prepare small meals in these rooms when you don't feel like going out to eat. Around the city you find plenty of supermarkets and natural food stores, as well as farmer's markets on Granville Island, Robson Street, and Lonsdale Quay.

✔ **Eat your vegetables.** Vancouver offers a healthy quantity of vegetarian restaurants to pick from, and one more hidden benefit of these good-for-you places are meals at a fraction of the cost of meat-oriented menus. Some Chinese restaurants in the city are also completely vegetarian, and offer shockingly realistic *faux* meat, poultry, and shellfish entrees that nearly outshine the real thing. Again, you pay less while eating more healthfully.

✔ **Go to school.** The Pacific Institute of Culinary Arts offers two-for-one lunch and dinner specials on Mondays. Executive chefs-in-training provide gourmet meals at a low price. This is especially a bonus, because many of the city's finest restaurants are closed on Mondays.

Vancouver's Ethnic Eats

Saying that Vancouver offers a large number of ethnic restaurants is an understatement. Here's just a sample of the cuisines available in just about any commercial block of the greater metropolitan area: Chinese, Japanese, Korean, Vietnamese, Thai, Malaysian/Indonesian, Native Canadian, East Indian, Greek, Italian, German, British, Spanish/Portuguese, Mexican, and maybe even Iranian. And that's just scratching the surface — new arrivals are staking their food claims every year, so this list could expand again. Check with us tomorrow for another update.

Asian invasion

Asian food remains the chief ethnic influence. Whether it's the large Hong Kong-style restaurants popping up in southern exurban shopping malls or the tiny, crammed-to-the-gills joints in Chinatown, you'll have no problem finding an authentic *dim sum* or *congee* (rice porridge) at any number of Chinese eateries.

However, Chinatown has lately been seeing more Vietnamese *pho* noodle shops and Thai eateries move in on its turf. Southeast Asian restaurants are also moving east to the Commercial Drive area, where rents are lower — as is the price of a good meal. Japanese restaurants are mostly concentrated downtown near the Robson Street shopping strip, and they tend to be more expensive as a result, but you can also find Japanese food in the Yaletown district. Finally, on both the eastern side of the city and the West Side, you find East Indian Punjabi markets with their spice markets and curry houses.

Given all these concentrated pockets of Asian food and ample choices, for me to even attempt any kind of definitive list is ridiculous. Nonetheless, I recommend a number of ethnic restaurants in "Vancouver's Best Restaurants," later in this chapter. Other standouts to watch for include:

Kam's Place, 1043 Davie Street (☎ 604-669-3389), serves food with a primarily Singaporean accent, although other influences are present as well. Lunches are cheap here.

Tien Than (Ten Thanks), 1063 Davie Street (☎ 604-687-7880), is one of my favorite lowbrow downtown eats. It's central, inexpensive, good — and friendly. The owner specializes in skewer of grilled meat dipped in Vietnamese sauces.

Zooropa: European eats

Germans and other Eastern Europeans immigrated to downtown Vancouver in the 19th century. In fact, Robson Street was once so full of old European delis featuring sausages, sauerkraut, and schnitzel that it was known as Robsonstrasse (*strasse* is German for "street"). Glitzy stores catering to moneyed tourists have largely replaced these shops, but you can still find European delis and eateries in other corners of the city.

The serious foodie can also locate numerous additional pockets of Euro-cooking in the city. Spanish and Portuguese communities are well served by authentic Spanish *tapas* bars and places serving Portuguese grilled meats, while Greek immigrants still congregate at authentic *tavernas* on the city's West Side. The city holds other surprises: Along Commercial Drive, long the bastion of Italian *trattorias,* Central Americans are filtering into the area and bringing their own unique food style with them; as a result, you can now nosh on *tacos, papusas,* and barbecued chicken at stands and joints up and down the drive.

Whew! That's a lot of ground — and a lot of calories — to cover. Here are some of the ethnic eateries I like.

Bavaria Restaurant and Deli, 203 Carrall Street (☎ 604-687-4047), is one of many Eastern European delis in the Gastown area, a good bet for solid German fare.

Fritz European House of Fries, 718 Davie Street (☎ 604-684-0811), is just what it sounds like: An emporium dedicated to the art of the fry, much like you'd find in any town square in Belgium, with a choice of flavored ketchups and mayonnaise-based sauces.

Minerva's, 3207 West Broadway (☎ 604-733-3956), is a Greek deli on Broadway that is good for aficionados of *moussaka* and *dolmathes.*

Nando's, 1301 Lonsdale Avenue, North Vancouver (☎ 604-990-1531), does a delicious meal of peppy Portuguese grilled chicken, good fries, and drinks to wash it down.

Omnitsky Kosher Foods, 5566 Cambie Street (☎ 604-321-1818). is, quite simply, an old-world Hebrew deli with caloric specials such as corned beef on marble rye, matzoh ball soup, gefilte fish, and brisket. The portions are bigger than enormous.

Vancouver's Best Restaurants

What follows are my recommendations of the best places to dine in alphabetical order.

The main course prices reflect the range of each restaurant's dinner menu. Drinks, tips, and appetizers are not included in this calculation. If the restaurant doesn't serve dinner, the price range applies to main courses at lunch, brunch, or breakfast, as appropriate to that particular eatery.

The dollar sign ratings represent the price of one dinner including drinks and tip and correspond with the following price ranges:

$	Less than C$10 (US$7)
$$	C$10–C$$20 (US$7–US$13)
$$$	C$20–C$30 (US$13–US$20)
$$$$	More than C$30 (US$20)

As in any large city, the finest restaurants are very popular, and reservations are not only sensible but often required. In each listing, I tell you which restaurants require you to call ahead to ensure you a table.

Dressing to dine

In Vancouver, almost anything goes. Almost. This is the West Coast, after all, so most restaurants are still pretty casual. You see everything from in-line skaters noshing on wrap sandwiches at a chic sidewalk cafe on Denman Street to sailors throwing back micro-brews at waterfront bars on False Creek.

That's not to say you shouldn't dress up on occasion, however. You may see the pre-theater crowd dining elegantly in the latest designer creations, for example, at the many fabulous downtown hotel restaurants. My general rule? If you plan to dine at a place where reservations are either required or recommended — I tell you which do in the restaurant listings later in the chapter — call ahead to find out if they have a dress code. Most places accept "refined casual," a fuzzy term that seems to have expanded generously to mean anything from Armani threads to pressed designer jeans with a $150 t-shirt. Otherwise, don't sweat it.

A Kettle of Fish

$$–$$$$ Downtown   SEAFOOD

This cheerful restaurant near the Burrard Bridge urges guests to "Eat Lotsa Fish," and here you can do it — easily. Naturally, the star attractions on the changing menu are all caught locally: British Columbia salmon, spotted prawns (people from the United States would called them "tiger shrimp"), sea scallops, and *mahi-mahi* all prepared with care and creativity. If you're feeling expansive, go for the combination seafood plate, which offers a chance to stretch your tastebuds and try a little of everything. The atmosphere is surprisingly casual in spite of the prices, and as a result the crowd can get a little tourist-heavy.

900 Pacific St. ☎ *604-682-6661. Reservations accepted and recommended. Main courses: C$15–C$32 (US$10–US$21). AE, DC, MC, V. Open: Lunch Mon–Fri only, dinner daily.*

Bacchus

$$–$$$ Downtown   CONTINENTAL

One of the top picks in town for a splurge, this place isn't for the faint of culinary heart. Sequestered in the terrific Wedgewood Hotel (see Chapter 10), it's designed with romance in mind with a limestone fireplace, lots of silk and velvet drapes, gorgeous wood paneling, and an illuminated bar. The food itself blends classic French and Italian cuisine with West Coast influences — risotto with salmon and caviar, for instance, or Chardonnay-steamed local clams — plus they offer a daily special of more traditionally French food. (Friday, of course, it's *bouillabaisse*.) There's a cigar room for smokers, excellent French pastries for dessert, and a *very* complete wine list; unusually, Bacchus also serves breakfast daily.

845 Hornby St. (in the Wedgewood Hotel). ☎ *604-608-5319. Reservations required. Main courses: C$13–C$30 (US$9–US$20). AE, DC, MC, V. Open: Breakfast, lunch, and dinner daily. Wheelchair-accessible.*

Bishop's

$$$ Kitsilano   PACIFIC NORTHWEST/FUSION

This Kitsilano star has been drawing big-ticket actors, politicians, and the like almost since the moment it opened (for dinner only) during the mid 1980s. Despite his A-list clientele, however, owner John Bishop prides himself on warm personal service and welcomes all to his mini-malist room. The kitchen features the best in fresh local ingredients; appetizers are straightforward (an endive salad topped with warm goat cheese, toasted pecans, and drizzled with a tangy raspberry vinaigrette) or a smoked-salmon salad, while the main dishes are hearty yet refined: roasted duck breast with sun-dried British Columbian fruits; pan-seared scallops with inventive sauces; roasted fish; and grilled lamb. All receive rave reviews — and return visits. The pastry staff is solid, too, fashioning ginger cake with toffee sauce and homemade apricot ice cream.

2183 West 4th Ave. ☎ *604-738-2025. Reservations required. Main courses: C$24–C$30 (US$16–US$20). AE, DC, MC, V. Open: Dinner daily.*

C

$$–$$$$ Downtown   SEAFOOD

The city's undisputed culinary leading light is this waterside seafood restaurant, which constantly raises the bar with its cutting-edge take on the genre. They don't fool around with fish-and-chips here: Caviar is one of C's best appetizers (served in a gold-leaf pouch), or you can try a seafood chowder with ingredients from the world over. Main courses show an interest in local Asian tastes, as well as some rather unexpected Indian and even Middle Eastern influences; look for grilled tuna served with samosas and spice-braised tomatoes; seared British Columbia sable-fish on couscous and lentils, and the like; a "taster box" pairs smoky tea-cured salmon or lobster with a wrap of seared Angus beef. The wine list here is heavy on Alsatian whites, while deserts show a light touch — or, if you want to finish heavily, select from a cart of French cheeses.

1600 Howe St. ☎ *604-681-1164. Reservations accepted and recommended. Main courses: C$15–C$35 (US$10–US$23). AE, DC, JCB, MC, V. Open: Lunch and dinner daily.*

Café de Paris

$$ West End   FRENCH

Stuck right amid the full-throttle activity along busy Denman Street, this bistro really does feel like one in 1920s Paris or Montréal, from the wall art to the smoky music in the air. Yet you won't have to worry about pronouncing menu items correctly; service is refreshingly unpretentious. Everything here is steadfastly Franco: densely cheesy onion soup, escargot, fish stew, steak and *frites,* and all the rest. Wash it down with something from the wine list (plenty of big bouncy reds and bubbly whites), and don't forget an aperitif or a coffee. Of course, it wouldn't be a French dining experience without a delectable dessert — say, the discomfortingly comforting chocolate cake. Feeling full? Pull those in-line skates out, strap 'em on, and race your pals around Stanley Park. If you dare.

751 Denman St. ☎ *604-687-1418. Reservations accepted and recommended. Main courses: C$15–C$20 (US$10–US$13). AE, MC, V. Open: Lunch Mon–Fri, dinner daily.*

Chartwell

$$–$$$ Downtown   PACIFIC NORTHWEST/FUSION

A superb restaurant inside the expensive Four Seasons Hotel (see Chapter 10) has the ambiance of an upper-crust British club — put it this way, the fireplace is accented with a portrait of Winston Churchill and leather chairs — yet without the stuffy service you may expect. This is a good spot for pre-theater meals, and staff time the service to ensure that you make the curtain call. During lunch, however, it's a wheeler-dealer's kind of place, with a little too much loud laughter and glad-handing. Anyhow, the food is stellar, running to the expected standards such as rack of lamb and prime rib, but also to lighter fare including glazed salmon with salsa and potatoes, local scallops, or free-range chicken sided with *ragoût.* Vegetarians are also well served here, and the wine list is among the very best in the city — a good place to try a local wine.

791 West Georgia St. (in the Four Seasons Hotel). ☎ *604-689-9333. Reservations accepted and recommended. Main courses: C$15–C$30 (US$10–US$20). AE, DC, DISC, JCB, MC, V. Open: Lunch daily except Sat, dinner daily. Wheelchair-accessible.*

Chili Club

$$ Downtown   THAI

Right beneath the Burrard Bridge, this restaurant offers great water views of chugging ferry boats (ask to be seated in the bar upstairs if you like floor-to-ceiling windows) and more-inventive-than-usual Thai food such as red curry chicken, deep-fried fish with chili sauce, and stuffed mussels. Herbs and spices are wonderfully balanced. Want an inside tip? The best time to dine here is during Sunday brunch, when a spectacular buffet with more than 20 different items is laid out.

1000 Beach Ave. ☎ *604-681-6000. Reservations not necessary. Main courses: C$9–C$15 (US$6–US$10). AE, DC, MC, V. Open: Lunch and dinner daily. Wheelchair-accessible.*

CinCin

$$–$$$$ Downtown ITALIAN

Robson Street doesn't suffer from a lack of glitz and glamour, but the Italian-fusion CinCin is the icing on the cake. A decidedly hip and trendy (and famous) crowd comes in search of inventive pizzas and pastas concocted in the open-concept kitchen's roaring, wood-fired ovens. Begin with complimentary fresh bread and olive tapenade spread, perhaps an appetizer of hand-formed *bocconcini* (that's fresh mozzarella) and organic tomato salad; then go for the gusto with a pizza of smoked salmon, caramelized onions, capers, and *crème fraîche*. Too much for you to handle? Well, the pasta is good, too, often featuring fresh local fish and shellfish, olives, basil, and creamy tomato sauces. The restaurant features quite a good vegetarian menu, as well, and the sweets afterward include melt-in-your mouth *panna cotta* or a three-nut caramel tart. Just remember to display your peanut-sized cell phone prominently at your table at all times, or you're nobody.

1154 Robson St. ☎ 604-688-7338. Reservations accepted and recommended. Main courses: C$12–C$36 (US$8–US$24). AE, DC, MC, V. Open: Lunch daily except Sun, dinner daily.

Diva at the Met

$$–$$$ Downtown PACIFIC NORTHWEST/FUSION

Another pre- and post-theater hotspot inside a hotel, Diva at the Met is quite simply one of the best meals Vancouver has to offer. (Its chef was featured on the popular Japanese television show *The Iron Chef,* a culinary match where two chefs go head to head creating their own dishes from the same ingredients.) The menu takes cuisines from France, Italy, and Asia and shakes them up with fresh, local ingredients: Alaskan black cod with *foie gras* and leek or pan-seared scallops with fennel, for instance. Whatever you do, don't forget to order from the extensive cellar of British Columbian wines, and don't leave without a slice of English cheesecake.

645 Howe St. (in the Metropolitan Hotel). ☎ 604-602-7788. Reservations accepted and recommended. Main courses: $12–$30 (US$8–US$10). AE, DC, JCB, MC, V. Open: Breakfast, lunch, and dinner daily. Wheelchair-accessible.

The Fish House in Stanley Park

$$ West End SEAFOOD

This venerable institution capitalizes on its equally venerable location — planted firmly in the heart of Stanley Park, away from tour buses and in-line skaters — then serves up great West Coast meals. The chef has created some *nouvelle* casual bites such as a salmon sandwich on a sesame seed bagel with horseradish-dill cream cheese and capers, and added Asian entrees such as crispy prawn spring rolls. The old favorites (such as a hearty, large portion of clam chowder or fresh salmon cakes sided with mashed potatoes) also remain on the menu, though. If you don't like seafood, or you're allergic to it, take heart: They make a mean ribeye steak, too. In good weather, enjoy your meal out on the porch.

2099 Beach Ave. ☎ 604-681-7275. Reservations accepted and recommended. Main courses: C$15–C$30 (US$10–US$20). AE, DC, JCB, MC, V. Open: Lunch and dinner daily;. Wheelchair-accessible.

Five Sails

$$$–$$$$ Downtown   PACIFIC NORTHWEST/FUSION

The mountain and water views alone would be reason enough to dine here, but the food is spectacularly fancy — come prepared to splurge. The excellent, restrained menu runs mostly to Canadian meat, seafood, and vegetables; think lobster ravioli in a white-wine sauce, scallops in a peppercorn crust, a local rack of lamb, or some poached oysters. They take the whiskey and wine lists very seriously here, and the chocolate ice cream bonbons served at the end of every meal are just sublime. Whatever your reasons to come here, you won't leave hungry, disappointed, or wealthy.

999 Canada Place. ☎ 604-891-2892. Reservations accepted and recommended. Main courses: C$20–C$45 (US$13–US$30). AE, DC, JCB, MC, V. Open: Dinner daily. Wheelchair-accessible.

Fleuri

$$–$$$ Downtown   PACIFIC NORTHWEST/FUSION

Change is in the air at Fleuri, located inside the Sutton Place Hotel (see Chapter 10), but it remains wonderful and a magnet for the celebrity clientele who stay at the hotel. What's interesting here is the preponderance of some rather lavish buffets: daily afternoon high teas with scones, clotted cream, and all the fixings; a seafood buffet offered on Friday and Saturday nights; a Sunday brunch widely applauded as the best in town; and a weekend dessert buffet — more on this last one in a moment. Dining here isn't limited to buffets, though; stand-alone entrees combine French and Italian tastes with British Columbian ingredients such as sea bass. Now to that Chocoholic Bar: Each Thursday, Friday, and Saturday the restaurant lays out a mouthwatering spread of chocolate creations, anything from mousse to truffles to daring creations such as a chocolate fruit pizza or non-chocolate crêpes with ice cream. Definitely a place to see and be seen — and eat well.

845 Burrard St. (in the Sutton Place Hotel). ☎ 604-682-5511. Reservations accepted and recommended. Main courses: C$15–C$30 (US$10–US$20). AE, DC, DISC, JCB, MC, V. Open: Lunch and dinner daily. Wheelchair-accessible.

Floata Seafood Restaurant

$–$$$ Chinatown CHINESE

Some of the city's best *dim sum* is served at this enormous Chinatown favorite, which actually has its roots in Honk Kong. The lunchtime cuisine, served from those ubiquitous carts, is just what you would expect — a wide variety of steamed buns filled with pork, stir-fries, roasted duck or pork, fried or steamed sprig rolls, and much more — and the dinner entrees are better than you may expect. Don't come for a quiet meal; this place gets mobbed at lunch. They have another — some say better — location in the southern suburb of Richmond ☎ **604-270-8889.**

180 Keefer St. (restaurant located on 3rd floor). ☎ 604-270-0368. Reservations accepted and recommended. Main courses: C$3–C$30 (US$2–US$20). AE, DC, JCB, MC, V. Open: Breakfast, lunch, and dinner daily. Wheelchair-accessible.

Gotham Steakhouse

$$$$ Downtown STEAK

Now that eating red meat is hip again, restaurateurs are capitalizing on the latest carnivore carnival — and Gotham Steakhouse delivers the goods in spades, albeit at top dollar. This is one of a small chain of local steakhouses, but by far the newest and most over-the-top. Diners here are young, urban, and wealthy and appreciate management's single-minded efforts to create an upscale ode to maleness and meat. Steak is the star (only the best aged beef from the United States and Canada makes it here), grilled in huge, tender cuts and paired with plenty of good red wine choices to match; sides are more filling then inventive, with creamed spinach, sautéed mushrooms, fries, and more. Given the size and expense, sharing a meal between two people is not out of the question — just try not to catch the eye of those young Internet whipper-snappers laughing at you and pointing.

615 Seymour St. ☎ 604-605-8282. Reservations accepted and recommended. Main courses: C$29–C$40 (US$19–US$27). AE, DC, MC, V. Open: Dinner daily. Wheelchair-accessible.

Gyoza King

$–$$ West End JAPANESE

Gyoza, a Japanese take on potstickers or ravioli, are practically the only menu item at this wildly popular West End eatery — but it offers about two dozen moderately priced variations. To make them, half-moon dumplings are filled with pork, veggies, or shellfish, tarted up with spices, then deep-fried. Also on the board: a few sushi items and daily specials such as *udon* and *o-den* soups. Beer and wine are available to drink, and the place sucks a constant stream of patrons in from Robson Street's busy stretch — anyone from Japanese students and tourists to residents of the local neighborhood. Be patient with the staff, though, as some speak rather limited English.

Chapter 11: Dining and Snacking in Vancouver *133*

1508 Robson St. ☎ 604-669-8278. Reservations not necessary. Main courses: C$6–C$12 (US$4–US$8). AE, DC, JCB, MC, V. Open: Lunch and dinner daily.

Hon's Wun Tun House

$–$$ Chinatown   CHINESE

Love it or hate it, the original Hon's is a legend in Vancouver — real Chinese served in a really crazy, communal atmosphere. It's fast, cheap, and tasty, and though some of the foods may be foreign to your palate, you have to try them; the kitchen knows how to handle a menu that run to more than three hundred dishes. Specialties include stir-fried shrimp — sorry, prawns — in black bean sauce, Shanghai fried noodles with shredded beef, a range of congee (rice porridge) dishes, and much more. Side dishes keep things interesting as well, with items such as curry beef brisket and potato, steamed sticky rice wrap, and mini flour buns — fun just to say, not to mention eat! (I'd avoid pork knuckles, though.) Finish off with a sweet dessert such as chilled coconut-and-red bean cake. Note that Hon's has become a local chain in recent years, and has another, more upscale branch at 1339 Robson Street ☎ **604-685-0871** — but it lacks the authentic, gritty feel of the original.

268 Keefer St. ☎ 604-688-0871. Reservations not accepted. Main courses: C$4–C$15 (US$2.68–US$10). Credit cards not accepted at this location. Open: Lunch and dinner daily.

Il Giardino di Umberto

$$–$$$$ Downtown   ITALIAN

Umberto Menghi is the proud founder of this Tuscan star, with a menu of simple yet satisfying cuisine and a restaurant itself resembling a villa from that fair land — all wood-beamed ceilings, garden flowers, and hushed tones. The menu focuses on classic pasta *primi piatti* (first courses) such as linguine with pesto, tortellini *con panna, cannelloni* filled with game meats, or spaghetti carbonara. The *secondi* (main courses) are heavy on game and other meat dishes such as roasted pheasant breast with wild mushrooms, roasted reindeer loin, rack of lamb, and beef filet with a pinot noir sauce. The wine list is pretty darned good, too. When you call to reserve, try for a choice seat in the garden terrace.

1382 Hornby St. ☎ 604-669-2422. Main courses: C$14–C$33 (US$9–US$22). Reservations required. AE, DC, MC, V. Open: Lunch Mon–Fri, dinner daily except Sun; closed daily 2:30–5:30 p.m.

La Bodega

$–$$ Downtown   SPANISH

Tapas, small plates of exquisite dishes that are Spanish in origin, have taken Vancouver by storm — and La Bodega's offers some of the best.

About a half-dozen restaurants in the city now feature them. Most places fuse the form with Pacific Rim styles. However, *this* tapas bar stays the course and remains traditionally Spanish: Menu items run to rabbit, garlic prawns, pan-fried squid, and plenty of salty olives. The room is rather low-lit — on the up side, a good place to snuggle, though you can't exactly make out all the foods or faces. Be sure to try a glass of Spanish or Portuguese wine.

1277 Howe St. ☎ 604-684-8814. Main courses: C$3–C$15 (US$2–US$10). AE, MC, V. Open: Lunch and dinner daily.

Landmark Hot Pot House

$$–$$$ Shaughnessy CHINESE

Hot pots are hot right now, and few places in town do them better than Vancouver's original hotpot hotspot, south of the city center but pretty close to Queen Elizabeth Park and its conservatory. You get to do the cooking for a change; yes, you. You're presented with a choice of soup bases — chicken and seafood are popular — that are heated on a gas burner at your table. You then dip raw meat, seafood, or live shellfish into the hot stock and hold it there until it's done, then pop it into your mouth. Simple, trendy, healthy — but why do I have to tip? Shouldn't *they* be tipping *me?*

4023 Cambie St. ☎ 604-872-2868. Reservations not necessary. Main courses: Main courses: C$10–C$20 (US$7–US$15). MC, V. Open: Dinner daily. Wheelchair-accessible.

Le Crocodile

$$–$$$ Downtown FRENCH

Run by a transplanted Alsatian, this bright restaurant features classic French cuisine with a slight nod to that region's German-tinged food as well. That means the menu is heavy on fatty, filling food; best bets are the onion tart, fried sole, and game dishes. You'll want to complement the meal with a glass of wine, mostly (of course) French, and it goes without saying that dessert will be a memorable chocolatey or cheesy something.

909 Burrard St. ☎ 604-669-4298. Reservations accepted and recommended. Main courses: C$12–C$28 (US$8–US$19). AE, DC, MC, V. Open: Lunch Mon–Fri, dinner Mon–Sat. Wheelchair-accessible.

Liliget Feast House

$$$ West End NATIVE CANADIAN

If there's one restaurant you've simply got to see while in Vancouver, this is it: an authentic Native Canadian house right in the city's hip West End with big platters of native cuisine. You sit at unusual tables in a dining room entered via a wooden path lined with stones; the meal begins with a warmed flatbread called *bannock,* and main dishes are simple yet full of flavor — grilled halibut, smoked cod, grilled salmon, barbecued duck, and platters of seafood. The "Liliget Feast" is made for sharing between two people: a buffalo or caribou main dish, plus sides of steamed fern shoots or seaweed and wild rice. Meals here are rather expensive — but you certainly leave with a knowledge of native West Coast foodways, as well as a full stomach.

1724 Davie St. ☎ *604-681-7044. Main courses: C$17–C$30 (US$11–US$20). Reservations accepted and recommended. AE, DISC, DC, MC, V. Open: Dinner daily.*

Lumière

$$$–$$$$ **Kitsilano   FRENCH**

The sunny cuisine of Provence is featured at this excellent West Side bistro, which also tosses in the occasional Asian or Pacific accent. The chef is so dedicated to his craft that he regularly visits the region to bone up on techniques and get fresh ideas. Everything's good, but sample the tasting menus if you can — they include vegetarian, seafood, or other combinations designed to give a range of tastes. If you're not feeling quite so flush, go for the satisfying and simple roasted chicken with potatoes: Just like *maman* used to make. And the dairy-heavy desserts are simply sinful.

2551 West Broadway. ☎ *604-739-8185. Reservations accepted and recommended. Main courses: C$25–C$35 (US$17–US$23). AE, DC, MC, V. Open: Dinner daily except Mon. Wheelchair-accessible.*

900 West

$$–$$$ **Downtown   CONTINENTAL**

This elegant restaurant, ensconced in Hotel Vancouver (see Chapter 10), does classic Continental cuisine as well as any other upscale hotel eatery. The chef begins with standard meals such as rack of lamb, grilled lobster, veal tenderloin, smoked salmon or trout, then goes to town with capers and dill crème fraîche, mozzarella, and *shiitake* mushroom terrine. It offers afternoon high teas as well as anyone, too, and sports an especially strong local wine list. If you have room left for dessert, try the sampler plate — enough decadent sweets to feed two, with some left over to take back to your room.

900 West Georgia St. (in Hotel Vancouver). ☎ *604-669-9378. Reservations accepted and recommended. Main courses: C$12–C$28 (US$8–US$19). AE, MC, V. Open: Lunch and dinner daily.*

The Naam

$–$$ Kitsilano   VEGETARIAN

The city's undisputed top vegetarian nosh, this Kitsilano standby has been serving up salads, sandwiches, and breakfast — and maintaining its hippie vibe — for 30 years now. Despite the yuppification of the neighborhood, you'll still feel the laid-back (maybe *too* laid-back) charm that this always-open health food emporium delivers. People come for a variety of meatless variations on ethnic cuisines, plus interesting side dishes, always served in big tasty portions; top sellers include the sesame-spiced fries (to which you can add miso gravy or cheese) and quesadillas on grilled whole wheat tortillas. Slow service has been a problem plaguing this institution since the early years, however — and it isn't getting any faster. My advice? Don't show up starving.

2724 West 4th Ave. ☎ 604-738-7151. Reservations not accepted. Main courses: C$4–C$11 (US$3–US$7). AE, MC, V. Open: Breakfast, lunch, and dinner daily; open 24 hours. Wheelchair-accessible.

Phnom Penh

$–$$ Chinatown   VIETNAMESE

Considered the most authentic of the many Vietnamese restaurants in Vancouver, Phnom Penh serves up delicious — dare I say, Phnom-enal? — and cheap food in a pleasant setting. You'll be amazed at the flavor of such dishes as marinated butter beef, deep-fried squid or prawns, garlic chili squid or hot-and-sour soup. Other standards for updated tastebuds include beef brochettes and deep-fried spring rolls; vegetarian offerings are imaginative and tasty, as well. All of it should be accompanied by sweet Vietnamese coffee, either hot or iced, and a subtly sweetened dessert such as white bean pudding with coconut milk. Another branch is in Kitsilano at 955 West Broadway ☎ **604-734-8898**.

244 East Georgia St. ☎ 604-682-5777. Reservations not accepted. Main courses: C$5–C$11 (US$3–US$7). DC, MC. Open: Lunch and dinner daily except Tue.

Pink Pearl

$$ Chinatown   CHINESE

A great place for *dim sum,* seafood or just something a little different, the Pink Pearl is the kind of place where big Chinese families congregate for both daily meals and big occasions such as weddings — those can get pretty raucous. Try to ignore the clamor, though, and focus on the food. You can't go wrong with dishes such as prawns with ginger and green onions, sautéed scallops with cream-filled crisps, sautéed crab, special chicken, wonton soup, or yin-yang vegetables with crab meat sauce. Are you sensing a more playful hand than is normal at a Chinese joint? Well, you're right — there is.

1132 East Hastings St. ☎ *604-253-4316. Reservations not accepted. Main courses: C$11–C$18 (US$7–US$12). AE, DC, MC, V. Open: Lunch and dinner daily. Wheelchair-accessible.*

Raincity Grill

$$–$$$ West End   PACIFIC NORTHWEST/FUSION

Locals and tourists love this pleasant restaurant with its great food and million-dollar view; they love it so much that you may not get to enjoy that quiet romantic meal as quietly as you had planned. The chef makes sure ingredients are fresh and interesting — try seared and roasted giant sea scallops, abalone, and hazelnut-grilled salmon with asparagus, buttermilk mashed potatoes, or roasted fish cakes with fennel carrot slaw. Or go for the duck or crab, prepared with French sauces. The wine list couldn't be fuller with locally produced bottles, and desserts are rich: Triple mint honey mascarpone cheesecake, dark chocolate paté, or a cheese plate are just a few of the caloric offerings.

1193 Denman St. ☎ *604-685-7337. Reservations accepted and recommended. Main courses: C$13–C$25 (US$9–US$17). AE, DC, MC, V. Open: Lunch and dinner daily.*

Salmon House on the Hill

$$–$$$ West Vancouver (North Shore)   SEAFOOD

A great place to top off a day of sightseeing on the North Shore, this restaurant serves up mostly seafood — in fact, mostly salmon, no surprise there — prepared a variety of ways. The ambiance is West Coast all the way, with indigenous art lining the cedar walls and an upscale menu. The Salmon House Sampler flanks the buttery, succulent fish with a variety of chutneys, salsas, and relishes. Another entree pairs salmon with prawns, fiddlehead ferns, and blueberry salsa. Sick of salmon? You can also order grilled tuna dusted with black pepper, free-range chicken, or sea bass in star anise sauce. Desserts are recommended, too, with West Coast touches applied to classics such as tiramisù topped with blueberries. The awesome views of the Strait of Georgia, Vancouver's skyline, and the Burrard Inlet make just-before-sundown the best time to come.

2229 Folkestone Way. ☎ *604-926-3212. Reservations accepted and recommended. Main courses: C$15–C$25 (US$10–US$17). AE, DC, MC, V. Open: Lunch and dinner daily.*

The Teahouse Restaurant at Ferguson Point

$$–$$$ West End   PACIFIC NORTHWEST/FUSION

One of the classic Vancouver experiences, dining at the Teahouse is a special affair. First, the setting within the greenery of Stanley Park is simply stunning; second, despite the hordes of tour buses unloading at the door, the food still rates highly. The best seats in the house are inside the all-glass conservatory — pleasant even on days when the weather isn't cooperating. You'll want to start your meal with the signature Teahouse button mushrooms packed with crab, prawns, scallions, and Emmental cheese or else try the carrot and chive Chantilly cream soup. The main menu runs to things such as rack of lamb with raspberry sauce and garlic mashed potatoes, but also contemporary West Coast items such as seafood risotto or seared prawns and scallops with leek risotto and a pinot noir butter sauce. Desserts such as the Delight of the King — a pastry swan filled with rum custard and cream, all gliding along in a pool of chocolate sauce — must be tried just for the fun of it.

7501 Stanley Park Dr. ☎ 604-669-3281. Reservations required. Main courses: C$11–C$28 (US$7–US$19). AE, MC, V. Open: Lunch and dinner daily.

The William Tell

$$–$$$ Downtown CONTINENTAL

Swiss food in Vancouver? Who'd have thunk it. Yet it's true — they serve anything from rösti to raclette at this opulent hotel restaurant, plus a good deal more Continental cuisine as well. Everyone from the resident glitterati to local office workers sing the praises of the top-notch menu, which includes such stunners as veal and mushrooms in wine sauce with *rösti* (a Swiss potato pancake); *raclette* (French cheese, melted and spread on split potatoes); châteaubriand with béarnaise sauce and potatoes; breast of duck with baked layered yams in a maple sauce; and jumbo tiger prawns cooked Provençal style with spinach and parmesan cheese risotto. Keeping in the European tradition, desserts are no-holds-barred including an exceptional array of crêpes, cherries jubilee, crème brûlée, and more.

*765 Beatty St. (in the Georgian Court Hotel). ☎ **604-688-3504**. Reservations accepted. Main courses: C$8–C$30 (US$5–US$20). AE, DC, JCB, MC, V. Open: Breakfast, lunch, and dinner daily; closed daily 2–5:30 p.m. Wheelchair-accessible.*

Yaletown Brewing Company

$–$$ Yaletown PUB FARE

One of a handful of brewpubs that have sprouted in the formerly working-class Yaletown district, this one serves good meals such as pizza, burgers, ribs, and salmon — all done with a slightly upscale touch to match the quickly yuppifying surroundings. It almost goes without saying that you come here more for the beer than for the food, so make sure to try a draught — they even have a classy sampler rack of a half-dozen tiny beers.

*1110 Hamilton St. ☎ **604-681-2739**. Reservations: Recommended for dinner. Main courses: C$8–C$15 (US$5–US$10). AE, MC, V. Open: Lunch and dinner daily.*

Index of restaurants by neighborhood

Chinatown
Floata Seafood Restaurant (Chinese, $–$$$)
Hon's Wun Tun House (Chinese, $–$$)
Phnom Penh (Vietnamese, $–$$)
Pink Pearl (Chinese, $$)

Downtown
A Kettle of Fish (Seafood, $$–$$$$)
Bacchus (Continental, $$–$$$)
C (Seafood, $$–$$$$)
Chartwell (Pacific Northwest/Fusion, $$–$$$)
CinCin (Italian, $$–$$$$)
Diva at the Met (Pacific Northwest/Fusion, $$–$$$)
Five Sails (Pacific Northwest/Fusion, $$$–$$$$)
Fleuri (Pacific Northwest/Fusion, $$–$$$)
Gotham Steakhouse (Steak, $$$$)
Il Giardino di Umberto (Italian, $$–$$$$)
La Bodega (Spanish, $–$$)
Le Crocodile (French, $$–$$$)
900 West (Continental, $$–$$$)
The William Tell (Continental, $$–$$$)

Kitsilano
Bishop's (Pacific Northwest/Fusion, $$$)
Lumière (French, $$$–$$$$)
The Naam (Vegetarian, $–$$)

West Vancouver (North Shore)
Salmon House on the Hill (Seafood, $$–$$$)

Shaughnessy
Landmark Hot Pot House (Chinese, $$–$$$)

West End
Café de Paris (French, $$)
The Fish House in Stanley Park (Seafood, $$)
Gyoza King (Japanese, $–$$)
Liliget Feast House (Native Canadian, $$$)
Raincity Grill (Pacific Northwest/Fusion, $$–$$$)
The Teahouse Restaurant at Ferguson Point (Pacific Northwest/Fusion, $$–$$$)

Yaletown
Yaletown Brewing Company (Pub grub, $–$$)

Index of restaurants by cuisine

Chinese
Floata Seafood Restaurant (Chinatown, $–$$$)
Hon's Wun Tun House (Chinatown, $–$$)
Landmark Hot Pot House (Shaughnessy, $$–$$$)
Pink Pearl (Chinatown, $$)

Continental
Bacchus (Downtown, $$–$$$)
900 West (Downtown, $$–$$$)
The William Tell (Downtown, $$–$$$)

French
Café de Paris (West End, $$)
Le Crocodile (Downtown, $$–$$$)
Lumière (Kitsilano, $$$–$$$$)

Italian
CinCin (Downtown, $$–$$$$)
Il Giardino di Umberto (Downtown,
    $$–$$$$)

Japanese
Gyoza King (West End, $–$$)

Native Canadian
Liliget Feast House (West End, $$$)

Pacific Northwest/Fusion
Bishop's (Kitsilano, $$$)
Chartwell (Downtown, $$–$$$)
Diva at the Met (Downtown, $$–$$$)
Five Sails (Downtown, $$$–$$$$)
Fleuri (Downtown, $$–$$$)
Raincity Grill (West End, $$–$$$)
The Teahouse Restaurant at Ferguson
    Point (West End, $$–$$$)

Pub Fare
Yaletown Brewing Company (Yaletown,
    $–$$)

Seafood
A Kettle of Fish (Downtown, $$–$$$$)
C (Downtown, $$–$$$$)
The Fish House in Stanley Park
    (West End, $$)
Salmon House on the Hill (West Vancouver
    [North Shore], $$–$$$)

Spanish
La Bodega (Downtown, $–$$)

Steak
Gotham Steakhouse (Downtown, $$$$)

Vegetarian
The Naam (Kitsilano, $–$$)

Vietnamese
Phnom Penh (Chinatown, $–$$)

Index of restaurants by price

$$$$
CinCin (Italian, Downtown)
Five Sails (Pacific Northwest/Fusion,
    Downtown)
Gotham Steakhouse (Steak, Downtown)
Lumière (French, Kitsilano)

$$$
A Kettle of Fish (Seafood, Downtown)
Bacchus (Continental, Downtown)
Bishop's (Pacific Northwest/Fusion,
    Kitsilano)
C (Seafood, Downtown)
Chartwell (Pacific Northwest/Fusion,
    Downtown)
Il Giardino di Umberto (Italian,
    Downtown)
Le Crocodile (French, Downtown)

Liliget Feast House (Native Canadian,
    West End)
900 West (Continental, Downtown)
The Teahouse Restaurant at Ferguson
    Point (Pacific Northwest/Fusion,
    West End)
The William Tell (Continental, Downtown)

$$
Café de Paris (French, West End)
Diva at the Met (Pacific Northwest/Fusion,
    Downtown)
The Fish House in Stanley Park (Seafood,
    West End)
Fleuri (Pacific Northwest/Fusion,
    Downtown)
Floata Seafood Restaurant (Chinese,
    Chinatown)

Landmark Hot Pot House (Chinese, Shaughnessy)
Pink Pearl (Chinese, Chinatown)
Raincity Grill (Pacific Northwest/Fusion, West End)
Salmon House on the Hill (Seafood, West Vancouver [North Shore])

$

Gyoza King (Japanese, West End)
Hon's Wun Tun House (Chinese, Chinatown)
La Bodega (Spanish, Downtown)
Yaletown Brewing Company (Pub Grub, Yaletown)
The Naam (Vegetarian, Kitsilano)
Phnom Penh (Vietnamese, Chinatown)

Vancouver's Best Snacks

Vancouver's chock-full of eats, treats, and food on the go. Whether it's swimming in grease, covered in ketchup — sorry there, old chap, I meant malt vinegar — sliced into wedges, eaten standing up in a park, or packed in a picnic basket, you'll find it somewhere in town. Here's where.

Gimme a pizza that pie

It's hard to believe you would head all the way to Vancouver on vacation and then eat pizza. Then again, sometimes the urge just strikes. For those times, the C$.99 (US$.66) pizza slice phenomenon is a real bargain, and something of a fad among young people in Vancouver right now. Just remember that quality isn't all that consistent.

Still, if you're looking for a quick, cheap bite, dozens of competing places downtown are falling over each other to offer you a drink and a slice for the lowest price. **Flying Wedge Pizza** is the easiest to find with several locations around town, including a popular Gastown spot, 3499 Cambie Street (☎ 604-874-8284), but also plenty of other locations in Kitsilano, South Granville, and downtown.

Burgers and fried

Vancouver loves its thick and juicy burgers, and you'll be a burgermeister in no time if that's your thing. Naturally, fries and milkshakes are always offered on the side.

The concession stand at Third Beach in Stanley Park is reputed to make some of the best French fries in the city.

Fresgo Inn, 1138 Davie Street (☎ 604-689-1132), a lowbrow West End cafeteria, grills up hamburgers, eggs, and other greasy-spoon fare, and it's open quite late on the weekends — though not 'round-the-clock like it once was.

Hamburger Mary's, 1202 Davie Street (☎ 604-687-1293) is the burger queen of Vancouver, with a hopping West End location in the midst of the Davie Street action, great fries and shakes, a genuine diner feel, and very late opening hours. The food's less greasy here than at the more divey places, too.

The **Red Onion,** 2028 West 41st Avenue (☎ 604-263-0833) is a true local's pick, buried in the otherwise upscale Kerrisdale neighborhood, not far from the University of British Columbia campus. They make burgers, fries, and sandwiches, but everyone comes for the "double dogs": two sausages packed into one bun, dripping with toppings, cheese, and sauce.

The one-of-a-kind **Tomahawk,** 1550 Philip Avenue (☎ 604-988-2612), simply can't be ignored when you're up in North Vancouver. They've gone *way* over the top with the native-motif decoration, the menu names, and especially the food, which leans heavily toward stacked burgers and huge wedges of good pie. It's also a solid breakfast option — if you like heavy, cooked breakfasts, that is. Note that this place isn't as cheap as a fast-food burger joint.

Finally, **White Spot,** 2518 West Broadway (☎ 604-731-2434) and 1616 West Georgia Street (☎ 604-681-8034), is the most locally famous place of all. This tasty provincial hamburger chain was born in the '20s and now boasts dozens of locations around the city; the one on West Broadway still does carhop-at-your-window service. It's justly famous for the secret sauce.

Fish and pub grub

Lowbrow chip shops are easy to find around town. Some chippies even still go so far as to swaddle this meal in the traditional newspaper wrapping — find that, and you've probably found a winner.

Bud's Halibut & Chips, 1007 Denman Street (☎ 604-683-0061), is okay, though perhaps a little more famous than it deserves to be. Still, portions are huge.

King's Fare Fish & Chips, 1320 West 73rd Street (☎ 604-266-3474), is practically out at the airport but makes for a good bite if you're incoming or outgoing; they're smart enough to serve English-style beers alongside the food.

Grease is the word: The best diners

Greasy-spoon cafés around the city serve up cheap, popular breakfasts and other meals too; concentrations of these high-fat dives can be found along Granville and Davie Streets, and also in the somewhat down-at-the-heels neighborhood of East Hastings, east of Gastown. Don't like grease? Don't despair. Another kind of healthier, upscale diner is popping up in Vancouver in increasing numbers — a higher-end sort that serves burgers and malts, but also offers eggs Benedict, granola, pecan-encrusted French toast, actual squeezed juice, and sumptuous brunches. Hamburger Mary's (see "Burgers and Fried," earlier in the chapter) is one classic example; Sophie's (see its listing coming up) is another.

The cleverly named **Elbow Room,** 560 Davie Street (☎ **604-685-3628**), is your quintessential sassy, hard-nosed (but ultimately soft-hearted) diner where breakfast rules no matter the time of day or night. You get the feeling staff is hired according to snob factor.

Joe's Grill, 2061 West 4th Avenue (☎ **604-736-6588**), out in Kitsilano, offers a refreshingly non-New Agey take on food: big portions, tasty breakfasts, and low prices — all of which are hard to find hereabouts.

Practically next door to Joe's Grill, **Sophie's Cosmic Diner,** 2095 West 4th Avenue (☎ **604-732-6810**), is your classic yuppie diner: rib-sticking food, but some concessions to taste, spicing, and health too. Prices tend to be a little higher here, and weekend brunch is wildly popular.

The Only Seafood Cafe, 20 East Hastings (☎ **604-681-6546**), is the oldest continuously operating eatery in the city; too bad it's in a horribly sketchy area — because of location I recommend coming here for lunch or at least by cab in the evening. Head here for wondrous fried fish, shellfish, and chowders.

The Templeton, 1087 Granville Street (☎ **604-685-4612**), in Yaletown, is more of the same — a diner that's tough with the talk and low in fiber — but with something different too, a spike of spices you don't normally find in a diner.

Restaurant rescue for vegetarians

Vegetarians that just skipped the last three sections are in good luck: in Vancouver, for once, you are *very* well taken care of. Any Asian restaurant offers plenty of tasty tofu entrees, and the local hippie population has outfitted itself with a range of self-defense eateries to keep out the meat. One of these restaurants, **The Naam,** is so famous and good that I include it earlier in the chapter in "Vancouver's Best Restaurants." Here are a few more choices for meat-, fish- and fowl-avoiding travelers.

Juice Zone, 1059 Denman Street (☎ **604-608-0220**), is just what it sounds like, a juice bar; the offerings here are barely enough to make a meal, but for a quick vegetarian lunch on the go, it will do. This place is open quite late, too.

Juicy Lucy's, 1420 Commercial Drive (☎ 604-254-6101), is smack dab in the middle of Commercial Drive's activity, and serves inventive veggie Indian — and more mainstream — meals.

O-Tooz the Energie Bar, 777 Dunsmuir Street (☎ 604-684-0202), is no longer just whipping up convoluted juice blends; now the place has added good veggie — well, mostly veggie — meal options to a successful chain of shops located downtown and in the West End.

Planet Veg, 1941 Cornwall Avenue (☎ 604-734-1001), sates the veggie-happy of Kitsilano by serving cheapo Indian meals and similar fare.

The coffee connection

Vancouver has so much good coffee, I don't know where to begin — I only know what to avoid (more on that in a moment). For starters, the best coffee "bars" — many with Italian names — line the old Italian neighborhood along Commercial Drive; these are good places for an *espresso, cappuccino,* or *panino.* Ultra-hip Robson and Denman Streets are each also packed with more beans per square foot than any other neighborhood in the city; you really can't go wrong.

Whatever you do, though, please avoid the encroaching U.S. chains from that city just to the south. They can't make good coffee: Good coffee does not come flavored with — what *was* that? Fake hazelnuts? Yuck. (And coffee shouldn't come in a cistern-sized cup, either.)

Café Calabria, 1745 Commercial Drive (☎ 604-253-7017), is a dyed-in-the-wool Italian coffee bar, which means they known exactly how to make a *real* cappuccino, macchiata, or espresso.

Joe's Café, 1150 Commercial Drive (☎ 604-255-1046), unrelated to Joe's Grill (mentioned earlier in the section on diners), is *the* place to drink, well, joe when in Vancouver. It's very boho, and the young staff has created some extremely hip alternative coffee-based drinks. Dare I say it? The coffee is exciting.

Murchie's Tea & Coffee, 970 Robson Street (☎ 604-669-0783), is a very English importer of some of the world's finest teas, plus java too and a mouth-watering dessert selection. Several branches are around town, including a very centrally located one on Robson Street.

Sweets to eat

Chocoholics abound, and you're never very far from a fix if you're also a member of the club. Kitsilano, in particular, seems to have become Chocolate Central. Don't worry if you're more of an ice cream fan. Vancouver has what you're looking for, too.

Chocolate Arts, 2037 West 4th Avenue (☎ 604-739-0475), is pretty unique: A partnership between a master chocolatier and a local native artist. The result: Chocolate masks and other intricately designed treats that look too good to eat — but you'll want to anyway.

Cows, 1301 Robson Street (☎ 604-682-2622), is a popular Canadian chain that has gone a little overboard with the t-shirts and other cow-spotted paraphernalia. The ice cream is certainly passable and fresh, though.

Death by Chocolate, 1001 Denman Street (☎ 604-899-2462) and 1598 West Broadway (☎ 604-730-2462), may force you to pry open your wallet. So what? This is perhaps the best locally made chocolate in Vancouver. Simply amazing.

Sure, the flagship scoop shop of **La Casa La Gelato,** 1033 Venables Street (☎ 604-251-3211), is way off the beaten path east of East Hastings — but ice cream freaks should find it anyhow. These folks, like a madly experimenting Mr. Wonka, crank out some of the weirdest ice creams known to mankind (wasabi (!) and wild asparagus, for example); try something. Other branches are around town.

The sweets at **True Confections,** 666 Denman Street (☎ 604-682-1292) and 3701 West Broadway (☎ 604-222-8489), aren't anywhere near cheap level, but boy are they good.

Urban guerrilla power picnicking

Vancouver is a picnickers' kind of town, the rainy weather not with-standing. At markets such as Granville Island Public Market, or others on Robson Street and the Lonsdale Quay SeaBus landing in North Vancouver, you can stock up on fresh fruit and veggies, smoked fish, desserts, and maybe a boxed iced tea or juice drink. This section takes a look at some of the city's other premiere picnic providers, most located off the downtown peninsula in either Kitsilano or adjacent South Granville. After picking up your supplies, head to nearby Wreck Beach, Kits Beach, Pacific Spirit Park, or the campus of the University of British Columbia.

Capers, 2285 West 4th Avenue (☎ 604-739-6685), is a kind of combina-tion gourmet food store and health food store, with a substantial gour-met takeout business on the side. Salmon, roasted chicken, exotic salads, pastas, and soups? No problem; they're all here, ready to go.

Lesley Stowe Fine Foods, 1780 West 3rd Avenue (☎ 604-731-3663), is a superior caterer with a justifiably high reputation for sweets, take-'em-and-eat-'em entrees, and high-quality beverages.

Meinhardt Fine Foods, 3002 Granville Street (☎ 604-732-4405), in South Granville is known for its ready-to-go goodies.

Urban Fare, 177 Davie Street (☎ 604-975-7550), is Yaletown's upscale neighborhood grocery store, where you find great produce, French breads — from France — and plenty of meals-ready-to-roll. This is a real winner.

Chapter 12

Exploring Vancouver

. . . .

In This Chapter

▶ Checking out the most popular destinations and rewarding activities

▶ Choosing guided tours on foot or wheels

▶ Tailoring your trip with four ready-to-follow itineraries

. . . .

C onsidered as a whole, Vancouver presents a lot of territory to
cover, but I'm here to help. Whether you're interested in strapping
on your walking shoes and checking out the coolest neighborhoods
and historic sights, or you just want to sit in a tour bus and let someone else narrate away, I tell you how to find the sights that make this
city special. I also devise several specific itineraries targeted at travelers with special interests. Ready? Let's go!

Discovering Vancouver's Top Sights from A to Z

Bloedel Floral Conservatory

Shaughnessy-Cambie

You'll be thankful for the warm, dry Plexiglas dome of this floral conservatory on a rainy Vancouver day. Under the dome away from the elements, a spectacular array of plant (5,000 species) and animal life thrives
in different types of climates. You find a desert oasis complete with
prickly cacti and a lush tropical jungle of banana trees, colorful plants,
and free-flying parrots (plus hundreds of exotic birds). These sights,
along with a pond stocked with colorful fish, will entertain the kids. The
rest of big Queen Elizabeth Park is also worth some time, too, for its walking trails and fun pitch-and-putt golf course (see "Finding More Cool
Things to See and Do" later in this chapter). Allow 1 hour.

Queen Elizabeth Park (33rd at Cambie St.). ☎ *604-257-8570. Internet:* www.city.
vancouver.bc.ca/parks. *Admission: Adults C$3.50 (US$2.35), seniors C$2
(US$1.34), children 6–17 C$1.65 (US$1.11). Family rate C$7.00 (US$4.69) for up to 2
adults and 4 children (max of 6 people). Open: Apr–Sept weekdays 9 a.m.–8 p.m.;
weekends 10 a.m.–9 p.m.; Oct–Mar daily 10 a.m.–5 p.m.*

Canadian Craft Museum

Downtown

This space, devoted to handmade crafts in all their various forms, is a folksy, welcome addition to the downtown corridor. Most of the collections represent Canadian artisans, although international temporary exhibits are wedged in from time to time; you can see works that deal in fibers (knitted clothing and needlepoint, for example), wood, pottery, and glassware. Workshops and lectures devoted to these arts and crafts are frequently held here, and the gift shop, one of the best in town, sells a range of handmade Canadian crafts. Allow 1 hour.

639 Hornby St. ☎ 604-687-8266. Admission: Adults C$5 (US$3.35), seniors and students C$3 (US$2), children under 13 free. Open: June–Aug Mon–Sat 10 a.m.–5 p.m. (until 9 p.m. Thurs), Sun and holidays 12–5 p.m.; Sept–May Mon, Wed–Sat 10 a.m.–5 p.m. (until 9 p.m. Thurs) and Sun noon to 5 p.m.

Capilano Suspension Bridge and Park

North Vancouver

This is *the* quintessential Vancouver experience for those who don't mind parting with a bundle of dough just to say they walked a narrow, swinging bridge high above a raging river. You certainly won't be alone — this place gets busy with tourists. More than just a bridge attracts visitors here; you can also find out about First Nations culture by watching traditional dancers perform or native carvers turn humble logs into noble totem poles. Other attractions include gardens, a forestry exhibit, and a center explaining the history of the bridge, plus hiking trails and the obligatory restaurant and gift shop. Allow 1 hour

Nearby Lynn River Canyon, which is less commercial, offers pretty much the same experience for free (see its listing later in this chapter).

3735 Capilano Rd. (To get there by car, take Hwy. 1 to exit 14 and follow road for approximately 1.2 miles (2 km). By bus from downtown Vancouver, take bus #246 directly to the bridge; from North Vancouver, take bus #236 from Lonsdale Quay.) ☎ 604-985-7474. Internet: www.capbridge.com. Admission: Adults C$10.75 (US$7), seniors C$8.75 (US$6), students with ID C$6.75 (US$4.52), children 6–12 C$3.25 (US$2.18). Open: Mid-May–Sept daily 8:30 a.m. to dusk; Oct–mid-May daily 9 a.m.–5 p.m.; closed Christmas day.

Chinatown

The most authentic of Vancouver's ethnic neighborhoods, Chinatown — bawling, boisterous, crowded, a little odd-smelling — simply must be experienced. It's so small that a tour doesn't take much time at all. Begin on Keefer Street, the center of the action and the location of any number of eateries, herb shops, and seafood markets. Here you find the Chinese Cultural Centre and the Dr. Sun-Yat Sen Classical Garden (see the next two listings). Don't forget to try a steamed bun or something more exotic at a place such as Hon's Wun Tun House (see Chapter 11). Finally, the 5-foot wide Sam Kee Building, at 8 West Pender Street, is the so-called narrowest building in the world, and everyone tromps over to take a look. Allow 1 to 2 hours.

Located along Keefer and Pender Streets, from Abbott St. to Gore Ave.

Chinese Cultural Centre

Chinatown

The newly opened Chinese Cultural Centre is a nice addition to the adjoining Dr. Sun Yat-Sen Classical Chinese Garden (see next listing). Through the center's extensive library, educational displays, archives, and even classes, you can discover the interesting history of Chinese immigrants who settled in this bustling neighborhood. A great time to visit is during the 2-week-long Chinese New Year festivities in late January and early February, which are sponsored and coordinated by the cultural center. Allow a ½ hour.

50 East Pender St. ☎ *604-687-0729. Internet:* http://cccvan.com. *Admission: Free. Open: Daily 9 a.m.–5 p.m. Wheelchair-accessible.*

Dr. Sun Yat-Sen Classical Chinese Garden

Chinatown

The first authentic classical Chinese garden built outside of China, this serene spot offers a place for contemplation right in the heart of busy Chinatown. All the materials used in the garden were shipped from China in nearly a thousand separate boxes — including the plants and building supplies. The aim of the garden is to present visitors with a vision of Taoist philosophy — a quiet place to contemplate the harmony in nature. The garden features architecture with exquisite carved windows and moon-shaped doors, twisting walkways, waterfalls, and trees, all of it carefully symbolic of something — ask someone to explain the code to you. Ironically, this island of serenity is one of the most visited attractions in Vancouver and may not be so serene when you get here; try for early morning or just before closing to get the most out of the experience. Allow 1 hour.

578 Carrall St. (east side of downtown core). ☎ *604-662-3207 or 604-689-7133. Internet:* www.discovervancouver.com/sun. *Admission: Adults C$7.50 (US$5), seniors C$6.50 (US$4.35), children 5–17 C$5 (US$3.35). Open: Mid-June–mid-Sept daily 9:30 a.m.–7 p.m.; mid-Sept–Apr daily 10 a.m.–4:30 p.m. ; May–mid-June daily 10 a.m.–6 p.m.*

Vancouver Attractions

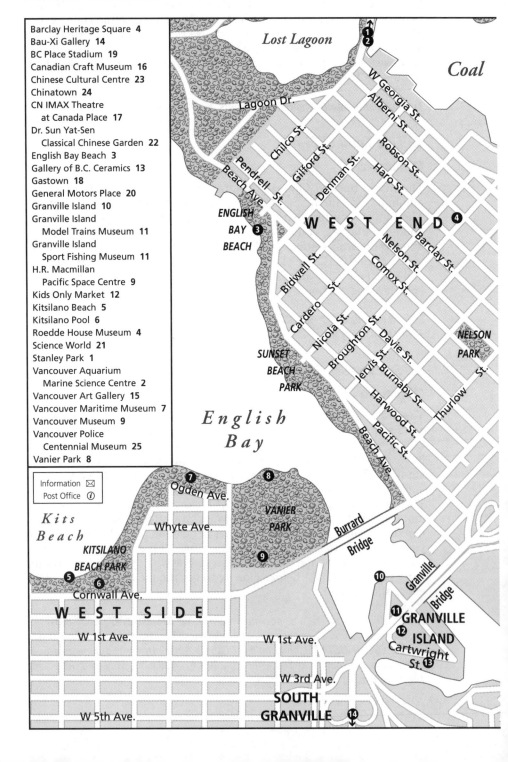

Barclay Heritage Square **4**
Bau-Xi Gallery **14**
BC Place Stadium **19**
Canadian Craft Museum **16**
Chinese Cultural Centre **23**
Chinatown **24**
CN IMAX Theatre
   at Canada Place **17**
Dr. Sun Yat-Sen
   Classical Chinese Garden **22**
English Bay Beach **3**
Gallery of B.C. Ceramics **13**
Gastown **18**
General Motors Place **20**
Granville Island **10**
Granville Island
   Model Trains Museum **11**
Granville Island
   Sport Fishing Museum **11**
H.R. Macmillan
   Pacific Space Centre **9**
Kids Only Market **12**
Kitsilano Beach **5**
Kitsilano Pool **6**
Roedde House Museum **4**
Science World **21**
Stanley Park **1**
Vancouver Aquarium
   Marine Science Centre **2**
Vancouver Art Gallery **15**
Vancouver Maritime Museum **7**
Vancouver Museum **9**
Vancouver Police
   Centennial Museum **25**
Vanier Park **8**

Information ✉
Post Office ⓘ

Lost Lagoon

Coal

W Georgia St.
Alberni St.
Lagoon Dr.
Chilco St.
Gilford St.
Robson St.
Pendrell St.
Beach Ave.
Denman St.
Haro St.
W E S T   E N D ❹

Nelson St.
Barclay St.
Comox St.
Bidwell St.
Cardero St.
Nicola St.
Broughton St.
Davie St.
NELSON PARK

SUNSET BEACH PARK
Jervis St.
Burnaby St.
Thurlow St.
Harwood St.

ENGLISH BAY BEACH ❸

English Bay

Pacific St.
Beach Ave.

❼
❽
Ogden Ave.
VANIER PARK
Whyte Ave.
Burrard Bridge
❾

Kits Beach
KITSILANO BEACH PARK
❺ ❻
Cornwall Ave.

❿
Granville

W E S T   S I D E
W 1st Ave.
W 1st Ave.

⓫ **GRANVILLE**
⓬ **ISLAND**
Cartwright St. ⓭
Bridge

W 3rd Ave.

W 5th Ave.
SOUTH GRANVILLE ⓮

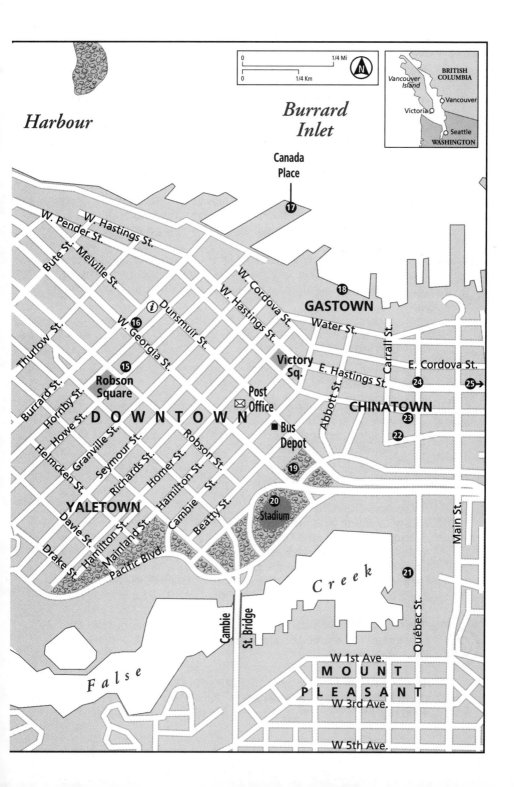

Harbour

Burrard
Inlet

BRITISH
COLUMBIA

Vancouver
Island

Victoria

Vancouver

Seattle
WASHINGTON

Canada
Place

17

W. Hastings St.

W. Pender St.

Bute St.
Melville St.

W. Cordova St.

W. Hastings St.

18

GASTOWN

Water St.

Carrall St.

E. Cordova St.

Dunsmuir St.

Thurlow St.

W. Georgia St.

16

Victory
Sq.

E. Hastings St.

24

25

15

Robson
Square

Burrard St.

Hornby St.

Howe St.

Post
Office

CHINATOWN

Abbott St.

23

D O W N T O W N

22

Granville St.

Seymour St.

Richards St.

Homer St.

Robson St.

Bus
Depot

Helmcken St.

19

YALETOWN

Hamilton St.

Cambie St.

Beatty St.

20

Stadium

Davie St.

Hamilton St.

Mainland St.

Main St.

Drake St.

Pacific Blvd.

C r e e k

21

Cambie

St. Bridge

Québec St.

W 1st Ave.

F a l s e

M O U N T

P L E A S A N T

W 3rd Ave.

W 5th Ave.

Gastown

The original historic center of Vancouver, Gastown was once presided over by the garrulous barkeep nicknamed (for his oration) "Gassy Jack" Deighton. His statue now stands in Maple Leaf Park, a slightly decrepit area of this part touristy, part seedy neighborhood. Attractions here include the Vancouver Police Centennial Museum (see "Finding More Cool Things to See and Do," later in this chapter); plenty of 19th-century architecture; the old-fashioned ambiance of shops, restaurants, and bars; and the closeness of downtown and the waterfront. The biggest draw, however, is a steam clock — which doesn't actually run on steam, though it does *emit* steam every 15 minutes for effect — at the corner of Water and Cambie Street. The Landing, a restored heritage building that has been transformed into an upscale mall at 375 Water Street, is worth a moment, as are excellent bars, cafés, and vintage clothing stores. Allow 1 hour; allow 2 hours or more if dining or visiting a bar.

Be wary though that East Hastings Street, which connects Gastown and Chinatown, is one of the city's worst — home to plenty of drug addicts and the like. Find another route to walk, or take a cab, if you visit at night.

Located along Water and Cordova Streets, just east of the SkyTrain's Waterfront station and just west of Chinatown.

Granville Island

Granville Island, teeming with houseboats and shop stalls, is a public space success story that has become one of the most visited areas in the Greater Vancouver region. Locals, art students, *and* tourists flock here. They come for the fantastic Granville Island Public Market, with its fresh food from British Columbia and the world over. Other stalls and stands sell ready-to-eat ethnic and specialty foods, anything from French cuisine to sushi. Kids enjoy the Kids Only Market here (see "Finding More Cool Things to See and Do," later in this chapter, for more on this). You can find outdoor seating with pleasant views of False Creek and the West End — although annoying street musicians and seagulls also seem to like these tables, and on those days you may actually hope for rain. Three worth-while indoor destinations are the Model Ships, Model Trains, and Sport Fishing Museums (see "Finding More Cool Things to See and Do"). Allow 2 or 3 hours if the weather's good; allow more time for visiting museums.

Don't even think of parking here during the weekend; instead take the convenient False Creek Ferries, tiny boats that whisk you from the West End.

☎ *604-666-5784. Internet:* www.granvilleisland.bc.ca. *Admission: Free. Open: Daily late May–early Oct 9 a.m.–6 p.m.; late Oct–early May Tues–Sun 9 a.m.–6 p.m.*

Greater Vancouver Attractions

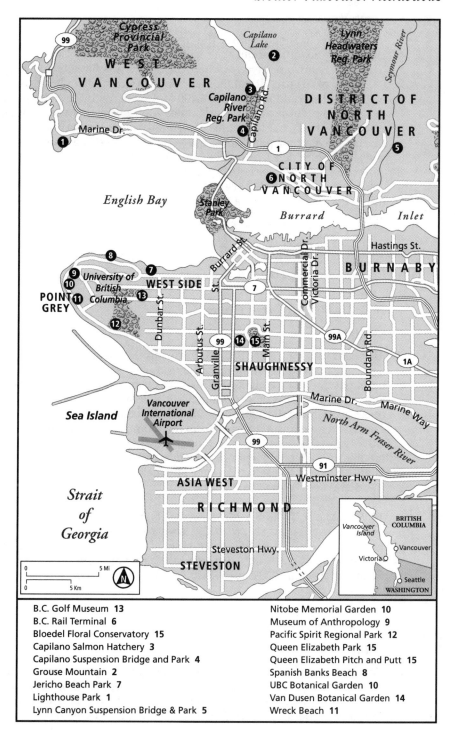

B.C. Golf Museum **13**	Nitobe Memorial Garden **10**
B.C. Rail Terminal **6**	Museum of Anthropology **9**
Bloedel Floral Conservatory **15**	Pacific Spirit Regional Park **12**
Capilano Salmon Hatchery **3**	Queen Elizabeth Park **15**
Capilano Suspension Bridge and Park **4**	Queen Elizabeth Pitch and Putt **15**
Grouse Mountain **2**	Spanish Banks Beach **8**
Jericho Beach Park **7**	UBC Botanical Garden **10**
Lighthouse Park **1**	Van Dusen Botanical Garden **14**
Lynn Canyon Suspension Bridge & Park **5**	Wreck Beach **11**

Grouse Mountain

North Vancouver

If you arrive in Vancouver for the first time at dusk, you may see twinkling lights hovering about the night sky above the city. No, they're not UFOs left over from the days when *The X-Files* was filmed here. They're the lights of Grouse Mountain, tempting you from high above to come have a bird's-eye look from the 3,700-foot peak. With the hefty price of the 8-minute journey up the mountain, you're best to make a day of it. Up top, you find a bar that hops year-round, a decent restaurant, a movie theater, playground, pony rides, and — in winter — skiing, snowboarding, and sledding, which are especially fun at night with the city lights below. You won't be bored, although you may be a little put off by the blatant commercialism of it all. Hikers and purists usually skip all that and do the steep "Grouse Grind," a near-vertical ascent of the peak. Allow 2 to 6 hours.

6400 Nancy Greene Way. ☎ *604-984-0661. Internet:* www.grousemtn.com. *Admission: Adults C$16.95 (US$11), seniors C$14.95 (US$10), children 13–18 C$10.95 (US$7), children 7–12 C$5.95 (US$4). Open: Daily 9 a.m.–10 p.m.*

H.R. MacMillan Space Centre

Kitsilano

Also known as the Pacific Space Centre, this thrill-a-minute museum manages to capture most visitors' attention with interactive exhibits that highlight Canada's contributions to space exploration. The real show-stopper is the Virtual Voyages Simulator, where for 5 heart-pounding minutes you're jolted through space like a character in *Star Wars;* the Cosmic Courtyard contains a real rock from the moon; and the Gordon Southam Observatory houses huge telescopes — you can take snapshots of the moon for C$10 (US$7) a pop. The Vancouver Museum (see listing in this chapter) shares the same entrance and makes a good bookend trip with this attraction. Allow 1 to 2 hours.

1100 Chestnut St. ☎ *604-738-7827. Internet:* www.hrmacmillanspacecentre. com. *Admission: Adults C$12.50 (US$8), seniors and children 11–18 C$9.50 (US$6), children 5–10 C$8.50 (US$6). Laser shows C$7.75 (US$5). Open: Sept–June Tues–Sun 10 a.m.–5 p.m.; July–Aug daily. Laser shows Sept–June Thurs–Sun 9 p.m. (second showing at 10:30 p.m. Fri–Sat); July–Aug daily 9:30 p.m. (second showing 10:45 p.m. Thurs–Sat).*

Jericho Beach Park

Point Grey

The first in a string of beaches that hug Point Grey, Jericho Beach is a quiet place to bring a Frisbee, dog, or a good book. What used to be a military complex is now a premier beach destination for families and would-be anglers. The view from the park is of mist-covered mountains and freight ships moored in English Bay. Playing fields are nearby, as well as a small playground and a youth hostel. In summer, the annual Folk Festival takes place here. Allow 1 to 2 hours.

At the foot of Point Grey Rd. and 4th Ave. (West, 3 miles east of Granville Bridge.) Admission: Free. Open: Daily dawn to dusk.

Kitsilano Beach

Kitsilano

The quintessential Vancouver Beach experience is a trip over to Kitsilano Beach, called "Kits" by the locals. The beach offers fantastic views of the mountains and the city skyline, a host of activities, and a shell-filled beach — not to mention proximity to the beautiful people and trendy cafes that line Cornwall Avenue. Allow 1 to 2 hours.

At the foot of Cornwall Ave. and Arbutus St. ☎ 604-731-0011. Admission: Free. Open: Daily dawn to dusk.

Lynn Canyon Suspension Bridge & Park

Lynn Valley

If you like scary heights but don't want to pay for the experience, visit Lynn Canyon Suspension Bridge rather than its nearby cousin, Capilano Bridge. This one's higher (though shorter). Here you're right in the thick of a beautiful rain forest of Douglas firs as you teeter more than 16 stories over a gorge. (Kayakers often run the river; no throwing stuff over the side to distract them.) You also find the Lynn Canyon Ecology Centre with films, slide shows, and displays as well as tours to explain the ecosystem around you. Make sure to pack a lunch, sturdy hiking shoes, trail maps, and bear whistles if you want to make a day of it and head down one of the surrounding trails. Allow 1 to 4 hours; 1 hour to cross the bridge and visit the Ecology Centre and up to 4 hours for hikes that radiate out from the park.

Take Trans-Canada Hwy. (Hwy. 1) to Lynn Valley Rd. exit. Continue north to Peters Rd. and make a right to parking lot at end of the road. ☎ 604-981-3103. Admission: Free. Open: Park daily dawn to dusk for cars and 24 hours for pedestrians and cyclists, Lynn Canyon Ecology Centre daily 10 a.m.–5 p.m.

Museum of Anthropology

Point Grey

Located on the green campus of the University of British Columbia, this may be the city's top sight. In a building inspired by the longhouses of First Nations villages, the museum has carved front doors that open into a great hall where totem poles welcome you. With the aid of a free booklet, you can examine some 15,000 artifacts in glass drawers. Most of the holdings relate to Native Canadian peoples, although you also find a wing of European ceramics. Highlights include carver Bill Reid's masterpiece *The Raven and the First Men,* which powerfully depicts a creation myth in which frightened humans emerge from a clamshell only to face a cackling Raven. Scary stuff. Outside stand two Haida big houses and more totem poles. While in the area, check out the UBC Botanical Garden (see listing in this chapter) and stroll through the university's campus, with its views of the mountains and sea. Allow 1 to 2 hours.

6393 Northwest Marine Dr. ☎ 604-822-3825. Internet: www.moa.ubc.ca. *Admission: Adults C$7 (US$5), seniors C$5 (US$3.35), students C$4 (US$2.68), children under 6 free; free Tues 5–9 p.m. Bring lots of small change for parking meters. Open: Late May–early Sept daily 10 a.m.–5 p.m. (Tues until 9 p.m.); late Sept–early May Tues–Sun 11 a.m.–5 p.m. (Tues until 9 p.m.).*

Pacific Spirit Regional Park

Point Grey

Formerly called the University Endowment Lands, this huge park with towering trees and mysterious paths embodies what the Canadian west is: green, leafy and vaguely spiritual. Located adjacent to the University of British Columbia, the park (which is even bigger than thousand-acre Stanley Park, and *much* less discovered) is a terrific place for a quiet stroll away from the madding crowds, amidst the towering and wonderful-smelling rain forest — just be sure not to get lost in the maze of trails. Allow 2 hours if hiking.

Bordered by Southwest Marine Dr., 16th Ave. West, and Imperial Rd., about 3 miles west of Granville St. Admission: Free.

Science World

Main Street Station

You have to be a science buff — or a kid — to really get into this geodesic dome (actually, it looks like a big golf ball) twinkling in the night sky across the street from Pacific Central Station in a forlorn industrial corner of downtown. The Matter and Forces gallery contains cool exhibits that fascinate young minds: The Plasma Ball (which tests your electrical conductivity) and the Shadow Wall (which holds your shadow in place using phosphorescent materials) are two of the more interesting ones. The mining exhibit is surprisingly pro-mining — well, this *is* Canada, after all — while natural science is tackled from a beaver lodge's point of view. Young kids (say, ages 3 to 6) enjoy the KidSpace Gallery with its brightly colored toys and giant building blocks. A giant-screen panoramic theater shows mostly science-themed films. Allow up to 2 hours, especially if seeing a film.

1455 Quebec St. ☎ 604-268-6363. Internet: www.scienceworld.bc.ca. *Admission including exhibits, laser theater, and OMNIMAX: Adults C$14.75 (US$10); seniors, students, and children C$10.50 (US$7); children under 4 free. Admission* *including exhibits and laser theater: Adult C\$11.75 (US\$8); seniors, students, and children C\$7.75 (US\$5). Open: July–early Sept daily 10 a.m.–6 p.m.; late Sept–June weekdays 10 a.m.–5 p.m., weekends and holidays 10 a.m.–6 p.m.*

Stanley Park

West End

Every city should be so lucky to have easy access to such a diverse and beautiful park. This thousand-acre green space, a wonderful respite from downtown traffic, is the one truly must-see attraction in Vancouver. You can bike, in-line skate, stroll, or sunbathe on the miles of paths and sea-wall that ring and crisscross the park. The park also features lawn bowling (for the ultimate British experience) and a par-three golf course. Begin at the park information booth near Lost Lagoon, the taking-off point for horse-drawn carriage tours (see "Seeing Vancouver by Guided Tour," later in this chapter) and bicycle rentals (see Chapter 9). As you drive, bike, or walk the 6-mile, one-way circuit, you pass Brockton Oval — a semi-circle of native Kwakiutl totem poles — and two native canoes carved from a cedar log. This area has the largest concentration of tour buses and camera-toting tourists. If you continue beyond the children's farm and a miniature train, things quiet again and you pass Deadman's Island, a former First Nations burial ground and quarantine during a late 19th-century epidemic of smallpox; the Empress of Japan figurehead; and then remote Third Beach and Ferguson point, home to The Teahouse Restaurant (see Chapter 11). Completing the circuit, you pass The Fish House in Stanley Park positioned strategically near Denman Street and English Bay (see Chapter 11). Allow 2 to 5 hours.

When you descend the stairs to Third Beach, turn right and walk down to the end of the beach. Any of the benches along that walk are secluded and have a great, kissable view of the sunset.

2099 Beach Ave. ☎ 604-257-8438. Internet: www.city.vancouver.bc.ca/ parks. *Admission: Park free, farmyard and train adults C\$2.60 (US\$1.74), seniors and children under 12 C\$1.30 (US\$.87). Open: Park year-round; farmyard daily 11 a.m.–4 p.m.; train May–Sept daily 11 a.m.–5 p.m.*

UBC Botanical Garden and Nitobe Memorial Garden

Point Grey

The University of British Columbia's eight botanical gardens and the separate (but sensational) Nitobe Garden ratchet up the green factor in a city already blessed with acres of green space. The UBC botanical circuit includes a 16th-century replica of a medicinal garden, native B.C. flowers and plants, and Alpine and food gardens. The Nitobe Memorial Garden, the most authentic Japanese garden in North America, consists of a large, informal Stroll Garden lined with a stone path bearing a passing resemblance to maps of the Milky Way — a subtle comment on the harmony running through nature, large and small. Here graceful bridges span the streams, while colorful *koi* fish swim through a placid pool. The garden's other section, the Tea Garden, has a stone path leading to a Tea House where tea ceremonies are held and a Japanese garden planted with native Japanese maples, cherry trees, azaleas, and irises; come in spring to see the cherries blossom or in fall to see the maples turning. Allow 1 to 2 hours.

6804 S.W. Marine Dr. ☎ *604-822-9666. Internet:* www.hedgerows.com. *Admission: Main Garden, Adults C$4.50 (US$3), seniors and students 14–18 C$2.25 (US$1.50), children 6–13 C$1.75 (US$1.18); Nitobe Garden, Adults C$2.50 (US$1.68), seniors and students 14–18 C$1.75 (US$1.18), children 6–13 C$1.50 (US$1). Open: Main Garden daily 10 a.m.–6 p.m.; Nitobe Garden Mar–mid-Oct daily 10 a.m.–6 p.m.; late Oct–Feb Mon–Fri 10 a.m.–2:30 p.m.*

Vancouver Aquarium Marine Science Centre
West End

You're instantly reminded that you are in the Pacific Northwest the moment you enter Vancouver's Aquarium and see the huge bronze killer whale looming. The aquarium features a tropical gallery, which simulates an Indonesian reef and tidal pool teeming with piranhas and black-tip reef sharks, and an Amazon gallery with an hourly tropical computer-generated "thunderstorm" and an impressive collection of rain forest fauna — three-toed sloths, scarlet ibis, toucans, boa constrictors, multi-eyed fish, and more. Another cool section — literally — highlights native Arctic species such as beluga whales. Here you can find a killer whale tank, though kids may get more of a kick out of the Steller sea lions in a nearby pool who share their home with a rescued harbor seal. (They do a lot of marine rescue and rehabilitation here.) . Other exhibits bring home the ecosystems of the Strait of Georgia and the Northern Pacific. Allow 2 hours.

Stanley Park. ☎ *800-931-1186 or 604-659-3474. Internet:* www.vanaqua.org. *Admission: Adults C$13.85 (US$9), seniors and students 13–18 C$11.70 (US$8), children 4–12 C$9.15 (US$6). Open: July–Sept daily 9:30 a.m.–7 p.m.; Oct–June daily 10 a.m.–5:30 p.m.*

Vancouver Maritime Museum
Kitsilano

This museum in Vanier Park isn't Vancouver's best-known or biggest, but it's actually pretty interesting if you're a marine buff. It highlights the region's maritime heritage, using the central exhibits of a restored Arctic exploring ship. Kids can pilot a remote-controlled deep-sea robot, visit a boatbuilding workshop, and check out model ships. This being Vancouver, a totem pole stands guard, and — appropriately enough — you can get here using the False Creek ferries from downtown or Granville Island. Allow 1 hour.

1905 Ogden Ave. (in Vanier Park). ☎ *604-257-8300. Internet:* www.vmm.bc.ca. *Admission: Adults C$6 (US$4), seniors and children under 19 C$3 (US$2). Family rate C$14 (US$9) for up to 2 adults and 4 children (max of 6 people). Open: Early Sept–late May Tues–Sun 10 a.m.–5 p.m.; June–Aug daily 10 a.m.–5 p.m.*

Vancouver Museum

Kitsilano

The Vancouver Museum, Canada's biggest city museum, has still more Native Canadian exhibits — the conical roof representing a Native cedar-bark hat, like the totem poles around town, is just another clue that you won't leave without learning plenty about its original inhabitants. The pioneer-era exhibits include a fur trading post, a replica of an immigrant ship, a hundred-year-old home — and then, what's this? A mummified child from Egypt. What that has to do with Vancouver city history is, well, beyond me. Anyhow, the First Nations heritage is well depicted with ceremonial masks, baskets, blankets, and all the rest. Recent exhibitions added material showcasing the large Asian immigration to Vancouver.

1100 Chestnut St. (in Vanier Park). ☎ *604-736-4431 or 604-736-7736. Internet:* www.vanmuseum.bc.ca. *Admission: Adults C$8 (US$5), seniors and children 4–19, C$5.50 (US$4). Open: July–Aug daily 10 a.m.–5 p.m., Sept–June Tues–Sun 10 a.m.–5 p.m.*

Index of top sights by neighborhood

Index of top sights by type

Galleries and museums
Canadian Craft Museum
H.R. MacMillan Space Centre
Science World
Vancouver Aquarium
Vancouver Maritime Museum
Vancouver Museum

Gardens and parks
Bloedel Floral Conservatory
Capilano Suspension Bridge and Park
Grouse Mountain

Jericho Beach Park
Kitsilano Beach
Lynn Canyon Suspension Bridge & Park
Pacific Spirit Regional Park
Stanley Park
UBC Botanical Garden & Nitobe Memorial
  Garden

Neighborhoods
Chinatown
Gastown
Granville Island

Finding More Cool Things to See and Do

More to do? You bet! I've only scratched the surface. With its miles of beaches and sprawling green parks, Vancouver is paradise for kids of all ages — or anyone who's a kid at heart.

Kid-pleasing spots

Before hitting these attractions, equip yourself by picking up the *Kids' Guide to Vancouver* at the **Tourist InfoCentre,** 200 Burrard Street, Waterfront Centre (☎ **800-663-6000** or 604-683-2000) and log on to the Web site (www.kidfriendly.org) of kid friendly!, a non-profit organization that accredits and reviews businesses especially good for kids and families.

If you're in Vancouver with your kids at the end of May or early June, don't miss the **Vancouver International Children's Festival (☎ 604-280-4444** tickets, 604-708-5655 information), a week-long event in Vanier Park.

Capilano Salmon Hatchery

North Vancouver

Come here to view the spawning of B.C.'s most famous fish. Along with tanks that contain tiny fry or baby salmon, kids can see the ladders that mature salmon climb to return to their streams of origin. Educational displays lay out the fish's life cycle. Note that the best time to visit is from July to November when the adult fish return. Allow 2 hours, including travel.

4500 Capilano Park Rd. ☎ *604-666-1790. Admission: Free. Open: Daily June–Aug 8 a.m.–8 p.m.; Sept 8 a.m.–7 p.m.; Oct 8 a.m.–6 p.m., Nov–May 8 a.m.–4 p.m.*

CN IMAX Theatre at Canada Place

Downtown

Most visitors come here to see bigger-than-life movies on the five-story-high screens at the IMAX theatre, a kid-oriented adventure probably not for people who frequent *avant-garde* film festivals. Expect cinematic views from mountaintops, deep space, rock concerts, and extreme sports. Allow 1 hour.

999 Canada Place. ☎ *800-582-4629 or 604-682-2384. Internet:* www.imax.com/ vancouver. *Admission: Adults C$8 (US$5), seniors C$7 (US$4.69), children C$6 (US$4). Showtimes: July–Aug daily 11 a.m.–10 p.m.; Sept–June noon to 10 p.m.*

Granville Island Model Trains Museum

Granville Island

It seems fitting that a museum dedicated to trains is in Vancouver, about as far west as you can go on the Canadian national train. (And Vancouver's original European and Asian population settled here to make a living building and working the rails.) In any event, kids and train fanatics alike enjoy the huge collections of model and toy trains here. An operational train diorama contains tunnels, trestles, mountains, and forests. Allow 45 minutes.

1502 Duranleau St. ☎ *604-683-1939. Internet:* www.modeltrainsmuseum.bc.ca. *Admission: Adults C$3.50 (US$2.35), seniors and students C$2.50 (US$1.68), children 6–18 C$2 (US$1.34), children under 6 free. Open: Tues–Sun 10 a.m.–5:30 p.m.*

Kids Only Market

Granville Island

The Kids Only Market is a unique concept, although everyone knows that the parents' money keeps the place afloat. The 26 stores — and not a chain among them — vend locally crafted products and toys. Older kids may be swayed by clothing stores that cater to their fickle tastes. Allow 60 to 90 minutes.

1496 Cartwright St. ☎ *604-689-8447. Open: Daily 10 a.m.–6 p.m.*

Kitsilano Pool

Kitsilano

The biggest outdoor swimming pool in Vancouver has a unique setting in Kitsilano beach, where stunning North Shore mountains gleam in the sun most summer days. The pool is extra large and graduated with a shallow end for kids. Allow 1 hour.

2305 Cornwall Ave. (at Yew St.). ☎ *604-731-0011. Admission: Adult C$4 (US$2.68), children C$2 (US$1.34). Open: Victoria Day (late May)–Labour Day (early Sept) Mon–Fri 7 a.m.–8:30 p.m.; Sat–Sun 10 a.m.–8:30 p.m. Park open all year.*

Teen-tempting attraction

Teens aren't left out when it comes to entertainment in Vancouver. I describe shopping options in Chapter 13; here is another.

Royal Hudson Steam Train

North Vancouver

This antique steam engine train, one of the last of its kind, makes a 2-hour coastal journey along Howe Sound to Squamish. Kids and teens may get a kick out of the scenery and the many opportunities for viewing wildlife along the tracks. Make the return trip to Vancouver even more interesting by taking a boat: The M.V. Britannia sails back to the city through splendid water views. Allow 6 hours, more if taking return boat.

B.C. Rail Terminal, 1311 West 1st St. ☎ *800-663-8238 or 604-984-5246. Internet:* www.bcrail.com/bcrpass/bcrhudsn.htm. *Round-trip fares: Adults: C$47.50 (US$32), seniors and children 12–18 C$41 (US$27), children 5–11 C$12.75 (US$9). Combination train and boat ticket: Adults C$78 (US$52), seniors and children 12–18 C$66 (US$44), children 5–11 C$22 (US$15). Trains operate mid-May–late Sept.*

Notable beaches, gardens, and parks

Vancouver's green space includes a lot more than just Stanley Park . . .

English Bay Beach

West End

English Bay Beach is a hectic swarm of well-heeled locals, all vying for a tiny plot of sand on which to savor nice weather or bring a takeout lunch from nearby Denman Street. You see it all here: Same-sex couples strolling arm in arm, blue-haired matrons walking their dogs, sun worshippers, Russian tourists, yuppies communing with their offspring, maybe even a movie star. Allow 30 minutes or more.

At the foot of Beach Ave. and Denman St. Admission: Free.

Lighthouse Park

West Vancouver

Named for Point Atkinson Lighthouse, this park is a popular family destination, especially on Sundays during the summer. The fir trees remain since the last logging in 1881, so you're getting an authentic look. Just don't expect any sandy beaches — this is strictly rocky shoreline, with great views of the Strait of Georgia and Stanley Park. My advice? Pack a lunch and come during the week when the crowds won't be as thick. Allow 2 hours, including travel.

Beacon Lane off Marine Dr. ☎ *604-925-7200. Admission: Free. Open: Daily year-round.*

Queen Elizabeth Park

Shaughnessy

Queen Elizabeth Park, notable for its Bloedel Conservatory (see listing earlier in this chapter), also boasts the Nat Bailey baseball stadium, interesting sculptures, flower gardens, and walking trails and benches. Still not convinced? Check this out: The park is the highest natural point of land within Vancouver's city limits. Allow up to 2 hours, including travel.

Cambie St. near 33rd Ave. Admission: Free. Open: Daily dusk to dawn.

Spanish Banks Beach

Point Grey

Extremely popular on summer weekends, this beach attracts families, thanks to a lifeguard and occasional checks for alcoholic beverages at the entrance. The beach has nice wide paths and views on sunny days of the mountains crowning the North Shore.

Northwest Marine Dr. (at the foot of Tolmie St.). ☎ *604-257-8400. Admission: Free. Open: Daily dawn to dusk.*

Van Dusen Botanical Garden

Shaughnessy

Located about 1½ miles from Queen Elizabeth Park in a wealthy neighborhood, this botanical garden occupies a former golf course. It consists of beautifully groomed theme gardens such as a topiary garden of whimsically designed plant-imals, a rhododendron walk, a rose garden, a children's garden, a Mediterranean Garden, and many others. Perhaps the biggest draw for kids and teens is the hedge maze, which allows them to "get lost" — and eventually find their way out. Allow 1 hour or more.

5251 Oak St. ☎ *604-878-9274. Admission: Adults C$5.50 (US$3.69); seniors, students, and children C$2.75 (US$1.84). Open: Daily 10 a.m. to dusk.*

Vanier Park

Kitsilano

In an enviable location squeezed in between Granville Island and Kitsilano Beach, this park has a serious air about it with three classy museums gracing its green lawns. During the last week of May, the Vancouver Children's Festival kicks up its heels here — and the Bard on the Beach Festival, held throughout summer, draws Shakespeare fans. This park is also a great place for flying kites. Allow 1 hour or more.

At the northern foot of Chestnut St. ☎ *604-257-8400. Admission: Free. Open: Daily dawn to dusk.*

Wreck Beach

Point Grey

North Americans are not typically associated with exhibitionism, but on the West Coast rules are thrown to the wind — and Wreck Beach is a place without many rules. Clothing is entirely optional, and the beach is a known haven for those living an alternative lifestyle. There must be lots of them: This beach gets *busy.* Some entrepreneurs have tapped into this unique market by vending a number of treats (tofu hot dogs anyone?). Do bring an open mind, a beach blanket, and plenty of sunscreen. The beach is out of public sight but accessible via a steep trail off the western side of Marine Drive, near the University of British Columbia. *Don't* bring binoculars, camcorders, or modesty.

Off Southwest Marine Dr., near the University of British Columbia campus. Admission: Free. Open: Daily dusk to dawn.

Intriguing museums

Museum addicts — and those who want to escape rainy weather — will be pleased with these specialty museums.

Barclay Heritage Square and Roedde House Museum

West End

Barclay Heritage Square, a four-block area of nine restored heritage houses from the 19th century, provides a welcome counterpoint to all the glass and steel downtown. You can tour one of them, the Roedde House, a good example of Queen-Anne architecture designed by Francis Rattenbury, who also designed The Empress hotel in Victoria. Period furnishings and gardens reflect the style of that time.

1415 Barclay St. ☎ *604-684-7040. Internet:* www.roeddehouse.org. *Admission: Roedde House Musuem, C$5 (US$3.35) per person. Open: Tours Tues–Fri at 2 p.m.*

B. C. Golf Museum

Point Grey

Golf enthusiasts may want to combine a quick tour of this small museum near the University of British Columbia with a visit to the Museum of Anthropology and the Botanical and Nitobe Memorial Gardens (see listings in this chapter). Located right at the university's golf course, the museum holds every manner of golfing paraphernalia, including an overload of clubs, trophies won by star B.C. golfers, and a reference library. Leave your bag at the door. Allow 30 to 45 minutes.

2545 Blanca St (at the University Golf Course). ☎ *604-222-4653. Admission: By donation. Open: Tues–Sun noon to 4 p.m.*

Granville Island Sport Fishing Museum

Granville Island

This museum is really only for fishing enthusiasts and not general public interest. Exhibits include a big collection of fishing rods, reels, paintings, and photographs — everything but the proverbial big one. You can also view the world's largest collection of fly fishing plates and hardy reels on public display, and a fishing simulator to determine if you've the right stuff to snag a big one in the near future. Allow 30 minutes.

1502 Duranleau St. ☎ *604-683-1939. Internet:* www.sportfishingmuseum. bc.ca. *Admission: Adults C$3.50 (US$2.35), seniors and students C$2.50 (US$1.68), children 6–18 C$2 (US$1.34), children under 6 free. Open: Tues.–Sun 10 a.m.–5:30 p.m.*

Vancouver Police Centennial Museum

Gastown

As "nice" as Vancouver is generally considered, it does have its steamy and seamy side, and the city's sordid past is hung out like dirty laundry at this quite intriguing Gastown museum. (Appropriately enough, it's housed in a former morgue and near a fairly down-at-the-heels neighborhood.) Exhibits include tools used by crooks — lock picks and the like — plus counterfeit money, surveillance equipment, and some interesting stories from the city's rough-and-tumble old days. Allow 30 to 45 minutes.

240 East Cordova St. ☎ *604-665-3346. Internet:* www.city.vancouver.bc.ca/ police/museum. *Admission: Adults C$5 (US$3.35), seniors and students C$3 (US$2); children under 6 free. Open: July–Aug Mon–Sat 10 a.m.–3 p.m.; Sept–June 9 a.m.–3 p.m.*

Recreation and spectator sports

Vancouver is nothing if not suited to active travelers: Literally hundreds of hikes, jogs, bikes, and walks are possible within or near the city limits. If you're feeling like a 'tator — a spectator, that is, not a couch 'tator — you're still in luck: The city boasts professional football (well, CFL football), hockey, and hoop teams. See Chapter 8 for my advice on how to get tickets to major sporting events.

BC Lions Football Team

Yaletown

Canada's version of football — on a bigger field than its U.S. counterpart, with slightly different rules and wild scoring — takes place in BC Place Stadium all summer.

777 Pacific Blvd. ☎ *604-589-7627. Internet:* www.bclions.com. *Tickets: C$14–C$45 (US$9–US$30). Season: June–late Oct.*

Queen Elizabeth Pitch and Putt

Shaughnessy

This par-three course takes in sweeping views of the city, and offers a short but beautifully undulating course on which to practice. It's a great place to practice your short game. You'll be charmed by the weeping willows that line the green fairways even if you don't hit 'em straight enough. Allow 90 minutes to 2 hours.

In Queen Elizabeth Park, on Cambie St. near 33rd Ave. ☎ *604-874-8336.*

Art-lovers' sights

Vancouver's art scene is alive in both new and old artistic traditions.

Bau-Xi Gallery

South Granville

Featuring Canadian artists such as Jack Shadbolt and adopting an open-storage concept — much like that of the Museum of Anthropology at the University of British Columbia. You have better access to exhibits here than at many galleries because of smaller crowds. Allow 1 hour.

3045 Granville St. ☎ *604-733-7011. Admission: Free. Open Mon–Sat.*

Gallery of B.C. Ceramics

Granville Island

This small gallery highlights pottery designed by local artists, some with rather quirky takes on what's usually considered to be a pretty conservative art form. Allow 45 minutes.

1359 Cartwright St. ☎ 604-669-5645. Open Tues–Sun.

Vancouver Art Gallery

Downtown

If you're a big fan of British Columbia painter Emily Carr, you'll love this downtown museum — it holds a large collection of her work detailing the provincial landscape and the First Nations people who inhabit it. If you're not so crazy about Emily Carr, the permanent collections are not short on big names. You can see a few 20th-century U.S. pieces by folks such as Andy Warhol and a Children's Gallery with a hands-on studio. Allow 1 hour.

750 Hornby St. ☎ 604-662-4700. Internet: www.vanartgallery.bc.ca. *Admission: Late June–Sept adults C$10 (US$7), seniors C$8 (US$5), students C$6 (US$4), children under 13 free; Oct–early June adults C$8 (US$5), seniors C$6 (US$4), students C$4 (US$2.68). C$5 (US$3.35) on Thurs nights during low season. Open: Easter–early Oct daily 10 a.m.–5:30 p.m. (Thurs until 9 p.m.); late Oct–Easter Tues–Sun 10 a.m.–5:30 p.m. (Thurs until 9 p.m.).*

Seeing Vancouver by Guided Tour

For those of you who want to be guided around Vancouver, I compiled a list of the best tour operators. Note that prices and policies are always subject to change, so check ahead to ensure that itineraries and prices are what you expect – and that the outfit hasn't gone out of business.

To tour or not to tour?

Should you take a tour in Vancouver? I think hard before committing time and money to a tour guide. I enjoy using my own feet, ears, and eyes to experience a new place just like a local. And you may feel the same way. On another continent, sure, I'd take a tour. Here in North America? That's a tough sell.

Here's why.

First, you can easily reach all Vancouver's splendors by car, feet, boat, or public transit. Second, with few historical sights, Vancouver's main attractions — mountains, parks, beaches, views, and neighborhoods —

require little to no explanation. The mere sight of the beach and mountains framing the skyscrapers is enough.

That said, however, I concede that plenty of you may enjoy a narrated tour, whether it's a guided walk through the rain forest, a high-speed tour by bicycle, or one of the many other options I list in the next few sections

Booking direct

Although I respect the humble hotel concierge, who may offer to arrange a tour for you, I always recommend booking a tour directly with the tour company. Some hotels, and/or their employees, receive a discreet "cut" of any tour business booked through their recommendations. In my opinion, this slants their judgment. Plus, to ensure that a tour meets your interests and budget, you really should talk with the company personally. Sure, doing so may require extra work, but think of it this way: A tour can take up 4 or 5 hours of your trip, so you want to make a wise decision.

Touring Vancouver

The varied topography that makes Vancouver such an interesting place means you can see it umpteen ways: by bus, boat, foot, horse-drawn carriage, mountain bike, airplane, floatplane, and ski.

I leave airplane tours out of this book, as they're mighty expensive, but the city's tourism office stocks plenty of information on the top providers if you want to go that route.

Most of the tours in this section run from spring (March, April, or May) through the end of summer (generally considered the end of September), but be sure to check with the individual company or operator — you may be pleasantly surprised.

Many of the tour companies that I list offer some form of a "family rate" that saves you money if you have two adults and two children. Inquire when making a booking.

By foot

Vancouver's a great city to tour by foot. The salt tang in the air, the smell of a Chinese restaurant, and the crowds of exuberant tourists can buoy you through hours of walking if that's what you want. The central peninsula even has a gentle grade, so you get a low-impact workout at the same time. Here are some great tour companies to try:

> ✔ **Architectural Institute of British Columbia Tours** (☎ **604-683-8588** or 800-667-0753 in British Columbia only; Internet: www.aibc.bc.ca) offers free walking tours of the city highlighting — what

else — interesting architecture in various neighborhoods. Call ahead, as the schedule and focus change each year.

✔ **Chinese Cultural Centre Tours** (☎ 604-687-0729) provides a concentrated look at the history of Chinatown. Tour fees are C$5 (US$3.35) adults, C$4 (US$2.68) seniors, and C$3 (US$2) children.

✔ **Gastown Business Improvement Society Tours** (☎ 604-638-5650) runs free walking tours of the city's oldest historic district from the end of May through September.

✔ **Pacific Running Guides** (☎ 877-728-6786 or 604-684-6464; Internet: www.pacificrunningguides.com) caters to those who want to pick up the pace with guided runs and jogs through the city, beginning at C$20 (US$13) per person.

By boat

One of the most pleasurable ways to get a look at the city is by taking one of several boat tours. Consider the following:

✔ **AquaBus Tours** (☎ 604-689-5858), Vancouver's short-shop ferry service, offers several tours of False Creek and the surrounding area. You can go anywhere from just out to Granville Island to all around the city waterfront — just don't feel silly in those bathtub-shaped boats. Fees are C$6 (US$4) adults, C$3 (US$2) children.

✔ **Harbour Ferries** (☎ 800-663-1500 or 604-688-7246; Internet: www.boatcruises.com) offers a more complete water tour than AquaBus Tours does, and on a cooler boat too — a paddle wheeler. You leave from the base of Denman Street, in the West End, and head for Stanley Park and other local points. A dinner-time cruise, with meals and music, departs every night at 7 p.m. for about 3 hours. Longer tours combine this itinerary with a ride on the Royal Hudson steam train. Admission is C$18 (US$12) adults, C$15 (US$10) seniors.

By horse

Touring by horse-drawn carriage is incredibly romantic, but it's really possible in only one part of town — Stanley Park, whose green paths are relatively unsullied by the traffic that makes carriage travel so unpleasant elsewhere around town.

Stanley Park Horse-Drawn Tours (☎ 604-681-5115; Internet: www.stanleyparktours.com) provides a very romantic way to see the famous park in an hour without feeling rushed. The horses do the work and the driver/guide does the talking as you pass Deadman's Island, the Lion's Gate Bridge, old-growth forests, totem poles, and lots more. As a bonus, you don't need to book this tour in advance; just show up at the carriage lineup near the tourism information kiosk on Park Drive and jump aboard. Rides are C$16.80 (US$11) adults, C$15.85 (US$11) seniors, C$10.95 (US$7) children.

By train

Pacific Starlight, which travels up the coast of Howe Sound and back, provides another romantic way to see the area's scenery. On board, you get dinner, stupendous views, and a taste of travel the way it used to be. The nightly run departs at 6:15 p.m. from North Vancouver station at 1311 West 1st Street and returns by 10 p.m. The train runs May through September from Wednesday through Sunday and in October from Friday through Sunday. Tickets, including dinner, cost from C$84 to C$100 (US$56–US$67) per person. Tickets for the glassed-in dome car cost more. You pay extra for tax, tips, and alcohol. The train has a recommended dress code. Call **BC Rail** (☎ 800-363-3733) for reservations and schedules, which may change.

By bus and car

Here are a few operators using buses and cars to view the city's hot spots:

- ✔ **Gray Line of Vancouver** (☎ 800-667-0882 or 604-879-3363; Internet: www.grayline.ca/vancouver), the huge bus tour company, weighs in with a huge selection of Vancouver itineraries, most of them geared toward groups of older folks. The popular Decker/Trolley tour uses both a bright red London-style bus and a green gas-powered trolley to trundle you around downtown, Chinatown, Stanley Park, Granville Island, and beyond. Other offerings include tours of Vancouver by night, a Native Canadian dinner, and sunset cruises. Prices vary.

- ✔ **Early Motion Tours** (☎ 604-687-5088) provides slightly corny, old-timey tours in the back seat of a top-down Model A Ford. Call for current tour offers and prices. Seats must be reserved in advance.

- ✔ **Pacific Coach Lines Tours** (☎ 800-661-1725 or 604-662-7575; Internet: www.pacificcoach.com), the other big bus tour in town besides Gray Line, goes by the nickname PCL. Their "Vancouver Grand City Tour" takes you from the downtown district's 550-foot lookout tower to Gastown, Chinatown, and Yaletown; through Stanley Park to English Bay and finally across the bridge to the West Side's Queen Elizabeth Park. They pick you up and drop you off at your hotel. Costs are C$41 (US$27) adults, C$39 (US$26) seniors, C$21 (US$14) children.

- ✔ **Vancouver Trolley Company** (☎ 888-451-5581 or 604-801-5515; Internet: www.vancouvertrolley.com), a continuous narrated circuit of stops through Vancouver's chief must-see points, makes this a good option for hop-on, hop-off sightseeing. (It's not an actual trolley running the rails, however, but instead more like a dolled-up bus.) Trolleys make 16 stops, spaced throughout downtown, Gastown, Chinatown, Vanier Park, and Stanley Park, among other places; if you don't get off at all, it takes 2 hours to do the circle. The tour runs daily from April through October, then from Fridays through Sundays only the rest of the year. Tours cost C$22 (US$15) adults, C$10 (US$7) children.

By bike

Now a bike tour is truly in the spirit of Vancouver, seeing as many, many locals commute to work on their bikes and ride them regularly for leisure no matter what the weather.

Velo-City Cycle Tours (☎ 604-924-0288; Internet: www.velo-city.com) offers an interesting tour for those who don't want to peddle the hills. They take you on a leisurely tram ride to the very top of Grouse Mountain, then set you loose for a bike ride back down through the foothills. It takes a long time, sure, but the terrain is beautiful and they even pick you up at your hotel. Other tours are more leisurely — a relaxed jaunt through Stanley Park — or more hardcore. Costs range from C$45–C$95 (US$30–US$64) adults.

Special-interest tours

The following identifies a few tour operators who are known for their ability to pinpoint special interests and lead you to particular slices of Vancouver city life:

✔ **All-Terrain Adventures (☎ 888-754-5601** or 604-434-2278; Internet: www.all-terrain.com) runs a variety of innovative hikes, bikes, and other adventure-type tours of Vancouver and the surrounding area. The Scenic Wilderness Adventure includes 4½ hours of touring in a 4 x 4 vehicle. The C$125 (US$84) price per person includes pickup from your hotel, snacks, and beverages.

✔ **Detours (☎ 604-646-6636;** Internet: www.detours.bc.ca) specializes in exploring Native Canadian culture. During the 5-hour Native Canadian tour, a Musqueam guide leads participants through the Museum of Anthropology and a native reserve at a cost of C$95 (US$64) for adults and C$85 (US$57) for seniors or children. Other tours combine visits to gardens, temples, markets, and historical sites.

✔ **LandSea Tours (☎ 877- 669-2277** or 604-669-2277; Internet: www.vancouvertours.com) is a very active local operator with lots of city and country half-day tours at rates of C$42 (US$28) for adults, C$39 (US$26) for seniors, and C$25 (US$17) for children.

✔ **Lotus Land Tours (☎ 800-528-3531** or 604-684-4922; Internet: www.lotuslandtours.com) offers 4-hour kayak paddling tours of Indian Arm, a fjord. The tour breaks midway for an island picnic featuring barbecued salmon on an uninhabited island. Hardier offerings and tours for groups that combine paddling with motorboat cruising are also available. Prices vary.

✔ **Rockwood Adventures** (☎ 604-926-7705; Internet: www.cool.mb.ca/rockwood) runs daily walking tours of the city — rain gear provided when necessary — plus a range of tours of the surrounding mountains and islands. It specializes in environmental destinations: You see big trees, rain forests, and the like. The company also offers a "Discover The Orient Tour" of Chinatown and a Granville Island tour. Prices vary.

✔ **Silver Challenger Tours** (☎ 604-943-3343) runs fishing tours on a commercial fishing boat. Participants get to navigate using the boat's radar, locate fish with sonar equipment, watch the catch — then dine on their own fresh-caught salmon and shellfish. Prices vary.

✔ **The X Tour** (☎ 888-250-7211 or 604-609-2770; Internet: www.x-tour.com) offers a look at the local buildings that were used in *The X-Files* television program — Scully's apartment, FBI buildings, CIA buildings, the whole shebang. The show may no longer be filmed in Vancouver, but die-hard fans may still want a brush with stardom. Prices vary.

Planning Four Great Vancouver Itineraries

Part of the fun in visiting Vancouver is that you can mix and match tastes and experiences all day and night long. You can go skiing in the morning and boating in the afternoon. You can feast on authentic *dim sum* in Chinatown for lunch and smoked salmon in a Native Canadian longhouse for dinner. The following daylong itineraries pull together some of the city's best experiences. These itineraries are grouped around themes so that you can more easily choose the one that's right for you.

Itinerary #1: Vancouver for beer lovers

Vancouver is a great place to fall in love with a beer. Here you may hear guys saying "look at the head on her" or "she's got legs" in reference to a glass of stout or India pale ale. If you're one of these people, this tour, my friend, is for you. It provides a quick sampling of the finest locally brewed beers in town.

Note that if you tend to linger at a bar, you will probably want to do this tour in reverse, as the last stop involves some ferry-riding and you can get stuck on the island if you miss the last ferry home. Alternately, you can skip every other stop on the itinerary to ensure you're home by dinnertime.

Itinerary #1: Vancouver for Beer Lovers

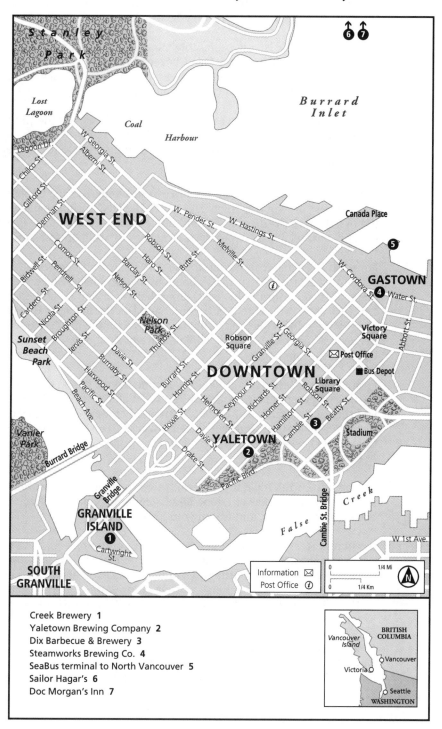

Creek Brewery **1**
Yaletown Brewing Company **2**
Dix Barbecue & Brewery **3**
Steamworks Brewing Co. **4**
SeaBus terminal to North Vancouver **5**
Sailor Hagar's **6**
Doc Morgan's Inn **7**

Because travel between some of these pubs is best done by car, rather than bus, make sure to travel with a designated driver. Choose a good friend . . . to whom you'll owe a big favor when this day is finished.

Begin on Granville Island, preferably after having consumed some lunch, at the **Creek Brewery** (see Chapter 14). Locals love hanging out at this place, not just for the good brews but also for the always-on-vacation feeling of the island and its market.

Now take a bus or cab, drive, or walk about a mile across the Granville Bridge into Yaletown. Here await two of the city's best brewpub experiences; turn right at Davie or Nelson Streets and continue to Mainland to find the first.

The massive, handsome **Yaletown Brewing Company** (see Chapter 11) was the first brewpub in town, and is still the city's primary player in the biz. Despite the great beers and fun atmosphere, the place is pretty big and can feel a little impersonal at times. Oh, well, bottoms up.

From here, it's just a short hop to the next microbrewery, which is actually a restaurant that brews beers on the premises. Beginning on Mainland Street, turn right (east) along Nelson or Smithe and continue two very short blocks to Beatty Street and **Dix Barbecue & Brewery** (see Chapter 14). This is a terrific spot to grab some much-needed barbecue to soak up the alcohol, while naturally sampling the house lagers at the same time.

From Beatty Street, you turn back west one teensy block, then angle north along Cambie Street. Continue almost all the way to the water, and turn at the last street — Water Street, of course — which leads you through the heart of Gastown to **Steamworks Brewing Co.** (see Chapter 14), where the beer's cold and the atmosphere is straight out of Fleet Street.

The area from Yaletown to Gastown is pretty rough, with plenty of streetwalkers, drunks, and dope fiends any time of day or night. Take a cab or drive at night, and watch yourself during the day.

I assume you still have your sea legs at this point; hope so, 'cause this next segment will be mighty interesting. Amble west (towards downtown) up Water Street a little ways until it ends at an angle, then continue the same direction along Cordova another block to the SeaBus station. Buy a ticket and take the SeaBus (see Chapter 8) across to North Vancouver.

Now safely on land again, walk two short blocks uphill and find **Sailor Hagar's** (see Chapter 14). This place is a virtual temple to the brewed beer, with house beers and a vast, superb selection of imports too.

Now, if you're not too tuckered, you have one more stop to make. Drive or take a bus west along Highway 1 to the Horseshoe Bay ferry docks.

At the docks, buy a ticket for Bowen Island, then jump on the Queen of Capilano ferry boat and take the scenic ride out to the island — it's normally pretty quick, unless seas are choppy or they're repairing the Bowen docks (as they were during much of 2000).

Off the boat, all you need to do is walk a few steps before you come to **Doc Morgan's Inn** (☎ **604-697-0707**). Owner Rondy Dike runs a classy, atmospheric place — and the Special Bitter is pretty darned good too. Haven't eaten? Tuck in to some pub grub. I warn you, though, you may like this island groove enough to want to stay over.

Itinerary #2: Vancouver as Hollywood North

Despite the recent loss of *The X-Files* to sunny L.A. — a sore subject around here — Vancouver is still a very popular spot for filming TV shows, feature films, and those dreaded TV movies. Celebrity spotting is becoming a common occurrence around town, particular in Yaletown and the West End.

You too can play Hollywood movie mogul with this quick-and-dirty tour.

Begin by contacting the **B.C. Film Commission** (☎ **604-660-2732;** Internet: www.bcfilmcommission.com). Its office, located on the main floor of the waterfront SeaBus/SkyTrain station at Granville and West Cordova Streets (open weekdays 8:30 a.m. to 4:30 p.m.), provides an updated list of current films in production around town. When you have the coordinates, simply head for the area and keep a sharp look-out for long white trailers and lots of people with sneakers, baseball caps, and cell phones. Hang out, don't bug them, sneak a look inside the catering trailer, and maybe you'll wind up as an extra in one of the numerous sci-fi shows that always seems to be filming in town. (Just don't blame me if your one shot at fame consists of being fried by alien goop or something equally glamorous.)

Done being a spectator? Now dig deeper into the city's tradition as a film (*The Sixth Day, Mission to Mars*) and television (*Wiseguy, The X-Files*, many more) stand-in for other cities. The folks at **X-Tour** (☎ **604-609-2770**; Internet: www.x-tour.com) have got it all down to a science. They know where all the scenes in *The X-Files* television show were shot, and they know just about every other snippet of local movie and television trivia under the sun. That should take up the better part of an afternoon.

The day wouldn't be complete, though, without a drink or a dinner at the **Alibi Room,** 157 Alexander Street (☎ **604-623-3383**), in Gastown, co-owned by Hollywood stars and the acknowledged hub of Vancouver's film community. (I can put it this way: The casual reading material here consists of a library of film scripts.)

Afterward, head for the **Chameleon Urban Lounge** (see Chapter 14), which despite its groovy, slightly divey feel is often *the* spot to sight famous rock and movie stars chatting or even taking the stage to belt out a few tunes. This is a good place to wind down from your day of stargazing. (Actually, if you *really* want to see Hollywood types in their, um, elements, head over to **No. 5 Orange,** 203 Main Street [☎ **604-687-3483**], a strip club in the seedier part of town. Sorry to say it, but the guest list at this place usually includes a virtual who's-who of famous actors, directors, and musicians.)

Itinerary #3: Vancouver for nature lovers

When in Vancouver, you're practically falling over abundant natural splendors, which you can always see from any point in town. This tour visits the major parks, canyons, and beaches around the Greater Vancouver area. Although I could have made this itinerary three times longer — countless parks fill the metro area — seeing these will certainly get your heart racing.

You can tailor this tour to your personality. If you're a morning person, just do it in reverse: After a big hotel breakfast, catch an early boat/bus and begin your day with the huffing, puffing, and splendiferous views of Grouse Mountain.

Although many of Vancouver's natural areas are accessible by public transit, this itinerary is probably best done with a car if you're pressed for time. However, if you're in town for a few days, you can take the bus and follow one or two segments each day.

Start by taking a bus or driving to the western tip of the lower peninsula, which is known as **Point Grey** and is dominated by the 70s architecture of the University of British Columbia, or UBC for short. UBC's campus is surrounded by some of the most amazing landscapes any student could ever imagine. (The campus lies within what are called "endowment lands," which basically means they're open and free to the public.)

Itinerary #3: Vancouver for Nature Lovers

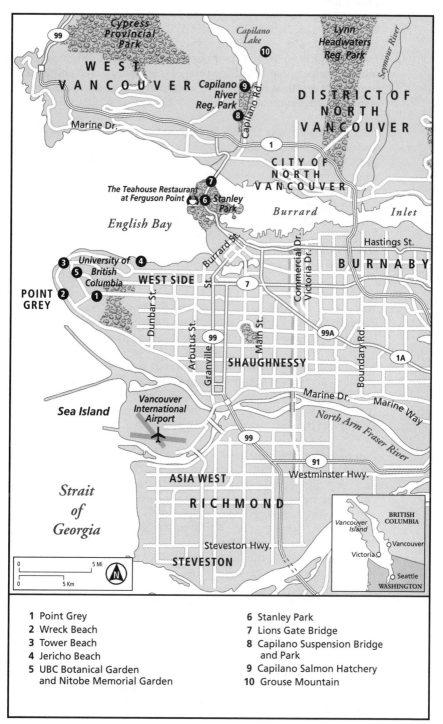

1 Point Grey	6 Stanley Park
2 Wreck Beach	7 Lions Gate Bridge
3 Tower Beach	8 Capilano Suspension Bridge
4 Jericho Beach	and Park
5 UBC Botanical Garden	9 Capilano Salmon Hatchery
and Nitobe Memorial Garden	10 Grouse Mountain

A morning walk on the beach isn't a bad way to begin. Beaches run pretty much around the entire point, and most are public property (check for signs, however). **Wreck Beach,** near the base of University Boulevard at Marine Drive, is one of the most popular. Although nice, this beach is almost a hippie carnival at times — nude sunbathers, old guys peddling weird stuff from carts, and so forth. Other beaches include **Tower Beach** and, on the northern shore, **Jericho Beach** — one of the prettiest beaches in Vancouver and party central for local dogs and dog owners.

Next make your way to **UBC Botanical Garden and Nitobe Memorial Garden** (see "Discovering Vancouver's Top Sights from A to Z," earlier in this chapter). Both spots sure look and smell good, and probably won't make for a long detour.

Now travel east along 4th Avenue to the Granville and Burrard Bridges, which you should cross. Follow signs to **Stanley Park** (see "Discovering Vancouver's Top Sights from A to Z," earlier in this chapter). You can spend hours (even days) here walking, sunbathing, beachcombing, reading plaques, and all that other stuff you're supposed to be do while on vacation. If you need a rest, this is also a good place for a nap.

You may also be ready for lunch. **The Teahouse Restaurant at Ferguson Point** in Stanley Park is a lovely spot for a cup of tea, glass of wine, or a luxurious full meal overlooking English Bay (see Chapter 11).

Next, drive straight across the high **Lions Gate Bridge,** a steeply pitched crossing with some rather spectacular (and vertiginous) views; it's definitely not for the heights-challenged. **Note:** Try to avoid the bridge at rush hour. When safely on the other side, exit onto Marine Drive East, then make the first left up Capilano Road.

You pass the **Capilano Suspension Bridge and Park** (see "Discovering Vancouver's Top Sights from A to Z") — pricey, but worth a look if you like drop-offs — and eventually come to the **Capilano Salmon Hatchery** (see "Finding More Cool Things to See and Do," earlier in this chapter), a dandy spot to watch little salmons coming into being. But the grand-daddy attraction lies a few hundred yards up this road: **Grouse Mountain** (see "Discovering Vancouver's Top Sights from A to Z"). Are you ready to tackle the nearly vertical "Grouse Grind"? Probably not on *this* itinerary — it takes a lot of huffing and puffing, and you have to be in excellent physical shape — but you can at least ride the gondola and check out the amazing geology on your way up.

Itinerary #4: Romantic Vancouver

Any city with mountains this big as backdrop — and whales and crashing ocean waves at its doorstep — doesn't need to work hard to enchant. This tour is best taken during warm weather.

Few places in downtown Vancouver are more romantic than **Stanley Park** (see "Discovering Vancouver's Top Sights from A to Z," earlier in this chapter), so if the weather's nice begin there. Consider touring the park by horse-drawn carriage (see "Seeing Vancouver by Guided Tour," earlier in this chapter) and make sure to ask the driver to drop you off for a walk along one of the beaches. **Third Beach** is the most secluded and romantic.

After the park, **Bacchus** is a good choice for lunch (see Chapter 11). The interior is decorated in cherry panels, silk, and velvet, and the house lights are always kept low.

Afterward, you can indulge in a sensuous chocolate dessert. **Death by Chocolate** (see Chapter 11) supplies an over-the-top chocolate experience.

Taking a boat tour of the harbor is a romantic way to spend the afternoon. **Harbour Ferries** (see "Seeing Vancouver by Guided Tour") offers a few excursions.

For dinner, if you like the romance of the rails, it's hard to beat the **Pacific Starlight** for a roughly 4-hour ride up the coast of Howe Sound and back (see "Seeing Vancouver by Guided Tour"). You get dinner, stupendous views, and a taste of travel the way it used to be. Consider booking two seats to finish up a perfectly romantic day.

If you want a less time-consuming — but no less romantic — option for dinner, try **C** or **CinCin.** A good choice up in North Van is the **Salmon House on the Hill,** a spot that piles on the atmosphere and gorgeous food. (See Chapter 11 for all three.)

To work off those dinner calories, try a nighttime skate at the **Robson Street Skating Rink,** 800 Robson Street, Downtown (☎ **604-482-1800**). Although the glass roofing provides views of the city, it's too bright to see stars, — but not too bright to steal a smooch.

The ice rink is open to the public Monday through Friday only, not weekends, and you can't rent skates. **Outa-Line Inline Sports,** 1251 Pacific Boulevard, between Yaletown and the West End (☎ **604-899-2257**), rents ice skates.

Finally, as a nightcap, it's hard to beat a drink in the high-altitude, revolving **Cloud 9 Lounge** (see Chapter 14). Looking out at the twinkling lights of the city, boats, and Grouse Mountain, you can begin to plan your own private ending to the day.

Chapter 13

A Shopper's Guide to Vancouver

In This Chapter

▶ Getting to know the scene

▶ Strolling the big names and markets

▶ Finding the best of the neighborhoods

*O*wing to its position as a gateway to Asia (and Asian tourists), not to mention its size and financial importance on the West Coast, the shopping in Vancouver is pretty good. Here you can find a tremendous variety of choice, high-quality, and lowbrow items available in abundance, and an exchange rate that will make you smile every time.

Checking Out the Scene

But hold on. Before you set off on a Vancouver shopping spree, you need to know the basics of the local scene. This section includes a quick rundown on shopping hours, specialty items, customs, and taxes.

You need to get used to the general shopping hours in Vancouver, which are similar to those in the rest of Canada — but a little different from standard hours in the United States. Stores usually open at 9:30 or 10 a.m. and close at 5 p.m. on Monday through Wednesday. On Thursdays and Fridays, however, they stay open much later than usual: until 9 p.m. Then, on Saturday, it's 9 to 5 again. Sunday, as you may expect, is a short shopping day, with most stores opening at noon and closing at 5 p.m. (or even 4 p.m. in the case of smaller merchants).

Vancouver Shopping

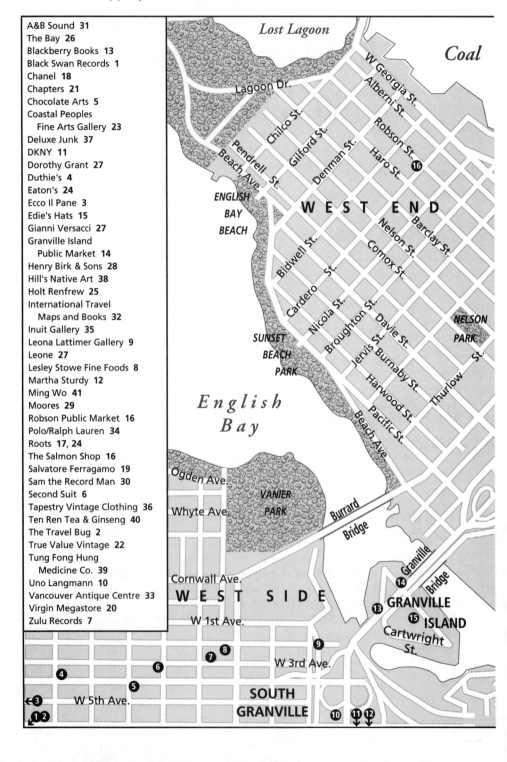

A&B Sound **31**
The Bay **26**
Blackberry Books **13**
Black Swan Records **1**
Chanel **18**
Chapters **21**
Chocolate Arts **5**
Coastal Peoples
  Fine Arts Gallery **23**
Deluxe Junk **37**
DKNY **11**
Dorothy Grant **27**
Duthie's **4**
Eaton's **24**
Ecco Il Pane **3**
Edie's Hats **15**
Gianni Versacci **27**
Granville Island
  Public Market **14**
Henry Birk & Sons **28**
Hill's Native Art **38**
Holt Renfrew **25**
International Travel
  Maps and Books **32**
Inuit Gallery **35**
Leona Lattimer Gallery **9**
Leone **27**
Lesley Stowe Fine Foods **8**
Martha Sturdy **12**
Ming Wo **41**
Moores **29**
Robson Public Market **16**
Polo/Ralph Lauren **34**
Roots **17, 24**
The Salmon Shop **16**
Salvatore Ferragamo **19**
Sam the Record Man **30**
Second Suit **6**
Tapestry Vintage Clothing **36**
Ten Ren Tea & Ginseng **40**
The Travel Bug **2**
True Value Vintage **22**
Tung Fong Hung
  Medicine Co. **39**
Uno Langmann **10**
Vancouver Antique Centre **33**
Virgin Megastore **20**
Zulu Records **7**

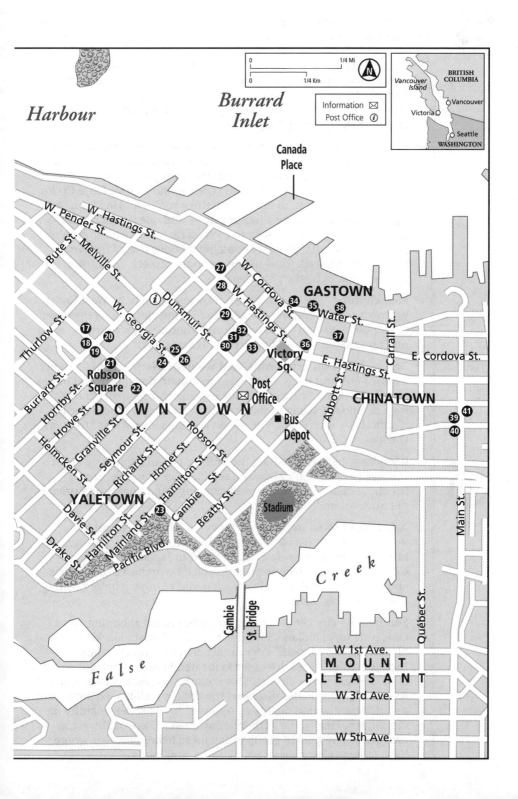

Harbour

Burrard
Inlet

0   1/4 Mi
0   1/4 Km

Information ⊠
Post Office ⓘ

BRITISH
COLUMBIA

Vancouver
Island

Vancouver

Victoria

Seattle
WASHINGTON

Canada
Place

W. Pender St.
W. Hastings St.
Bute St.
Melville St.
Dunsmuir St.
W. Georgia St.
Thurlow St.
Burrard St.
Hornby St.
Howe St.
Granville St.
Seymour St.
Richards St.
Homer St.
Hamilton St.
Robson St.
Helmcken St.
Davie St.
Drake St.
Hamilton St.
Mainland St.
Pacific Blvd.
Cambie St.
Beatty St.

W. Cordova St.
W. Hastings St.
Water St.
GASTOWN
Carrall St.
E. Cordova St.
E. Hastings St.
Abbott St.
CHINATOWN
Victory
Sq.
Post
Office ⊠
■ Bus
Depot

Robson
Square

DOWNTOWN

YALETOWN

Stadium

Creek

Cambie

St. Bridge

Québec St.

Main St.

False

W 1st Ave.
MOUNT
PLEASANT
W 3rd Ave.
W 5th Ave.

17 18 19 20 21 22 23 24 25 26 27 28 29 30 31 32 33 34 35 36 37 38 39 40 41

Vancouver offers a few **specialty items** at great prices. The city is probably best known for the following stuff:

✔ **Vintage clothing.** Vancouver really delivers in the vintage clothing department: Just head on down to Cordova Street (on the edge of Gastown) and troll through the lineup to get your very own hipster *Shaft*-era hat, granny glasses, bowling shirt, leather coat, or crinoline skirt. Or anything Elvis.

✔ **Compact discs.** Using some form of econometric analysis I can't quite fathom, local tourism officials have somehow determined (or decided) that Vancouver is the cheapest place in the free world to buy CDs I'm pretty sure I once found a Steve Earle CD for C$5 in Montreal, but no matter. Whether you're looking for new or used, this town is crazy about music — and one bonus of shopping in Canada is the chance to pick up rare "imports" that were pressed in Canada, possibly containing bonus tracks that you never knew existed. Robson and Seymour Streets, downtown, are the best places to start hunting.

✔ **Fine clothing.** The city has big bucks, and despite its West Coast groove, you can find a good selection of fine clothing on the downtown peninsula and occasionally elsewhere. Shoes, however, are a different matter — nothing terrific presents itself.

✔ **Native Canadian arts, crafts, and woolens.** Native items are a big export here, and good selections are around downtown and out in politically correct Kitsilano. Look especially for Indian candy (a type of smoked salmon) and Cowichan sweaters, hand-woven in distinctively native patterns. Begin looking along Water Street, at the foot of Gastown.

If you're going to be visiting the Museum of Anthropology at the University of British Columbia (see Chapter 12), pick up a brochure called Publication #10 explaining the quality and pricing of native art and other crafts.

✔ **Asian and Indian items.** The city overflows with cheap, fun imported little things from China, Hong Kong, Korea, and India — but also some higher-class stuff too, from Japan and China. Chinatown is the obvious place to start; be prepared for crowds and confusion, and try to know what you're buying before tasting it or paying big bucks.

South of the city center are several other Asian shopping areas. One, a string of Indian shops, is called the Punjabi Market (see "To Market, To Market," later in this chapter). An even larger — though harder-to-reach — area is located in Richmond, not so far from the Vancouver airport. This complex consists of four adjacent Asian shopping malls, all geared toward the well-heeled immigrant Asian. Here you find quality as opposed to the sheer quantity in Chinatown. Finally, the authentic Japanese village of Steveston — first settled by a small group of Japanese fishermen — is where local stores sell Japanese art, clothing, and foods.

✔ **Salmon.** Buying a cut of salmon is absolutely *de rigueur* when visiting Vancouver, and it's better and cheaper (relatively speaking) here than anywhere else on the continent except maybe Maine or Nova Scotia. Salmon is smoked in a number of different ways, and you can try them all. See "Gourmet foods," later in this chapter, for a list of my recommended salmon shops.

Remember to keep careful track of whatever you buy in Canada. U.S. Customs regulations require an accounting of everything you bring home across the border, so keep those receipts and be honest when they question you. Assuming you stayed at least 2 days (and if you didn't, you probably don't own this book), your first US$400 of merchandise is duty-free. That includes 45 ounces (a little more than a liter) of alcohol. After you pass that magic US$400 mark, however, you have to pay a small tax — calculated as a percentage of what you spent (converted into U.S. dollars, of course).

If you stay in Canada less than 48 hours, your duty-free limit drops to US$200 per person.

And don't forget about taxes. You pay a surcharge totaling 14% for the privilege of shopping in Canada. For more information on taxes and how to receive a General Sales Tax refund, totaling half of that 14%, see Chapter 3.

Meeting the Big Names

For such a large and well-heeled city, surprisingly few big-name department stores are left in Vancouver; in fact, now only three remain — and all of 'em are Canadian:

✔ **The Bay,** 674 Granville Street, Downtown (☎ **800-661-2290** or 604-681-6211), also known as the **Hudson's Bay Company,** anchors the corner of Georgia and Granville Streets. It contains a smattering from all the big-name fashion houses that you would expect at any respectable big-league department store, plus a variety of other stuff too. You even find some Canadiana-type items such as colorful woolen blankets from the far north that bring back thoughts of the days when this was a rough-and-tumble, trapping and trading outfit.

✔ **Eaton's,** 701 Granville Street, Downtown (☎ **604-687-7112**), on the third level of Pacific Centre, experienced a miraculous comeback of sorts when a U.S. retailer bought it in 2000, reopening doors that had been closed only a year before. It's still getting back on its feet, but you can expect the same sorts of mid-priced cosmetics, men's and women's clothing, and housewares as in any other department store, with the added attraction that some of the fashions are Canadian-made.

✔ **Holt Renfrew,** 633 Granville Street, Downtown (☎ **604-681-3121**), is the other biggie still standing downtown, and it remains a classy (though not through-the-roof expensive) place to shop for fashions, particularly men's fashions, which are probably a cut above those you find across the street at The Bay. The store also has a very good shoe selection.

While visiting the big name stores, don't panic if you don't recognize some of the designers on the labels, or feel tentative about buying the house labels. Canada's fashion industry (based in Montreal) is going strong, with a number of designers and tailors imported from France or Italy. These are quality clothes.

You can also find outlet stores for many big-name designers downtown and along Robson Street, including — but certainly not limited to — **Gianni Versace,** 757 West Hastings, Downtown (☎ **604-683-1131**); **Salvatore Ferragamo,** 918 Robson Street, Downtown (☎ **604-669-4495**); **Chanel,** 755 Burrard Street, Suite #103, West End (☎ **604-682-0522**); **DKNY,** 2625 Granville Street, Shaughnessy (☎ **604-733-2000**), and **Polo/Ralph Lauren,** 375 Water Street, Gastown (☎ **604-682-7656**).

Going to Market

Vancouver is blessed with an amazing concentration of urban markets — clothing, ethnic, food, and more — and, in fact, they're so good that they may actually provide you with more pleasure than the usual big-name and big-street shopping described in this chapter. They are *certain* to supply more cultural stimulation, because these are the places where the Vancouver local shops, browses, and just generally hangs out. Dozens of Asian markets dispersed throughout the city, to take just one example, provide ample opportunity to pick up that exotic gift of ginseng jelly, lacquered chopsticks, or hard-to-find box of bonito flakes you've been dying to find — or, at the very least, to watch other people do it instead.

By all means, make the time to explore at least one of the markets described in this section.

Chinatown markets

The markets of Chinatown are a special case, because you won't find one centralized Asian market. So many interesting individual merchants pack into these compact blocks between Powell, Keefer, and Main Streets that seeing them is absolutely essential, even on a short visit to the city. Thankfully, the area is fairly close to downtown. Just dive in and sift through the mounds of straw mats and hats, cotton slippers, candy, cookware, exotic spices, and veggies laid out in barrels.

The majority of these places are inexpensive, chaotic, and pretty similar to one another.

A few local favorites include **Ming Wo,** 23 East Pender Street (☎ **604-683-7268**), the flagship of local cookware chain and a cut above the rest; **Ten Ren Tea & Ginseng,** 550 Main Street (☎ **604-684-1566**), a tea, herb, and spice shop; and **Tung Fong Hung Medicine Co.,** 536 Main Street (☎ **604-688-0883**), a similar place of more epic contents. (Don't visit these places if you have a weak stomach, though, as some of the odder spices are, um, animal-derived.)

A second, much smaller district of odds-and-ends Asian markets is along a stretch of Broadway.

Though you may think so, bargaining isn't really kosher here.

One of the real joys of visiting the Chinatown markets, in summer, is a chance to experience the so-called "night market," when several blocks centered around Keefer, Main, and East Pender Streets are closed to traffic on Friday, Saturday, and Sunday evenings from 6 p.m. until around midnight to allow pedestrians the full run of the area. That's when the good street food comes out, sold by the piece — no need to dine at a restaurant *this* night. If you don't mind a little jostling, you'll feel like you've penetrated the essential heart of Asian Vancouver.

Walking here from downtown or Gastown at night is certainly possible, logistically speaking, but the intervening area is a bit of a marginal one in terms of safety. Take a cab after hours.

Granville Island Public Market

When the weather's good, the **Granville Island Public Market,** 1669 Johnston Street (☎ **604-666-6655;** Internet: www.granvilleisland. bc.ca), in a former factory complex, is by far the city's largest and most interesting market — a beautifully located concentration of produce, flower, and other markets rolled into one. The appealing waterside package also offers the bonus of a microbrewery on-site. And the daily carnival of locals, tourists, performers, and panhandlers guarantees no people-watcher can possibly go home unsatisfied. The market is open daily from 9 a.m. to 6 p.m.; closed Mondays during January only.

With so much food from which to choose, sample takeout from several of a mind-boggling array of international offerings — then pick up something for dessert and sit by the waterside benches. If the buskers (who could be professional singers in training, but also basically panhandlers in disguise) bug you too much, rent a canoe from the kayak shop on Duranleau Street and paddle out of earshot

Street parking is tight on the island, however, especially on weekends, in summer, or (egads) on summer weekends. You can pay to park in the big garage if room exists. It's probably more intelligent and less headache, though, to get here via the cute little AquaBus tugboats that run from the downtown peninsula, or by city bus #51 (see Chapter 9). If feasible, walking's a good option too.

Lonsdale Quay Market

Across the water in North Vancouver, and conveniently right on the SeaBus ferry dock, the smaller **Lonsdale Quay Market,** 123 Carrie Cates Court (☎ **604-985-6261**), gives a good fix of food and scenery if you're en route to or coming back from Grouse Mountain, the Capilano Bridge, the Nanaimo Ferry, or the drive up to Whistler. The market is open daily from 9:30 a.m. to 6:30 p.m. and until 9 p.m. Friday. Restaurants generally open until 9 p.m. on weekdays, later on weekends.

The ground floor is dedicated to eats. Particularly good are the Chinese food stalls; you can find some excellent produce in the markets here, too, which makes it the perfect en-route stop for picnic planning. You'll probably have to wait until you officially relocate to Vancouver to take advantage of the excellent fish market, though. Upstairs, a collection of shops offers decent books, clothes, and knickknacks. A special children's area called Kids' Alley is also here.

The evening rush hour can be a busy time here, as homeward-bound North Shore commuters scurry to pick up the evening's supper. Do your shopping before 4:30 p.m. if you can.

The easiest way to get here is by taking the scenic SeaBus ride from the Vancouver waterfront to the North Vancouver landing; the market is right next to the landing.

Robson Public Market

The glass-enclosed **Robson Public Market,** 1610 Robson Street (☎ **604-682-2733**), up the street from the too-expensive shops along central Robson Street, is a real find. The market includes a tasteful collection of some of the city's better gourmet food offerings, all assembled under a long and airy roof that lets in the summer sunlight. Think trays of Okanagan cherries and apples, fresh-packed Pacific salmon and just about anything else you could want — designer chocolate, good beer and wine, croissants, just-squeezed juice. And that's just the bottom floor; upstairs, you find takeout fare of every stripe. This should be a locals' kind of place by now, but the truth is that locals don't really come here as much as one might expect — perhaps it's too fancy? If I were lucky enough to live in this neighborhood (stay tuned, I'm working on it), I'd come here. The market's open daily from 9 a.m. to 9 p.m.

Punjabi Market

If you have more energy, the **Punjabi Market,** a hard-to-reach but visually interesting Indian market, is along four blocks of Main Street between 48th and 52nd Streets south of downtown, in an area sometimes called South Vancouver. As with Chinatown, this place isn't contained under one central roof, but consists of a string of lookalike shops. Sure, the location is several miles south of the city, but nowhere else (save New York or Toronto, perhaps) can you find such an abundance of Indian fabrics, hot spices, Hindi hit tunes, and more at such amazing prices.

Strolling the Best Shopping Neighborhoods

The city is full of good shopping neighborhoods and specialty stores. This section includes my recommendations. If you're hunting for a particular item, jump ahead to the index at the end of this chapter to find the store, and neighborhood, that fills your need.

Downtown and West End

Downtown is where most of the heavy hitters are concentrated, mostly in a series a malls with unexciting names like Pacific Centre and Sinclair Center and Harbour Centre. You also find several worthwhile shopping streets: Granville Street — with its too-urban mixture of department stores, record stores, and peep shows — and the much classier Robson Street, which has been taken over by chain stores (think: The Gap), but still offers great people-watching, cafés, and upscale merchandise. What follows are the highlights of the downtown shopping scene.

For antique hunting, hit **Vancouver Antique Centre,** 422 Richards Street (☎ **604-669-7444**), a sprawling collection of shops and dealers in two unremarkable buildings. Some of the stuff for sale here is trash, some of it's treasure, but if it's pouring rain and you want to go a-hunting, this is the place to do it. Opening hours vary by dealer.

It's fashionable around town to knock new-kid-on-the-block **Chapters,** 788 Robson Street (☎ **604-682-4066**), the supposed big bad bookstore monster that will destroy the independent bookstore owner, but I'm not so sure that criticism's fair. After all, who said people would stop going to the little store? If you need a title and need it fast, however, chances are excellent that this place will have it when others may need to put in a special order. Granville Street has another branch (☎ **604-731-7822**).

International Travel Maps and Books, 552 Seymour Street (☎ 604-687-3320), is *the* place to come in town for topographic or other maps — the selection's enormous — plus a big selection of specialty books you would never find anywhere else because they were basically published in someone's kitchen. Need a hiking, skiing, or wildflower guide to some obscure B.C. mountain range? Come here first.

When you shop for clothes here, you may want to dress your best even before you get to **Leone**, 757 West Hastings Street (☎ 604-683-1133), a high-end and beautifully designed store, with every famous European designer you would expect or want to find — each in its own carefully designated area. Head downstairs from Leone's main entrance for house-label clothes that don't have Italian names stitched on them, but are still pretty good.

The men's clothing store **Moores,** 524 Granville Street (☎ 604-669-1712), is one of the better choices in the downtown district — not the most expensive in town, but stocked nevertheless with quality shirts, suits, neckties, and more.

The Canadian clothing store of the moment is **Roots,** 1001 Robson Street (☎ 604-683-4305) and Pacific Centre, 701 West Georgia Street, West End (☎ 604-683-5465). Not a new store, Roots transformed its look from post-hippie to simply hip (just as San Francisco's The Gap did). Everything here is casually cool, with an inclination toward clothes you can wear comfortably outdoors; an Olympic gold-medal snowboarder from Whistler is the store's hot poster child of the moment. With nothing fusty here, it's no surprise that Asian tourists pile in during their Robson Street walks to stock up.

You can find beads, leather, and odd garments galore at **True Value Vintage,** 710 Robson Street (☎ 604-685-5403), a subterranean little showroom. Asian tourists love the place — I'm not sure why.

The Salmon Shop, 1610 Robson Street (☎ 604-688-3474), is a convenient location to pick up smoked salmon before hopping back on your plane home. The Robson Street location means you may pay more than you should.

Henry Birk & Sons, 698 West Hastings Street (☎ 604-669-3333; Internet: www.birks.com), an upscale Canadian jeweler, is a good choice for reliable watches, engagement rings, and other traditional jewelry.

Despite the tough competition around town, music store **A&B Sound,** 556 Seymour Street (☎ 604-687-5837), succeeds by giving you a variety of experiences to keep you in the store. Pop music greets you as you enter, but the store also has a book section upstairs, a small movie area where a film's always playing, classical music, and videos for sale. Periodic sales lower prices even further.

Sam the Record Man, 568 Seymour Street (☎ 604-684-3722), the other big record store on Seymour Street, is a four-story Canadian-owned behemoth featuring low, low prices and astounding quantity of selection. This store is very strong on Canadian and other "import" albums containing different cuts than the versions you know and love from the U.S. of A. You can get movies here, too.

Virgin Megastore, 788 Burrard Street (☎ 604-669-2289), isn't a department store, but it may as well be. A warehouse-like altar to recorded music (which was once a library), Vancouver's Virgin branch has been dressed out in typically Virgin — that is to say, flamboyant — style and located very centrally to the city's poshest shopping district. Woe be to you, though, if the next-big-thing boy band should happen to be here in the lobby signing t-shirts and body parts for hundreds of screaming teenaged girls. In that case, disappear quickly to the basement, hook up some headphones, and listen to the latest CDs in relative obscurity. Open Monday through Thursday from 9:30 a.m. to 11 p.m., Friday and Saturday until 12 midnight, Sunday until 10 p.m.

 Located inside the upscale Sinclair Centre complex, **Dorothy Grant,** 757 West Hastings Street (☎ 604-681-0201), highlights the collaborative clothing of Native Canadian designer Grant and her husband Robert Davidson. You find truly distinctive vests, coats, native jewelry, and more here.

Gastown

Gastown is the place to go for vintage clothing or modern art (not to mention camera-clicking tourists). Like Granville Street, this area is a blend of over-the-top tacky and gone-to-seed local characters. Cordova Street, in particular, serves up secondhand clothing stores — including great leather coats and some wild '70s fashions — as well as a handful of top-flight little *avant garde* fashion shops and artsy galleries too. What follows are my top recommendations.

 Of all the joints along Cordova Street, **Deluxe Junk,** 310 West Cordova Street (☎ 604-685-4871), probably offers the best vintage clothing. There's a crazy-quilt of stuff to dig through, some of it truly deserving of the moniker "junk" and some of it just about to come back in vogue — maybe. Note that prices here, which can seem high at first glance, drop over time as the item hangs out and waits for a home. Check the tag to see if the "freshness" of the item has expired but staff forgot to mark it down.

Tapestry Vintage Clothing, 321 Cambie Street (☎ 604-687-1719), a Gastown lowbrow option on grungified Cambie Street, seems to specialize in women's stuff (as many retro stores do). Think '40s, '50s, and '60s, for starters. This store has bell-bottoms, too, of course.

Hill's Native Art, 165 Water Street (☎ **604-685-4249;** Internet: www. hillsnativeart.com), does resemble a former trading post, but get beyond the slightly campy look and you find quality items such as Native Canadian sweaters, totem poles, sculptured stone, masks, jewelry, and the like. Former President Bill Clinton shopped here once . . . for Monica.

Inuit Gallery, 345 Water Street (☎ **604-688-7323**), sells an amazing collection of Inuit art. The selection is top-drawer, so don't come expecting a bargain-basement find. In fact, coming here is like going to a museum without actually having to buy a ticket, and for that alone — the exposure to such wonderful work — you ought to make time for a visit.

Chinatown

Chinatown is just what you'd expect, a concentration of shops, eateries, and produce markets where nearly all the signs are in Chinese. The only real shopping you can do here is for exotic herbs, spices, and food, or for inexpensive souvenir-type items such as bamboo flutes or chimes. See "Chinatown markets," earlier in this chapter, for my recommended shops.

Granville Island

Granville Island is beloved by locals — it's just a fun place to hang out, eat, watch the water (and each other), and shop in the stalls, which purvey everything from organic produce to hand-knit clothing. Here are a couple of my favorite stores.

Everyone raves about **Blackberry Books,** 1663 Duranlea Street (☎ **604-685-4113** or 604-685-6188), a good local favorite. It stocks upscale cookbooks — you know, the ones with nice pictures throughout, not the ones with ring-binders and grease stains — plus a selection of art, photography, and other titles.

Edie's Hats, 1666 Johnston Street (☎ **604-683-4280**), is all hats — but what fine (and expensive) women's hats these are, some designed by Edie and others selected from the best of Paris, London, and other fashion hotspots.

South Granville

Just south of Granville Island is the surprisingly upscale South Granville neighborhood, really a locals' kind of neighborhood but with some quality stores if you know where to look.

You can tell right away, from the short hours that antique dealer **Uno Langmann,** 2117 Granville Street (☎ 604-736-8825), deals in exclusive stuff. The high-priced antiques here run to European silver, porcelain, furniture, and other items, all from *way* before you were born. Open Wednesday through Saturday only, 10 a.m. to 5 p.m.

Martha Sturdy, 3039 Granville Street (☎ 604-737-0037), purveys some of the finest jewelry in North America designed by Martha Sturdy herself. You're more likely to see her wares, though, in the pages of *Cosmo* or on the runways of Paris than about town. Earrings and finger rings have long been two of her specialties, but now she has also branched out to design furnishings and other household items.

Leona Lattimer Gallery, 1590 West 2nd Avenue (☎ 604-732-4556), is the place to come for higher-priced Native-Canadian goods — such as your very own totem pole. Don't forget your checkbook. This isn't the place for a stocking-stuffer, but rather a serious gift.

Kitsilano and Point Grey

Kitsilano is the place to come for gourmet foods: Every street corner, it seems, has another café, coffee shop, sushi shop, natural foods store, or chocolatier. The main shopping area extends west along West 4th Avenue from Granville Street. Only a few blocks south, **Broadway** runs parallel to the west and offers a somewhat more variable, alternative mix of businesses: dubious Chinese restaurants and junk shops, but then also a store selling excellent all-natural cosmetics. What follows are my picks for the neighborhood's best stores.

Duthie's, 2239 West 4th Avenue (☎ 604-732-5344), is Vancouver's best-loved bookstore — heck, it may be Canada's best-loved bookstore — but apparently it's not being loved enough, because the cozy down-town store (big ladders and all) has closed, leaving only this Kits location as the last holdout. Still, it's well worth a stop if you're looking for Canadian history or travel titles, or books that were published abroad. The staff should be licensed as private detectives they're so good at tracking down obscure or out-of-print stuff. *Generation X* author Douglas Coupland has been sighted working one shift a week here.

The Travel Bug, 2667 West Broadway (☎ 604-737-1122), may not be the largest travel bookshop in Canada, but it's probably the most personable. Dwight Elliot runs a fabulous little place stocked with his choices of the big-name guidebook titles, plus some little-name ones too, and a few travel supplies — including globes, although you're unlikely to take one of *those* to Europe in your backpack — as well. And if, like me, you're a fan of narrative travel books that make great reading on the train or plane, well, he has lots of those too.

Second Suit, 2306 West 4th Avenue (☎ **604-732-0338**), takes lightly used suits and fancy accessories — who knows, maybe they were worn by a mannequin once — on consignment, then marks them way down. Your eyes will pop at the big names and small prices, so don't be shy. It's not like you came all the way to Canada to pay top price on an Italian suit, is it?

Chocolate Arts, 2037 West 4th Avenue (☎ **604-739-0475**), is hands-down the most interesting and best chocolate shop in a city that seems obsessed with the cocoa bean. Check out this recipe: Begin with one inventive chocolatier (that would be Greg Hook) — who doesn't mess around with fillers in his product, using only organic fruits and the best cocoa butter. Then stir in one wonderful collaborating partner, Native Canadian artist Robert Davidson. The result? High-quality chocolates formed into native masks and other distinctively Pacific Northwestern shapes and patterns. Plus, they taste great.

One of the best bakeries in the city, **Ecco Il Pane,** 238 West 5th Avenue (☎ **604-873-6888**) and 2563 West Broadway (☎ **604-739-1314**), is a good-smelling place perfect for olive breads, foccacias, and similar artisanal breads. Knock yourself out with the fruity raisin bread or the too-sinful chocolate cherry bread.

There may be no better place to stock up for a luxurious picnic — from appetizer to finish — than at **Lesley Stowe Fine Foods,** 1780 West 3rd Avenue (☎ **604-731-3663**). The sweets are especially good.

Jazzheads, world music fans, and folkies know there's only one place in town you go for the best, and it's tiny **Black Swan Records,** 3209 West Broadway, (☎ **604-734-2828**). Acid jazz, Herb Alpert, Miles Davis? Natch. World music? Jah, mon. Good folk and blues sections, too. They have new and used records, tons of personality, and — they get a prize for this — they still actually sell *records.* You know, those round things?

Just in case you happen to be after something *really* different and loud, come to **Zulu Records,** 1972 West 4th Avenue (☎ **604-738-3232**); they probably have it. Punk, hip-hop, new wave, and all those other styles or tiny labels that don't fit neatly into a corporate-music bin — anything that's the opposite of wimpy music, basically — can be found here. They sell used records, tapes, and CDs, too.

The University of British Columbia's **Museum of Anthropology,** 6393 NW Marine Drive (☎ **604-822-5087**), located just west of Kitsilano in Point Grey, has a very good store where you can stock up on books about the Native Canadian arts and crafts you purchased while in Vancouver. They also sell assorted prints and jewelry, among other items. Staff may even be able to give you some free advice on where to mount that totem pole that you're bringing back to Milwaukee.

Yaletown

Yaletown is a booming district of brewpubs, art galleries, and dance clubs, once an industrial area but now slowly developing more and better shops. Stay tuned as this compact neighborhood becomes increasingly hip and tech types begin moving in.

 A small boutique in the new crop of Yaletown contenders, **Coastal Peoples Fine Arts Gallery,** 1072 Mainland Street, Yaletown (☎ **604-685-9298;** Internet: www.coastalpeoples.com), specializes in native-designed jewelry, especially jewelry featuring whales, ravens, bears, and other animals and sea creatures related to native oral traditions.

Index of Stores by Merchandise

Antiques
Uno Langmann (South Granville)
Vancouver Antique Centre (Downtown)

Asian items
Ming Wo (Chinatown)
Ten Ren Tea & Ginseng (Chinatown)
Tung Fong Hung Medicine Co. (Chinatown)

Books and maps
Blackberry Books (Granville Island)
Chapters (Downtown)
Duthie's (Kitsilano)
International Travel Maps and Books (Downtown)
The Travel Bug (Kitsilano)

Clothing (fine fashions and vintage)
Chanel (West End)
Deluxe Junk (Gastown)
DKNY (Shaughnessy)
Edie's Hats (Granville Island)
Gianni Versace (Downtown)
Leone (Downtown)
Moores (Downtown)
Polo/Ralph Lauren (Gastown)
Roots (Downtown, West End)
Salvatore Ferragamo (Downtown)
Second Suit (Kitsilano)
Tapestry Vintage Clothing (Gastown)
True Value Vintage (Downtown)

Department stores
The Bay (Downtown)
Eaton's (Downtown)
Holt Renfrew (Downtown)

Gourmet foods
Chocolate Arts (Kitsilano)
Ecco Il Pane (Kitsilano)
Lesley Stowe Fine Foods (Kitsilano)
The Salmon Shop (Downtown)

Jewelry
Henry Birk & Sons (Downtown)
Martha Sturdy (South Granville)

Markets
Granville Island Public Market (Granville Island)
Lonsdale Quay Market (North Vancouver)
Robson Public Market (Downtown)
Punjabi Market (South Vancouver)

Music
A&B Sound (Downtown)
Black Swan Records (Kitsilano)
Sam the Record Man (Downtown)
Virgin Megastore (Downtown)
Zulu Records (Kitsilano)

Native Canadian items
Coastal Peoples Fine Arts Gallery
 (Yaletown)
Dorothy Grant (Downtown)
Hill's Native Art (Gastown)
Inuit Gallery (Gastown)
Leona Lattimer Gallery (South Granville)
Museum of Anthropology (Point Grey)

Chapter 14

Living It Up after the Sun Goes Down: Vancouver Nightlife

· ·

In This Chapter

▶ Getting down with the music scene

▶ Visiting the best clubs and bars

▶ Discovering the city's performing arts

· ·

*G*et one thing straight from the get-go: Nightlife is not hard to find in Vancouver, but it takes limited forms. Basically, I'm talking about a few true dance clubs — quite hip, however — plus a good supply of live music venues (where the city shines) and bars and pubs with character. You also find a decent slate of theater offerings.

This chapter offers my insider's list of the best of the city's nightlife. For convenience, I divide the places into those featuring music, those specializing in a particular social scene or beverage, and those catering to a primarily gay and lesbian clientele. I follow these listings with a rundown of the city's performing arts venues and companies.

Where should you go to find nightlife? Dance clubs increasingly litter the Yaletown, Robson Street, and downtown districts, while Kitsilano is more a place for an organic brew or a glass of wine. More upscale areas such as South Granville and the West End offer the sorts of bars where you may want to wear a jacket, or at least shuck your sneakers — places where a drink can cost more than a meal in other parts of town. Finally, strip joints have long been fixtures on the fringes of downtown, Yaletown, and East Hastings — not that you were thinking of going to one of *those*.

Your search for higher culture will take you all around town, because Vancouver does not have a central theater district. You may even find yourself watching Shakespeare on the beach!

 Closing time for a Vancouver bar or club is usually 2 a.m. — earlier on Sundays — although exceptions exist and are noted throughout the chapter.

Vancouver Nightlife

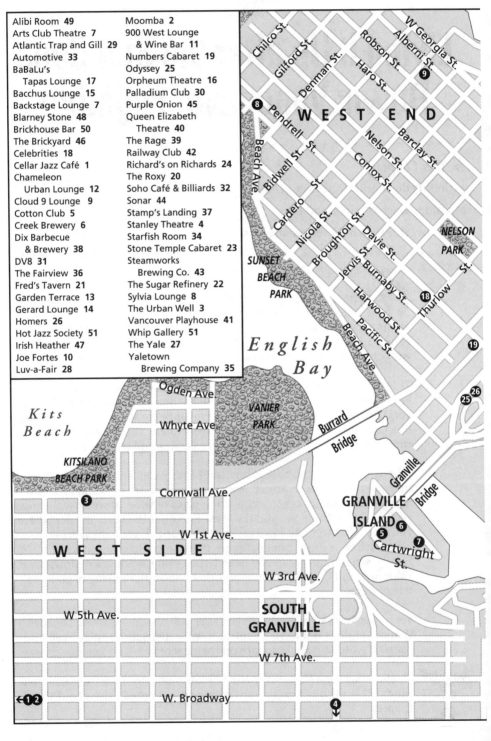

Alibi Room **49**
Arts Club Theatre **7**
Atlantic Trap and Gill **29**
Automotive **33**
BaBaLu's
   Tapas Lounge **17**
Bacchus Lounge **15**
Backstage Lounge **7**
Blarney Stone **48**
Brickhouse Bar **50**
The Brickyard **46**
Celebrities **18**
Cellar Jazz Café **1**
Chameleon
   Urban Lounge **12**
Cloud 9 Lounge **9**
Cotton Club **5**
Creek Brewery **6**
Dix Barbecue
   & Brewery **38**
DV8 **31**
The Fairview **36**
Fred's Tavern **21**
Garden Terrace **13**
Gerard Lounge **14**
Homers **26**
Hot Jazz Society **51**
Irish Heather **47**
Joe Fortes **10**
Luv-a-Fair **28**

Moomba **2**
900 West Lounge
   & Wine Bar **11**
Numbers Cabaret **19**
Odyssey **25**
Orpheum Theatre **16**
Palladium Club **30**
Purple Onion **45**
Queen Elizabeth
   Theatre **40**
The Rage **39**
Railway Club **42**
Richard's on Richards **24**
The Roxy **20**
Soho Café & Billiards **32**
Sonar **44**
Stamp's Landing **37**
Stanley Theatre **4**
Starfish Room **34**
Stone Temple Cabaret **23**
Steamworks
   Brewing Co. **43**
The Sugar Refinery **22**
Sylvia Lounge **8**
The Urban Well **3**
Vancouver Playhouse **41**
Whip Gallery **51**
The Yale **27**
Yaletown
   Brewing Company **35**

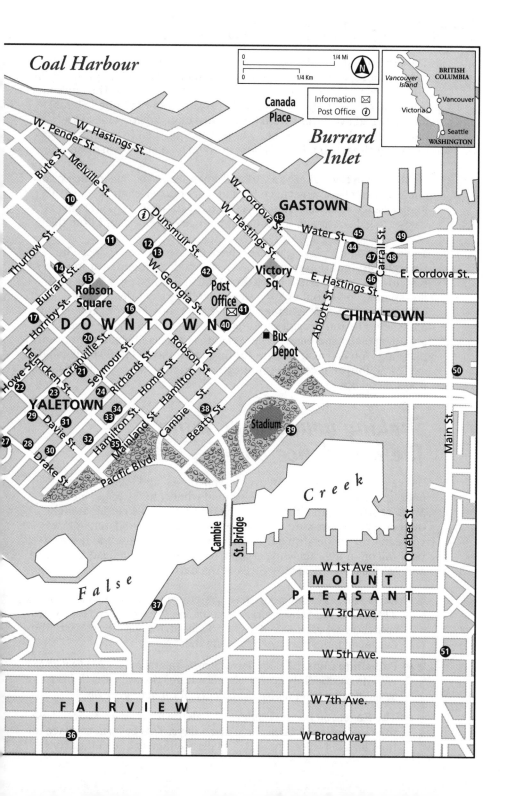

Checking Out the Music Scene

The city's most popular music can be described by one of two Rs: rootsy (blues, rock, Irish-tinged folk, acoustic folk, punk) or refined (in other words, classical). But the choices don't end there. The city's multicultural character (and, frankly, its proximity to the United States) has spawned everything from Euro-dance clubs to jazz clubs to a hardcore-punk scene. In other words, whatever you're looking for is probably already established here in some pocket of town or another.

Most clubs in town charge a variable cover fee to see live music performances (better-known acts command higher cover charges), and the hipper dance clubs also require a C$5 to C$10 (US$3.35–US$7) cover charge to gain entrance — though women are often exempt from this.

To find out who's playing where, check the weekly newspaper **The Georgia Straight** (Internet: www.straight.com), found in stores, bars, restaurants, and tourist offices. **Xtra! West,** the city's gay and lesbian newspaper, comes out every 2 weeks and lists gay-oriented club events. **Vancouver Magazine** (Internet: www.vanmag.com) comes out once a month and provides in-depth coverage of the music scene including clubs and bands. The Web site is especially handy for pre-trip planning. You can also call the **Talking Telus Pages** (☎ **604-299-9000,** ext. 2489) for pre-recorded (although not comprehensive) club listings; press menu option #6.

Shaking your groove thing: The best dance clubs

Dance clubs are hotter than ever in Vancouver, and long lines will undoubtedly greet you on any weekend when you try to get into one. My best advice is to either go during the week, or go earlier at night than everyone else; sure, the dance floor may be a void, but at least you can wait inside, drinking and socializing, as opposed to freezing your tail off in the rain while arguing with some musclehead in a t-shirt and flak jacket. Here are my picks of the hottest spots:

✔ **Luv-a Fair,** 1275 Seymour Street, Yaletown (☎ **604-685-3288**), offers a little something for everyone as the week goes on, and the crowd somehow retains its coolness throughout. It nods more toward the European industrial scene than anything else.

✔ **Palladium Club,** 1250 Richards Street, Yaletown (☎ **604-688-2648**), with its astounding variety of dance tunes pounding forth from ear-assaulting speakers, provides plenty of room to get jiggy.

✔ **The Rage,** 750 Pacific Boulevard, Yaletown (☎ **604-685-5585**), is the rage, as it has been since disco days. This cavernous place on the Plaza of Nations near B.C. Place Stadium is one of the city's biggest and most popular clubs, with a hair-raising sound system and live radio broadcasts. Open weekends only, but call about special concert performances too.

✔ **Sonar,** 66 Water Street, Gastown (☎ 604-683-6695), probably the top dance club in British Columbia, established a name for itself far and wide by attracting top DJs to spin eclectic hip-hop tunes and island rhythms — for once, much more than just droning, bass-fueled dance music — within a gorgeously designed space. Closed Sundays.

✔ **Stone Temple Cabaret,** 1082 Granville Street, Downtown (☎ 604-488-1333), your good old-fashioned disco, does everything — music, lighting, flashpots — on a grand scale. Only the hairstyles have changed. Closed Mondays.

✔ **The Urban Well,** 1516 Yew Street, Kitsilano (☎ 604-737-7770) delivers with a surprisingly good range of music and a top-notch drink selection. As with so many other popular Vancouver spots, though, the crowd may annoy with its perfection. The high-tone crowd jacks up drink prices, too.

Focusing on the music: The best folk, jazz, and blues clubs

Jazz appears spottily on bills around town. For up-to-date performance info, consult the **Jazz Hotline** (☎ 604-872-5200). If you're a real diehard fan, try to visit town during June as the annual Vancouver Jazz Festival is blowing full-force. The blues and folk are harder to find, but it can be done. Here are my recommendations for enjoying all three styles:

✔ **Cellar Jazz Café,** 3611 West Broadway, Kitsilano (☎ 604-738-1959) presents musicians playing much more than jazz, although Sunday is reserved for jazz brunch. You also hear blues, soul, funk, and related forms, all among the usual Kitsilano cooler-than-thou scene and some wild decor — think red, seriously red.

✔ **The Fairview,** 898 West Broadway, Fairview (☎ 604-872-1262), among the best blues bars in town, hides within a chain hotel. Sundays, various musicians play free-form with each other.

✔ **Hot Jazz Society,** 2120 Main Street, Mount Pleasant (☎ 604-873-4131), a longstanding jazz joint, is pretty authentic, which may explain its devoted following and staying power. Dixieland is big here, and so is dancing.

✔ The **Cotton Club,** 1833 Anderson Street, Granville Island (☎ 604-738-7465) is good enough that it actually books players of different forms of jazz. Outdoor performances in summer on the patio are a definite bonus — this is one of those Vancouver experiences that you shouldn't miss if you like jazz.

✔ The **Purple Onion,** 15 Water Street, Gastown (☎ 604-602-9442) is one of the city's top jazz clubs (when jazz is playing, which isn't always), with several areas to dance, drink, or just enjoy the sounds. Unfortunately, the club has become something of see-and-be-seen spot of late, and you may have trouble getting inside during weekends. Call ahead to check the schedule. If you come on the wrong night or walk into the wrong part of the club, you may be subjected to Top 40 or something equally unexpected, and unwanted.

✔ **The Yale,** 1300 Granville Street, Yaletown (☎ 604-681-9253) is a very good blues club stuck amid an otherwise down-at-the-heels stretch of Granville. Acoustics and sight lines aren't exactly top-quality, but what do you expect? This *is* a blues dive, after all.

Turning up the volume: The best rock-'n-roll bars

Rock and roll is alive and well, although it may not always seem so. You have to scout a bit to find its beating pulse in Vancouver, however, sometimes descending into grottier neighborhoods to hear up-and-coming stars. Frankly speaking, the town's just too politically correct and overly polite to appreciate hard rockers. (The biggest musical star ever to come out of here was Bryan Adams, after all, so maybe it's just not a hard-rock town.) Here are some places where you can really "r-a-w-k" — don't forget the earplugs:

✔ **The Brickyard,** 315 Carrall Street, Gastown (☎ 604-685-3922), yet another gritty, down-to-earth joint in Gastown, rocks out part of the week and throbs to house and dance music the other. Definitely not for the beautiful people.

✔ **The Roxy,** 932 Granville Street, Downtown (☎ 604-684-7699), attracts a young, happy crowd with cover music, unchallenging drinks, and silly bartenders juggling hard liquor. The operative word is fun, and they do actually pull it off — hey, you just may win a trip to Cuba or something — but don't expect anything musically or culturally original.

✔ The **Starfish Room,** 1055 Homer Street, Yaletown (☎ 604-682-4171), squarely in the middle of revitalized Yaletown, is a good place to pick up on the city's youthful energy. Local bands of a hungry and non-commercial streak supply most of the music, as well as proof that shards of talent exist out there among the rubble. Visiting acts of surprisingly high caliber and renown also hit the stage. Closed Sundays and Mondays.

Dipping into Watering Holes

If you don't care much for music but enjoy kicking back with a drink, you're in luck — this is definitely not a dry town. The central business core is home to a preponderance of hotel bars, most of them pretty good for atmosphere, local character, and a draft of something cold. Gastown in particular offers some grungy examples. Yaletown experienced a recent explosion of brewpubs; you almost feel stupid here ordering a brew that *wasn't* made in Vancouver. Sports bars do exist in the city, but they're mostly confined to the suburbs. And despite the city's English roots, the central city has surprisingly few authentic pubs — go to Victoria if you're craving true bangers 'n' mash and a pint of some terrific but obscure British ale.

Pubs and bars normally don't charge a cover, unless some sort of event is going on, and then there may be a small charge.

See-and-be-seen spots

Despite its laid-back charms, Vancouver certainly has its fair share — okay, maybe more than its share — of nightspots where patrons are simply there to make deals and connections, get noticed, and basically ignore anyone else who can't further their ends in life. That said, living like the other half for a night can be fun. And you may spy someone famous shooting a film or TV series in town; film stars are much more likely to hang out publicly here than in Los Angeles, as polite Canadians tend not to rush at them with popping flashbulbs, plastic grins, and boorish autograph requests. Here are the top places to get an eyeful:

✔ **Alibi Room,** 157 Alexander Street, Gastown (☎ 604-623-3383), is ground zero for U.S. film industry types. Every wannabe Hollywood screenwriter and actor in town — a larger group than you'd guess — knows this place. Industry types drink upstairs in the restaurant section or, less frequently, downstairs in the lounge area. *X-Files* note: Co-star (now main star) Gillian Anderson is part owner of the place.

✔ **Gerard Lounge,** 845 Burrard Street, Downtown (☎ 604-682-5511), housed inside the Sutton Place Hotel (see Chapter 10), attracts a star-studded and blasé crowd to its posh surroundings. Try not to drop your drink when some mega-movie star saunters by on his/her way to the john. Tuesdays, a locally famous Chocoholic's Buffet lays out treats of a different kind.

✔ **Moomba,** 3116 West Broadway, Kitsilano (☎ 604-737-8980), hoping for hipness, is still figuring out its groove. The level of pretension is already off the meter. You're unlikely to have metaphysical conversations on the dance floor (if you even get past the doormen); at least everybody looks good talking about nothing.

✔ **Richard's on Richards,** 1036 Richards Street, West End (☎ 604-687-6894) features various incarnations of dance and rock, sometimes played by local bands and sometimes by world-renowned acts. But you don't just come to listen: You come to look. This is *the* place to be seen in the city, so wildly popular among its surgically enhanced and overdressed clientele that it needs to open only 2 nights a week — Friday and Saturday, of course — plus for concert performances.

English and Irish pubs

Finding an authentic pint being drawn in downtown Vancouver is amazingly hard. All the expatriate Brits and Irish appear to have headed for the 'burbs, and indeed several excellent pubs are in outlying areas. I don't assume that you're such a hardcore Anglophile that you'd head to the Canadian equivalent of Hoboken just for a beer. Bearing that in mind, here are the best of the central places, all somewhat geared to tourists but nevertheless kind of fun:

✔ **Atlantic Trap and Gill,** 612 Davie Street, West End (☎ 604-806-6393), is an Irish bar where the glass of stout reigns supreme and live Celtic music is almost a sure thing.

✔ **Blarney Stone,** 216 Carrall Street, Gastown (☎ 604-687-4322), another Irish pub, sometimes features live fiddle players. Even without music, the pub stocks enough Harp and Guinness to make one teary for the Emerald Isle. It's closed Sunday through Tuesday, yes, but open until 2 a.m. the rest of the week.

✔ The **Irish Heather,** 217 Carrall Street, Gastown (☎ 604-688-9779), one of several Irish pubs in this touristy part of town, nevertheless delivers in spades — not too bright and clean. In other words, like a real Irish pub.

✔ **Stamp's Landing,** 610 Stamp's Landing, Mount Pleasant (☎ 604-879-0821), is an almost-authentic British pub — except with much better food — that offers an array of draft beers that you normally find only in your dreams. Your fellow drinkers are wannabe boaters, however, so unless you enjoy boat talk and stock tips you may want to cut out after a couple pints. It's across False Creek from Yaletown, a bit hard to reach.

Cue-crackin' poolrooms

Sometimes you've just gotta shoot some pool, and Vancouver's not short on places to do it. Here are two of the best:

✔ **Automotive,** 1095 Homer Street, Yaletown (☎ 604-682-0040), a pool hall much yuppified since its early days, becomes more active the later the night goes.

✔ **Soho Café & Billiards,** 1144 Homer Street, Yaletown (☎ 604-688-1180), is a very classy place to shoot some stick and sip twee drinks among the beautiful people. If you're looking for a dive in which to hustle some barflies, look elsewhere.

Neighborhood bars

Sometimes you really do want to go where everybody knows your name. Loads of neighborhood bars await in the residential neighborhoods of Vancouver, including these three for starters.

✔ **Fred's Tavern,** 1006 Granville Street, Downtown (☎ 604-605-4350), is the definition of a corner bar in look and feel — sometimes almost suspiciously so, what with the made-for-TV layout and luscious staff. Yet it works. Closed Sundays.

✔ **Brickhouse Bar,** 730 Main Street, Main Street Station (☎ 604-689-8645), is a good neighborhood bar in what has long been a pretty rugged area. Things are gradually improving hereabouts, and the bar owners deserve mucho kudos for leading the charge. This place has everything you want and more — good drinks, comfy seating, superlative snacks, and everyone remarks on the long fish tanks.

✔ **Sylvia Lounge,** 1154 Gilford Street, West End (☎ 604-681-9321), a lovely hotel bar, is loved by West Enders, and not only for its tranquil water views. The feeling is actually neighborhoody, and — thank goodness — no bad music is piped in to overwhelm attempts at conversation or matchmaking.

Hip alternative bars

I don't know what else to call this hodgepodge of a category; it simply denotes a place where the vibe is young, alternative, artsy . . . the kind of places where granny glasses, Gram Parsons, Elvis Costello, and Elvis Presley are still in.

✔ **Backstage Lounge,** 1585 Johnston Street, Granville Island (☎ 604-687-1354), is frequented by young locals — and, yes, budding artists — for its water views, theater-company ties, and exceptionally happy atmosphere. The live music on weekends gets pretty good too.

✔ **Chameleon Urban Lounge,** 801 West Georgia Street, Downtown (☎ 604-669-0806), should be in the "dance" category perhaps, because that's what the DJs play — except when they're messing with Latino rhythms, jazz, and other funky stuff. But the mellow atmosphere, setting, and famous drop-by clientele are so cool it really belongs here instead. Important tip: The door to this basement spot is actually around the corner on Howe Street.

✔ **DV8,** 515 Davie Street, West End (☎ 604-682-4388), a very late-night spot, attracts young, rich rebels busy rebelling on their parents' money. Dress like you're at a rave (or a prison break) and you're more likely to fit in than if you're sporting fancy threads. Seriously, though, the live music can be a cut above many other places.

✔ **Joe Fortes,** 777 Thurlow Street, West End (☎ 604-669-1940), a hopping, healthy place named for a heroic Jamaican lifeguard, attracts a youthful, *St. Elmo's Fire*-type crowd flaunting some serious wealth.

✔ **The Sugar Refinery,** 1115 Granville Street (☎ 604-683-2004), stays open later than any other Vancouver hotspot. In early summer you can nearly see the sun rise upon stumbling out after last call. Refusing to be defined by any one genre, this hip space offers a mishmash of food, drink, art, and performance.

✔ **Whip Gallery,** 209 East 6th Avenue, Mount Pleasant (☎ 604-874-4687), is hip, sure — hip enough to be a coffee shop or design-school graduate's crash pad. Instead, it's a bar with a decent (if small) drink selection, light eats, occasional jazz, and interesting art. The feeling is more laid-back and mature than you may expect from the living-room-furniture motif.

Chic bars and lounges

If you like to feel right at home in a stylishly decorated lounge sipping martinis and other shaken or stirred drinks, you'll find places aplenty around town. Here are some of the best:

✔ **Bacchus Lounge,** 845 Hornby Street, Downtown (☎ 604-689-7777), in the plush Wedgewood hotel (see Chapter 10), almost demands a dress code, it's so well-appointed. Think of it as a potential pre- or post-dinner spot to snuggle over a drink. Quite expensive and trendy.

✔ **Cloud 9 Lounge,** 1400 Robson Street, West End (☎ 604-687-0511), revolves high, high above the city's main shopping drag — and, no, it doesn't whip around so fast that you'll get seasick. Views of the mountains, the water, and even Washington state can be incredible if clouds are absent, and nighttime jazz sessions add to the already ethereal atmosphere. To find the club from street level, enter at the Empire Landmark Hotel and take the elevator.

✔ **Garden Terrace,** 791 West Georgia Street, Downtown (☎ 604-602-0994) is the only place in town that you can sit beneath foliage imported from the African subcontinent. Housed within the ultra-pricey Four Seasons hotel (see Chapter 10), it's an extremely *precieux* place in which to sip a drink — save it for a special occasion. Closed Sundays.

✔ **900 West Lounge & Wine Bar,** 900 West Georgia Street, Downtown (☎ 604-669-9378), the smartest wine bar in town, serves glasses, carafes, and bottles of some terrific vintages — plus great martinis if you don't feel like wine. Huge chandeliers and wingback chairs fill out the mood. Located in the Hotel Vancouver (see Chapter 10), it's a nice place for a snack with your drink, too, but wear your nicest clothes and bring your wallet.

Thirst-quenching brewpubs

You may find no hotter trend, this moment, than the brewpub in Vancouver — and most of the action is tightly concentrated in Yaletown, although it's beginning to spread to other hip quarters of the city as well. I love sampling the freshly brewed products of a micro while chatting with the owners, and the atmosphere in such a place is almost always reliably genteel, too. Here are my top picks:

✔ **Creek Brewery,** 1253 Johnston Street, Granville Island (☎ 604-685-7070), is a fine spot to sip local beer and meet what passes for the city's high rollers.

✔ **Dix Barbecue & Brewery,** 871 Beatty Street, Yaletown (☎ 604-682-2739), a microbrewery near B.C. Place Stadium, is as attractive as all the others in Yaletown, with good period photographs lining the walls. The crowd is pretty (though it morphs into Testosterone Central on hockey or hoop nights), and the beer isn't bad at all.

✔ **Steamworks Brewing Co.,** 375 Water Street, Gastown (☎ 604-689-2739) brews such good drafts that you may not notice the sometimes smarmy clientele. Explore several comfortable seating areas before settling down. This is Vancouver's original brewpub.

✔ **Yaletown Brewing Company,** 1111 Mainland Street, Yaletown (☎ 604-688-0064 or 604-681-2739), yet another Yaletown micro-brewery, may be a bit of a scene, but the beer's the thing. You can drink outside when it's warm and dry, too, and the hip location for once doesn't preclude casual dress.

Beer joints

I love great beer, and I really like bar owners who know the huge differ-ence between drinking a can of imported beer and savoring a hand-drawn pint of the same stuff. At the following places, you can count on superb choice of beers and a staff that knows how to serve each and every one of 'em:

✔ **The Rusty Gull,** 175 East 1st Street, North Vancouver (☎ 604-988-5585), is one of those bars that seems to exist simply for the pleasure of quaffing. Ownership has put together a knowledgeable beer list, and you'll want to sample as much of it as possible. Live music complements the atmosphere.

✔ **Sailor Hagar's,** 221 West 1st Street, North Vancouver (☎ 604-984-3087 or 604-984-2567), seems to have everything under the sun. If you're a connoisseur of hard-to-find Bavarian dark beers, northern English ales, Irish cream stouts, or Belgian lambics, this is your place. They use authentic pub equipment to keep it fresh; and the bartenders know their stuff. Views of the city back across the water are astounding, and a restaurant is on the premises too. Don't feel like driving to North Van? No problem — the bar's just a short walk from the SeaBus (see Chapter 9) landing.

Gay bars and clubs

Vancouver is a very gay-friendly town. And a network of bars and clubs has sprung up to knit together the area's growing gay population. Here are some of the hottest places for gays and lesbians to meet:

✔ **Celebrities,** 1022 Davie Street, West End (☎ 604-689-3180) is an enormous and central gay club, the city's biggest, with a number of everyone-welcome nights too — but Saturday is absolutely not one of them. Friday is. Closed Sundays.

✔ **Homers,** 1249 Howe Street, Downtown (☎ 604-689-2444), is low-key and friendly and has pool tables and a kitchen.

✔ **Numbers Cabaret,** 1098 Davie Street, West End (☎ 604-685-4077), a multi-level complex of loud and quiet spots, is a prime spot for gay trawlers to sip beers, taste cocktails, cruise the scene, or just go nuts on one of several dance floors.

✔ **Odyssey,** 1251 Howe Street, Downtown (☎ 604-689-5256), rages all night, every night, with everything from cultural events to disco DJs to some truly outrageous stuff as well — I'll just say that showers and drag queens are involved. Not really a place for straight folks, not at all.

Exploring Something Different

Finally, if you're bored with the previous listings, try one of these places for a different stroke:

✔ **BaBaLu's Tapas Lounge,** 654 Nelson Street, Downtown (☎ 604-605-4343), capitalizes on Canada's snuggly ties to Cuba by hosting some mighty fine swing bands and jazz combos that you'd never have a chance to hear in the U.S. of A. If you liked the film *Buena Vista Social Club,* you'll love the Latino feel of this bar. And, unlike in so many other hipper-than-hip places sprinkled around town, you don't need to be wet behind the ears to get in or feel at home, either. Find it inside the Hotel Dakota (see Chapter 10).

> ✔ **Railway Club,** 579 Dunsmuir Street, Downtown (☎ 604-681-1625) is a nice spot thanks to a train theme, eclectic tunes, and famous musicians popping in. You pay a little extra to get inside if you're not already a member of the "club."

Getting Artsy: The Performing Arts

Vancouver's sophisticates enjoy a major symphony orchestra, a world-class opera company, several theater companies, and an arena large enough to host such mega-groups as the Rolling Stones.

To find out what's happening in venues big and small, just check *The Georgia Straight,* a free weekly newspaper. Its entertainment listings are beyond reproach. Or buy a copy of *Vancouver* magazine, which does a good job laying out each month's offerings — which in recent years have included such things as a rare Joni Mitchell show and the great annual folk festival.

Trying to plan in advance? Check the publications' Web sites at www. straight.com and www.vanmag.com.

Or (and this is really covering your bases) call the **Vancouver Cultural Alliance's Arts Hotline** (☎ 604-684-2787). The Alliance's office, located downtown at 938 Howe Street (Suite #100), can provide the same information in visual, carryable form.

While in a way endorsing its rip-off surcharges, I feel duty-bound to report that **TicketMaster** (☎ 604-280-4444 for general information, 604-280-4400 for sports events, 604-280-3311 for arts events; Internet: www.ticketmaster.ca) is the easiest place to snag an advance ticket for major events. They have dozens of outlets scattered around the city. Remember that you pay something like five bucks extra per ticket for the "privilege" of shelling out.

Raise the curtain: Vancouver's theater scene

Vancouver's theater scene bumps along, usually pretty decent but occasionally a little rough for stretches. Current offerings include a mixture of retreads, which don't seem to do too well in this town, and more exciting work, some of it locally penned. The city does not have a compact theater district, so plan ahead before heading out for the evening. The four major theater spaces to check out are:

> ✔ The **Arts Club Theatre,** 1585 Johnston Street, Granville Island (☎ 604-687-1644), the home of a big regional company, produces an interesting array of plays. The Backstage Lounge is here, too

(see "Hip alternative bars," earlier in this chapter). Tickets start at C$20 (US$13) per performance.

✔ **Stanley Theatre,** 2750 Granville Street, Shaughnessy (☎ **604-687-1644**), the best-looking of these four theaters, is a renovated Art Deco-style movie house. The same company that performs at the Arts Club Theatre also performs here, but the shows are glitzier. Tickets generally run C$20 to C$40 (US$13–US$27) per show.

✔ The **Frederick Wood Theatre,** 6354 Crescent Road at Gate 4 (☎ **604-822-2678**), part of the University of British Columbia, offers student work at serious bargains (usually C$15 [US$10] per person) — and it's not all just *Carousel* reruns, either.

✔ The **Vancouver Playhouse,** 600 Hamilton Street, Downtown (☎ **604-665-3050**), is another place to see local and experimental work; sightlines are especially good here. Tickets are a steal at C$10 to C$15 (US$7–US$10) most nights. The theater is adjacent to the Queen Elizabeth Theater (see the next section).

If you happen to be in town during summer and like Shakespeare, don't even think about missing the fun **Bard on the Beach** (☎ **604-737-0625**) series. The Bard's plays are performed right out there in Vanier Park at the 1100 block of West Broadway, and also inside a smaller enclosed space.

A similar series (without the Shakespearean focus) is the **Theatre Under the Stars** (☎ **604-687-0174;** Internet: www.tuts.ba.ca) series in Stanley Park during July and August. This open-air theater can be very romantic — although a brisk wind is usually blowing in from the ocean. Picnicking is encouraged.

If you're coming in September, be aware of the *avant-garde* **Fringe Festival** (☎ **604-237-0350;** Internet: www.vancouverfringe.com), a spin-off from the popular Edinburgh festivals centered around Commercial Drive east of downtown.

Wings and strings: Opera, dance, and classical music

Patrons of the higher art forms find the city well stocked with these offerings:

The **Vancouver Symphony Orchestra** (☎ **604-876-3434** for information, 604-280-4444 for tickets) gets classical — yet stays accessible with pops concerts, big-name guest soloists, and children's shows — at the venerable **Orpheum Theatre,** 800 Granville, Downtown (☎ **604-655-3050**). Tickets run anywhere from C$20 to C$55 (US$13–US$37) per person.

The talented **Vancouver Opera** (☎ 604-683-0222) performs four or more times annually before gorgeous set pieces at the busy **Queen Elizabeth Theatre,** 600 Hamilton Street, Downtown (☎ 604-665-3050), adjacent to the Vancouver Playhouse (see previous section). This venue is worth consulting for its other performances, too. Tickets generally cost from as little as C$35 (US$24) to as much as C$90 (US$60) per person — but, hey, you just may see one of those famous tenors you've only ever seen on PBS.

For dance fans, **Ballet British Columbia** (☎ 604-732-5003) stages a number of challenging performances — check out the light shows — around town, often at the Queen Elizabeth (see previous listing). And some very good visiting companies often show up to join in the fun. Tickets for a performance usually cost between C$20 and C$50 (US$13–US$34) per person.

If you're tired of paying big bucks for nosebleed seats, head over to the University of British Columbia (UBC) in Point Grey. The university's **Chan Centre for the Performing Arts** (☎ 604-822-9197; Internet: www. chancentre.com) hosts a pretty good bill of student and guest performances, sometimes free, sometimes at cost — but still at a better deal than in the big venues, and you definitely can hear the sounds better. (The concert hall is said to be world-renowned for its acoustics.) Performances happen year-round on weekends, more often in summer.

Chapter 15

Exploring Beyond Vancouver: Three Great Day Trips

*A*lthough Vancouver has plenty to offer, you may want to get out of town to experience the beautiful countryside. Those snow-capped mountains visible from downtown are one possibility, as is nearby Victoria (see Part IV), but a host of lesser-known day trips awaits as well — all within an hour's drive or ferry ride from the city. These trips are so good that you may prefer one of them to staying an extra day in the city. This chapter presents three of my favorite trips.

Day Trip #1: The Road to Whistler

One of the finest single-day trips you can do in western Canada is a drive north up Highway 99 from North Vancouver to (or, if you like, beyond) the popular ski resort town of Whistler.

Getting there

This two-lane road is known as the Sea to Sky Highway, and sections are indeed spectacular — especially the first half, where you skirt the water of Howe Sound (a fjord) from atop cliffs. As the road begins climbing, you notice sturdy gates like those at a railroad crossing. These gates are closed when sudden winter snowstorms sweep in from the mountains or the Pacific, closing the route off. How to avoid these potential road-blocks? Go in summer or early fall to eliminate the possibility.

The route passes through tiny Britannia Beach — mostly just a handful of homes and a diner — and past trailheads and campgrounds. Halfway to Whistler, you pass through the only town of size en route, Squamish; fast-food restaurants announce your brief return to civilization, where backpackers and other outdoorsy folks stock up on climbing gear and snacks before pressing onward. You may not think to linger or to climb the pinnacle known as The Chief, but a short detour west down an unmarked side road (ask locals how to find it) brings a surprising sight in winter: one of North America's finest eagle-viewing areas. The **West Coast Railway Heritage Park** (☎ 604-898-9336), also in Squamish, showcases a collection of train equipment and restored train compartments. The park is open daily 10 a.m. to 5 p.m.; admission is C$4.50 (US$3) for adults and C$3.50 (US$2.35) for seniors and children 5 to 15.

Just north of Squamish, Tantalus pullover is a great spot to shoot pictures of the mountains.

After another 30 or 35 miles of driving, you reach the highly (and very recently) developed town of Whistler. Internationally famous for its two ski mountains and world-class snowboarding, this resort shouldn't be overlooked during the summer months.

If you want to explore farther, continue driving north to Pemberton, a one-time logging town that has undergone a startling transformation into a hip West Coast outdoor playground. It's cheaper than Whistler, and far more pristine and authentic. Plenty of inns, B&Bs, and fine-dining establishment are here, as well as a winery (with suites on the premises) and various farms selling produce and baked goods. For information on Pemberton's attractions and lodging, call ☎ 604-894-6175.

Seeing the sights

This day trip is most convenient to do by car, because you have the freedom to turn off at various lookout points, trailheads, and shops. If you happen to drive through Squamish in winter, remember to get directions to the eagle lookout sights at Easter Seal Camp, a few miles west of the downtown strip.

When in Whistler, **hiking trails** are the prime attraction. You can get information on the area's best hikes from the **Whistler Activity and Information Center** (☎ 800-944-7853 or 604-932-2394), at the corner of Lake Placid Road and Highway 99, or from **Whistler Alpine Guides Bureau** (☎ 604-938-3228). Another major attraction is the relatively new **Nicklaus North golf course,** 8080 Nicklaus North Boulevard (☎ 604-938-9898), open from early May to mid-October.

Exploring Beyond Vancouver

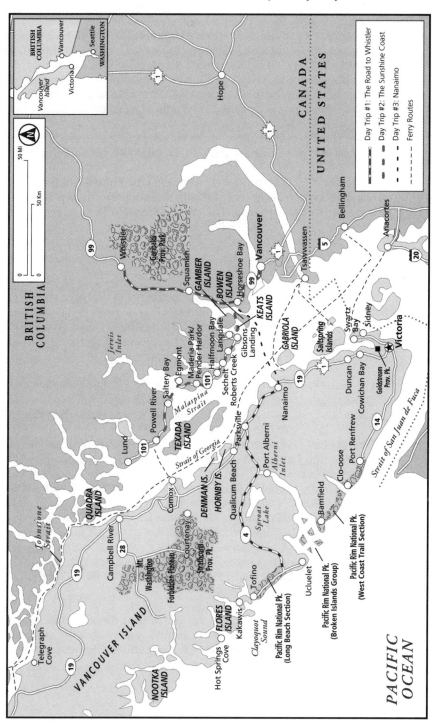

You can also take a look at pretty Alta Lake and think about riding up the **Whistler Gondola** (☎ 800-766-0449 or 604-932-3434); you may see bears roaming below. The gondola travels up Whistler Mountain from the center of town to the Roundhouse Lodge and operates from 8:30 a.m. to 8:00 p.m. Cost of a round-trip, including tax, is C$23.54 (US$16) for adults, C$21.40 (US$14) for seniors, C$14.98 (US$10) for children 6 to 18 (children under 6 are free). To ride with a mountain bike — mountain bike trails are at the top — costs C$41.73 (US$28) adults, C$34.24 (US$23) seniors and children. The gondola is handicapped-accessible.

If you simply want to linger in the village for a few hours, plenty of pubs, bistros, and pricey stores are in the various Whistler complexes.

If you don't feel like driving up from the city, but wish only to see the sights along the lower half of this route, another — considerably more romantic — option exists. The **Pacific Starlight Dinner Train** runs once per day. See Chapter 12 for details.

Where to stay

Along the Sea to Sky Highway, few lodgings break the journey outside campgrounds and Squamish hotels. Whistler, however, is another story — the town offers almost a glut of choices, most geared toward a seasonal well-heeled ski crowd. That means, in summer, you can find deals on certain condominiums or resorts.

Chateau Whistler, 4599 Chateau Boulevard (☎ **800-606-8244** or 604-938-8000), is the town's luxurious *grande dame* — not the place to ask about discounts — while the somewhat remote **Durlacher Hof,** 7055 Nesters Road (☎ **604-932-1924**), is a more homey-feeling inn. The **Chamber of Commerce** (☎ **604-932-5528**) or **Whistler Activity and Information Center** (☎ **800-944-7853** or 604-932-2394), both at the corner of Lake Placid Road and Highway 99, can quickly point you toward many rustic ski lodge-style accommodations, which are more mid-priced than super-expensive. **Edelweiss,** 7162 Nancy Green Drive (☎ **604-932-3641**), and the **Timberline Lodge,** 4122 Village Green (☎ **800-777-0185** or 604-932-5211), are two that get good reviews. Finally, you can find even less expensive cabins scattered around town, although some cater to a younger, more boisterous crowd. **Swiss Cottage B&B,** 7321 Fitzsimmons Drive (☎ **604-932-6062**), is one of the quieter examples.

In Pemberton, I suggest checking first with the **Pemberton Valley Vineyard Inn** (☎ **604-894-5857**) about room availability and local restaurant recommendations — not to mention their current vintage.

Where to dine

You can't possibly go hungry in Whistler, although you need to choose carefully to avoid overspending. Fine dining establishments (with big-time prices to match) abound; try the **Wildflower** (☎ **604-938-8000**) in the Chateau Whistler hotel complex, **Joel's** (☎ **604-932-1240**) at the golf course, or **Araxi** (☎ **604-932-4540**) in Whistler Village Square to sample some *nouveau* West Coast cuisine, which is strong on Asian flavors and local fish and shellfish.

If you'd rather mix with locals than tourists, however, head instead for one of the many cozy pubs, delis, and pizza joints around town. You may have to search to find one, but persevere; these places are definitely a cut above greasy-spoon diners. **Auntie Em's,** 4340 Lorimer Road (☎ **604-932-1163**), serves a fine all-day breakfast and good lunches as well to Whistlerians and tourists alike. Or just ask a local for a recommendation.

You also find the **Roadhouse Diner** (☎ **604-892-5312**) in Britannia Beach and a small brewery, **Howe Sound Inn and Brewing Company** (☎ **604-892-2603**), in Squamish on the way up or back if you simply can't wait to eat.

Day Trip #2: The Sunshine Coast

Vancouverites call it the "Sunshine Coast," and locals swear the weather's better here than in the city proper. Casting a skeptical eye skyward, I take their word for it.

But there's certainly no quibbling about the scenery on this stretch of the mainland, which follows the tortuous folds of Howe Sound as it twists and stretches in drop-dead-gorgeous curves west from Vancouver. These inlets are so indented and wild, in fact, that the entire region is cut off from Vancouver by road; you must fly in (prohibitively expensive for most of us) or else take the regular ferries from Horseshoe Bay. The entire length of the Sunshine Coast (which is basically Highway 101) is 95 km (60 miles). The closest town to Vancouver along this stretch is Langdale; other towns here are Gibsons Landing, Sechelt, Halfmoon Bay, Madeira Park, and Powell River.

If you're in the city for a week or more, try to find half a day to visit — this is small-town British Columbia at its most beautiful.

Getting there

The ferry from Horseshoe Bay, near West Vancouver, to Langdale runs on a variable schedule — check with **BC Ferries** (☎ **888-223-3779;** Internet: www.bcferries.bc.ca) for the latest schedules and fares. It takes about 40 minutes each way.

To get to Horseshoe Bay from downtown Vancouver, drive across the Lions Gate Bridge from the West End and merge onto the Trans-Canada Highway (Highways 1 and 99). Follow the highway west to Horseshoe Bay.

Seeing the sights

From the Langdale landing most visitors, choose to make the short drive of a mile or so over to **Gibsons Landing** (locals just call it "Gibsons"), a decent if overly precious first look at the coast. Canadians love visiting this town, because a hotel here was featured in a popular seaside television program for years. You may find the town worth a look too — if only to stock up on essential supplies and gifts or to check out the **Sunshine Coast Maritime Museum,** on Molly's Lane (☎ **604-886-4114;** open daily July through August 10 a.m. to 4 p.m., September through June 11 a.m. to 3 p.m.).

There's only one main road (Highway 101) to speak of along the Sunshine Coast. Highway 101 goes west past **Roberts Creek Provincial Park** (about 7½ miles west of Gibsons), which has good hiking trails and a beach, and on through the hamlet of Roberts Creek and the larger Sechelt, a base for **golf** and other outdoor activities, such as **kayaking, canoeing, boating, bicycling, mountain biking, fishing, diving, and cross-country skiing.** The **Sunshine Coast Golf & Country Club** (☎ **877-661-2288** or 604-885-9212) in Sechelt is open year-round. Another Sechelt attraction, **House of Hewhiwus** (☎ **604-885-2273**), showcases the culture and crafts of the local Sechelt Indians.

Writers, musicians, and artists are thick on the ground in this part of the coast. From Sechelt, Highway 101 continues to Halfmoon Bay, with its authentically aging general store, and then finally to a series of settlements on Pender Harbor — starting point for **boating and fishing excursions,** should you have the time, or a walk to the rapids at the interestingly named Skookumchuck Narrows. One company offering boat trips in the area is **Ketchalot Charters** (☎ **604-883-9351**).

For more information on activities along the Sunshine Coast, contact the office of the **Sunshine Coast Regional District** (☎ **604-885-2261**) or one of the town tourism offices, such as **Gibsons Tourist InfoCentre** (☎ **604-886-2325**), **Powell River Tourist InfoCentre** (☎ **604-485-4701**), or the **Sechelt Tourist InfoCentre** (☎ **604-885-0662**).

Where to stay

Because the coast is largely residential, few lodging choices are available. Bed-and-breakfasts and off-the-beaten-track cabins predominate, with few truly luxurious accommodations available; I'd probably make this a long day trip from Vancouver.

Where to dine

This lightly populated area offers a surprising range of dining options, from country store picnic fare to highfalutin' gourmet meals.

Gibsons Landing offers the most choice. Go fancy or simple, burgers or French; it's all concentrated on the main street. Farther down the road, everyone in Roberts Creek ends up, sooner or later, at **Gumboot Garden** (☎ 604-885-4216), a plain-looking place concealing a terrific bakery and hearty lunch menu. In Sechelt, farther still, splurge at the widely renowned **Blue Heron** (☎ 800-818-8977 or 604-885-3847).

Day Trip #3: Nanaimo

Nanaimo may not seem, at first glance, like an obvious day-trip destination after you've experienced the splendors of Vancouver and Victoria. But if you want to get a quick taste of adjacent Vancouver Island, the island's second largest city (after Victoria) is a convenient ferry ride away from North Vancouver.

Getting there

You reach Nanaimo by one of two ferries, both operated by **BC Ferries** (☎ 888-223-3779; Internet: www.bcferries.bc.ca). The **Horseshoe Bay-Nanaimo** ferry departs from the terminal at Horseshoe Bay, about 15 miles north and west of central Vancouver (take the Lions Gate Bridge from the West End and follow the Trans-Canada Highway to Horseshoe Bay). The ferry departs eight times daily for the 95-minute trip to Nanaimo. The **Mid-Island Express** departs six times daily from Tsawwassen for a 2-hour crossing to Duke Point, just outside Nanaimo. The Tsawwassen docks are south of Vancouver on Highway 17. Contact BC Ferries for fares, schedules, and reservations.

Seeing the sights

In Nanaimo, most everything is close to the docks. The working waterfront is the main sight here, although you can find a couple other worthwhile attractions, such as a fort on Front Street called the **Bastion** (☎ 250-753-1821) — complete with booming cannon — open mid-May to October daily 10:30 a.m. to 4:30 p.m. Admission is only C$1 (US$.67) for adults and seniors, and C$.50 (US$.34) for children. You can also find the **Nanaimo District Museum,** 100 Cameron Road (☎ 250-753-1821), a good little museum open mid-May to October, Monday through Friday, 9:00 a.m. to 5:00 p.m., and weekends from 10:00 a.m. to 6:00 p.m.; and November through early May, Tuesday through Saturday 9:00 a.m. to

5:00 p.m. Both the Bastion and the museum are wheelchair-accessible. Additionally, Nanaimo's shopping district is compact, walkable, and reasonably quaint.

By car, you're very close to **Cathedral Grove,** a forest of ancient trees. To get here, about 20 miles from Naniamo, take Highway 19 north and then exit onto Highway 4, going west. You're also near excellent swimming at beaches such as **Qualicum Beach.** Moreover, the area is the hub of Vancouver Island's growing golf tourism business. If you're interested in playing a few rounds, one course to try is **Nanaimo Golf Club** (☎ 250-758-6332).

Or just take a second ferry to **Gabriola Island,** gathering point for artists, environmentalists, and another self-sufficient types. A 20-minute ferry ride from Gabriola Ferry Wharf (right at the very end of Front Street), the island is full of beaches and parks, and has a pub. If you're interested in the arts, plenty of galleries and studios are also on hand. But my favorite pick would be to play a round of golf at the island course, **Gabriola Golf and Country Club** (☎ 250-247-8822), or to stroll around the weird rocks known as the Malaspina Galleries, located about 6 miles north of the Taylor Bay Road turnoff.

Where to stay

Nanaimo itself probably isn't interesting enough to warrant an overnight stay, but the surrounding area is. You can find plenty of farms, hills, and beaches within a short drive of this tiny city. A range of motels, inns, bed-and-breakfasts, and more luxurious choices are both inside and outside the city. For information on accommodation choices, contact **Tourism Nanaimo,** 2290 Bowen Road (☎ 800-663-7337 or 250-756-0106).

Where to dine

Nanaimo is decidedly gritty rather than flashy, and as such many of the dining options are of the fried-seafood variety rather than the gourmet. Still, the tourism traffic and the presence of a small university mean you can find good food here with a little poking around. On Gabriola Island, a pub is right next to the ferry landing; it serves the pub food and English ales you'd expect in a place like this.

Although they won't make a meal, don't forget to try a so-called "Nanaimo bar," a chocolate-and-butter confection invented by a local bakery and available everywhere around town.

Part IV
Exploring Victoria

The 5th Wave   By Rich Tennant

"...which reminds me— is your cousin's family still planning to visit us this summer?"

In this part . . .

*J*ust a ferry ride away from Vancouver is lovely Victoria, an English stronghold surrounded by beauty. In this part I first orient you to the city by telling you what's where and how to find information and get around. I then introduce you to the city's many charms and give you the lowdown on hotels, restaurants, attractions, and nightlife. I also provide an itinerary for the Anglophiles among you who want to enjoy the city's strong English heritage.

Chapter 16

Orienting Yourself in Victoria

*V*ictoria, being much more compact than Vancouver, is even easier to get around. The airport and ferry terminals are a fair distance outside the city, but clearly marked roads and some public transit make getting into town relatively easy. In this chapter, I tell you how to get here, give you a quick outline of the city's layout, and point you toward the helpful tourist information folks. Finally, I show you how to best get around Victoria by foot, car, or cab.

Arriving in Victoria

Upon arrival in Canada, you first have to pass through Customs and Immigration. See Chapter 8 for what you can expect at these points.

Getting from Vancouver International Airport to your hotel

En route to Victoria, you'll most likely fly into **Vancouver International Airport** (☎ 800-668-3141), abbreviation: YVR. For information on what to expect at the airport and the location of information booths, see Chapter 9. To get to Victoria from this airport, you have several choices.

By ferry

Many travelers simply rent a car at the airport and then drive straight to the Victoria ferry at Tsawwassen (pronounced SAH-WAH-sen, although you sometimes hear TAH-WAH-sen). This way is convenient, but if you go this route you spend time driving to and from the ferry, waiting for the ferry, riding the ferry, and worrying about traffic and parking in Victoria. Then you need to reverse the process before leaving. Still, if you have to fly into Vancouver International Airport and you have the need for a car, this may be your best option.

Several major rental car companies have representatives at the airport (see the Appendix for their toll-free numbers). After you pick up your car, drive out of the airport, and turn onto Highway 99 South (*away* from Vancouver). Continue approximately 8 miles south to the junction with Highway 17, then turn south on Highway 17. Now you roll through suburbs and then miles of peaceful farmland. After about ten miles, the highway ends at the Tsawwassen dock of **BC Ferries** (☎ **888-223-3779;** Internet: www.bcferries.bc.ca). Drive right onto the dock and take a place in the lineup. If you're lucky, there won't be a huge backup; however, you may need to wait a while. The ferry ride across the Strait of Georgia and through several small channels to Swartz Bay takes about 90 minutes. (See Chapter 5 for ticket information for BC Ferries.)

From the Swartz Bay terminal, take Highway 17, the Patricia Bay Highway, directly south into downtown Victoria, where it becomes Blanshard Street. To reach Old Town and the Inner Harbour, turn right at Yates Street. To reach the Empress, turn right at Burdett Avenue or Humboldt Street.

By plane or helicopter

Much easier — and cooler — is to fly from Vancouver International Airport straight to downtown Victoria via either a seaplane (also called a floatplane) or a helicopter. Both land right in Victoria's Inner Harbour, steps from nearly all the major sights. The options include **Harbour Air, Helijet,** and **West Coast Air,** and costs range between C$80 (US$54) and C$105 (US$70) each way. For more details on these services, see Chapter 5.

By bus

You can even get to Victoria from the airport without lifting off *or* driving (yourself, that is). **Pacific Coach Lines** (☎ **800-661-1725** or 604-662-8074; Internet: www.pacificcoach.com), known as PCL, runs three buses each day directly from Vancouver International Airport to downtown Victoria — the bus drives right onto the ferry. Just remember that all departures tend to take place in the middle of the day, which is inconvenient if your flight is early- or late-arriving. The bus costs about C$25 (US$17), though it varies depending on the season because of fluctuating ferry fares. The trip takes about 3½ hours from the airport to Victoria's bus depot. Call or check the Web site for up-to-the-minute reservation, schedule, and fare information.

Getting from Victoria International Airport to your hotel

In every situation I can think of, flying into Vancouver's airport is cheaper than flying into Victoria's. Assume, however, that you decide to value convenience over cost and fly into Victoria — either directly (which is actually possible from a handful of cities in the northwestern United States), or on a connecting flight from Vancouver.

Victoria International Airport (abbreviation: CYYJ; ☎ 250-953-7500) is a small facility located about 15 miles north of the city on Highway 17, up on the Saanich Peninsula. Several short-hop airlines, as well as various special charter flights, land here. The facility is small enough that you won't get lost, and everything is clearly marked and signed. For a list of airlines that fly to this airport, see the Appendix.

Surprisingly, public transit does not connect the airport to Victoria. Therefore the quickest, though certainly not cheapest, way to travel from the airport into the city is by cab. The 40-minute ride costs roughly C$30 to C$45 (US$20–US$30); a 15% tip is usually appropriate. The major cab companies include **Blue Bird** (☎ 800-665-7055), **Empress** (☎ 250-381-2222), and **Victoria Taxi** (☎ 888-842-7111). Empress usually has cabs waiting at the airport, but you can pre-arrange for any other cab company to pick you up if you call in advance.

The privately operated shuttle bus known as **Airporter** (☎ 877-386-2525 or 250-386-2525) is also a good choice, as it leaves regularly from the terminal and makes stops at many of the key downtown hotels. You may have to wait a half-hour or more for a departure, however, depending on your timing. The fare is C$13 for adults (C$11.70 for seniors) and the ride takes about an hour.

Although you won't need a car in Victoria, several rental car agencies are at the airport, including **Avis, Budget, Enterprise, Hertz,** and **National** (see the Appendix for their toll-free numbers). For directions from the airport into the city, see the next section.

Driving to Victoria

If you drive into Victoria, you'll either be coming from the Inner Harbour ferry docks, the Swartz Bay terminal north of the city, the airport, or elsewhere on Vancouver Island.

From the Inner Harbour ferry docks, simply drive two short blocks along Belleville Street to Douglas Street, just past the huge Empress hotel; here, you turn left to reach the heart of the Old Town or right to reach Beacon Hill Park or the ocean loop through James Bay and Oak Bay.

From the Swartz Bay terminal, drive off the ferry and onto Highway 17, the Patricia Bay Highway, which runs directly south into downtown Victoria, where it becomes Blanshard Street. To reach Old Town and the Inner Harbour, turn right at Yates Street. To reach the Empress, turn right at Burdett Avenue or Humboldt Street.

From the Victoria International Airport, you also drive Highway 17 south for about 15 miles into downtown Victoria, following the same directions as in the previous paragraph.

From elsewhere on Vancouver Island, simply proceed south on Highway 1, which becomes Douglas Street and runs right into the heart of town.

Finding Information after You Arrive

Victoria has one central place for picking up comprehensive tourism information, but thank goodness it's well stocked. The **Visitor InfoCentre,** 812 Wharf Street (☎ **250-953-2033** or 250-382-6539; 800-663-3883 to book accommodations only), located right on the harbor at the corner of Government and Wharf Streets, is open daily all year long. The hours are 8:30 a.m. to 7 p.m. in summer and 9 a.m. to 5 p.m. the rest of the year. (And by the way, it looks sorta like a gas station because it *was* once a gas station. Fill 'er up!)

The friendly staff offers plenty of brochures and other printed material, covering nearly every aspect of Victoria. Beyond this, the office can also find accommodations for you at no extra charge; book tours, boat excursions, and theater tickets; and offer recommendations. Note that the office also distributes information for the rest of Vancouver Island, as well.

A smaller, seasonal InfoCentre on the Patricia Bay Highway (Highway 17) is about 16 miles north of town. This is a more convenient first stop if you're coming into town from the north — that is, from the Vancouver-to-Swartz Bay ferry or from the Victoria airport. This office is open from March through the end of November, daily, 9 a.m. to 5 p.m.

Victoria by Neighborhood

Compact Victoria is less confusing than spread-out Vancouver. The city's three central neighborhoods are all connected, and as you walk or drive, they tend to blur into one another. Staying in this area is the best option if you're on a short visit, although you do pay extra. Victoria's suburbs tend to be almost exclusively residential, although one or two of these outlying areas have hotels. Finally, you can find chain motels and hotels on Highway 17 north of Victoria, but consider these only if you're strapped for cash or in a hurry to leave the following morning.

Victoria Neighborhoods

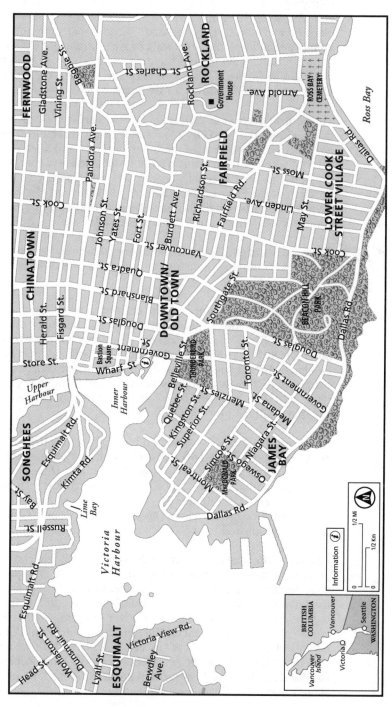

The **Inner Harbour** (note the British/Canadian spelling) is the area surrounding the city's small inner harbor, where ferry boats, floatplanes, and whale-watching boats arrive and depart. Accommodations are plentiful and wonderfully situated. The views are splendid, and you're no more than a few minute's walk to such important sights as the Empress Hotel, government buildings, and — of course — the waterfront and its ferries. This is, not very surprisingly, the most expensive place in town to bed down for the night.

The central portion of Victoria consists of an area along the waterfront, within five or so city blocks of it in any direction. This is the next-priciest location after the Inner Harbour, and it isn't a quiet place (except when bars shut down), but it does possess good atmosphere. Think of this area as two adjacent parts: **Old Town**, first up walking north from the Empress and including Bastion and Market Squares, and then **Downtown**, which contains the bulk of the city's commerce — shopping, restaurants and bars, plus hotels.

Downtown and Old Town are so interwoven that, for the purposes of this book, I combine them into a single area called "Downtown/Old Town."

The adjacent neighborhoods are hit-or-miss when it comes to bedtime. The tiny and slightly grubby **Chinatown** (surprisingly, the continent's oldest in spite of its small size) occupies only a few narrow blocks north of Old Town, and I don't recommend any lodgings here. A few blocks northeast lies **Fernwood,** a once down-at-heels but now up-and-coming area, that is swiftly revitalizing itself through the arts, restaurants, and the like; again, however, I don't recommend any accommodations here. Stay tuned.

Just west of Old Town, connected by a bridge, lies the neighborhood of **Songhees** (pronounced SONG-eeze) and then the separate municipality called **Esquimalt** (pronounced ess-KWHY-malt). Once an industrial area, this section is hot stuff today — home to North America's first microbrewery (see Chapter 21), but also several excellent lodgings, all with stupendous water views. Throughout this book, I combine these neighborhoods and refer to them as "Esquimalt/Songhees."

Finally, a little south and east of the central area you can find a number of residential neighborhoods harboring excellent, and quieter, lodgings. **James Bay,** directly south of downtown (to the right as you leave the ferries) is quietly attractive and offers a handful of distinctive lodgings to go with terrific views over water of islands and mountains. You can also wander nice Beacon Hill Park from your front door. The next neighborhood to the west is **Lower Cook Street Village,** a narrow strip that runs along the eastern side of Beacon Hill Park. **Rockland** and **Fairfield** are situated just north of here, composed of quiet and elegant streets and a handful of nice bed-and-breakfasts.

And **Oak Bay,** farther still to the east, is a friendly and British-feeling neighborhood with excellent beaches, golf courses, and a pleasant mixture of older and newer homes. Surprisingly posh accommodations are here. Think about staying here if you crave a quieter, more local experience. Reach the area by looping east and then north from the Inner Harbour along Dallas Road, a very scenic drive.

Getting around Victoria

You're most likely to see Victoria by your own power, in a car, by private transportation, or as part of some sort of a tour. However, the city does have a small, public transportation system. In this section, I let you know about each mode of transport.

By foot

You can reach many of the key sights — including all the Inner Harbour, the Old Town, James Bay, and Chinatown — by foot, and in fact the vast majority of your fellow visitors will be walking also.

By bicycle

In a city possessing as many beaches, parks, and gardens as Victoria — without big-city traffic — bicycling turns out to be one of the best ways to see the local charms if you have the energy. Bike lanes have thoughtfully been provided in key locations, and a day's rental costs only about C$20 (US$14), with an hour's rental about C$6 (US$4).

Some companies that rent cycles include **Cycle Victoria** on Wharf Street (☎ 250-385-2453), **Harbour Rentals** at 811 Wharf Street (☎ 250-995-1661), and **Sports Rent** at 611 Discovery (☎ 250-385-7368).

A number of bike repair shops are in Victoria as well, although they're almost all on the outskirts; the most central are probably **James Bay Bicycle Works,** 331 Menzies Street (☎ 250-380-1664), conveniently near the popular ocean loop, and the slightly hard-to-find but helpful **Fairfield Bicycle Shop,** 1275 Oscar Street (☎ 250-381-2453).

By car

Having a car in Victoria is convenient if you plan to get out into the countryside. But if you're concentrating on downtown, I recommend that you leave the wheels at home. If you do drive, you'll find that drivers here are exceptionally polite. You should drive — and act — in the same fashion. Traffic rules are mostly the same as those of the United States: You drive on the right and stop at red lights. Plus, you can turn right on a red light if no traffic is coming. Blinking green arrows can be confusing — they simply mean "Proceed with caution" not "Go for it! Turn left! (heh-heh)" Headlights must be on at all times, although on Canadian rental cars this happens automatically, and seat belts are always required. The speed limit within Victoria's limits is generally 50 kilometers per hour (that's about 30 mph), sometimes less.

Traffic backs up downtown at rush hour, which occurs from perhaps 4:00 to 6:00 p.m., as downtown employees make an exodus for the northern, eastern, and western suburbs, and the one-way street system can be confounding. Parking is also often a hassle due to the compactness of the tourist area. On-street meters are expensive and nearly impossible to find during the high summer season — if you do manage to snag one, have plenty of change at the ready (a Canadian dollar only gets you a half-hour). Parking in a garage or lot is a better option than a meter. Several facilities are along Blanshard and View Streets, for example. You should always ask your restaurant, hotel, or merchant if they'll validate your parking slip.

Watch for parking spots that "disappear" at rush hour; you'll be towed if you stay too long in these. Parking fines in Victoria run about C$20 (US$13) — you can pay online if you're nabbed.

By public transportation

BC Transit's Victoria arm, known as the **Victoria Regional Transit System** (☎ 250-382-6161; Internet: www.bctransit.com), consists almost solely of a bus network you may never use, but the agency still does a good job of collecting local maps and transportation information together in one package. You can pick up booklets such as the *Victoria Rider's Guide* or *Explore Victoria by Bus* at the waterfront tourist information center. If you've already been to Vancouver, that city's transit guide also includes a section covering Victoria.

City buses do go to some tourist destinations, such as the ferry docks and Butchart Gardens. Buses are clean, but they're slow and make lots of stops.

As in Vancouver, multiple fare zones determine prices: A ride costs either C$1.75 or C$2.50 per adult, depending on how far you go, less for seniors and children. Drivers don't carry change, so you need exact fare — a possible headache if you've just arrived. Day passes, available at both the tourist information center and certain stores, cost C$5.50 for adults (only C$4.00 for children and seniors) and allow you to avoid the exact-change dance, but otherwise aren't a good deal as you're unlikely to use the bus system enough to justify buying one.

You can get transfers for one-time use if you're continuing in the same direction on a different bus. If you venture out of zone one, which is downtown Victoria, you have between 30 to 45 minutes before a transfer becomes invalid. If you get off the bus and do not take the very next bus running the same direction, however, you have to purchase a new ticket. For a one-zone ticket, you have between 15 to 20 minutes to use the transfer and the same rules apply. For more info on the zones, log on to www.bctransit.com.

By taxi

You probably won't need a cab in Victoria, but if you do here's the skinny. Taxis cost C$2.10 to start the meter and C$1.10 for each additional kilometer (which is a little more than half a mile). Downtown trips generally cost about C$5 to C$6; from the airport, it varies from C$30 to C$45 (US$20–US$30). A 15% tip is appropriate. The major cab companies include **Blue Bird** (☎ 800-665-7055), **Empress** (☎ 250-381-2222), and **Victoria Taxi** (☎ 888-842-7111). Call ahead if at all possible, rather than simply trying to hail a cab in the street; they may not stop.

Chapter 17

Victoria's Best Hotels

In This Chapter

▶ The rundown on Victoria's best hotels

▶ Runner-up options if the top choices are full

▶ At-a-glance lists arranged by neighborhood and price

*T*his chapter includes the best sleeps in Victoria. If you can't get into one of these places, you can check out the runner-up listings toward the end of the chapter. See also Chapter 7 for my strategies on how to find a room at the last minute.

Each listing includes a $ symbol that indicates the price range of the hotel's rack rates. Prices are for a standard double room for one night, not including taxes. The $ signs correspond with the following ranges (for more information about these symbols and ranges, see Chapter 7):

$	less than C$100 (US$67)
$$	C$100–C$200 (US$67–US$134)
$$$	C$200–C$300 (US$134–US$201)
$$$$	more than C$300 (US$201)

Remember that the $ symbols are guidelines. A great off-season rate or package deal can knock a hotel down a category or two, and a popular citywide event can drive up prices even at modest establishments. (See Chapter 7 for pointers on getting the best rates.)

This icon indicates hotels that are especially family friendly. I use it to indicate those with plenty of room for families to spread out, plus features such as kitchens, laundry, free breakfast, as well as special programs, rates, or facilities for kids.

Victoria Accommodations

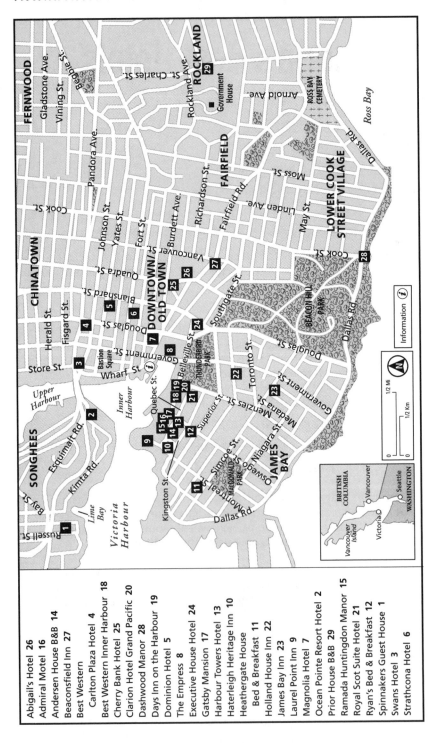

Abigail's Hotel **26**
Admiral Motel **16**
Andersen House B&B **14**
Beaconsfield Inn **27**
Best Western
Carlton Plaza Hotel **4**
Best Western Inner Harbour **18**
Cherry Bank Hotel **25**
Clarion Hotel Grand Pacific **20**
Dashwood Manor **28**
Days Inn on the Harbour **19**
Dominion Hotel **5**
The Empress **8**
Executive House Hotel **24**
Gatsby Mansion **17**
Harbour Towers Hotel **13**
Haterleigh Heritage Inn **10**
Heathergate House
Bed & Breakfast **11**
Holland House Inn **22**
James Bay Inn **23**
Laurel Point Inn **9**
Magnolia Hotel **7**
Ocean Pointe Resort Hotel **2**
Prior House B&B **29**
Ramada Huntingdon Manor **15**
Royal Scot Suite Hotel **21**
Ryan's Bed & Breakfast **12**
Spinnakers Guest House **1**
Swans Hotel **3**
Strathcona Hotel **6**

Victoria Hotels from A to Z

Abigail's Hotel

$$–$$$ Downtown/Old Town

This Tudor mansion has been converted into one of the most romantic little hotels in the city in spite of its position off the water. The suites come with extravagant touches such as four-poster beds, leather love seats, wood-burning fireplaces, and double whirlpool baths, while the remaining pastel-colored rooms are outfitted with standard furnishings and comfortable down pillows and duvets. The rooms do not have televisions, so you won't be distracted from that special someone if you come for the romance. Marvel at the blossoming gardens and crystal chandeliers, and meet fellow guests at the nightly "sherry hour" where snacks are served in the library and sitting room. Next morning, don't rush out to sightsee without tasting the excellent full breakfast — which they bring to your bed by prior arrangement.

906 McClure St. (from The Empress hotel, walk 2 blocks away from water along Burdett, turn right at Quadra, go 1 block to McClure, turn right again). ☎ **800-561-6565** *or 250-388-5363. Fax: 250-388-7787. Internet:* www.abigailshotel.com. *Parking: Free. Rack rates: C$160–C$290 (US$107–US$194) double, C$265–C$330 (US$178–US$221) suites. Rates include full breakfast. AE, MC, V.*

Admiral Motel

$$ Inner Harbour

This is not the fanciest place in town, and that's exactly why people (especially traveling families) come here. It's just plain amazing that you can spend this little for million-dollar harbor views, and still bring the family, too. Management has kindly added fridges and microwaves for those who may be dining in, pull-out sofa beds for tuckered-out kids to crash on, and such bonuses as balconies and free local calls. Other thoughtful, almost youth-hostel-like, amenities include: free bikes — a boon in the parking-strapped downtown — free Internet access, a laundry room, and loads of great advice from the friendly Margison family (and their staff) on what to see and do in the city.

257 Belleville St. ☎ **888-823-6472** *or 250-388-6267. Fax: 250-388-6267. Internet:* www.admiral.bc.ca. *Parking: Free. Rack rates: C$99–C$169 (US$66–US$113) double and suites. Rates include continental breakfast. AE, MC, V.*

Andersen House B&B

$–$$$ Inner Harbour

Truly a British Columbia kind of place, this small bed-and-breakfast offers nice guest rooms and the additional option of sleeping on your own private boat. The four onsite rooms are spacious, include extras such as CD players and interesting art, and possess individual charms — from the Casablanca Room's private stairway, French doors, window seat, and views of the Parliament Buildings to the claw-foot tub, wet bar, and extra bedroom that comes with the Captain's Apartment. The Southside Room is notable for its garden entrance, while the more luxurious Garden Studio has extras such as a hot tub and antiques. The full breakfast is truly sumptuous: You choose from such entrées as cheese soufflé, breakfast quesadillas, baked salmon with potato pancakes, or Dutch apple pancakes — and some of the fruits and berries on the side come right from the garden. If you're feeling nautical, request information about sleeping on the bobbing yacht moored in the harbor.

301 Kingston St. ☎ *250-388-4565. Internet:* www.andersenhouse.com. *Parking: Street. Rack rates: C$95–C$250 (US$64–US$168) doubles. Rates include full breakfast. MC, V.*

Beaconsfield Inn

$$ Downtown/Old Town

A nice bed-and-breakfast located a few short blocks from the harbor, the Beaconsfield is well-positioned and small enough to remain personable. There's a pleasantly English feel to the place, as well. The hotel was designed by famed local architect Samuel McClure in 1908, and the Emily Carr Suite remains one of the showpiece rooms with its romantic double hot tub in front of a fireplace, queen bed, and separate sitting area. Another suite features a flowery patio and similar double hot tub. As a bonus, the full breakfast, afternoon tea, and evening sherry in the sitting room are all complimentary.

998 Humboldt St. (from The Empress hotel, walk 2 blocks east away from the water along Humboldt). ☎ *250-384-4044. Fax: 250-721-2442. Internet:* www.islandnet.com/beaconsfield. *Parking: Free. Rack rates: C$125–C$175 (US$84–US$117) double, C$175–C$350 (US$117–US$235) suites. Rates include full breakfast, tea, and evening sherry. MC, V.*

Best Western Inner Harbour

$–$$ Inner Harbour

As long as you understand exactly what you're getting yourself into — an unspectacular chain motel — there's no harm staying here if you want to save some money and still get harbor views. The hotel's suites are a good choice for traveling families, with a queen bed and two pullout sofa beds apiece, plus full kitchen facilities, dual televisions, and big balconies, among other amenities. A laundromat, sauna, and pool are on the premises.

412 Quebec St. ☎ *800-383-2378 or 250-384-5122. Fax: 250-384-5113 Internet:* www.victoriabestwestern.com. *Parking: Free in underground garage. Rack rates: C$95–C$155 (US$64–US$104). Rates include continental breakfast. AE, DC, DISC, MC, V.*

Cherry Bank Hotel

$ Inner Harbour

The Cherry Bank is the sort of kitschy place you stay to save money or to tell stories about later. This former boarding house isn't a bad place at all though, just not nearly as fancy as all the other options in town. At least it's centrally located across from both the Federal Law Courts building and Christ Church Cathedral, and only a block from The Empress and the harbor. Most rooms are furnished with canopy beds, and all guests are entitled to a full English (which means filling, if not exactly gourmet) breakfast. On the premises are an off-track betting parlor and a good rib restaurant called Bowman's (see Chapter 18). A welcome sense of humor prevails throughout — think of it as a thumb in the eye of The Empress.

825 Burdett Ave. ☎ *800-998-6688 or 250-385-5380. Fax: 250-383-0949. Parking: Free. Rack rates: C$60–C$110 (US$40–US$78) double. Rates include full breakfast. AE, JCB, MC, V.*

Clarion Hotel Grand Pacific

$$–$$$$ Inner Harbour

A relative newcomer, the Clarion is one of the most comfortable upscale options around the Inner Harbour. The more expensive rooms are worth the splurge, with lots of little extras (a cordless phone to walk around with? Natch!) and guaranteed balconies; regular rooms are nice enough, but the suites really pile on the luxury — think whirlpool tubs that fit two, plug-ins for laptop modems, fireplaces, and multiple patios with views. The hotel's top-notch athletic club features a lap pool, workout machines, and even racquetball courts.

450 Quebec St. (from The Empress, walk south to Belleville St., turn right on Belleville and walk two blocks to Oswego St., turn left and continue to Quebec St.). ☎ *800-663-7550 or 250-386-0450. Fax: 250-386-8779. Internet:* www.hotelgrand pacific.com. *Parking: Free. Rack rates: C$150–C$400 (US$101–US$268) double and suites. AE, DC, DISC, JCB, MC, V. Wheelchair-accessible.*

Dashwood Manor

$–$$$$ Lower Cook Street Village

A pretty little Tudor inn with superb positioning on both a park and the ocean, this sleeper is outside the tourist bustle of downtown Victoria yet within a half-hour's walking distance of the Inner Harbour. Built in 1912, the inn features 14 rooms, many with close-up views of the bay and, 25 miles across the water, Washington's Olympic Peninsula. The inn's gardens — and big Beacon Hill Park itself — are literally outside your door, and you can make a fine day by cycling, walking, or driving around the water's edge through Oak Bay and beyond. For breakfast, staff has tried something quite novel that I like: Rather than serving it in a stuffy room, they simply stock the refrigerator in your room each night, and you cater to yourself the next morning. Some rooms also have whirlpools.

1 Cook St. (from back of The Empress hotel, travel south away from downtown along Douglas St. less than 1 mile to water; turn left, and continue north on Dallas Rd. ½ mile to corner of Cook St.). ☎ *800-667-5517 or 250-385-5517. Fax: 250-383-1760. Internet:* www.dashwoodmanor.com. *Parking: Free. Rack rates: C$85–C$385 (US$57–US$258) double. Rates include full breakfast. AE, DISC, DC, MC, V.*

Dominion Hotel

$–$$ Downtown/Old Town

This place is much nicer than it has to be, considering its very low rates and accessibility to downtown shops, restaurants, and tours. Plus, it has some history on its side: This is now the oldest standing accommodation in the city. Some recent renovation work really cleaned up the place, too, polishing the copious marble, mahogany, etched glass, and crystal to something like its former glory. Standard hotel rooms aren't huge, but they're nicely decked out in vintage furnishings; the suites here *are* big. As if that weren't enough, family-style restaurants make this an attractive options for families. All in all, this hotel qualifies as a find for budget-hunters.

759 Yates St. ☎ *800-663-6101 or 250-384-4136. Fax: 250-382-6416. Internet:* www.dominion-hotel.com. *Parking: C$5–C$10 (US$3.35–US$7). Rack rates: C$65–C$175 (US$44–US$117). AE, CB, DC, DISC, JCB, MC, V. Wheelchair accessible.*

The Empress

$$$–$$$$ Inner Harbour

You don't necessarily have to be "somebody" to stay here, but you do have to have somebody's mighty thick wallet. One of the crown jewels in the Canadian Pacific (CP) chain stretching across Canada, this huge hotel is fancy in every possible way; you'll feel stupid standing around in jeans (though tourists do it) trying to figure out how to get to the restaurants, pool, sauna room, or business center. The Empress has more than 500 rooms and suites, and the cheaper-end ones can be considered spacious only by 1908 standards; you would probably be unpleasantly surprised, so pay even more for an upgrade or stay somewhere else. Even if you can't afford the splurge, though, visit the top-notch shopping gallery attached to the hotel — see Chapter 20 for details on that — as well as the amazing Bengal Lounge (described in Chapters 18 and 21), good for a drink or a relatively inexpensive meal. Services are doting, including buzzing valets, concierge service, an on-call masseur, business services, a special children's pool, and much more.

721 Government St. ☎ *800-441-1414 or 250-384-8111. Fax: 250-381-4334. Internet:* www.cphotels.ca. *Parking: Valet parking in underground garage, $15. Rack rates: C$200–C$500 (US$134–US$335) double, C$400–C$1,500 (US$268–US$1005) suites. AE, CB, DISC, DC, JCB, MC, V. Wheelchair-accessible rooms.*

Executive House Hotel

$$ Downtown/Old Town

The bland, high-rise exterior of the Executive House conceals unbeatable luxuries, room to roam, and suites perfect for the traveling family that can afford one. The location is close to perfect, too — nearly across the street from The Empress, a mere block from the Inner Harbour and the Royal B.C. Museum — while rooms are big and comfortable enough to satisfy even high-rollers. All suites come with full kitchen facilities and pullout beds, and there are three restaurants on the premises too if you don't feel like cooking. The suites on the 17th floor are beyond luxurious with terraces, posh furnishings, and private hot tubs. Because this is primarily a business hotel (note the banquet room and upscale health spa), ask about weekend discounts — the high prices can drop by as much as half.

777 Douglas St. ☎ *800-663-7001 or 250-388-5111. Fax: 250-385-1323. Internet:* www.executivehouse.com. *Parking: C$2 (US$1.34). Rack rates: C$175 (US$117) doubles, C$195–C$695 (US$131–US$466) suites. AE, CB, DISC, DC, JCB, MC, V.*

Gatsby Mansion

$–$$$$ Inner Harbour

A rather plush little B&B overlooking Victoria's harbor, the Gatsby probably gets less attention than it deserves. It harkens back to the roaring '20s, certainly, with fine linens and a dashing hand throughout; they don't skimp on the little things here. The design is full of clever exterior and interior details — a "pepper-shaker" tower, crystal chandeliers, stained-glass windows, and frescoed ceilings — while rooms have nice extras such as thick duvets, harbor views, and antique furnishings, though they do vary a good deal in size. (You can generally trade ocean views for extra space.) A delicious full breakfast is included each morning, and the kitchen staff will even fashion picnic baskets to take out — or eat in bed — on request.

309 Belleville St. ☎ *800-563-9656 or 250-388-9191. Fax: 250-920-5651. Parking: Free. Rack rates: C$95–C$330 (US$64–US$221) double. Rates include full breakfast. AE, DC, MC, V.*

Haterleigh Heritage Inn

$$–$$$$ Inner Harbour

One of the city's top bed-and-breakfast choices, with prices to match, this restored mansion is located only two blocks from the harbor and the action. Innkeepers Paul and Victoria Kelly have thought of everything: sherry and chocolates at night, gourmets breakfasts each morning, extra pillows, carefully restored leaded and stained-glass windows throughout, and other touches that make for a *very* turn-of-the-century Victoria experience. It's a great place for honeymooners, too — every room has a hot tub, with the Secret Garden and Day Dreams suites being especially decadent. Just remember to book early; the place has only six rooms.

243 Kingston St. ☎ *250-384-9995. Fax: 250-384-1935. Internet:* www.haterleigh. com. *Parking: Free. Rack rates: C$150–C$325 (US$101–US$218) doubles. Rates include full breakfast. MC, V.*

Holland House Inn

$–$$$ Inner Harbour

Very close to everything you could possibly want to visit in downtown Victoria, this bright yellow English-style B&B is beautifully furnished throughout with antiques. Many of its rooms and suites come with four-poster beds, soaker tubs, fireplaces, and balconies. The Florenza, with wood-burning fireplaces, a claw-foot tub, and a garden deck, is typical of the higher-end rooms, while the spacious Venicia is the equivalent of a honeymoon suite with its romantic double hot tub. Among the 14 total choices are a number of rooms with twin beds or canapy beds.

595 Michigan St. ☎ *800-335-3466 or 250-384-6644. Fax: 250-384-6117. Internet:* www. hollandhouse.victoria.bc.ca. *Parking: Free. Rack rates: C$95–C$295 (US$64–US$198) doubles. Rates include full breakfast. AE, MC, V.*

James Bay Inn

$–$$ James Bay

Granted, this isn't the Ritz. But it *is* one of downtown Victoria's few budget steals, even without the off-season discounts that slash prices even more — don't mind the fading aura about the place, and you'll be fine. As a bonus, you can say you slept in Emily Carr's house. That's right. One of Canada's most beloved painters lived here for a time late in her life. There are few extras or amenities, but rooms are surprisingly large. Hotel guests get a discount at the on-premises restaurant and pub.

270 Government St. (from The Empress, walk 4 blocks south on Government St.). ☎ *800-836-2649 or 250-384-7151. Fax: 250-385-2311. Internet:* www.jamesbayinn. bc.ca. *Parking: Free. Rack rates: C$70–C$190 (US$47–US$127) double. AE, MC, V.*

Laurel Point Inn

$$–$$$$ Inner Harbour

Well-heeled Japanese tourists love this luxurious new hotel sticking out into the Inner Harbour, and no wonder: The design touches, wall art, and even the robes are largely Japanese in style. The giant structure comes with tremendous, unencumbered views of the Inner Harbor and the Strait of Juan de Fuca. Suites are in a newer addition and big and wonderful; rooms in the older building aren't, frankly, as large or modern, but everything here is well appointed. All the rooms — from the standard doubles

to a wide assortment of suites with quickly escalating rack rates —
feature scenic balconies, marble bathrooms, quality furniture, high-speed
Internet access, down duvets, and Japanese kimonos. More expensive
suites add soaker tubs, and the Panoramic Penthouse Suites cost a mint
but also come with wrap-around balconies giving 360-degree views of the
city, Italian linens, and a double whirlpool tub.

680 Montreal St. ☎ 800-663-7667 or 250-386-8721. Fax: 250-386-9547. Internet:
www.laurelpoint.com. *Parking: Free. Rack rates: C$115–C$225 (US$77–
US$151) doubles, C$175–C$745 (US$117–US$499) suites. AE, CB, DC, JCB, MC, V.*

Magnolia Hotel

$$–$$$$ Downtown/Old Town

Perhaps the most centrally located, this beautiful boutique hotel has
plenty of touches — including one of the city's best spas. Most of the
rooms, from the executive suites with fireplaces to standard rooms, have
been outfitted with floor-to-ceiling windows, two-poster beds covered in
duvets and feather pillows, wet bars, refrigerators, and — now *here's*
thoughtfulness — umbrellas. Large desks come with two-line cordless
phones, data ports, and speakerphone capability. The marble bathrooms
are stocked with fine linens, terrycloth bathrobes, and classy toiletries;
some executive rooms are also equipped with soaker tubs and gas fire-
places. The Aveda spa is the real star, though, with a range of services —
massage, hydrotherapy, a Vichy shower, among many others. A restau-
rant and Hugo's brewpub are on the ground floor, as well.

623 Courtney St. ☎ 877-624-6654 or 250-381-0999. Fax: 250-381-0988. Internet:
www.magnoliahotel.com. *Parking: Valet parking, C$8 (US$5). Rack rates:
C$169–C$419 (US$113–US$281) double and suites. AE, DISC, DC, JCB, MC, V.
Wheelchair-accessible*

Oak Bay Beach Hotel

$$–$$$$ Oak Bay

Right on the ocean and directly across the street from a golf course, this
Tudor-style resort hotel offers one of the most relaxing locations possible — though it is 3 to 4 miles from most of the main sights. Public rooms
are furnished in elegant antiques and a baby grand piano, while the 51
rooms are each unique. Some are decorated with more antiques and
flower prints, some contain brass or canopy beds, and others are more
modern-looking; some are outfitted with gas fireplaces, double soaker
tubs, and balconies; some come with views of Haro Strait (and
Washington state's mountains and islands beyond). I recommend an
upstairs suite to get the best of all these things, although you pay quite
a bit more for the privilege. Appropriate considering its position on the
water and a pebbly beach, the hotel offers marine activities: You can
book kayaking or whale-watching outings at the front desk. Or, if the
weather's inclement, wander into the little on-site pub.

1175 Beach Dr. (from The Empress, follow Douglas St. south away from downtown to water; turn left and follow Dallas Rd. along coast approximately 5 miles to golf course). ☎ ***800-668-7758*** *or 250-598-4556. Fax: 250-598-6180. Internet:* www.oakbaybeachhotel.bc.ca. *Parking: Free. Rack rates: C$155–C$450 (US$104–US$302) doubles and suites. AE, DC, MC, V.*

Ocean Pointe Resort Hotel

$$$–$$$$ Esquimalt/Songhees

The "OPR" makes for a great splurge, where you'll be pampered almost beyond belief with huge rooms and the best bedding money can buy. You're not exactly right downtown — but you can see it spread out before you, and you're just a short ferry ride away from everything. All 250 rooms have been designed with high-speed Internet, a cordless phone, terry robes and, for an extra fee, access to squash and tennis courts, a massage service, and the terrific in-house spa. The hotel also offers childcare facilities. One of the city's top restaurants, the Victorian (see Chapter 18), is located on the premises and the excellent Spinnakers Brewpub (see Chapter 21) is also a short walk away from the front door. Note that off-season and low demand-day "promotional rates" can cut your bill by up to 50% if you book in advance, although the availability of those rates is quite limited; be sure to ask.

45 Songhees Rd. (from downtown Victoria, proceed north to Johnson St. and cross Johnson St. bridge; hotel is on left, at corner of Songhees Rd.). ☎ ***800-667-4677*** *or 250-360-2999. Fax: 250-360-1041. Internet:* www.oprhotel.com. *Parking: Valet parking in underground garage, C$9 (US$6). Rack rates: C$258–C$518 (US$173–US$347) doubles and suites. AE, DC, DISC, JCB, MC, V. Wheelchair-accessible rooms.*

Prior House B&B

$$ Rockland

Out in the quiet and pretty Rockland neighborhood, this is one of the city's most luxurious B&Bs — and it's not too pricey. The area's not the place for nightlife or a party, but rather a place for a contemplative stay. The oak-paneled rooms all come with goose-down comforters, duvets, pillows, and robes, but their individual character is quite different. You enter the Hobbit Room from a patio through a round-topped door to find a bar, queen bed, and fireplace; bathroom fixtures are all done in marble and there's a whirlpool tub. The Arbutus (sea views) and Linden Lea (which has a loveseat) Rooms each include antiques, linens, fireplaces, and canopy beds, plus televisions and VCRs. The suites are even more luxurious. As a final nice touch, hotel staff serves a complimentary afternoon tea daily in the public sitting rooms.

620 St. Charles St. (from downtown Victoria, follow Fort St. 1½ miles away from water to St. Charles, turn right, and continue 1 block to Rockland). ☎ ***877-924-3300*** *or 250-592-8847. Fax: 250-592-8223. Internet:* www.priorhouse.com. *Parking:*

Free. Rack rates: C$160–C$195 (US$107–US$131) double, C$215–C$285 (US$144–US$191) suites. Rates include breakfast and afternoon tea. MC, V.

Royal Scot Suite Hotel

$$–$$$ **Inner Harbour**

This extremely kid-friendly and centrally located hotel is a favorite with families. You do find standard rooms, but most are roomy suites; the larger ones split between a living room, dining room, and a full kitchen — a great arrangment for large families. The Royal Scot is a good pick if you're traveling with little ones and don't care about impressing friends back home with tales of The Empress. Other handy amenities include a do-it-yourself laundry, free parking, indoor pool, an exercise room, and a game room (with pool tables); though this isn't far from downtown, they run a courtesy shuttle to the central shopping and touring areas.

425 Quebec St. ☎ **800-663-7515** _or 250-388-5463. Fax: 250-388-5452. Internet:_ www.royalscot.com. _Parking: Free. Rack rates: C$135–C$220 (US$90–US$147) doubles, C$165–C$380 (US$111–US$255) suites. AE, DC, MC, V._

Ryan's Bed and Breakfast

$–$$ **Inner Harbour**

This pretty Victorian home, only three blocks from the Inner Harbour and downtown, is a relative bargain. The 1892 structure was recently renovated by the Ryan family, then designated as a heritage property — it's not hard to see why. Oil paintings in gilded frames, china cabinets, and chaise lounges decorate the public areas. The six guest rooms, while not especially large, are certainly comfortable — and furnished in period antiques and rugs. The family serves breakfast in a dining room, which retains its original oak buffet and fir mantelpiece. Outside, the garden has plenty of sitting space.

224 Superior St. ☎ **877-389-0012** _or 250-389-0012. Fax: 250-389-2857. Internet:_ www.ryansbb.com. _Parking: Free. Rack rates: C$65–C$185 (US$44–US$124) double. Rates include full breakfast. MC, V._

Spinnakers Guest House

$$–$$$ **Esquimalt/Songhees**

This spot, with tremendous service and room options, is a good choice among Victoria's guest houses. The complex has three buildings, including the original 1884 home. Most of the guest rooms have luxurious double whirlpool tubs, while some have fireplaces. The Garden Suites, added in 1998, include a queen bed, down duvets, patio overlooking the garden and harbor, and a hot tub (with candles); two contain wood-burning fireplaces; use of kitchen facilities is also an option. Breakfast is served in the brewpub restaurant that made the place famous; it's also a great spot for dinner or lunch (see Chapter 18).

308 Catherine St. (from downtown Victoria, proceed north to Johnson St.; cross the Johnson St. bridge and continue ½ mile to Catherine St.). ☎ *877-838-2739 or 250-384-2739. Fax: 250-384-3246. Internet:* www.spinnakers.com. *Parking: Free. Rack rates: C$150–C$250 (US$101–US$168). Rates include full breakfast. AE, MC, V.*

Strathcona Hotel

$ Downtown/Old Town

Possibly *the* cheapest recommendable hotel in downtown Victoria, the Strathcona is a city within itself. The rooms are clean and adequate, if rather plain and charmless — the sort you would expect in a bland, mid-priced European city hotel, for instance. The price is the reason you're staying here. Be aware, however, that the sprawling five-story complex also contains no less than nine hopping pubs, clubs, and restaurants — how do you *think* they make a profit? The offerings include a pool hall, a British pub, a divey bar, and an off-track horse betting parlor (see Chapter 21 for more on these). All this commotion means that the lower floors are quite noisy, so try to avoid them with an upper-floor room if at all possible.

919 Douglas St. ☎ *800-663-7476 or 250-383-7137. Fax: 250-383-6893. Internet:* www.strathconahotel.com. *Parking: Free. Rack rates: C$54–C$99 (US$36–US$66) double, C$75–C$119 (US$50–US$80) suites. AE, DC, DISC, MC, V.*

Swans Hotel

$$$–$$$$ Downtown/Old Town

Once an ugly duckling, but now a swan — that's the story of this former grain warehouse, which is now a real sleeper in the Victoria accommodations game. An award-winning renovation of the building created 29 apartment suites — some of the biggest rooms per dollar in the city — each decorated with original Pacific Northwestern art. On the top (third) floor, all nine rooms have skylights. Five rooms scattered throughout the property have private terraces. All rooms have kitchens, however, and either one or two bedrooms. No expense was spared in the renovation — chandeliers from The Empress Hotel, beer engines imported from England in the excellent Swans Pub microbrewery on the main floor, and a jazz bar in the cellar (see Chapter 21 for more details on these last two).

506 Pandora Ave. (from downtown, walk north along harbor on Wharf St. ½ mile to Johnson St. and cross; hotel is at corner of Pandora and Store. ☎ *800-668-7926 or 250-361-3310. Fax: 250-361-3491. Internet:* www.islandnet.com/~swans. *Parking: C$8 (US$5). Rack rates: C$135–C$190 (US$90–US$127) suites. AE, DC, MC, V.*

Runner-Up Hotels

Best Western Carlton Plaza Hotel

$$ **Downtown/Old Town**

This modern hotel, near several brewpubs and clubs, is a surprisingly good deal — and rooms have kitchens or kitchenettes. 642 Johnson St. ☎ **250-388-5513.** Fax: 250-388-5343. Internet: www.bestwesterncarlton.com.

Days Inn on the Harbour

$$–$$$ **Inner Harbour**

This pinkish property is blocky, predictable, and filled with tourists who appreciate both its centrality and the family-friendly amenities. 427 Belleville St. ☎ **205-386-3451.** Fax: 250-386-6999. Internet: www.daysinnvictoria.com.

Harbour Towers Hotel

$$–$$$ **Inner Harbour**

Another Inner Harbour winner, this place offers a choice of nearly 200 rooms of varying styles and rates from plain to plush. 345 Quebec St. ☎ **250-385-2405.** Fax: 205-385-4453.

Heathergate House Bed & Breakfast

$$ **Inner Harbour**

A typically simple yet elegant British-style B&B, this is one of the Inner Harbour's most affordable options — but it has only four rooms, so book early. 122 Simcoe St. ☎ **250-383-0068.** Fax: 250-383-4320.

Ramada Huntingdon Manor

$$–$$$ **Inner Harbour**

Close to the ferry docks, this chain offers a choice of standard rooms, split-level suites, and small apartment-style kitchenette units. 330 Quebec St. ☎ **250-381-3456.** Fax: 250-382-7666. Internet: www.bctravel.com/huntingdon.

Index of Accommodations by Neighborhood

Downtown/Old Town

Abigail's Hotel ($$–$$$)
Beaconsfield Inn ($$)
Best Western Carlton Plaza Hotel ($$)
Cherry Bank Hotel ($)
Dominion Hotel ($–$$)
Executive House Hotel ($$)
Magnolia Hotel ($$–$$$$)
Strathcona Hotel ($)
Swans Hotel ($$$–$$$$)

Esquimalt/Songhees

Ocean Pointe Resort Hotel ($$$–$$$$)
Spinnakers Guest House ($$–$$$)

Inner Harbour

Admiral Motel ($$)
Andersen House B&B ($–$$$)
Best Western Inner Harbour ($–$$)
Clarion Hotel Grand Pacific ($$–$$$$)
Days Inn on the Harbour ($$–$$$)
The Empress ($$$–$$$$)
Gatsby Mansion ($–$$$$)
Harbour Towers Hotel ($$–$$$)
Haterleigh Heritage Inn ($$–$$$$)
Heathergate House Bed & Breakfast ($$)
Holland House Inn ($–$$$)
Laurel Point Inn ($$–$$$$)
Ramada Huntingdon Manor ($$–$$$)
Royal Scot Suite Hotel ($$–$$$)
Ryan's Bed and Breakfast ($–$$)

James Bay

James Bay Inn ($–$$)

Lower Cook Street Village

Dashwood Manor ($–$$$$)

Oak Bay

Oak Bay Beach Hotel ($$–$$$$)

Rockland

Prior House B&B ($$)

Index of Accommodations by Price

$$$$

Clarion Hotel Grand Pacific (Inner
   Harbour)
Dashwood Manor (Lower Cook Street
   Village)
The Empress (Inner Harbour)
Gatsby Mansion (Inner Harbour)
Haterleigh Heritage Inn (Inner Harbour)
Laurel Point Inn (Inner Harbour)
Magnolia Hotel (Downtown/Old Town)
Oak Bay Beach Hotel (Oak Bay)
Ocean Pointe Resort Hotel
   (Esquimalt/Songhees)
Swans Hotel (Downtown/Old Town)

$$$

Abigail's Hotel (Downtown/Old Town)
Andersen House B&B (Inner Harbour)
Days Inn on the Harbour (Inner Harbour)
Harbour Towers Hotel (Inner Harbour)
Holland House Inn (Inner Harbour)
Ramada Huntingdon Manor (Inner
   Harbour)
Royal Scot Suite Hotel (Inner Harbour)
Spinnakers Guest House
   (Esquimalt/Songhees)

$$

Admiral Motel (Inner Harbour)
Beaconsfield Inn (Downtown/Old Town)
Best Western Carlton Plaza Hotel
(Downtown/Old Town)
Best Western Inner Harbour (Inner
Harbour)
Dominion Hotel (Downtown/Old Town)
Executive House Hotel (Downtown/Old
Town)
Heathergate House Bed & Breakfast (Inner
Harbour)
James Bay Inn (James Bay)
Prior House B&B (Rockland)
Ryan's Bed and Breakfast (Inner Harbour)

$

Cherry Bank Hotel (Downtown/Old Town)
Strathcona Hotel (Downtown/Old Town)

Chapter 18

Dining and Snacking in Victoria

*W*hen you say the word Victoria, you don't immediately picture culinary decadence. It just doesn't carry the cachet of a Paris, a London, a New Orleans, or a San Francisco. But the city's thriving tourist trade ensures a larger choice of restaurants than you'd expect to find in a city this size. And that's good news — you can find *something* to eat no matter what you crave.

For the locations of the majority of the places mentioned in this chapter, see the Victoria Dining and Snacking map on the next page.

What's Hot Now

Tea is still hot. Heh, heh.

No, but really. Victoria is staunchly traditional and anti-trendy in character, and this trait extends to its restaurants; it has taken some time for even nouvelle cuisine to reach the place, and in many British quarters a hamburger is still considered about as high art as a meal will go.

Now, at least, ethnic foods have arrived in force, and you're as spoiled for variety as you would be in any cosmopolitan city. Meals of Indian, Italian, Mexican, Californian and the like can easily be had. You can even find a flurry of activity on the — horrors! — *health-food* front, as popular **Re-bar** serves up the best smoothies and vegetarian meals in British Columbia. (See "Victoria's Best Restaurants," later in this chapter.)

Victoria Dining and Snacking

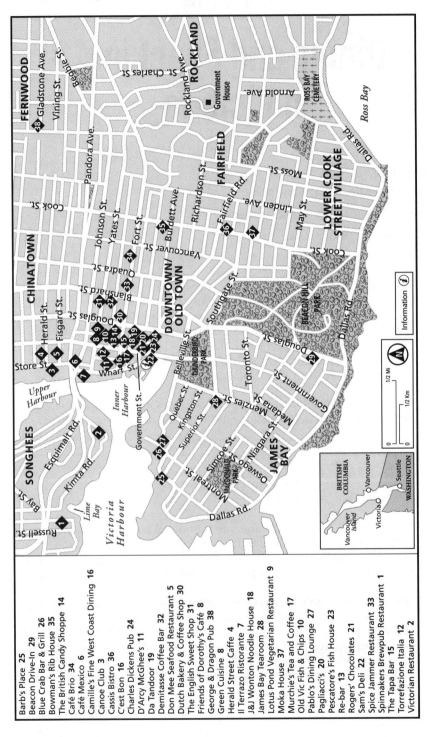

Barb's Place 25
Beacon Drive-In 29
Blue Crab Bar & Grill 26
Bowman's Rib House 35
The British Candy Shoppe 14
Café Brio 34
Café Mexico 6
Camille's Fine West Coast Dining 16
Canoe Club 3
Cassis Bistro 36
C'est Bon 16
Charles Dickens Pub 24
D'Arcy McGhee's 11
Da Tandoor 19
Demitasse Coffee Bar 32
Don Mee Seafood Restaurant 5
Dutch Bakery & Coffee Shop 30
The English Sweet Shop 31
Friends of Dorothy's Café 8
George & Dragon Pub 38
Green Cuisine 8
Herald Street Caffe 4
Il Terrazo Ristorante 7
J&J Wonton Noodle House 18
James Bay Tearoom 28
Lotus Pond Vegetarian Restaurant 9
Moka House 37
Murchie's Tea and Coffee 17
Old Vic Fish & Chips 10
Pablo's Dining Lounge 27
Pagliacci's 20
Pescatore's Fish House 23
Re-bar 13
Rogers' Chocolates 21
Sam's Deli 22
Spice Jammer Restaurant 33
Spinnakers Brewpub Restaurant 1
The Tapa Bar 15
Torrefazione Italia 12
Victorian Restaurant 2

Is all that just a tad too adventurous for you? Well, you can always stick to seeking out and ordering what the Victorians themselves long preferred to fancy foods: tea, high tea (which comes with loads of sweets and snacks), pub food (steak-and-kidney pie, bangers, and mash, and so forth), and fish-and-chips. Or, if you're willing to test your taste buds — and your intestinal fortitude — Chinese, which tends to be less Westernized here.

Finally, seafood is always a good middle-ground item to order in Victoria. The city's position right on the sea ensures a constant supply of finny fun coming in on the docks, and you can order it prepared every which way but loose: anything from lowbrow (fried and stuck between two hamburger buns) at a dockside shack to grilled or sautéed in the finest restaurants in town.

Where the Locals Eat

Figuring out where to eat in Victoria is easy: Either read the listings later in this chapter and take copious notes, or simply track down a real Victorian, wait 'til he or she gets hungry, and then surreptitiously shadow this person to his/her favorite eatery. Where to begin hunting? (For descriptions of the restaurants mentioned in this section, see "Victoria's Best Restaurants," later in this chapter.)

Inner Harbour

Right on the Inner Harbour, places tend to fall into one or two categories: They're either very, very pricey (that is, hotel restaurants) or else dirt-cheap (for example, **Barb's Place,** a fish-and-chips hole-in-the-wall).

Old Town/Downtown

The eateries in the Old Town and Downtown districts are quite a mixture. You can find a large number of overpriced tourist traps (often sporting oh-so-English spellings lyke thys: Yee Olde Drynkyng & Ryppyng-Offe Thee Custoumer Pubbe). But a number of extremely good restaurants downtown are also here (such as **Camille's Fine West Coast Dining, Herald Street Caffe,** and **Il Terrazzo Ristorante**), for which you pay more for the privilege of dining within, and a supply of middling other places not worth mentioning.

Then there are the local haunts, which may not advertise with splashy signs or charge big prices, but they do the job nicely in the pinch for a breakfast, brunch, or lunch. These kinds of places may even be tucked within larger shopping centers such as Market Square or Bastion Square.

Dressing to dine

Generally speaking, Victoria has loosened up its act since the Colonial days. Years of sweatshirted, short-shorted U.S. tourists have helped soften up the locals, and you'll rarely be hassled about your attire except in the very finest hotel restaurants and bistros. If a restaurant is very expensive, then it probably operates some sort of official or unofficial dress code. Call if you're in doubt. Otherwise, though, don't sweat it.

Note: Although West Coast casual works in many places around town, it definitely does not work in The Empress hotel's tearoom. Don't even think about wearing tennies, jeans, shorts, or other typically touristic garb. They'll escort you — politely, of course — back to the door.

Chinatown

Victoria's Chinatown is so tiny that you can practically log the total restaurant count here on two hands. Yet the quality is extremely variable, so if you're going to dive in, you need to choose carefully. I recommend **Don Mee Seafood Restaurant.**

Outlying districts

Oak Bay is the district most worth mentioning, as it sports a number of authentic English pubs and tearooms, such as **Windsor House Tea Room.** Many of these also serve food, and thus double as restaurants despite their names. Plus, the neighborhood's oceanside position has led to the construction of several luxury hotels, and each has an exemplary — although not inexpensive — restaurant on the premises.

Victoria's Best Restaurants

What follows are my recommendations of the best places to dine.

The main course prices reflect the range of each restaurant's dinner menu. Drinks, tips, and appetizers are *not* included in this calculation. If the restaurant doesn't serve dinner, the price range applies to main courses at lunch, brunch, or breakfast, as appropriate to that particular eatery.

The dollar sign ratings represent the price of one dinner including drinks and tip and correspond with the following price ranges:

$	less than C$10 (US$7)
$$	C$10–C$$20 (US$7–US$13)
$$$	C$20–C$30 (US$13–US$20)

For ways to trim the fat from your bill, see the money-saving tips in Chapter 11, which also apply to dining in Victoria. See also my ideas for where to find snacks and meals on the go later in this chapter.

The majority of Victoria's restaurants are fairly casual, and reservations won't be necessary. However, every rule naturally has exceptions — and so, too, does this one. In the listings, I note which restaurants require or recommend reservations year-round. During Victoria's high season (from June through September), you'll want to call early for a table at some of the primo places.

Barb's Place

$ Inner Harbour   SEAFOOD

Actually located out on Fisherman's Wharf, this little place (okay, shack) is Victoria's favorite lowbrow eatery — a place as famous as the city's gardens. You come for sandwiches of fried fish hauled onto the dock that very morning, just-fried fries, or (if you're feeling fancy) maybe fried oysters. Don't expect linen napkins or candlelight. Though a bit off the downtown tourist track, Barb's is right near one of the stops for those tiny ferries that constantly circle the Inner and Outer Harbours.

310 St. Lawrence St. (from The Empress, walk along Belleville St. to Kingston St., then continue to docks). ☎ *250-384-6515. Reservations not accepted or necessary. Main courses: C$3–C$9 (US$2–US$6). Credit cards not accepted. Open: Lunch and dinner daily.*

Beacon Drive-In

$ Old Town/Downtown   BARBEQUE/BURGERS

Not a true drive-in in the sense that there isn't carhop service (this is right downtown, after all, where parking is a nightmare), the Beacon nevertheless captures the flavor of good ol' American burgers-and-fries. They also do rib-sticking breakfasts that will weigh you down all day, plus milkshakes, hot dogs, dinners of fried fish or chicken, and — naturally — soft-serve ice cream.

126 Douglas St. ☎ *250-385-7521. Reservations not accepted. Main courses: C$3–C$8 (US$2–US$5). Credit cards not accepted. Open: Lunch and dinner daily.*

Blue Crab Bar & Grill

$$$ Inner Harbour   SEAFOOD

If I were to pick one fancy restaurant for a piece of grilled salmon or something else from the sea, this place — located inside the Coast Harbourside Hotel — would be it. The kitchen here is never short of daring, using the daily catch as its guide and then improvising wildly. Local oysters, prawns (basically, big shrimp), and salmon are the obvious stars, presented in a variety of interesting crusts, stir-fries, or bisques; then there are other specials — crab cakes in jalapeño sauce, tuna kabobs, pistachio-encrusted swordfish. Desserts are very good, the view of the harbor is unbeatable, and — interestingly — they also serve breakfast daily and do a Sunday brunch.

146 Kingston St. (inside Coast Harbourside Hotel; from The Empress, walk along Belleville to Kingston). ☎ **250-480-1999.** *Reservations accepted and recommended. Main courses: C$16–C$30 (US$11–US$20). AE, DC, MC, V. Open: Breakfast, lunch, and dinner daily.*

Bowman's Rib House

$$ Downtown/Old Town   BARBEQUE/BURGERS

A little bit out of the way, sure, but Bowman's is one of Victoria's top barbecue joints — and fun enough to avoid being stuffy. Homesick Southerners can compare their home-cooked "Q" to the rib racks here, which come with all the starchy, caloric sides you'd expect in a U.S. restaurant but not in a prim and proper town like this. If you're not feeling like baby back ribs, they also offer fried chicken, broiled salmon, steak, and combinations thereof. The restaurant is located inside the budget-conscious Cherry Bank Hotel.

825 Burdett Ave. (from The Empress, travel due east along Burdett approximately 1 mile). ☎ **250-385-5380.** *Reservations accepted. Main courses: C$12–C$20 (US$8–US$13). AE, DC, MC, V. Open: Lunch and dinner daily; closed daily 2–5 p.m.*

Café Brio

$$ Old Town/Downtown   PACIFIC NORTHWEST/ITALIAN

This place takes fusion to dizzying heights: An Italian chef and a Canadian one have put their heads together to create, well, a Pacific-Italian experience. In practice, that means anything from smoked albacore tuna, sablefish, or grilled sockeye salmon to upscale treatments of pastas, Italian sausages, gnocchi, prosciutto, or fava beans. The more expensive — and expansive — chef's taster menu brings in potato and chive blossom ravioli, local lamb, polenta, and other surprises. Definitely one of the city's top bites.

944 Fort St. ☎ **250-383-0009.** *Reservations accepted and recommended. Main courses: C$13–C$23 (US$9–US$15). AE, MC, V. Open: Lunch Tue–Fri, dinner Mon–Sat; closed Tue–Fri 2–5:30 p.m.*

Café Mexico

$–$$ Old Town/Downtown   MEXICAN

You don't normally think Mexican in a British town, but if you're hankering for a taste, this is the place in town to try it. Expect the usual decor, and the food — at first glance the same assortment of burritos, fajitas, nachos, and tacos as at a hundred other places — actually turns out to be prepared a tad classier than you'd have had any right to expect, even experimenting a bit with Pacific Northwest fusion elements. Check the specials before ordering, and wash it all down with sangria, margaritas, or Mexican beer.

1425 Store St. ☎ 250-386-1425 or 250-386-5454. Reservations not accepted or necessary. Main courses: 6–15 (US$4–US$10). AE, DC, MC, V. Open: Lunch and dinner daily.

Camille's Fine West Coast Dining

$$–$$$ Old Town/Downtown   PACIFIC NORTHEST

One of the city's most romantic fine restaurants, Camille's prides itself on using local ingredients, and as such the menu tends to abound with the highly seasonal: tender fiddleheads in spring, blackberry desserts in summer, wild salmon and pumpkin in fall. The kitchen isn't afraid to use the local wild mushrooms, Canadian bison, or caribou when they're in season, either. Start with pan-seared scallops, onion-and-Stilton-tart, jambalaya, or a lemony prawn bisque, then move on to the daring entrees — fillet of sole with garlic confit and fennel cakes in champagne sauce, ostrich with smoky creamed potatoes, or just paella. The brick-walled room is lit with candles, softened with blues and jazz, and set with silver, linens, and fresh blossoms, making it a good honeymoon or anniversary meal. And Sunday evenings are special, as samples from the wine cellar are laid out for tasting.

45 Bastion Square. ☎ 250-381-3433. Reservations accepted and recommended. Main courses: C$14–C$22 (US$9–US$15). AE, MC, V. Open: Dinner Tue–Sun.

Canoe Club

$$ Downtown/Old Town   PUB FARE

A former warehouse now converted into a combination brewpub and restaurant space, this is yet another successful Victoria renovation story. It has the usual brick, timber and skylights to set off the industrial look of the place, plus a menu that ranges from pizzas and burgers to pasta, tuna, and more. The on-premises beers here are every bit as good as the others around town.

450 Swift St. (walk north along Store St. to Swift, turn left, and continue to water). ☎ 250-361-1940. Reservations accepted and recommended. Main courses: 6–16 (US$4–US$11). MC, V. Open: Lunch and dinner daily.

Cassis Bistro

$$$ Fairfield   FRENCH

This romantic little bistro, tucked in the Fairfield neighborhood on the yonder side of Beacon Hill Park, serves the best French food in town. The *prix fixe* menu (C$24 [US$16] per person) runs to things such as potato-encrusted salmon, fish soup, calf's liver, and pasta in a sauce of hazelnut, sherry butter, and wild mushrooms. Specials such as cassoulet, coq au vin, rabbit in mustard, and sweetbreads vary daily. And even the regular menu is five-star, with starters such as mussels, paté, or frisée with warm bacon vinaigrette and poached egg; wonderful carts of mouth-watering French cheeses, some of these little-known to North Americans; and entrees such as braised lamb shank, steak with *frites,* or roasted chicken with truffles. Dessert choices, naturally, include cream tarts, bittersweet chocolate terrine, and sorbet.

253 Cook St. ☎ 250-394-1932. Reservations accepted and recommended. Main courses: C$13–C$24 (US$9–US$16). MC, V. Open: Dinner daily; Sun brunch 10 a.m.–2 p.m.

Da Tandoor

$$ Downtown/Old Town   INDIAN

The exotic interior invites you to take a seat and taste the best Indian food in town, with an East Indian slant and menu items such as biryani, tandoori, chili chicken, and — drawing on the city's maritime heritage and daily fishing catch — even a small selection of seafood dishes. Several sampler plates offer the chance to try a little of everything, a good idea in a place this good; the chef's specials include small amounts of lamb, , fish, chicken, beef, and vegetables, each prepared a different way. Desserts include typical offerings such as Indian-style mango ice cream and fried cheese dunked in sugared rosewater.

1010 Fort St. ☎ 250-384-6333. Reservations accepted and recommended. Main courses: 7–16 (US$5–US$11). MC, V. Dinner daily.

Don Mee Seafood Restaurant

$–$$ Chinatown   CHINESE

In a town where the Chinese food varies tremendously in quality, every-one raves about this place. You come for seafood — fried, stir-fried, sea-soned, or poached any number of ways — or the classiest *dim sum* in town from the long menu. They also offer delivery and takeout from a much shorter, more touristy menu that's heavy on chop suey, egg foo yong, and the like. But get a *prix fixe* combo meal for two to eight people, and you both save money and get to sample and share lots of different things.

538 Fisgard St. ☎ 250-383-1032. Reservations accepted. Main courses: C$6–C$12 (US$4–US$8). AE, DC, MC, V. Open: Lunch and dinner daily; closed daily 2:30–5 p.m.

Herald Street Caffe

$$–$$$ **Downtown/Old Town** **PACIFIC NORTHEST**

A fixture on the local scene for almost 20 years now, owner Mark Finnigan cooks plenty of local seafood, pastas, and West Coast cuisine at this hopping bistro; it's got that rare buzz that truly great bistros possess. Swirl in a super wine list that's acknowledged as one of the city's best, and you have a winner. You can find anything from British Columbian lamb to local salmon, shellfish, and fresh-picked berries on the menu, while Finnigan shows off influences from Italian to Asian. The Sunday brunch is especially interesting, delicious — and popular. Call to make a booking as early as possible.

546 Herald St. (from The Empress, walk north along Wharf or Store St. ¾ mile to Herald and turn right). ☎ *250-381-1441. Reservations required. Main courses: C$15–C$20 (US$10–US$13). AE, MC, V. Open: Lunch and dinner Wed–Sun until 2 a.m.; closed daily 3–5:30 p.m. Wheelchair-accessible.*

Il Terrazzo Ristorante

$$–$$$ **Downtown/Old Town** **ITALIAN**

Actually down a cute little alley between Yates and Johnson Streets, this place has been voted Best Italian Restaurant in town by locals umpteen times by now, and not without reason. It's simply terrific, bursting with good pastas, risotto, seafood, steaks, osso buco, and other mostly northern Italian specialties. They also have a solid wine list, specializing (no surprise here) in wines from Tuscany, Umbria, and the Veneto. Ask for a table out on one of the city's better patios if the weather's halfway decent.

555 Johnson St. ☎ *250-361-0028. Reservations accepted and recommended. Main courses: C$15–C$31 (US$10–US$21). AE, MC, V. Open: Lunch Mon–Sat, dinner Sun. from 5 p.m. Wheelchair-accessible.*

J&J Wonton Noodle House

$–$$ **Old Town/Downtown** **CHINESE**

I'd eat Chinese a lot more often if more places were like this one. Fun, casual, visual — you get to see the noodle-makers in action — and a real bargain to boot, J&J's delivers a mix of Chinese and Asian specialties such as wontons, hot pots, and stir fries. Everything's very fresh, and more inventive than at most Chinese restaurants in this or any other town.

1012 Fort St. ☎ *250-383-0680. Reservations not accepted or necessary. Main courses: C$6–C$17 (US$4–US$11). MC, V. Open: Lunch and dinner Tue–Sat; closed Tue–Sat. 2–4:30 p.m. Wheelchair-accessible.*

James Bay Tearoom

$–$$ Inner Harbour   ENGLISH

Despite the name, this is not the fanciest place in town, not at all; in fact, it's just a little bit like a tripped-up English version of a U.S. diner. Rather than being served dainty little sandwiches, you're more likely to feel at home noshing on heavy, caloric foods: eggs, meats with Yorkshire pudding, fried fish, and the like. Sure, *some* of the diners will be sipping tea and eating light, but that doesn't mean *you* have to do it. (This place is not related to the James Bay Inn in Chapter 17.)

332 Menzies St. (from The Empress, walk south along Government St. to Belleville, go one block west on Belleville, then turn south on Menzies; continue four short blocks). ☎ *250-382-8282. Reservations accepted and recommended. Main courses: C$12–C$16 (US$8–US$11). AE, MC, V. Open: Breakfast, lunch, and dinner Mon–Sat. Wheelchair-accessible.*

Marina Restaurant

$$–$$$ Oak Bay   SEAFOOD

The panoramic water views from this hotel restaurant couldn't be finer, and although the seafood here probably isn't the very best in the city, it's good enough. Roasted salmon, steamed halibut, grilled tuna, and a lemongrass seafood bowl are all typical dinner entrees, and the oyster and sushi bars are nice touches too. But you come here for the sight of boats on water. The Sunday all-you-can-eat brunches *are* something, though, an event in and of themselves — come if you want to gorge on oysters, eggs, and more.

1327 Beach Dr. (from downtown Victoria, drive along Fort St. away from the water about 1.5 miles to Oak Bay Ave.; turn right and continue 1½ more miles to Beach Drive). ☎ *250-598-8555. Reservations accepted and recommended. Main courses: 8–27 (US$5–US$18). AE, DC, JCB, MC, V. Open: Lunch daily, dinner Mon–Sat. Partly wheelchair-accessible.*

Pablo's Dining Lounge

$$ Inner Harbour   CONTINENTAL

The feel is partly Spanish at this off-the-track place inside an attractive house, but French food such as grilled lamb has been thrown into the mix too, with good results — locals have been coming here for decades. Live music on weekends and other nights accentuates the mood, the paella is just dynamite, and the desserts are suitably sweet too.

225 Quebec St. (from The Empress, walk about ½ mile down Belleville St. to Montreal St., turn left, and continue to Quebec St.). ☎ *250-388-4255. Reservations accepted and recommended. Main courses: 13–30 (US$8–US$20). AE, MC, V. Open: Dinner daily.*

Pagliacci's

$$ Old Town/Downtown ITALIAN

There's nothing quiet or pretentious about this Italian place — no reservations are taken — so that means it's okay in my book. Apparently everyone in Victoria agrees, because the place has some of the longest pre-meal lineups (even in rainy weather) that you find in the city. The secret to this success? Elegant simplicity: Meals are fun here, whether they're pasta, prawns, steak, or seafood. It's a great break from the formality of certain other, more expensive places around town — and kids won't feel like they have to keep quiet, either.

1011 Broad St. ☎ 250-386-1662. Reservations not accepted. Main courses: C$11–C$19 (US$7–US$13). AE, MC, V. Open: Lunch and dinner daily; snacks only 3–5 p.m. Wheelchair-accessible.

Pescatore's Fish House

$$ Inner Harbour SEAFOOD

Superb seafood and shellfish in every guise is the draw here, in a room decorated with eye-catching and thought-provoking murals and artwork. Whether it's crab, clams, , salmon, oysters on the half shell at a raw bar, or thick soups and chowders you like, you'll find something to stick a fork in here. All items are well handled: they know what they do best. They also have some non-fish entrees — such as meat and lamb — and they're said to be very good, but I'd order those only if I were allergic to seafood.

614 Humboldt St. (across street from The Empress). ☎ 250-385-4512. Reservations accepted and recommended. Main courses: 10–20 (US$7–US$13). AE, DC, MC, V. Open: Lunch Mon–Sat, dinner daily. Wheelchair-accessible.

Re-bar

$–$$ Old Town/Downtown VEGETARIAN

King among a smattering of veggie restaurants in this town is Re-bar, a brightly painted throwback to the '70s. Their fresh-squeezed vegetable and fruit juice combinations make an energizing, Technicolor snack, but they also have breakfast, lunch, and brunch meals such as omelettes — which aren't strictly vegetarian, I must point out — sandwiches, Mexican, and more.

50 Bastion Square (downstairs). ☎ 250-361-9223. Reservations not accepted or necessary. Main courses: C$7–C$14 (US$5–US$9). AE, MC, V. Open: Breakfast, lunch, and dinner Mon–Sat; Sun brunch.

Sam's Deli

$ Downtown/Old Town DELI

This little delicatessen, which serves healthy sandwiches, tasty soups, and chili, is the most popular lunch nosh in town. And it's a mighty good deal, from the desserts to the snacks to the unusual prawn sandwich — just get there early, *really* early, because everyone in town eats lunch here at some point. No worries, though: If the tables are full (and it isn't pouring), get takeout and head for the waterfront.

805 Government St. ☎ 250-382-8424. Reservations not accepted. Main courses: C$4–C$10 (US$2.68–US$7). MC, V. Open: Breakfast, lunch, and dinner daily. Wheelchair-accessible.

Spice Jammer Restaurant

$-$$ Downtown/Old Town INDIAN

Along with Da Tandoor (see earlier listing), this is best Indian bite in town. The East Indian food is good, everything from tandoori-oven specials to tasty curries, filling samosas, hot vindaloo dishes, and vegetarian dishes such as coconut lentils. They offer a few non-Indian dishes too — concessions to tourist tastes such as steak, grilled chicken, and stir-fried prawns — but also a couple surprises: Ever tried some mogo (East African-style fried cassava root with chutney)? Probably not; well, here you can.

852 Fort St. ☎ 250-480-1055. Reservations not necessary. Main courses: 5–12 (US$3.35–US$8). AE, MC, V. Open: Lunch and dinner Tue–Sat; closed 2:30–5 p.m. Wheelchair-accessible.

Spinnakers Brewpub Restaurant

$-$$ Esquimalt/Songhees PUB FARE

This restaurant, housed in the same building as the award-winning (and original) North American brewpub, serves plenty of pub-grub meals of burgers, smoked sausages, fish-and-chips, pizzas, ploughman's lunches, and steak sandwiches. But they also do more upscale meals, as well, taking good advantage of the supply of locally raised beef, lamb, and chicken that's available on Vancouver Island — and combining these foods with the house ales, lagers, and stouts for flavoring.

308 Catherine St. (from downtown Victoria, proceed north to Johnson St.; cross the Johnson St. bridge and continue ½ mile to Catherine St.). ☎ 250-386-2739. Reservations accepted and recommended. Main courses: C$8–C$20 (US$5–US$13). AE, DC, MC, V. Open: Breakfast, lunch, and dinner daily. Wheelchair-accessible.

Victorian Restaurant

$$$ Esquimalt/Songhees   PACIFIC NORTHEST

Rich, full meals of local game, fish, and shellfish highlight the menu at one of the city's finest restaurants, which combines Pacific Northwest food (and its Asian accents) with some French touches such as cream sauces, truffles, onion tarts, and a good list of French red wines. Ask about the *prix fixe* menu of the night.

45 Songhees Rd. (inside Ocean Pointe Resort; from downtown Victoria, cross Johnson St. Bridge and continue to Songhees Rd. on left). ☎ 250-360-5800. Reservations recommended and accepted. Main courses: 20–30 (US$13–US$20). AE, DC, JCB, MC, V. Open: Dinner daily.

Windsor House Tea Room

$–$$ Oak Bay   ENGLISH

Good views and an authentic feeling — yes, that's real lace on the table and the Queen Mother staring at you from the wall — highlight this Oak Bay tearoom, which offers tea and crumpets all afternoon but also serves full meals. (As with any classic tea room, the high tea here is practically a meal in and of itself.) The entrees are mostly English favorites. Or should I say favourites? Welsh *rarebit* (bread in a cheese-beer sauce) and meat pies are the stars, with lighter fare such as quiche and salads too.

2540 Windsor Rd. (from downtown Victoria, follow Fort St. away from water approximately 1½ miles to Oak Bay Ave., turn right, and continue almost to water; bear right at Newport and continue 1 block to Windsor Rd.). ☎ 250-595-3135. Reservations required for meals. Main courses: C$7–C$13 (US$5–US$9). MC, V. Open: Lunch to 5 p.m. Mon–Sat. Wheelchair-accessible.

Index of restaurants by neighborhood

Chinatown
Don Mee Seafood Restaurant (Chinese, $–$$)

Downtown/Old Town
Beacon Drive-In (Barbeque/Burgers, $)
Bowman's Rib House (Barbeque/ Burgers, $$)
Café Brio (Pacific Northwest, $$)
Café Mexico (Mexican, $–$$)
Camille's Fine West Coast Dining (Pacific Northwest, $$–$$$)
Canoe Club (Pub Fare, $$)

Da Tandoor (Indian, $$)
Herald Street Caffe (Pacific Northwest, $$–$$$)
Il Terrazzo Ristorante (Italian, $$–$$$)
J&J Wonton Noodle House (Chinese, $–$$)
Pagliacci's (Italian, $$)
Re-bar (Vegetarian, $–$$)
Sam's Deli (Deli, $)
Spice Jammer Restaurant (Indian, $–$$)

Esquimalt/Songhees
Spinnakers Brewpub (Pub Fare, $–$$)
Victorian Restaurant (Pacific Northwest, $$$)

Fairfield

Cassis Bistro (French, $$$)

Inner Harbour

Barb's Place (Seafood, $)
Blue Crab Bar & Grill (Seafood, $$$)

James Bay Tearoom (English, $–$$)
Pablo's Dining Lounge (Continental, $$)
Pescatore's Fish House (Seafood, $$)
Oak BayMarina Restaurant (Seafood,
  $$–$$$)
Windsor House Tea Room (English, $–$$)

Index of restaurants by cuisine

Barbecue/Burgers

Beacon Drive-In (Downtown/Old Town, $)
Bowman's Rib House (Downtown/Old
  Town, $$)

Chinese

Don Mee Seafood Restaurant (Chinatown,
  $–$$)

J&J Wonton Noodle House (Downtown/Old Town, $–$$) Continental

Pablo's Dining Lounge (Inner Harbour, $$)

Deli

Sam's Deli (Downtown/Old Town, $)

English

James Bay Tearoom (Inner Harbour, $–$$)
Windsor House Tea Room (Oak Bay, $–$$)

French

Cassis Bistro (Fairfield, $$$)

Indian

Da Tandoor (Downtown/Old Town, $$)
Spice Jammer Restaurant (Downtown/Old
  Town, $–$$)

Italian

Il Terrazzo Ristorante (Downtown/Old
  Town, $$–$$$)

Pagliacci's (Downtown/Old Town, $$) Mexican

Café Mexico (Downtown/Old Town, $–$$)

Pacific Northwest

Café Brio (Downtown/Old Town, $$)
Camille's Fine West Coast Dining
  (Downtown/Old Town, $$–$$$)
Herald Street Caffe (Downtown/Old Town
  $$–$$$)
Victorian Restaurant
  (Esquimalt/Songhees, $$$)

Pub Fare

Canoe Club (Downtown/Old Town, $$)
Spinnakers Brewpub
  (Esquimalt/Songhees, $–$$)

Seafood

Barb's Place (Inner Harbour, $)
Blue Crab Bar & Grill (Inner Harbour, $$$)
Marina Restaurant (Oak Bay, $$–$$$)
Pescatore's Fish House (Inner Harbour, $$

Vegetarian

Re-bar (Downtown/Old Town, $–$$)

Index of restaurants by price

$$$

Blue Crab Bar & Grill (Seafood, Inner Harbour)
Camille's Fine West Coast Dining (Pacific Northwest, Downtown/Old Town)
Cassis Bistro (French, Fairfield)
Herald Street Caffe (Pacific Northwest, Downtown/Old Town)
Il Terrazzo Ristorante (Italian, Downtown/Old Town)
Marina Restaurant (Seafood, Oak Bay)
Victorian Restaurant (Pacific Northwest, Esquimalt/Songhees)

$$

Bowman's Rib House (Barbeque/Burgers, Downtown/Old Town)
Café Brio (Pacific Northwest, Downtown/Old Town)
Café Mexico (Mexican, Downtown/Old Town)
Canoe Club (Pub Fare, Downtown/Old Town)
Da Tandoor (Indian, Downtown/Old Town)

J&J Wonton Noodle House (Chinese, Downtown/Old Town)
James Bay Tearoom (English, Inner Harbour)
Pablo's Dining Lounge (Continental, Inner Harbour)
Pagliacci's (Italian, Downtown/Old Town)
Pescatore's Fish House (Seafood, Inner Harbour)
Spinnakers Brewpub (Pub Fare, Esquimalt/Songhees)

$

Barb's Place (Seafood, Inner Harbour)
Beacon Drive-In (Barbeque/Burgers, Downtown/Old Town)
Don Mee Seafood Restaurant (Chinese, Chinatown)
Re-bar (Vegetarian, Downtown/Old Town)
Sam's Deli (Deli, Downtown/Old Town)
Spice Jammer Restaurant (Indian, Downtown/Old Town)
Windsor House Tea Room (English, Oak Bay)

Victoria's Best Snacks

As a tourist town, Victoria is necessarily loaded with on-the-fly snacking opportunities. Whether it's a scone with tea, a fruit smoothie, a chocolate truffle, or a neighborhood café, your tank never need run too low here.

Tearooms and cafés

The quintessential Victorian snack is a quick stop into a tearoom, sipping hot tea while nibbling on a finger sandwich or scone and watching the raindrops run down the windows. You can eat as little as you like, or go whole hog with high tea — almost a meal, and you pay accordingly. The city has lots of non-English cafes scattered around, too, also good for a quick muffin or sandwich.

Blethering Place Tearoom & Restaurant, 2250 Oak Bay Avenue, Oak Bay (☎ **250-598-1413**), is one of the grande dames of Victorian teaosity, with all the decorations, pretensions, and nibbles you would expect. You need a car, bike, or bus to get here from downtown.

Friends of Dorothy's Café, 615 Johnson Street (☎ **250-381-2277**), is a find — a funky interior theme (*Wizard of Oz*) and three classy meals a day right in the heart of downtown. This is a great place to meet a broad cross-section of un-stuffy Victorians.

Murchie's Tea and Coffee, 1110 Government Street (☎ 250-383-3112), offers the best selection of teas in the city, plus good coffee and everything from tea snacks to full-blown sandwiches and salads.

Burgers, fish, and pub grub

Without a doubt, the most plentiful quick food in Victoria is its pub grub. The only problem is that quality can be highly variable, and the grease factor is always a problem.

The **Charles Dickens Pub,** 633 Humboldt Street (☎ **250-361-2600**), practically beneath The Empress, is the most central pub and a pretty good pick for your first beer or Scotch in town — it's not a stuffy sort of place.

D'Arcy McGhee's, 1127 Wharf Street (☎ **250-380-1322**), one of the only honestly Irish pubs in town, goes nuts on St. Patty's Day. Besides the requisite Guinness and Harp, they do fish-and-chips and similar ribsticking food.

The **George & Dragon Pub,** 1302 Gladstone Avenue (☎ **250-388-4458**), is much more eclectic than you'd expect — American, Asian, and other influences mingle with the usual English favorites.

Old Vic Fish & Chips, 1316 Broad Street (☎ **250-383-4536**), an alternative to Barb's Place in the very heart of the downtown area, offers a selection of fish, oysters, and chicken, all very good.

The Tapa Bar, 620 Trounce Alley (☎ **250-383-0013** or 250-383-0086), is a restaurant, a bar, and snack stop all in one; load up on various kinds of Spanish tapas. Remember that the price can escalate quickly as you pile on the chow.

Restaurant rescue for vegetarians

An English town is a meat-eating town, certainly, but this is also the West Coast: You're never too far from a plate of organic vegetables, and several restaurants specialize in vegetarian or vegan dishes.

Even if you can't get to one of these places, always ask at any restaurant about veggie menu items. Some cafés — and *every* Asian restaurant — will gladly cook something meatless for you.

Green Cuisine, 560 Johnson Street (☎ 250-385-1809), the undisputed center of Victorian veggie life, is wildly popular for its good hot buffet, salad bar, and baked goods. The spot is tucked away from street activity on the courtyard level of the Market Square shopping complex.

Lotus Pond Vegetarian Restaurant, 617 Johnson Street (☎ 250-380-9293), is a newish vegan eatery — run by Buddhists, so this is the real deal — which stakes its claim on "mock" meats, a hot lunch buffet, and plenty of Chinese-influenced menu items.

The coffee connection

You don't need to cave into U.S. chain-coffee imperialism here, no sir. You're spoiled for choice and quality in Victoria; every new block seems to offer another take on the roasted bean.

C'est Bon, 10 Bastion Square (☎ 250-381-1461), is a croissant shop with a great selection of breakfast and lunch croissants, plus coffee to wash it down. More popular as a takeout spot, really.

Demitasse Coffee Bar, 1320 Blanshard Street (☎ 250-386-4422), is almost too cool for its own good, with superb grinds of coffee blends, interesting wall art, good food — and quite the crowd.

Dutch Bakery & Coffee Shop, 718 Fort Street (☎ 250-385-1012), is the epitome of good snacking, Victoria-style: They make their own chocolates, serve good coffee, and a range of other eats and treats as well. Seating is a bit rudimentary, but so what?

Moka House, 345 Cook Street (☎ 250-388-7377), in Cook Village is a fair piece from downtown — but a beautiful walk it is, and you're rewarded with trays of sweets and eats alongside the java.

Torrefazione Italia, 1234 Government Street (☎ 250-920-7302), is among the classiest coffee shops in the city; the Italian management demands a perfect cappuccino, and brews one. Mineral water and Italian nibbles complement the atmosphere.

Sweets to eat

This town has a sweet tooth, and you'll easily find chocolates, penny candy, and more. The central tourist area is thickest with sweets, but outlying neighborhoods have their own local candy shops too.

The British Candy Shoppe, 635 Yates Street (☎ **250-382-2634**), and **The English Sweet Shop,** 738 Yates Street (☎ **250-382-3325**), maintain that old-time candy store feel with a wide choice of penny candies, toffee, jelly beans, and the like.

Rogers' Chocolates, 913 Government Street (☎ **800-663-2220** or 250-384-7021), makes its own exquisite cream-filled chocolates in an old-candy-shop atmosphere, though they're not cheap.

Chapter 19

Exploring Victoria

● ●

In This Chapter

▶ Previewing Victoria's best attractions

▶ Exploring the city by guided tour

▶ Following a British -based itinerary

● ●

*V*ictoria's compact downtown area means that its sights are easily covered in a day or two, linked to each other by cab, bus, horse-drawn carriage, or some walking. Actually, though, downtown has fewer impressive sights than you may expect. As a result, several of my recommended must-sees lie on the fringes of the city, and two (Butchart Gardens and Victoria Butterfly Gardens) are located more than 15 miles northwest of it.

Exploring Victoria's Top Sights from A to Z

Art Gallery of Greater Victoria

Fairfield

Very near Craigdarroch Castle (see listing later in this chapter), the AGGV — as it's known in shorthand — holds more than 15,000 pieces of art in its permanent collection, including a strong selection of local painter Emily Carr's works. Six wings of this museum feature more than 30 exhibitions each year; permanent exhibits include a life-sized dollhouse and a genuine Shinto shrine, part of Canada's most extensive Japanese art collection. Allow 1 to 1½ hours.

1040 Moss St. (from downtown Victoria, walk along Fort St. away from downtown approximately 1 ¼ miles to Moss St. and turn right). ☎ *250-384-4101. Admission: C$5 (US$3.35) adults, C$3 (US$2) seniors. Open: Mon–Sat 10 a.m.–5 p.m., Thurs to 9 p.m., Sun 1–5 p.m. Wheelchair-accessible.*

Victoria Attractions

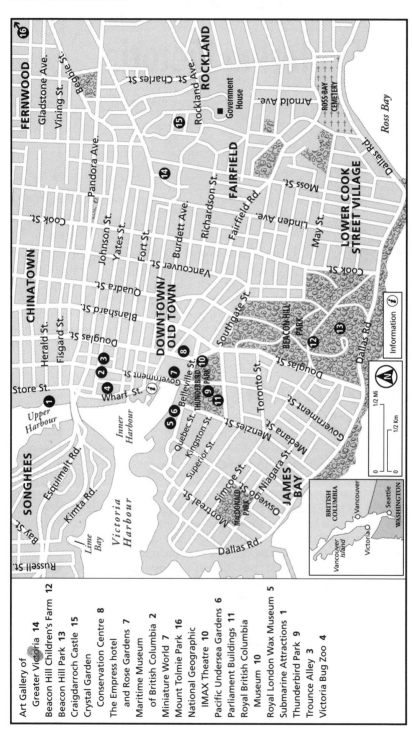

Art Gallery of
Greater Victoria **14**
Beacon Hill Children's Farm **12**
Beacon Hill Park **13**
Craigdarroch Castle **15**
Crystal Garden
Conservation Centre **8**
The Empress hotel
and Rose Gardens **7**
Maritime Museum
of British Columbia **2**
Miniature World **7**
Mount Tolmie Park **16**
National Geographic
IMAX Theatre **10**
Pacific Undersea Gardens **6**
Parliament Buildings **11**
Royal British Columbia
Museum **10**
Royal London Wax Museum **5**
Submarine Attractions **1**
Thunderbird Park **9**
Trounce Alley **3**
Victoria Bug Zoo **4**

Beacon Hill Park

Inner Harbour

Without a doubt the top park in downtown Victoria, Beacon Hill park does the city proud. It's a sprawling, green oasis of flowers, fields, trees, ponds, views, and totem poles — some of it very ordered, but some of it left to nature's devices. A Scotsman, John Blair, won a competition to design the park in 1889; the descendants of rhododendrons he planted that year around Fountain Lake still thrive more than a century later. One particularly tall totem pole marks the endpoint (called Mile Zero) of the Trans-Canada Highway, and rose gardens, canals, a band shell, a small zoo, and even (oh, those English) a cricket pitch are also interspersed throughout the grounds. Children especially adore the Beacon Hill Children's Farm; if you want a taste of the salt air, you can even walk all the way through the 150-acre park — about a mile long — and come out the other side on the ocean, facing Washington state. Allow 1 to 2 hours.

Corner Southgate St. and Douglas Blvd. (from The Empress, walk south to Belleville St., turn left, continue to Thunderbird Park, and turn right on Douglas; continue 1 block to park). Admission: Free. Open: Daily dawn to dusk. Wheelchair-accessible.

Butchart Gardens

Brentwood Bay (12 miles northwest of Victoria)

An amazing testament to one woman's love for gardening, these gardens are *the* top tourist draw to Victoria, despite their remoteness, and rightly so. Jenny Butchart planted 50 acres of gardens in her husband's exhausted marble quarry, stocking much of it with rare imported plants and showing a deft design touch as she created a rose garden, Japanese garden, "sunken garden," and more. Amazingly, thanks to the temperate maritime climate, something's in bloom all 12 months of the year — all carefully color-coordinated, trimmed, and precisely timed to blossom — most of it illuminated with night lighting during the high summer months, then again with special Christmas lighting during that season. A gardening store and Saturday night fireworks in summer complete the experience, which is worth every pretty penny you pay for it. Note that if you want to dine at the more upscale of the two restaurants on the estate grounds, you need to reserve in advance (☎ 250-652-8222). Also know that after dark it's much less crowded here. Allow 3 hours, including travel time, longer if dining.

800 Benvenuto Ave. (from downtown Victoria, drive away from town along Blanshard St., which becomes Hwy. 17; after about 6 miles, exit onto Hwy. 17A and continue 5 miles to Wallace Dr. turnoff; then either follow Wallace Dr. 3 miles to Benvenuto, following signs to gardens, or continue 3 more miles on Hwy. 17A to Benvenuto Ave. turnoff and follow Benvenuto to gardens). ☎ 250-652-4422. Admission: C$11.75–C$16.50 (US$8–US$11) adults, C$5.75–C$8.25 (US$4–US$6) children 13–17, C$1.50–C$2.00 (US$1–US$1.34) children 5–12. Open: Daily at 9 a.m, closing times vary seasonally. Wheelchair-accessible.

Craigdarroch Castle

Fairfield

One-time British Columbia coal magnate Robert Dunsmuir built this Victorian "castle" during the late 1800s for his wife, decking it out with almost 40 rooms and plenty of eye-popping furniture, statuary, carpeting, and exotic wood. Dunsmuir passed away just before its completion, and so never lived in the house, but his wife did for years. The oak staircase is a real looker — and a real climb, at 87 stairs. (This is one attraction that isn't fully wheelchair-accessible.) You have to show yourself around, as guided tours aren't available. Allow 1 to 2 hours.

1050 Joan Crescent (from downtown Victoria, follow Fort St. approximately 1½ miles away from the water to Joan Crescent turnoff). ☎ *250-592-5323. Internet: www.craigdarrochcastle.com. Admission: C$7.50 (US$5) adults, C$5 (US$3.35) students, C$2 (US$1.34) children 6–12. Open: Daily 10 a.m.–4:30 p.m. Not fully wheelchair accessible.*

The Empress Hotel and Rose Gardens

Inner Harbour

The Empress is, for all practical purposes, the hub of Victoria's substantial tourist trade. This rambling waterside Canadian Pacific hotel with its handsome mansard roofs is the best, most obvious point to orient yourself on the Inner Harbour; the congregating point for every manner of double-decker tour bus, tour guide, and camera-clicking visitor; and a must-see, inside and out. Designed by English architect Frances Rattenbury, this place is so big that is has three entrances — though the front stairs are no longer one of them. It's almost unnecessary to tell you that the wood, marble, stained-glass, and crystal chandeliers are all of the highest quality. (Some of the hotel rooms *are* a bit on the small side, though.) There are no tours — not unless you're a paying guest, of course, in which case you get a *real* inside look — but most of the ground floors are open to the public, including a shopping gallery, a lush conservatory, lavish sitting rooms, two restaurants, and the wonderfully overdone Bengal Lounge (see Chapter 21), which serves tea, alcoholic drinks, and Indian meals. Outside, walk around to find the rose gardens, a fragrant and peaceful retreat from the touristic buzz of the harbor. Allow about 1 hour, 2 hours if taking tea. See Chapter 17 for information on staying here.

721 Government St. Admission: Free. Wheelchair-accessible.

Fort Rodd Hill and Fisgard Lighthouse

Colwood (8 miles west of Victoria)

As the crow flies, this lighthouse and fort practically overlook the twin peninsulas of Victoria and Esquimalt, and that's precisely why they were built here during the late 1800s: to guard the strategic harbor from invaders. The lighthouse, constructed first, is the oldest on Canada's west coast. Inside the keeper's house (everything is automated now), a small museum gives you some sense of what life was once like here. The fort was added later, very close by, with three batteries of guns, barracks, underground magazines, the whole bit. And local volunteers drop by the complex during summer to demonstrate the old blacksmithing ways. If you're not into all this history, you can still come for the oak meadows, blacktail deer, bobbing seals, and sea lions — it's a scenic place for a picnic. Allow 2 to 3 hours, including travel time.

603 Fort Rodd Hill Rd. (8 miles west of downtown Victoria; drive north on Douglas St. to Hwy. 1, continue 3 miles, take exit 10 for Colwood and follow Hwy. 1A another 1.2 miles. Turn left at Ocean Blvd. and follow signs.) ☎ *250-478-5849. Admission: C$6 (US$4) adults, C$3 (US$2) children 6–16. Open: Mar–Oct daily 10 a.m.–5:30 p.m., Sept–Feb daily 9 a.m.–4:30 p.m. Mostly wheelchair-accessible.*

Maritime Museum of British Columbia

Old Town/Downtown

This museum, containing pretty much exactly what you would expect, is housed in the province's former courthouse. Various low-tech galleries explain the early history of marine exploration in the province, the story of Captain Cook, naval history, and the role of BC Ferries in modern-day island life. Among the most interesting exhibits are a dugout canoe, marine charts, and ship bells. But the *really* interesting stuff has to do with the courthouse itself, a beautiful structure paneled in exotic woods that holds plenty of its own history. One especially tough judge made a name for himself by sentencing dozens of criminals to death in the oak chambers, then ordering them hanged right out in front of the steps; the same judge designed the rather ornate elevator — Canada's oldest — supposedly because His Ampleness couldn't fit up the building's narrow stairway. Allow about 1 hour.

28 Bastion Square. ☎ *250-385-4222. Admission: C$5 (US$3.35) adults, C$4 (US$2.68) seniors, C$2 (US$1.34) children 11 and under. Open: Daily 9:30 a.m.–4:30 p.m. All wheelchair-accessible except Special Exhibition Gallery.*

Parliament Buildings

Inner Harbour

Basically the Canadian equivalent of a state capital building, Victoria's dual Parliament Buildings house the workings of its provincial legislators. A fresh-faced Englishman named Frances Rattenbury blew into town and somehow won the local design competition, overseeing the huge stone buildings' construction during the late 1890s; Rattenbury would go on to design nearly everything else of note in the city, including The Empress. The exterior is notable for thousands of small light bulbs, which illumine the facade at night, as well as a statues of early explorer George Vancouver topping the centermost dome and another of Queen Victoria.

Inside, it's all wood, marble, and stained glass. Free tours are given three times each hour during the summer, once an hour during the winter months. The chamber upstairs is chock-full of reminders of that not-so-bygone day when Canada was tied at the hip to England. If legislature is in session you can watch the lively give-and-take of parliamentary procedure, which peaks around 2 in the afternoon — probably too dull for the kids, but architecture and history buffs will certainly want a look. Otherwise just wander through the halls looking like an important politician. Allow about 1 hour.

501 Belleville St. ☎ 250-387-3046. Admission: Free. Open: Daily 9 a.m.–5 p.m. Wheelchair accessible except restrooms.

Royal British Columbia Museum

Inner Harbour

Victoria's downtown tourist offerings offer lots of dogs, but this science, nature, and history museum isn't one of them — rather, it's a truly eye-opening experience, one of the highlights of a visit to the city. The displays include a *serious* collection of Native Canadian artifacts, a re-created rainforest, a mini-train, actual seals, a mockup of Chinatown, and much more. The attached National Geographic IMAX Theatre (see "Finding More Cool Things to See and Do," later in this chapter), with its panoramic screen and sound, is a must-visit if you're bringing kids. Almost everything here is life-like, fascinating, and thought-provoking for all ages — kids, teens, and adults. Allow 2 hours.

675 Belleville St. ☎ 888-447-7977 or 250-356-7226. Admission: 10.65 (US$7) adults, C$7.65 (US$5) seniors, C$4–C$5 (US$2.68–US$3.35) children 6–18. Open: Sat–Wed 9 a.m.–5 p.m., Thurs–Fri 9 a.m.–7:45 p.m. Partially wheelchair-accessible.

Thunderbird Park

Inner Harbour

Absolutely free and fascinating, this park's collection of totem poles is a wonderful introduction to the island, and it's enhanced by the summertime presence of carvers making new ones — as you watch. Sometimes they even answer questions. A single carver revived the nearly lost art of making these poles right here in the park. Allow a half-hour.

Corner of Belleville and Douglas Streets (from The Empress, walk south a short distance to Belleville and turn left). Admission: Free. Open: Daily dusk to dawn. Wheelchair-accessible.

Trounce Alley

Old Town/Downtown

There's not a lot to Trounce Alley, but it's still a quick and fun stroll into a bit of Victoria's past. Once the city's, er, red-light district (okay, that's something the kids don't really need to know), this narrowest of streets — which you may still have little trouble squeezing through — is today much scrubbed and polished up, lit with quaint lanterns and so forth. The alley now holds little nook-and-cranny shops, some of them among Victoria's most interesting, as well as a Spanish tapas restaurant, The Tapa Bar (see Chapter 18). Kid usually get a kick out of the novelty of the alley, as well as some of the shops. Allow a half-hour.

Runs from Government St. to Broad St., between Yates and View Streets. Admission: Free. Wheelchair-accessible.

Victoria Butterfly Gardens
Brentwood Bay (12 miles northwest of Victoria)

The motto here is, "Ever been kissed by a butterfly?" Well, have you? If not, it just may happen in this walk-through greenhouse full of specially selected tropical blossoms and exotic butterflies from all over the world. You won't believe the color and variety here, and some of the bigger critters approach a foot. Wanna kiss? Here's a sneaky inside tip: Women with bright lipsticks stand the best chance. This makes a good day trip when combined with nearby Butchart Gardens, which is less than 2 miles west. Allow about 1 hour.

1461 Benvenuto Ave., Brentwood Bay (from downtown Victoria, drive away from town along Blanshard St., which becomes Hwy. 17; after about 6 miles, exit onto Hwy. 17A and continue about 8 more miles to gardens on left). ☎ *250-652-3822. Admission: C\$7.50 (US\$5) adults, C\$6.50 (US\$4.35) seniors, C\$4.50 (US\$3) children 3–12. Open: Mar–Oct, daily 9:30 a.m.–5 p.m., rest of the year call for hours. Wheelchair-accessible.*

Index of top sights by neighborhood

Fairfield
Art Gallery of Greater Victoria
Craigdarroch Castle

Inner Harbour
Beacon Hill Park
The Empress Hotel and Rose Gardens
Parliament Buildings
Royal British Columbia Museum
Thunderbird Park

Old Town/Downtown
Maritime Museum of British Columbia
Trounce Alley

Outside Victoria city limits
Butchart Gardens
Fort Rodd Hill and Fisgard Lighthouse
Victoria Butterfly Gardens

Index of top sights by type

Art museums
Art Gallery of Greater Victoria

Streets
Trounce Alley

Historic attractions and museums
Craigdarroch Castle
The Empress Hotel and Rose Gardens
Fort Rodd Hill and Fisgard Lighthouse
Maritime Museum of British Columbia
Parliament Buildings
Royal British Columbia Museum

Parks and gardens
Beacon Hill Park
Butchart Gardens
Thunderbird Park
Victoria Butterfly Gardens

Finding More Cool Things to See and Do

What? There's more?

Of course, although — frankly speaking — after you cover Victoria's central attractions and day trip out to its gardens, you've hit everything major. But say you're staying in town for an extended period of time and want to see and do more. Well, you're in luck. What follows are a few more things you can pencil into your itinerary.

Kid-pleasing spots

Beacon Hill Children's Farm

Inner Harbour

Kids love this little zoo-like corner of Beacon Hill Park, where they can ride, coddle, and otherwise get up-close and personal with farm animals. A small pool is on hand for cooling off during the hot weather, too, after riding the ponies; all things considered, the petting zoo is a great alternative to hot, boring (to kids) afternoons pounding the pavement doing the city walking-tour thing — and it's both very central and practically free.

Circle Dr. (in Beacon Hill Park). ☎ 250-381-2532. Admission: C$1 (US$.67) suggested. Open: Daily mid-Mar–Sept 10 a.m.–5 p.m. Wheelchair-accessible.

Crystal Garden Conservation Centre

Inner Harbour

You'll be amazed, especially by the four-inch-tall monkeys in this conservatory, located right behind The Empress hotel. This is one of those times when a hyped-up destination actually delivers a certain quantity of information and fun — while treading on a fine line between interesting and tacky. You may find it hard to believe that this was once a vast saltwater pool where socialites swam and a ballroom where they danced and drank the nights away, but it was.

713 Douglas St. ☎ 250-953-8818. Admission: C$7.50 (US$5) adults, C$6.50 (US$4.35) seniors, C$4 (US$2.68) children 5–16. Open: July–Aug daily 8:30 a.m.–8 p.m. and Sept–June 10 a.m.–4:30 p.m. Wheelchair-accessible.

Miniature World

Inner Harbour

This openly corny attraction frankly is just a curiosity, with things such as the smallest (supposedly) working sawmill, two very large doll houses, and a very long model railway. The attractions are divided into sections with Disney-like names: Circus World, Space 2201, Frontierland, Fantasyland. You get the picture.

649 Humboldt St. ☎ 250-385-9731. Admission: C$7 (US$4.69) adults, C$5 (US$3.35) children. Open: July–Sept daily 9 a.m.–9 p.m., Oct–June daily 9 a.m.–6 p.m. Wheelchair-accessible, except for the restrooms.

Pacific Undersea Gardens

Inner Harbour

Extending more than 10 feet down to the floor of Victoria's Inner Harbour, the gardens offer a chance to view all sorts of sea life and a live scuba diving show. You can see live fish — salmon, sturgeon, snapper — swimming, eating, mating, and otherwise doing their thing amid the ruins of a sunken ship, not to mention brightly colored sea anemones, huge octopi, and other odd and carnivorous creatures in their natural environs.

490 Belleville St. ☎ 250-382-5717. Admission: C$7 (US$4.69) adults, C$6.25 (US$4.19) seniors, C$5 (US$3.35) children 5–11. Open: July–Aug daily 10 a.m.–7 p.m.; Sept–June daily 9 a.m.–5 p.m. Not wheelchair-accessible.

Royal London Wax Museum

Inner Harbour

This collection of more than 300 wax figures shipped over from Madame Tussaud's original (and better) wax museum in London, England, is a bit schlocky. I don't find it worth the effort or money — but kids sometimes

enjoy it, especially those unintentionally hilarious figures that are supposed to depict gruesome doings.

*470 Belleville St. ☎ 250-388-4461. Admission: C$8 (US$5.36) adults, C$7 (US$4.69)
seniors, C$3.00–C$6.50 (US$2–US$4.35) children. Open: Mid-May–Aug daily 9
a.m.–7:30 p.m., Sept–Dec daily 9:30 a.m.–6 p.m., Jan–early May daily 9:30 a.m.–5
p.m. Wheelchair accessible.*

Victoria Bug Zoo

Downtown/Old Town

The squeamish won't want to visit this place; kids, not being squeamish,
often get a kick out it, though. The "zoo" features live scorpions, taran-
tulas, centipedes, stick insects, exotic beetles, grasshoppers, and more.
You can even — ugh — cradle some of these comely creatures if you like.
Not feeling up to it? Then you'll want to slide over to the gift shop and
buy some chocolate-covered insects (maybe not) or local honey.

*1107 Wharf St. ☎ 250-384-2847. Admission: C$6 (US$4) adults, C$4 (US$2.68) chil-
dren 3–16. Open: July–Aug daily 9:30 a.m.–9 p.m.; Sept–June daily 9:30 a.m.–5:30
p.m. Wheelchair accessible.*

Teen-tempting attractions

Many teens seem to prefer shopping and hanging out at the Eaton
Centre or in Market Square, but you can find a few other teen-friendly
attractions, such as these:

Dominion Astrophysical Observatory

Saanich (7 miles north of Victoria)

The white domes atop Little Saanich Mountain are visible from parts of
Victoria, and the two large telescopes here — with 3½-foot and 5-foot mir-
rors — are used to stargaze by professionals on about 200 nights each
year; the larger of the two, in fact, was once the largest telescope in the
world. Tours lasting about 75 minutes are offered Monday to Friday by
advance reservation, and Saturday night talks and public stargazing are
also available on an irregular schedule. Always call ahead before ven-
turing, however; at press time, one of the telescopes was closed to public
view for repairs.

*West Saanich Rd. (from downtown Victoria, drive north out Blanshard St. to Hwy.
17 and continue approximately 4.5 miles; exit onto Hwy. 17A north and continue 2.5
more miles on West Saanich Rd. to observatory). ☎ 250-363-0001 for information;
250-363-0012 for tour reservations. Admission: Free. Open: Tours Mon–Fri 9 a.m.–
5 p.m. by appointment only; special events on weekends, call for information. Not
fully wheelchair-accessible.*

National Geographic IMAX Theatre

Inner Harbour

One of the hippest, highest-tech attractions in Victoria is the six-story, panoramic IMAX movie screen housed inside the Royal British Columbia Museum (see "Exploring Victoria's Top Sights from A to Z," earlier in this chapter). Science, nature, and popular films screen every hour on the hour all day long; the pounding surround-sound brings another dimension to the huge wraparound images on the screen above.

675 Belleville St. (inside Royal British Columbia Museum). ☎ *250-480-4887. Admission: C$9 (US$6) adults, C$8 (US$5) seniors, C$6 (US$4) children. Open: June–Sept, daily 10 a.m.–9 p.m., Oct–May 10 a.m.–8 p.m. Wheelchair-accessible.*

Submarine Attractions

Downtown/Old Town

Kids will likely get a kick out of the innards of this 300-foot man-o-war submarine docked at the foot of Swift Street. The boat, once crewed by Russian naval officers and known as U-521, was long ago decommissioned. Now visitors can walk through the actual torpedo rooms, crew quarters, sonar, and radar rooms.

450 Swift St. (on water, docked at Old Town Marina). ☎ *250-382-3022. Admission: C$10 (US$7) adults, C$8 (US$5) seniors and children 12 and under. Open: June–Aug 9 a.m.–9 p.m., Sept–May 10 a.m.–5 p.m. Not wheelchair-accessible.*

Notable parks and gardens

Almost nothing is better in Victoria than wandering through one of numerous parks, many snuggled into residential neighborhoods (see the next section). Here are three of the loveliest:

Horticulture Centre of the Pacific

Saanich (6 miles north of Victoria)

One of the better botanical gardens in the Greater Victoria region, this center is made up of more than 100 acres of property with hundreds of identified plants, trees, and flowers. It's a great deal less expensive than Butchart Gardens, if less spectacular.

505 Quayle Rd. (from downtown Victoria, drive north out Blanshard St. to Hwy. 17 and continue approximately 4½ miles; exit onto Hwy. 17A north and continue 1½ more miles and make a left on Beaver Rd., just after Beaver Lake Elementary school; at end of Beaver Rd., make a right on Quayle Rd.). ☎ *250-479-6162. Admisstion: C$5 (US$3.35) per person. Open: Apr–Oct daily 8 a.m.–8 p.m., Nov–Mar 8:30 a.m.–4:30 p.m. Limited wheelchair access.*

Mount Douglas Park

Saanich (3 miles north of Victoria)

Called "Mount Doug," this reclaimed copper-mining hill is perhaps the most impressive park of all in Victoria nowadays, though it does take a little finding — it's nestled within farms and suburbs a couple miles north of the city center. The 640-foot summit (which you can walk or drive to) has panoramic views of the city, the strait, and the mountains. The park has an ocean section with rocky tide pools and genuine cliffs, and hiking trails that pass through fragrant ferns, wildflowers, Douglas firs, and cedar trees. A great spot to get away from the city for a few hours.

Cordova Bay Rd. (from downtown Victoria, proceed to Johnson St. and turn right, traveling away from bridge; remain on main road for 3 miles — street changes name to Begbie, then Shelbourne, then Cordova Bay Rd.). ☎ 250-744-5341. Admission: Free. Open: Daily dawn to dusk.

Mount Tolmie Park

Mayfair

Several walking trails ascend the 350-foot summit in this small park — not a long climb, but high enough on this flat peninsula to reward the walker with good views of Victoria and the Olympic Mountain Range.

Mayfair Dr. (from downtown Victoria, drive 2 miles east on Fort St. and turn left on Richmond Rd.; continue 1½ more miles north to Mayfair Dr., turn right onto Mayfair and continue 1/2 mile to park). ☎ 250-744-5341. Admission: Free. Open: Daily dawn to dusk.

Stroll-worthy neighborhoods

After you're done combing through the Inner Harbour, downtown, Old Town, and Antique Row, a few more areas await your inspection.

Chinatown is almost too small to explore for long, but Fan Tan Alley — a narrow passageway now filled with shops — is fun with the kids during the daytime. **Bastion Square,** on Government Street, was the original site of Fort Victoria, a fort constructed in 1843 by the Hudson's Bay Company but later torn down; it was also, for a time, a rough-and-tumble district of bars and houses of ill repute. Today the square has mostly cafés and shops.

Beyond the central attractions, you can tour the nearby neighborhoods of **Lower Cook Street Village, James Bay, Oak Bay, Uplands,** and **Mayfair.** To do it, begin at Beacon Hill Park and cycle or drive along Dallas Road, which becomes Beach Drive and passes through gorgeous mansions and a golf course. The breakwater at **Ogden Point** is a good early spot to break this journey, with seafood available to eat and a shore path for walking. Other recommended spots for breaks are (in succession) **Clover Point, Trafalgar Park, Willows Beach Park,** and big **Uplands Park,** all right on the same beach route. **Ross Bay Cemetery,** on the dry side of the road just after Clove Point, contains 27,000 graves including those of notable locals Robert Dunsmuir, a Scottish mining baron, and Emily Carr, a painter.

Turning inland at Cadboro Bay (site of the Royal Victoria Yacht Club) you pass the **University of Victoria** campus, which — in springtime — is ablaze with the blossoms of rhododendron gardens. From here, you can turn and follow Cadboro Bay Road south back into town, where it becomes Fort Street.

Seeing Victoria by Guided Tour

If you're pressed for time, a guided tour of Victoria may be a good idea. And for such a small city, a greater variety of tours are available than you would probably expect — everything from walks through moonlit cemeteries to sailboat tours. Take note that almost all of them, however, operate only during the summer season, which here runs approximately from the beginning of June to the beginning of October. Some tour companies may also operate during spring and fall as well, so it's always worth checking, but a winter visitor will find the tour offerings very much reduced.

Touring by foot

Those who want to hoof it around Victoria, have a few options. The cheapest tour is the one you make for free by yourself, using maps gleaned at the Visitor InfoCentre, 812 Wharf Street. But even if you're a poor route-planner, you can get free guided tours, beginning at the Visitor InfoCentre, any afternoon during summer from the local chapter of the **Architectural Institute of British Columbia** (☎ **800-667-0753**).

Several tours given by private companies point out Victoria's spookier side, among them **Victoria's Haunted Walk** (☎ **250-361-2619**), a 90-minute tour of reputedly haunted spots that leaves from the Visitor InfoCentre. The cost is for C$8 (US$5) for adults and C$7 (US$4.69) for children and seniors. Other options are the **Murder, Ghosts, and Mayhem Walk** (☎ **250-385-2035**) from Bastion Square each summer night at 8 p.m., which costs C$7 (US$4.69) per person with children free, and the **Ghostly Walks** tour (☎ **250-384-6698**) each summer night at 7:30 p.m. for C$10 (US$7).

Equally spine-tingling are the offerings of the **Old Cemetery Society of Victoria** (☎ **250-598-8870**), which hosts lantern-lit walks through the Old Burying Ground on summer nights. Meet at the Cherry Bank Hotel on Burdett Street and pay C$5 (US$3.35) each; family discounts are available for groups of three or more. The Society also operates other walks, including Sunday afternoon daylight walks for the timid and tours of another city cemetery.

Touring on wheels: Bus, carriage, pedicab, and limo

Gray Line of Victoria (☎ **800-667-0882** or 250-388-5248; Internet: www.grayline.ca/victoria) is the old standby. Among its offerings are the usual bus tours: A 90-minute "Grand City" tour costing C$13.75 (US$9) for adults and C$6.95 (US$4.66) for children, as well as more expensive packages combining the standard city tour with such destinations as Butchart Gardens, Butterfly Gardens, and Craigdarroch Castle. Call for details. Tours generally run from April through October, but check ahead to be certain.

Gray Line also runs a small trolley around town, hitting many of the major points of interest; an all-day ticket on this hop-on, hop-off circuit costs C$7 (US$4.69) for adults, C$4 (US$2.68) for children, and can be quite convenient if you haven't rented a car.

Pacific Coach Lines Tours (☎ **800-661-1725** or 250-385-4411) offers several bus tours from Vancouver. The Royal Victorian & Butchart Gardens tour, for instance, is for flower-lovers and includes 2 hours' time at Butchart Gardens; the Royal Victorian & Grand City Tour takes place on a London double-decker bus that drives through almost all Victoria's neighborhoods; and the Royal Victorian Excursion is shorter and not narrated. Prices vary according to such factors as where your tour begins and how old you are, but all prices include ferry costs.

Horse-drawn tours are also an option in Victoria. **Tallyho Horse Drawn Tours** (☎ **250-383-5067**) provides that old-fashioned feeling in turn-of-the-last-century carriages clip-clopping around town from March through September. Group tours in a carriage holding up to 20 strangers cost C$14 (US$9) per adult, C$12 (US$8) for seniors, and C$9.50 (US$6) for children. Or you can rent an entire, smaller carriage for somewhat more — a half-hour will cost you about C$60 (US$40), for example. You can find the carriages waiting in front of The Empress hotel or at Belleville and Menzies Streets, next to the ferry docks. **Black Beauty Carriages** (☎ 250-361-122) is a smaller firm, with smaller and more intimate carriages (they hold up to six people) and more route flexibility. Call about pricing and itineraries.

Perhaps the most fun and interesting way to see Victoria is inside a *pedicab* — a kind of small rickshaw propelled by a cycling "driver" in front of you — although it isn't cheap. These vehicles, operated by **Kabuki Kabs** (☎ **250-385-4243**; Internet: www.kabukikabs.com), are tiny, quick, and maneuverable. Expect to pay from C$60 to C$90 (US$40–US$60) per hour for a pedicab holding two to four people; shorter tours are certainly possible, charged at a rate of at least a dollar per minute. You can pick up a pedicab most easily in front of The Empress hotel — or just hail any empty one you see returning to the waterfront.

More expensive limousine tours are also possible through **Heritage Tours** (☎ **250-474-4332**), but once again these cost approximately

C$60 (US$40) per hour. One advantage of a limo rental, on the other hand, is that it holds up to six people at a time for the same price as the much smaller pedicab.

Going by other means

Victoria Harbour Ferries (☎ **250-708-0201**) also runs touring boats around the waterfront from late spring until early autumn. A tour up the inlet known as the Gorge costs C$12 (US$8) and takes 45 minutes. Inner Harbour tours cost C$12 (US$8) for adults and C$7 (US$4.69) for children, and you can jump on and off.

Finally, perhaps the most exhaustive (which is not to say exhausting) tour I found is the aptly named Grand Circle Tour offered by **Great Northwestern Adventure** (☎ **800-665-7374** or ☎ 250-480-7245) in Cowichan Bay. For about C$100 (US$67) per person, you get a ten-hour, all-day tour that uses everything from an excursion train to a British-style, double-decker bus to a sailboat. The surrounding parts of Vancouver Island are included, as is lunch. This is great fun!

Discovering Victoria for Anglophiles

This city is as English as they come in North America, and any stroll through town is bound to bring you past dozens of reminders of this. The following itinerary consists of sights that you can mix and match in whatever order you choose. No matter how you go about it, you're sure to have a jolly good time.

Your English day in Victoria must at some point pass through the doors of **The Empress hotel** (see "Exploring Victoria's Top Sights from A to Z," earlier in this chapter). This is a particularly good spot for refreshments. High tea costs C$29 (US$19) and basically includes a full meal of sweets, treats, finger sandwiches, plus, of course, a pot of tea. Or you can stop by in the evening — it gets no more colonial than a drink or an Indian meal in the **Bengal Lounge** (see Chapter 21).

If that's too rich for your blood, you can pop into the nearby **James Bay Tearoom,** an Anglo stronghold near the Inner Harbour (see Chapter 18). They serve high tea at a fraction of what you'd pay at The Empress, though it's probably even better as a lunchtime stop for some fish-"n-chips, Yorkshire pudding, or a glass of bitter.

If it's something stronger that you crave, the **Charles Dickens Pub,** not far from The Empress, has the look and the feel of a rather classy British taproom, with ale of course but fine whiskey, too (see Chapter 18).

Some 10 miles north of Vancouver, **Butchart Gardens** with its very English landscaping and flower collections is one must-see stop on this itinerary (see "Exploring Victoria's Top Sights from A to Z"). You can also enjoy high tea here, too, for C$18 (US$12) per person.

Victoria for Anglophiles

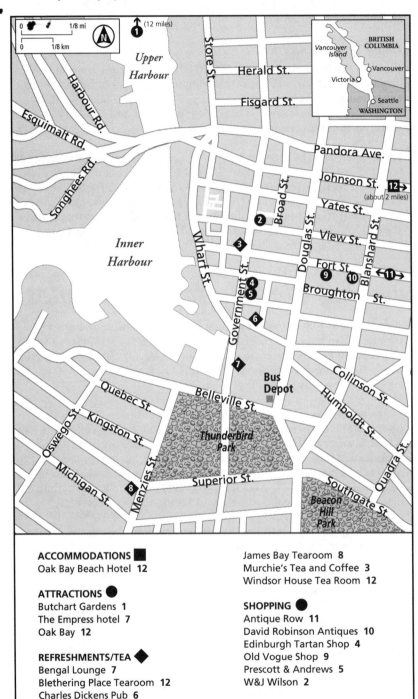

0 1/8 mi
0 1/8 km

(12 miles)

Upper Harbour

Store St.

Herald St.

Fisgard St.

Vancouver Island

BRITISH COLUMBIA

Vancouver

Victoria

Seattle

WASHINGTON

Harbour Rd.

Esquimalt Rd.

Songhees Rd.

Pandora Ave.

Johnson St. **12**→
(about 2 miles)

Broad St.

Yates St.

Douglas St.

View St.

Blanshard St.

Inner Harbour

Wharf St.

2

3

Fort St.

9 **10** ←**11**→

Government St.

4
5

Broughton St.

6

7

Bus Depot

Collinson St.

Humboldt St.

Quebec St.

Belleville St.

Kingston St.

Oswego St.

Thunderbird Park

Menzies St.

8

Michigan St.

Superior St.

Beacon Hill Park

Southgate St.

Quadra St.

ACCOMMODATIONS ■
Oak Bay Beach Hotel **12**

ATTRACTIONS ●
Butchart Gardens **1**
The Empress hotel **7**
Oak Bay **12**

REFRESHMENTS/TEA ◆
Bengal Lounge **7**
Blethering Place Tearoom **12**
Charles Dickens Pub **6**

James Bay Tearoom **8**
Murchie's Tea and Coffee **3**
Windsor House Tea Room **12**

SHOPPING ●
Antique Row **11**
David Robinson Antiques **10**
Edinburgh Tartan Shop **4**
Old Vogue Shop **9**
Prescott & Andrews **5**
W&J Wilson **2**

English-style shopping is easy to find, beginning right outside the door of The Empress on Government Street. Whether it's a kilt from the **Edinburgh Tartan Shop** or a Scottish sweater from **Prescott & Andrews** or **W&J Wilson,** you can't possibly go home empty-handed. **Murchie's Tea and Coffee** is a good pit stop for a snack, accompanied by something from the finest tea selection this side of the Atlantic. (See Chapter 20 for these stores.)

Other Anglo shops of note are along Fort Street, also known as **Antique Row.** Here you find plenty of English silver, porcelain, and furniture dating from the 18th and 19th centuries. **David Robinson Antiques** and the **Old Vogue Shop** are two of the best. (See Chapter 20 for these stores.)

Now it's time to really dive in — head for the area where the expat Brits have resettled. Take a #1 or #2 bus or an "Oak Bay Explorer" tour bus a few miles out to the **Oak Bay** neighborhood, Victoria's most English of all. Walking, riding, or driving along the main drag — simply called Oak Bay — you pass more than a half-dozen tea rooms and a number of bookshops, British importers, candy shops, and antique dealers as well, not to mention plenty of fine residential homes and gardens (which are off-limits to the public). You also find a long scenic beach and marina with fishing boats, yachts, seals, seagulls, and crashing waves — all, except the yachts, serving as additional reminders of Old England.

You can spend the better part of an afternoon here just wandering. Some of the high points include the **Blethering Place Tearoom,** where high tea costs from C$9 to C$12 (US$6–US$8), and the very authentic **Windsor House Tea Room** (Chapter 18). Captivated by the Anglo-feel, but stumped for ideas on where to spend the night? It's a splurge, sure, but the **Oak Bay Beach Hotel** makes a good one (see Chapter 17). Bentley's on the Bay, inside the hotel, also serves its own good tea.

 If you need a break during this tour, and you're a fan of English bitters, ales, and other beers — a good bet, given your card-carrying Anglophile status — swing by **Spinnakers Brewpub Restaurant,** the first brewpub in Canada, or **Swans Pub,** which specializes in British ales (see Chapter 21).

Chapter 20

A Shopper's Guide to Victoria

· ·

In This Chapter

▶ Getting to know the scene

▶ Visiting the big names

▶ Checking out the neighborhoods

· ·

*V*ictorians love to shop in any weather, and the handsome downtown buildings — once banks, warehouses, and offices — are now full of careful shopkeepers who ensure orderly stores. They also import a higher-than-usual level of quality goods, especially from the British Isles. Locals were cheered when Eaton's — an English-Canadian institution, their equivalent of, say, Macy's — emerged from bankruptcy proceedings and reopened a handful of stores across the country. One of them is here in Victoria.

Checking Out the Scene

In terms of specialties to look for in Victoria, the city is probably best known for two things — **English and Native Canadian goods.** Both are available, surprisingly, in more quantity and quality than in Vancouver, and often at bargain prices compared to elsewhere. Genuine Georgian pewter and similar British Empire antiques, not to mention tea sets, Aran sweaters, Celtic crests, kilts, shortbreads, and other Anglo items are very easy to find. You can score deals on many of these items if you look hard enough. Given the city's rather English bent, the availability of English goods is not unexpected. However, the strong selection of Native Canadian art and trade does come as a pleasant surprise. I'm always amazed by the number of native galleries and shops within a very small area of the downtown, and it's hard to visit any of them without taking home at least a little bit of native art, jewelry, clothing, or food. Some is very expensive, and some almost tacky, but for sheer concentration and choice this is *the* place to go.

Victoria Shopping

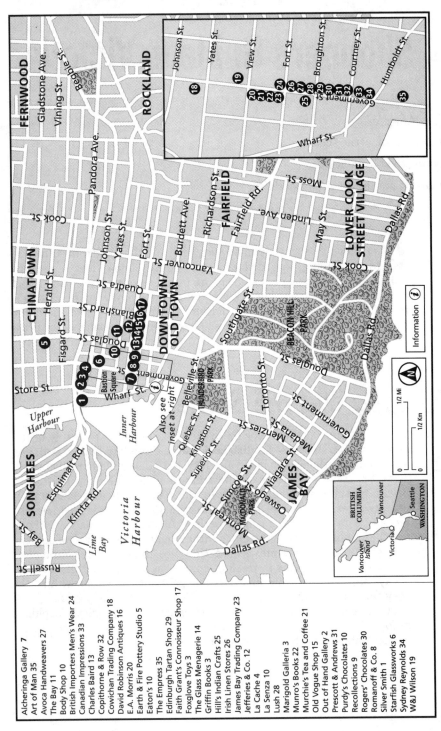

Alcheringa Gallery 7
Art of Man 35
Avoca Handweavers 27
The Bay 11
Body Shop 10
British Importers Men's Wear 24
Canadian Impressions 33
Charles Baird 13
Copithorne & Row 32
Cowichan Trading Company 18
David Robinson Antiques 16
E.A. Morris 20
Earth & Fire Pottery Studio 5
Eaton's 10
The Empress 35
Edinburgh Tartan Shop 29
Faith Grant's Connoisseur Shop 17
Foxglove Toys 3
The Glass Menagerie 14
Griffin Books 3
Hill's Indian Crafts 25
Irish Linen Stores 26
James Bay Trading Company 23
Jefferies & Co. 12
La Cache 4
La Senza 10
Lush 28
Marigold Galleria 3
Munro's Books 22
Murchie's Tea and Coffee 21
Old Vogue Shop 15
Out of Hand Gallery 2
Prescott & Andrews 31
Purdy's Chocolates 10
Recollections 9
Rogers' Chocolates 30
Romanoff & Co. 8
Silver Smith 1
Starfish Glassworks 6
Sydney Reynolds 34
W&J Wilson 19

The store hours in Canada are different from those in the United States. Victoria's stores usually open at 9 a.m. and close at 5 p.m. or 6 p.m. from Monday through Wednesday. On Thursdays and Fridays, however, they stay open much later than usual: until 9 p.m. Then, on Saturday, it's 9-to-5 again. Sunday is a short shopping day, with most stores opening at noon and closing at 5 p.m. (or even 4 p.m. in the case of smaller merchants).

Remember to keep careful track of whatever you buy in Canada. **U.S. Customs** regulations require an accounting of everything you bring home across the border, so keep those receipts and be honest when they question you. Assuming you stayed at least 2 days (and if you didn't, you probably don't own this book), your first US$400 of merchandise is duty-free. That includes 45 ounces (a little more than a liter) of alcohol. After you pass that magic US$400 mark, however, you have to pay a small tax — calculated as a percentage of what you spent (converted into U.S. dollars, of course).

If you stay in Canada less than 48 hours, your duty-free limit drops to US$200 per person.

And don't forget about **taxes.** You pay a surcharge totaling 14% for the privilege of shopping in Canada. For more information on taxes and how to receive a General Sales Tax refund, totaling half that 14%, see Chapter 3.

Shopping the Big Names

Victoria is a relatively small city, and as such the really "Big Name" department stores (Macy's, Bloomingdale's, and the like) simply don't exist here. For those, try Vancouver — or, actually, Seattle. But you can still find all the usual department-store offerings at two longtime Canadian institutions.

Eaton's, 1150 Douglas Street (☎ **250-382-7141**), in Eaton Centre (see its description later in the chapter), was a Canadian fixture from its founding until it closed its doors in 1999. New owners stepped in, however, and Victoria's Eaton's has just reopened. It's nothing spectacular, more a sentimental favorite with Canadians now, but certainly adequate as downtown department stores go.

The Bay, 1701 Douglas Street, Downtown/Old Town (☎ **250-385-1311;** Internet: www.thebay.ca), is the new, hipper name for what used to be known as the fur-trading Hudson's Bay Company. No longer a place of beaver pelts and rabbit furs, today it merely carries the same upscale fashions, housewares, perfumes, and the like that you would expect at any quality department store. But you do find some unique Canadian-heritage items such as wool blankets.

Strolling the Best Shopping Neighborhoods

There are three or four areas where you can concentrate your Victoria shopping, and — happily — all of 'em are within a short walk of the ferry docks on the Inner Harbour.

For ease of organization in this compact city, I describe the shopping options by region or street. If you're in search of a particular specialty item, see the index at the end of this chapter. The first shopping stop (The Empress hotel complex) sits right on the harbor. The next four shopping areas (Government Street, Antique Row, Yates/Douglas, and Market Square) may seem geographically separate but they're actually all close to one another, and all are considered to be in Victoria's Old Town; I'm separating them here because each has a unique character. Chinatown, the last area, is attached to Old Town but everyone treats it as a separate and distinct area, and I do the same. Finally, I touch briefly on Oak Bay, an upscale residential area located a few miles from the harbor on Dallas Road.

Inner Harbour

You can't go wrong by starting right at Victoria's harbor, inside a hotel that's so interesting that it also qualifies as one of the city's best sights (see Chapter 19). Why not double your efficiency by doing two things at once?

The Empress hotel complex, 721 Government Street (☎ **800-441-1414** or 250-384-8111), offers several floors of displays and shopping spread throughout the hotel. You find expensive chocolate, clothing, porcelains, and much more; the real star is the **Art of Man** (☎ **250-383-3800**), a Native Canadian art gallery, with carvings, paintings, and masks, among other items.

Connected to The Empress by a passageway, the Victoria Convention Centre maintains its own distinctive shopping galleries as well as an art gallery.

Government Street

The first main shopping area you come to off the harbor runs along Government Street, a red-bricked road that runs from The Empress hotel to Chinatown and beyond. Here you find a mixture of touristy shops stocking knickknacks and truly fine goods, including one of western Canada's best bookstores; a little weeding out is necessary, and I show you where to look.

This street is one of the two best (also see "Antique Row," later in this section) in North America to find anything British, Scottish, or Irish you could ever want without actually buying a ticket to those fair islands. One of the best of these is **Sydney Reynolds,** 801 Government Street (☎ **250-383-3931**), an elegant yet whimsical shop selling wonderful china, British tea sets, porcelains, dolls, and more from the Isles. For Scottish clothing, the **Edinburgh Tartan Shop,** 921 Government Street (☎ **250-953-7790**), stocks just what you'd expect — Scottish kilts, tartans, clan crests, and more — as does nearby **Prescott & Andrews,** 909 Government Street (☎ **250-953-7788**), which is strong on woolens.

Ireland is well-represented, too, by classy **Avoca Handweavers,** 1009 Government Street (☎ **250-383-0433**), which offers genuine Irish sweaters, jewelry, capes, and tweed coats, plus a section of Irish books as well; **Irish Linen Stores,** 1019 Government Street (☎ **250-383-6812**), a longstanding shop selling fine Irish laces, sweaters, bowties, and more; and **W&J Wilson,** 1221 Government Street (☎ **250-383-7177**), an excellent men's clothing store carrying sweaters from Scotland and Ireland plus other European imports. Finally, **Copithorne & Row,** 901 Government Street (☎ **250-384-1722**), is one of the city's top china and crystal shops.

Intermingling with this Anglo overload, is an almost overwhelming concentration of Native Canadian shops along the same stretch of Government Street — ironic, isn't it? The most popular such shops offer a mixture of cheap souvenirs and pricier but authentic marks, carving, jewelry, and more; you need to weed through the tawdry to get to the good stuff. These shops include the **Cowichan Trading Company,** 1328 Government Street (☎ **250-383-0321**), and **Hill's Indian Crafts,** 1008 Government Street (☎ **250-385-3911**), a spot for truly inspiring native art (everything from kayak paddles to drums) from British Columbia's coastal peoples with an emphasis on quality.

Another good trading company that carries quality Canadian goods is **Canadian Impressions,** 811 Government Street (☎ **250-383-2641**), which is strong on such Canadiana as native carvings, woolens, and packed salmon, plus it stocks a good selection of imported goods from the British Isles as well.

Also worth a visit is **British Importers Men's Wear,** 1125 Government Street (☎ **250-386-1496**), with its continental imports of the highest quality in an exceptionally stylish showroom; think Armani suits and you have the picture. This is *the* place to buy fine men's clothing in Victoria.

Some of the other unusual and interesting shops you find along this stretch of Government include the old, old **James Bay Trading Company,** 1102 Government Street (☎ **250-388-5477**), which stocks Canadian items such as native crafts and foods and thick Maritime wool sweaters; **Earth & Fire Pottery Studio,** 1820 Government Street (☎ 250-380-7227), a working studio where you can watch the ocean-themed pots being thrown, fired, and glazed right on site; **Rogers' Chocolates,** 913 Government Street (☎ 800-663-2220 or 250-384-7021), a wonderful old-candy shop which hand-concocts delicious cream-filled chocolates so good the Queen of England has ordered them; **Lush,** 1001 Government Street (☎ 250-384-5874), an all-natural cosmetics company based in Vancouver that sells bath soaps and other wholesome (and handmade) personal care products in bulk; **E.A. Morris,** 1116 Government Street (☎ 250-382-4811), the place to pick up hand-rolled cigars and pipe tobacco.

Finally, I'd be remiss if I didn't mention **Munro's Books,** 1108 Government Street (☎ 250-382-2464). Housed in a handsome old structure, packed with books amid elegant furnishings, this shop is perhaps the province's best locally owned bookstore. The selection is strong on local history, but offers plenty of everything else too. And the staff is incredibly knowledgeable. After a browse, head next door to **Murchie's Tea and Coffee,** 1110 Government Street (☎ 250-383-3112) for wonderful teas and coffees from around the world.

Two complexes just off Government Street also deserve a visit, because you're in the area. Between Fort and View Streets (it can also be reached from Douglas Street), you find the **Eaton Centre** (☎ 250-382-7141). This modern shopping gallery — a four-story building with a central atrium and giant clock telling the time around the world — is anchored by the newly revived **Eaton's** (see "Shopping the Big Names," earlier in the chapter). But it also includes other merchants such as the **Body Shop,** the **La Senza** lingerie chain, locally made **Purdy's Chocolates** (☎ 250-361-1024) and a host of other leather, gift, and apparel shops — everything you'd expect in an upscale gallery. Eaton Centre is open daily from 9 a.m. to 9 p.m.

Also just off Government Street is **Trounce Alley,** Victoria's former red-light district (although it's hard to believe now, given the current look of the area). The short alley now holds all sorts of little stalls and shops, plus a few eateries too.

Antique Row (Fort Street)

Victoria's Antique Row is a sterling — pardon the pun — place to shop for antiques, especially those of British origin such as porcelains, estate jewelry, and top-quality silver. It stretches about 3 blocks east along Fort Street. To get here, walk due east from the Eaton Centre's south side along Fort Street two blocks until you reach Blanshard; this is where the district begins.

There are so many choices here, one hardly knows where to begin. It's probably best to just wander at your leisure, popping in whenever a shop strikes your fancy.

Charles Baird, 1044A Fort Street (☎ 250-384-8809), runs a skinny but well-stocked shop of antique furniture and good humor; **The Glass Menagerie,** 1036 Fort Street (☎ 250-475-2228), carefully shelves a huge array of collectible plates, plus china, and pottery; **Jefferies & Co.,** 1026 Fort Street (☎ 250-383-8315), is the city's top silver shop, with everything you could want in fine silversmithing; **Romanoff & Co.,** 837 Fort Street (☎ 250-480-1543), run by a proprietor who comes from a family of dealers, is stronger in coins and jewelry than most; **David Robinson Antiques,** 1023 Fort Street (☎ 250-384-6425), deals classy (and pricey) furniture, silver, rugs, and other fine antiques; and the **Old Vogue Shop,** 1034 Fort Street (☎ 250-380-7751), is a good generalist's antique shop of china, pottery, and a hodgepodge of other items.

Two more must-sees located along Fort Street but outside Antique Row are the **Alcheringa Gallery,** 665 Fort Street (☎ 250-383-8224), which features the work of many native peoples from the world over — all of superior quality and expensive — and **Faith Grant's Connoisseur Shop,** 1156 Fort Street (☎ 250-383-0121), which is wonderfully stocked with antique furniture. Finally, don't miss **Recollections,** 817A Fort Street (☎ 250-385-1902), a sort of upscale flea market compressing together a mishmash of dealers and styles.

Yates and Douglas area

One of the largest shopping areas stretches north-south along big Douglas Street and east-west along the cross street called Yates; so many restaurants, bars, and shops are packed into this area (which also includes a few other side streets such as Broughton and Johnson) that you could easily spend hours here.

Perhaps the most intriguing of these stores is **Starfish Glassworks,** 630 Yates Street (☎ 250-388-7827), located in a former bank now containing its own kiln — you can watch them firing from an interesting viewpoint — and terrific pots and glassware. (Note that they only blow glass during the afternoon, and not at all on Mondays or Tuesdays.)

Market Square

Market Square, a former warehouse and shipping-goods complex at 560 Johnson Street near the Esquimalt Bridge and Chinatown, is today one of the city's most interesting little shopping complexes. When it was legal, opium was once manufactured here; today many of the several dozen shops offer eclectic choices. (Two examples: an all-dog treats shop and a hilarious yet tasteful, er, condom shop.) Plus the central courtyard area often hosts music and other arts performances in summer. **Marigold Galleria** (☎ 250-386-5339), which sells ceramics and glasswork; **Foxglove Toys** (☎ 250-383-8852); and **Griffin Books**

(☎ 250-383-0633) are three good examples of the more conventional stores in the complex. You can eat anything from wholesome vegetarian meals to more typical fast-food fare at food stalls.

Outside the Market Square building but close by, **Silver Smith,** 360 Johnson Street (☎ 250-383-7979), is Victoria's other good silver shop; **Out of Hand Gallery,** 566 Johnson Street (☎ 250-384-5221), purveys interesting hand-crafted home furnishings and art from mostly regional artists; and if for some reason you're hankering for Paris instead of London, **La Cache,** 562 Johnson Street (☎ 250-384-6343), offers Francophiles linens, clothing, and the like.

Index of Stores by Merchandise

Art and antiques

Alcheringa Gallery (Antique Row)
Charles Baird (Antique Row)
David Robinson Antiques (Antique Row)
Faith Grant's Connoisseur Shop
   (Antique Row)
The Glass Menagerie (Antique Row)
Jefferies & Co. (Antique Row)
Old Vogue Shop (Antique Row)
Recollections (Antique Row)
Romanoff & Co. (Antique Row)

Arts and crafts

Earth & Fire Pottery Studio (Government
   Street)
Out of Hand Gallery (Market)
Starfish Glassworks (Yates and Douglas
   area)

Books

Griffin Books (Market Square)
Munro's Books (Government Street)

British and Irish goods

Avoca Handweavers (Government Street)
Edinburgh Tartan Shop (Government
   Street)
Irish Linen Stores (Government Street)
Prescott & Andrews (Government Street)

Canadian specialties

Canadian Impressions (Government
   Street)
James Bay Trading Company
   (Government Street)

Candy

Purdy's Chocolates (Government Street)
Rogers' Chocolates (Government Street)

China and glassware

Copithorne & Row (Government Street)
Marigold Galleria (Market Square)
Sydney Reynolds (Government Street)

Clothing and lingerie

British Importers Men's Wear
   (Government Street)
La Cache (Market)
La Senza (Government Street)
W&J Wilson (Government Street)

Cosmetics

Body Shop (Government Street)
Lush (Government Street)

Department stores

Eaton's (Government Street)
The Bay (Downtown/Old Town)

Food
Murchie's Tea and Coffee (Government
  Street)

Jewelry
Silver Smith (Market)

Malls
The Empress (Inner Harbour)

Native Canadian items
Art of Man (Inner Harbour)
Cowichan Trading Company (Government
  Streets)
Hill's Indian Crafts (Government Streets)

Tobacco
E.A. Morris (Government Streets)

Toys
Foxglove Toys (Market Square)

Chapter 21

Living It Up after the Sun Goes Down: Victoria Nightlife

In This Chapter

▶ Getting the beat on the music scene

▶ Swinging through the clubs and bars

▶ Stopping by the performing arts venues

*A*t first glance, the chief enjoyments around here would seem to be on the stodgy side — classical music, opera, theater . . . stuff like that. And it's true. Live music probably plays second fiddle here to tunes written back in the Renaissance.

Nevertheless, Victoria does actually let its hair down at night. You find a thriving folk and jazz scene, for example, and more dance clubs in the downtown area than you would ever believe possible after walking the prim streets of the city by day. Hate music but like beer? Ah, but you're in luck. The microbreweries here are world-class; there may be no finer place in the hemisphere to do a mini-tour of local brewers while having so much fun. The pubs aren't bad, either, and there are even a few cocktail bars of some renown.

All the listings in this chapter are concentrated within a small area, close to the Inner Harbor or the Old Town. For convenience, I divide the listings into those clubs and bars where music is the primary draw and those spots where beer, cocktails, and socializing are the reason to go. I follow these with my top recommendations for where to enjoy the performing arts, including theater, opera, and classical music venues.

The envelope, please . . .

Victoria Nightlife

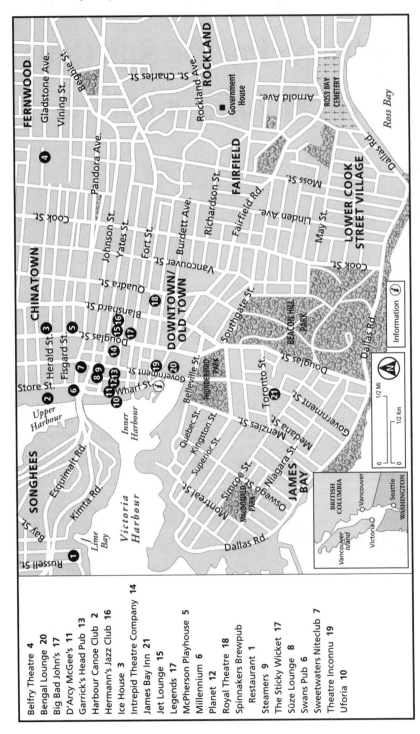

Belfry Theatre **4**
Bengal Lounge **20**
Big Bad John's **17**
D'Arcy McGee's **11**
Garrick's Head Pub **13**
Harbour Canoe Club **2**
Hermann's Jazz Club **16**
Ice House **3**
Intrepid Theatre Company **14**
James Bay Inn **21**
Jet Lounge **15**
Legends **17**
McPherson Playhouse **5**
Millennium **6**
Planet **12**
Royal Theatre **18**
Spinnakers Brewpub Restaurant **1**
Steamers **9**
The Sticky Wicket **17**
Süze Lounge **8**
Swans Pub **6**
Sweetwaters Niteclub **7**
Theatre Inconnu **19**
Uforia **10**

Getting the Beat on the Music Scene

To find out who's playing where, check the weekly newspaper **Monday Magazine** (Internet: www.monday.com), the best source for entertainment listings. The local daily paper **The Times-Colonist** is also good, although it doesn't have a Web site. Another option is to call the **Community Arts Council of Greater Victoria** (☎ 250-381-2787).

Some clubs in town charge a variable cover fee to see live music performances, and the hipper dance clubs also require a C$5 to C$10 (US$3.35–US$7) cover charge to gain entrance — although women are often exempt from this.

The best folk, jazz, and blues clubs

As befits its strongly English heritage, this town loves a good sad folk tune strummed away on something stringy. The undisputed event of the year for folkies is **Folkfest** (☎ 250-388-4728), each June in Centennial Square; a disproportionate number of the English- and Irish-themed pubs also offer live music, usually on weekends but sometimes during the week as well.

Surprisingly, Victorians also really like their jazz. The biggest musical soirees of the summer season are probably the oddly named **TerrifVic Jazz Party** (☎ 250-953-2011), an annual collection of performances at the end of April, and the very experimental **International Jazz Fest** (☎ 250-388-4423), which includes more than just jazz and begins in late June. As if that weren't enough, a third jazz-oriented festival called **Sunfest** (☎ 250-953-2033) wraps up the summer in late August.

The local Jazz Society operates a recorded hotline (☎ 250-388-4423) to keep abreast of all local performances.

Here are some of the hotspots for blues and jazz music:

- **Hermann's Jazz Club,** 753 View Street, Downtown/Old Town (☎ 250-388-9166), costs more than a hole-in-the-wall joint, because you have to buy dinner, but the music comes free and it's always good. You sometimes hear other kinds of music here, but it's mainly jazz. Closed Sundays.

- **Swans Pub,** 506 Pandora Street, Downtown/Old Town (☎ 250-361-3310), a top-notch microbrewery with an amazing art collection, offers the added attraction of good rootsy musical performances on an ongoing basis. Among the top drafts is a dynamite Bavarian-style beer. Don't forget to catch some jazz in the basement night-club or to try the superb restaurant food. Finally, if you're just too full of beer to move along, the operation has a top-flight guest-house (see Chapter 17).

✔ **Steamers,** 570 Yates Street, Downtown/Old Town (☎ **250-381-4340**) is undergoing a somewhat surprising renaissance as a top-flight blues club (it was once a strip club). The visiting acts pack more talent than you'd expect to find in Victoria.

The best spots to shake your groove thing

Now this is a real surprise: Young folks, dressed like they just got off planes from London or Milan, shaking their butts to house music? Gawd! Surely this can't be Victoria? What would the Queen Mother think? But, yes, it is and they do. Some of the trendy dance clubs of the moment include

✔ **Millennium,** 506 Pandora Street, Downtown/Old Town (☎ **250-360-9098**), hidden beneath the main floor of the Swans brewpub, was once a jazz club but now has found success with blander dance fare, plus occasional peppier live bands. The crowd is far from young. Closed Monday through Wednesday.

✔ **Ice House,** 1961 Douglas Street, Downtown/Old Town (☎ **250-382-2111**), tucked within the otherwise sedate Horizon West Hotel, rocks with plenty of trippy house music. You'll be amazed that such cool kids live in this town.

✔ **Jet Lounge,** 751 View Street, Downtown/Old Town (☎ **250-920-7797**), is one of the few very places where Victoria flaunts its wealth. It's a very young, very hip crowd and you will no doubt be made to feel at least a little out of place.

✔ **Sweetwaters Niteclub,** 560 Johnson Street, Downtown/Old Town (☎ **250-383-7844**), is a fancy and fun place to hang if you're unattached and looking to boogie with similarly unattached locals. There's nothing spectacular about the music, though. Closed Sundays and Mondays.

✔ **Uforia,** 1208 Wharf Street, Downtown/Old Town (☎ **250-381-2331**), beckons you to dance the night away like the '80s never left. Whatever's popular is what's gonna be playing in this club near the water. Don't expect the latest experimental trip-hop master to blow in; it ain't that kind of place. You're here to bow down to the pop music charts, past and present.

The best spots for rockin' the night away

Victoria isn't really a hard-rocker's kind of town, although pockets of long-haired guys belting out Loverboy covers — wait a minute, that actually was Loverboy — can be found in the 'burbs. If you really crave ear-splitting noise, go to Vancouver instead. Stuck here? Try these places for size:

- ✔ **Legends,** 919 Douglas Street, Old Town/Downtown (☎ 250-383-7137), once a slightly grotty and overly loud palace of Goth, has rounded out its tastes and now offers something for everyone in the basement floor of the huge Strathcona Hotel.

- ✔ **Planet,** 15 Bastion Square, Old Town/Downtown (☎ 250-385-5333), is really a catch-all venue, so you won't necessarily catch loud rawk music here. It can be anything else from dance music spun by house DJs to the blues, too.

Visiting the Watering Holes

You can find many fine spots to quench your thirst in Victoria, especially if you're in search of a cold brew. What follows are my favorite spots in a few different categories.

English and Irish pubs

This is no surprise at all: Pubs are thick on the ground in Victoria. Some of them are authentically Anglo or Celtic and others, well, basically consist of a veneer of Irishness (say a few Harp posters and pictures of the Emerald Isle) pasted over watered-down, pricey drinks. Those places are for tourists. Head for one of *these* places, instead:

- ✔ **D'Arcy McGee's,** 1127 Wharf Street, Old Town/Bastion Square (☎ 250-380-1322), awaits with pints of Irish beer and traditional Celtic music.

- ✔ **Garrick's Head Pub,** 69 Bastion Square, Old Town/Bastion Square (☎ 250-384-6835), in the Bedford Regency Hotel, is a pleasant place to get away from the *faux*-British pubs elsewhere around town. The food is authentically Brit, and the beer is darned good.

- ✔ **James Bay Inn,** 270 Government Street, Downtown (☎ 250-384-7151), yet another British pub, is attached to a decent hotel and quietly goes about the business of pulling good pints and maintaining a reasonably low profile.

- ✔ **The Sticky Wicket,** 919 Douglas Street, Old Town/Downtown (☎ 250-383-7137), is one of many bars inside the Strathcona Hotel. Transplanted — and I mean piece by piece — from Ireland, it really scores with its basement-pub ambience.

Outstanding brewpubs

This is why you came to Victoria: To sip a tall cold one, marveling at the skill of the master brewer, while warming up your darts hand and looking out over the harbor.

Any of the following three brewpubs would top any "best-of" list in another city, but because they're all in Victoria I stay out of that debate:

✔ **Harbour Canoe Club,** 450 Swift Street, Old Town/Downtown (☎ 250-361-1940), wasn't the first microbrewery in town but it's one of the best. Live music, a pleasant atmosphere, and good — make that great — snacks make you want to stay as long as you can.

✔ **Spinnakers Brewpub,** 308 Catherine Street, Esquimalt/Songhees (☎ 250-386-2739), is it: The very first brewpub in Canada, and one that continues to amaze with what are now dozens of home brews — almost every one of them delicious. That's to say nothing of the tremendous water views, first-rate inn attached to the premises (see Chapter 17), or the active dart games. This is probably the most fun you can have in one place in town, and it's even walking distance — just — from the Old Town. Head across the Esquimalt Bridge to get here.

✔ **Swans Pub,** 506 Pandora Avenue, Old Town/Downtown (☎ 250-361-3310), is as fun as Spinnakers; it's almost as if the two have a happy rivalry to be the best at everything. Well, let's call it a tie. Terrific beers, a happy crowd, amazingly intriguing wall art, music downstairs, and plenty of different spaces and moods in which to relax all add up to a must-drink kind of place. Hard to believe this was once a warehouse.

Neighborhood bars

Sorry, although plenty of pubs and bars are tucked in outlying neighborhoods, Victoria has only one neighborhood bar that must be visited. And, although it's in a very good neighborhood, it sure acts like it's in Seed Central:

Big Bad John's, 919 Douglas Street, Old Town/Downtown (☎ 250-383-7137), another bar in the big Strathcona Hotel, attracts a lowbrow clientele. *Really* lowbrow — you may hear country music. A no-nonsense decor, wisecracking bartenders, and refreshingly unstarched ambience combine to make this the rowdiest place for miles around.

Chic bars and lounges

The Bengal Lounge, quite simply, is *the* place to sip a cocktail when in Victoria. Other lounges exist, but none can compare to this one.

✔ **Bengal Lounge,** 721 Government Street, Inner Harbour (☎ 250-384-8111), inside The Empress hotel, simply must be seen to be believed. Basically, you haven't been to the real Victoria until you've sipped a mixed drink here in an atmosphere of dark wood and lush plants designed to conjure up the British Empire's heyday in India. (They also serve meals spiced with Indian curry if you're hungry.) The exotic tiger pelt is either incredibly bad taste or incredibly cool, depending on your view of animal rights, but you can't deny that this is one the holdouts of the city's colonial past.

✔ **Süze Lounge,** 515 Yates Street, Downtown/Old Town (☎ 250-383-2829), may not be welcoming — you have to be "somebody," or at least dress like one, to feel at home here — but if you're not intimidated by the crowd, it's a fine place for a drink. The adjacent restaurant is pretty good too.

Enjoying the Performing Arts

Victoria's arts patrons are vigorous enough to have created a pretty solid network of events despite the small size of their city. For example, the annual **Victoria International Festival** brings a whole bunch of different forms together from mid-July through mid-August. Tickets cost C$10 to C$25 (US$7–$US17) per show, or you can save and buy a pass for the entire 5-week series if you're really making a long visit to the city. Call **Tourism Victoria** (☎ 250-953-2033) for schedule, ticket, and venue information. Even if you don't make it to town for the festival, several opera and theater companies, a small orchestra, and plenty of other diversions can provide you with an arts fix while you're here.

To get the skinny on what's happening consult the free weekly *Monday Magazine,* or else call the **Community Arts Council** (☎ 250-381-2787). You can access calendars on the Internet, too, at www.monday.com or www.victoriatourism.com.

Tickets for events are usually most easily purchased from the city's tourism center at 812 Wharf Street (☎ 800-663-3883 or 250-382-2127). The same helpful folks can also provide you with events calendars and lots of other information about the arts.

Calling all thespians: Victoria's theater scene

You may expect the decidedly Shakespearean bent you find here, but experimental companies remain strong, too, and you don't need to spend megabucks to enjoy local theater as you do in nearby Seattle or Vancouver.

Don't miss the **Victoria Fringe Festival** (☎ 888-374-6432 or 250-383-2663), a series of performances around town that runs from spring until just after Labor Day, or the **Shakespeare Festival** — no surprise there — at St. Ann's Academy on Humboldt Street during August. Tickets for both events are cheap.

Hereforth, a few of the city's top theater companies:

- ✔ The **Belfry Theatre,** 1291 Gladstone Avenue, Fernwood (☎ 250-385-6815), in a renovated church, is reason enough to come to town if you like small, local companies. Try to call ahead, as these performances are wildly popular with locals and Vancouverites alike. Tickets usually cost from C$15 to C$25 (US$10–US$17) per person.

- ✔ **Intrepid Theatre Company,** 1205 Broad Street (☎ 250-383-2663), also runs an interesting theater. Tickets tend to cost very little, perhaps C$12 (US$8) per person.

- ✔ **Theatre Inconnu** (☎ 250-380-1284) is edgier and smaller than the other theaters mentioned here. Tickets runs just C$10 per show.

Locating high art: Opera, dance, and classical music

The city is well supplied with opera and classical offerings. However, there's more variety than you may think — and nothing stodgy about it.

The **Victoria Symphony Orchestra** (☎ 250-385-9771) performs a free waterside show called Symphony Splash from a stage floating on the Inner Harbour. The orchestra follows this event, which takes place on the first Sunday of August, with a full season of orchestral performances at the **Royal Theatre** at 805 Broughton Street, Old Town/Downtown (☎ 250-381-0820 for schedules or 250-386-6121 for tickets). What the orchestra lacks in size, it makes up for in talent — and famous guests occasionally drop by. As orchestra prices go, tickets are amazing low, usually no more than C$15 to C$30 (US$10–US$20).

The **Pacific Opera Victoria** (☎ 250-385-0222) sings at the **McPherson Theatre,** 3 Centennial Square (☎ 250-386-6121), an overwrought house from the early 20th century. The season comprises three different works, each presented about half a dozen times; you may hear classical or an operetta. Either way, ticket prices vary wildly — anywhere from C$20 to C$80 (US$13–US$54) per person — so check carefully before whipping out the credit card.

The smaller **Victoria Operatic Society** (☎ 250-381-1021) isn't so much opera as musical theater, and tends to perform extremely well-known works, probably those you sang back in high school. Performances are held at the McPherson Theatre. Tickets cost from C$12 to C$20 (US$8–US$13).

Part V
The Part of Tens

WHALE WATCHING IN VANCOUVER

@RICHTENNANT

WHALE WATCH CAFE

"Would you like to watch the whale a little longer, sir, or should I ask him to leave?"

In this part . . .

In this part I get to have a little fun. I let you know a bit more about the characters of the two cities by telling you what you can't live without here. Although you may think twice about some of my suggestions — okay, so you're not sure about that tattoo — you also find some real advice: An umbrella *is* a must. Finally, I wrap up the section with a rundown on some of the surprisingly famous folks who hail from here.

Chapter 22

Ten Things You *Can't* Live Without in Vancouver

*O*kay, you're ready to go to Vancouver. You're psyched. You've put the mail on hold, the cat food in the dish, the car in the garage. All that's left to do now is go, right? Not necessarily. Before you close the front door for the final time, make a last-minute check of that suitcase: Do you *really* have everything you'll need? Not sure? Read on as I give you an insider's look at how to fit in, deflect raindrops, and otherwise equip yourself for the getaway of a lifetime.

Umbrella

After a few days in the city, this need will become extremely self-explanatory. Although summers are generally bright and (relatively) dry, any walk out of doors the rest of the year is a potentially rainy one — think London and you get the idea. Actor David Duchovny from the X-Files television program famously remarked that it rains "400 inches a day" in Vancouver, a snarky remark that quickly transformed him from a local icon to *persona non grata* around here; that was a little off-base, but you get the idea. Why do you think it's so green, anyway? You want a tan, go to the south of France instead.

Don't trust the weather reports, either, unless they call for days of high pressure. Just because it isn't raining now doesn't mean it *won't* be in 5 minutes. I don't mean a buckets-full, get-the-sandbags-and-head-for-the-levee kind of rain. No, Vancouver's rain is special. Imagine a fine mist, building itself up to an annoying drizzle and then, occasionally, spatterings of large drops. The kind that gets inside of your shirtsleeves — and, after awhile, your psyche.

Bring an umbrella.

Coffee Cup

Have you ever seen people drink so much coffee? No, you haven't (except down the road in Seattle). In Vienna, they sit for hours over a single cup. That's because they're in Vienna. Here, coffee is consumed as frequently as possible, in a wide variety of ways — iced, frozen, lattéd, mélanged, espressoed, double decaf capped — whatever you want, really. Organic, shade-grown, handpicked by Ecuadorians? Yep, Vancouver's got that. Hawaiian? Arabica? No sweat. Soy milk instead of cream, organic raw turbinado sugar on the side? Come on, that's an easy one. (About the only thing you won't find here is instant coffee.) All mainlined directly into the veins, if possible.

To get your fill, pop into any of the dozens of local coffeehouses or, of course, the "cozy" little branches of those monster coffee chains whose names I won't mention here for fear of giving them the free publicity they so richly do not deserve. Suffice to say that they've taken over the place. (One busy downtown corner even has *two* They-Shall-Remain-Nameless coffee shops facing off against each other across the traffic lights; both are always full. At last report no price war has broken out between them.)

Ring/Stud/Tattoo

Actually, I'm going easy on you here. The true Vancouver slacker has at least one tongue, nose, or possibly another hidden body part pierced with a ring or stud. I'm giving you the tattoo as an out. For temporary cool, try a henna tattoo; they wash off.

Hiking Shoes

Very few cities in the world can boast that they're positioned at the base of a spectacular mountain range, *and* contain miles of beach within the city limits, *and* are a ferry ride away from even greener islands. But Vancouver can. And if you visit for more than a couple days, you owe it to yourself to live like the locals.

If you're in excellent shape, you should make a point of heading on over to Grouse Mountain (the one with the ski lift that's lit up at night, which seems to hover right over the city) and walk right up the side of it. It will take you about an hour if you're super-fit . . . a lot longer if you're not. That's too much? Okay, fine. Take the cable car up and walk back down — though that may hurt even more. Still too tough? Fine. Just walk the hilly parks, streets, and beaches of the West Side. And, of course, don't forget the hiking shoes.

Chopsticks

Vancouver has an amazing proliferation of Asian food, due no doubt to the city's westward-facing position on the Pacific Rim. But in recent years it seems to have become even more pervasive. A virtual tidal wave of Japanese eateries has hit, adding to an arsenal of Chinese places that may be second to none in North America.

Chopsticks: Get 'em, and learn how to use 'em.

Jeans

This has to be one of the all-time casual-dressing towns. Of course, if you're dining at a place like, say, Diva at the Met, you'll want (and need) to break out the fancy duds. But in most other situations, jeans and a designer t-shirt — or a tie-dye, let's face it — will get you by just fine.

And those jeans will come in mighty handy for the dirty work of climbing onto and off of ferries, bellying up to the bar for a pint, or poking around in the gardens and parks.

Bike

Vancouver is an extremely bike-friendly town, in theory, although in practice the combination of lots of cars, high bridges, and wet roads doesn't always mean the biking is actually fun. Think about it, though — would you rather drive to and around Stanley Park, or bike there? That's a no-brainer. And, as a huge bonus, you can bring your bike onto the BC Ferries, then use it to get around the islands at little financial — and no environmental — cost. Some hardbodies even bike up the side of Grouse Mountain, though I'm not ready to suggest that.

Sweater

Did I mention the weather? Summer nights are unlikely to ever get hot, and with a fresh sea breeze blowing they can even be a bit chilly. That's when it's dry out. When it's wet, the temperature always feels colder than it is (even though Vancouver doesn't get a hard freeze in winter). So carry along a sweater no matter what time of year you choose to visit.

Organic Cotton/Hemp Mesh Bag

If you really want to live like a local, you must check out the city's markets at least once. Begin at Granville Market, just off the main peninsula, and stuff that eco-correct bag with all the fruits and veggies you can fit in there. Another time, take the bus out to Broadway and find a little Asian food market — then go wild. This is probably the best place on the continent to locate authentic, made-in-the-East bonito flakes, tofu, ginseng royal jelly, and all the rest, not to mention plenty of spices, nuts, and snacking materials in bulk.

Frisbee

So many parks are here that it would be a shame to neglect them. So don't. Get yourself out to Wreck or Kitsilano Beach, borrow a local dog, and go nuts with the flying disc.

Chapter 23

Ten Things You *Can't* Live Without in Victoria

Sure, you can be a tourist in Victoria, but why not try to blend in a little? All you need are a few props — and a little attitude adjustment.

Teacup

No place in North America is as English as Victoria, and tea is an integral part of locals' wanna-be ritual. Whether you're taking morning tea, afternoon tea, or high ("with-the-works") tea, you need something to put it in, right?

Malt Vinegar Shaker

All this English heritage also means you can find a surprising number of fish-and-chips (er, fish-and-French-fry) shops here. But the English don't slather tartar sauce all over their fish, and ketchup all over their chips. No, they use the one thing they always have plenty of — malted vinegar — on both.

Beer Stein

As you may guess if you read the rest of this book, this town is loaded down with better-than-average brewpubs. So be like a Boy Scout — prepared.

Golf Clubs

Vancouver Island contains some downright terrific golf courses in beautiful terrain, and whether you bring your own bag of sticks or rent 'em on the spot, any golfer will want to take advantage.

Camera or Camcorder

You rarely get a chance to film such nice scenery (maybe some whales or sales on the ferry over from Vancouver), fine architecture (hello, The Empress and Parliament Buildings), and cheesy gotta-show-the-family-later tourist sights (all those English pubs and double-decker buses) in one concentrated place while still in North America. Take full advantage.

Allergy Medication

Hey, they call this the city of roses, right? And for good reason — everybody and their cousin has a garden, in a climate in which flowers can bloom 12 months out of the year. And *that* means lots and lots of pollen at odd times. Come prepared if this affects you.

Boat Shoes

Chances are pretty good that, at some point, you'll clamber onto a boat, perhaps a big Vancouver ferry, a smaller island ferry, or a whale-watching expedition boat. But bring waterproof shoes, for goodness' sake. You don't want to know what saltwater can do to fine shoes.

Cricket Wicket

Nah, just kiddin'. You'll be surprised, though, how often this English thing keeps repeating itself in Victoria. A little cricket "pitch" (playing field) is in Beacon Hill Park, and who knows? Hang around long enough and some polite someone may actually volunteer to teach you the rules — after carefully explaining why the sport is so much more, well, civilized than baseball.

Chinese Phrasebook

As in Vancouver, you will no doubt be bowled over by the diversity of a place you may have thought was only lily-white. Don't shy away from it. Instead, celebrate the diversity here, and dive in while you have the chance.

Umbrella

Although Victoria proclaims to be British Columbia's sunniest spot, that's not saying much. Sure, the "rain shadow" of the Lions Mountains keeps out a little rain. But it's still soggy as heck for much of the year. Don't forget the umbrella.

Chapter 24

Ten Celebrities You Didn't Realize Were from Vancouver

*V*ancouver rules! And that's why so many people you meet here — Aussies, Ontarians, transplanted U.S. citizens — have abandoned their homelands for this watery paradise. At times it seems as if nobody in Vancouver actually grew up in these parts. So who knew that a handful of famous people actually did.

Bryan Adams

Perhaps the wimpiest rocker in the history of pop music — wait a minute, is Michael Bolton still alive? — Bryan Adams hails from Vancouver's North Shore and reportedly worked as a burger carhop during his teen years.

Pamela Anderson

The former Mrs. Tommy Lee was just a Vancouver teenybopper at a football game when she got caught on screen in the stands. Soon she was the darling of Western Canadian beer ads; a local talent scout for a certain U.S. men's magazine — think bunny ears — got wind of her, and the rest is surgically enhanced history.

Raymond Burr

Old Ironsides, a Canuck? Say it ain't so! Well, it *is* so. The portly actor who so brilliantly portrayed both Ironsides and Perry Mason — and, I'll be honest, I occasionally thought they were the same guy, but that's another matter — hailed from New Westminster, a Vancouver 'burb now but actually a fairly old part of the city just east of downtown. He passed away in 1993 but remains a solid television presence thanks to the magic of cable reruns.

Douglas Coupland

Okay, that one was easy. Lots of people know that the guy who coined the term *Generation X* came up with it while hanging out among Vancouver's sizable, suitably alienated slacker population. For a time, during the height of his fame, he even kept working a regular shift at the Duthie's bookstore.

James Doohan

I bet you that 99 out of 100 people who've seen *Star Trek* thought the actor who played chief engineer "Scottie" was actually from Scotland. Wrong! He's from good old Vancouver, and for a bit part he sure made a pretty good career out of it, didn't he?

Paul Kariya

This one requires sports knowledge, but if you're Canadian you'll have known about this guy ten years ago. Hockey is the national sport up here — actually, it's more like the national religion — and the Asian-Canadian Kariya's exploits as a young Vancouver sharpshooter on skates were legend long before he became a star in our national spotlight. He may be little, but he sure can skate and score, as he demonstrated with both the University of Maine Black Bears and then the Anaheim Mighty Ducks.

Carrie-Ann Moss

Hip movie buffs will likely recognize the name of the young, up-and-coming actress who made a splash in the futuristic hit film *The Matrix*. Moss was born and raised in Vancouver. Rumor has it, she'll star in two sequels to the movie that made her famous.

Jason Priestley

Yep, the "big" — which is not necessarily equal to "talented" — names just keep coming. The former *Beverly Hills 90210* heartthrob, now said to be doing other projects, has no detectable accent. Still, yes, he's from Vancouver.

And More. . .

And, finally, a cheer for all the rest — famous folks who weren't born in Vancouver or on Vancouver Island, but spent significant time here — everyone from members of the Spandex-rocker band **Loverboy** to scary black-and-white-era actor **Boris Karloff.**

Appendix

Quick Concierge

• •

Fast Facts: Vancouver

AAA

The British Columbia affiliate of AAA, known as BCAA, has an office on the West Side at 999 West Broadway (☎ 604-268-5600) open weekdays 9 a.m.–5:30 p.m. and Saturdays 9 a.m.–5 p.m. Members of AAA can pick up maps, tour books, and traveler's checks at no charge; they can also make travel arrangements here (☎ 604-268-5622). Emergency road service and towing (☎ 604-293-2222) are also free for certain members.

American Express

The main office is located on the ground floor of the Park Place Building at 666 Burrard Street (☎ 604-669-2813). Open hours: Monday–Friday 8 a.m.–5:30 p.m., Saturday 10 a.m.–4 p.m. AMEX cardholders may cash traveler's checks and pick up mail (envelopes only); there's also a travel agency. For lost or stolen credit cards, call ☎ 800-668-2639. For lost or stolen traveler's checks, call ☎ 800-221-7282. A second AMEX office is downtown at 674 Granville Street, corner of Georgia (☎ 604-687-7688), on the fourth floor of the The Bay department store. Hours are Monday–Friday 8:30 a.m.–4:30 p.m.

Area Code

The telephone area code for the Greater Vancouver area and Whistler is **604**.

ATMs

The most common places to find a major bank's machine are the major shopping and business districts, including Robson, Denman, Davie, Granville, and West Georgia Streets and Gastown. Major banks in Canada don't charge a user fee if you're not an account holder. But make sure the network logo on the back of your card matches that of the machine; Cirrus ☎ 800-424-7787 and Plus ☎ 800-843-7587 can both tell you which ATMs work with cards in their respective systems.

Baby-sitters

Most hotels either have someone on staff who looks after children, or can make arrangements to care for your child — just be certain to advise them of your child's special needs well in advance. If you stay somewhere that doesn't happen to provide this service, try one of the following child sitting services:

Kids Included (☎ 604-803-3337) at 5450 Ash Street in Kitsilano minds children and keeps them entertained by taking them on trips or preparing special programs.

Moppet Minders (☎ 604-942-8167), another option, is at 1075 Dolphin Street in Coquitlam — far from downtown.

Cribs & Carriages (☎ 604-988-2742) rents items like a car seat or crib, and delivers them to your hotel, though many hotels may have these items on hand free of charge — ask first.

Camera Repair

Lens & Shutter (☎ 604-684-4422), on the lower level of the Pacific Centre at 700 Dunsmuir Street, provides repairs, supplies, and 1-hour film processing. Another branch is in Kitsilano at 2912 West Broadway (☎ 604-736-3461).

Leo's Camera Supply (☎ 604-685-5331), downtown at 1055 Granville Street, does repair and has supplies.

For less expensive supplies, film, and processing, pharmacies such as the ubiquitous Shopper's Drug Mart (☎ 800-363-1020) or London Drug (☎ 604-272-7645) are usually well-stocked. Each has plenty of branches around town.

Convention Center

The Vancouver Convention & Exhibition Centre (☎ 604-689-8232; Internet: www.canconex.com) is located at 999 Canada Place, the building with the distinctive white "sails" atop it.

Credit Cards

For lost or stolen cards, contact the following: Visa (☎ 800-847-2911), MasterCard (☎ 800-307-7309), or American Express (☎ 800-668-2639).

Currency Exchanges

The following exchanges are in Vancouver: American Express, 666 Burrard Street (☎ 604-669-2813); Custom House Currency Exchange, 375 Water Street, Gastown (☎ 604-482-6007; Internet: www.customhouse.com); Thomas Cook Foreign Exchange, 999 Canada Place, Suite #130 (☎ 604-641-1229) and 777 Dunsmuir Street, in Pacific Centre (☎ 604-687-6111); Vancouver Bouillon and Currency Exchange, 402 Hornby Street (☎ 604-685-1008); and Money Mart, 1195 Davie Street (☎ 604-606-9555).

Customs

Canada Customs & Revenue (☎ 604-666-0545) and U.S. Customs (☎ 604-278-1825), both located at Vancouver International Airport.

Dentists

For dental emergencies, call ☎ 604-736-3621 to locate a dentist nearest you. Walk-in dental care is provided by Dentacare (☎ 604-669-6700) in the Bentall Centre at Dunsmuir and Burrard Streets; open Monday–Friday, 9 a.m.–5 p.m.

Doctors

All major hotels should either have a doctor on call, or be able to refer you to one.

Care Point Medical Centre, 1175 Denman Street (☎ 604-681-5338) and 1623 Commercial Drive (☎ 604-254-5554), offers walk-in services and accepts all major credit and debit cards. Open daily 9 a.m. –9 p.m.

Kits Medical Clinic, 2678 Broadway, Kitsilano (☎ 604-737-2699) is open Monday–Friday, 9 a.m.–5 p.m. (A doctor is also on call for emergencies during weekends and accepts cash payments).

Electricity

Canada's electrical outlets put out 110 volts AC (60Hz), same as those in the United States

Embassies and Consulates

You can find consolates at the following locations: U.S. Consulate, 1095 West Pender Street, downtown (☎ 604-685-4311); British Consulate, 1111 Melville Street (☎ 604-683-4421); and Australian Consulate, 888 Dunsmuir Street. The local Yellow Pages contain listings for other countries' consulates under the heading "Consulates & Other Foreign Government Representatives."

Emergencies

Dial ☎ 911 for all emergencies including fire, police, and ambulance.

For questions about possible poisons, dial ☎ 604-682-5050 or ☎ 604-682-2344.

Hospitals

The closest hospital to downtown is St. Paul's Hospital, 1081 Burrard Street (☎ 604-682-2344). You can find the city hospital, Vancouver General at 855 West 12th Street (☎ 604-875-4111), just south and east of the Granville Bridge.

Hotlines

For emotional distress, call the Crisis Centre ☎ 604-872-3311.

For sexual assault, call the Rape Crisis Centre ☎ 604-255-6344 or Rape Relief ☎ 604-872-8612.

If you see a crime happening, call Crime Stoppers ☎ 604-669-8477.

For animal emergencies, call the SPCA ☎ 604-879-7343.

For non-emergencies, dial ☎ 604-717-3321 for police, ☎ 604-665-6000 for fire, and ☎ 604-872-5151 for ambulance.

See also "Emergencies" earlier in this section.

Information

The Travel InfoCentre (☎ 604-683-2000; Internet: www.tourism-vancouver.org) is located near Canada Place on the Plaza Level in the Waterfront Centre at 200 Burrard Street. Summer hours are daily 8 a.m.–6 p.m. During the rest of the year, hours are Monday–Friday 8:30 a.m.–5 p.m. and Saturday 9 a.m.–5 p.m. You can call toll-free (☎ 800-663-6000) for information prior to your arrival.

Other Travel InfoCentres are locoated at Vancouver International Airport on the arrivals area on level 2 (open daily 6:30 a.m.–11:30 p.m) and at Granville Island, 1398 Cartwright Street (☎ 604-666-5784; open daily 9 a.m.–6 p.m. during the summer and closed Mondays the rest of the year).

Internet Access and Cyber Cafes

Most hotels have two-line telephones, and some have high-speed Internet access. Make sure to check the hotel's policy for in-room phone charges.

The Vancouver Public Library, 350 West Georgia Street (☎ 604-331-3600), dedicates three computer terminals to checking e-mail, free of charge. Users must sign up and wait in a (sometimes-long) line for 30 minutes of access. The library also has a Computer Lab (☎ 604-331-3685) on the seventh floor, which closes a half-hour before the library shuts down. Here you pay $2.50 per half-hour but there's no advance signup or limit. Bring photo identification and leave the disks at home. Library hours: Monday–Wednesday 10 a.m.–9 p.m., Thursday–Saturday 10 a.m.–6 p.m., Sundays October– April only 1–5 p.m.

Kinko's two Vancouver locations, 1900 West Broadway, Kitsilano (☎ 604-734-2679) and 789 West Pender Street, downtown (☎ 604-685-3338) offer 24-hour computer access.

Internet cafes are variable in quality, and I never recommend one as a first resort — the equipment is sometimes iffy, and you may have to order food or drink. But you can check the Web site www.cyberiacafe.net for a comprehensive listing of Vancouver locations. Here are at least two good options: Digital U Cyber Café, 1595 West Broadway, Kitsilano (☎ 604-731-1011) and Webster's Internet Café, 340 Robson Street, downtown (☎ 604-915-9327).

Liquor Laws

You must be 19 years old to legally drink in British Columbia. You can purchase spirits at government-controlled LCBC (Liquor Control British Columbia) stores, found throughout the city. To locate one near you, look in the Yellow Pages under the heading "Liquor Stores." Beer and wine are sold in restaurants, hotel lounges, taverns, and nightclubs as well as privately owned stores sporting a "Licensed Premises" sign on the door. LCBC stores are open Monday to Saturday from 10 a.m.–6 p.m., some until 11 p.m.

Mail

Stamps for mailing letters within Canada cost C46¢, letters to the US cost C55¢ and letters overseas cost C95¢.

The central post office, 349 West Georgia Street, corner of Homer (☎ 604-662-5722 is), is open weekdays 8 a.m.–5:30 p.m. You can also buy postage at any store with the red-and-white Canada Post logo, such as Shoppers Drug Marts, 1125 Davie Street (☎ 604-685-0246; open 24 hours); Denman Place Mall, 1020 Denman Street (☎ 604-669-8053, open until midnight) and 2302 West 4th Street, Kitsilano (☎ 604-732-1587, open 24 hours).

Another option is the Downtown Postal Outlet, 1014 Robson Street (☎ 604-684-4011), open Monday–Friday 9 a.m.–7 p.m. and Saturday 10 a.m.–5 p.m. Also check the Yellow Pages under "Postal Services" for additional locations, and ask at your hotel; some provide stamps or mailing services.

Maps

Maps of the city are available for free from the Travel InfoCentre (see "Information" earlier in this section). Maps are also in the Yellow Pages as well as in the free visitor's guides you find in your hotel room. You can purchase useful and more detailed street maps such as the *Greater Vancouver Streetwise Map Book* of Vancouver and the surrounding area at most gas stations and convenience and grocery stores. Bookstores such as Chapters, 788 Robson Street (☎ 604-682-4066), and Duthie Books, 2239 West 4th Street (☎ 604-732-5344), carry maps as well, or try bookstores dedicated entirely to travel such as Travel Bug, 2667 West Broadway, Kitsilano (☎ 604-737-1122), and International Travel Maps and Books, 552 Seymour Street (☎ 604-687-3320).

Newspapers/Magazines

For mainstream news, try the *Vancouver Sun* which is published Monday to Saturday and *The Province* published Sunday to Friday. You can find these at corner stores or newspaper boxes for which you need exact change. *The Globe and Mail* or *The National Post* keep you in the loop for Canada and world coverage as well. On Thursdays, you may also want to pick up the free *Georgia Straight* at any coffee house, grocery store, or on-street newspaper box for entertainment and dining recommendations.

Other publications include:

The Westender /Kitsilano News for a slice of community life found throughout the city at similar venues.

Of special interest to gays are the publications *Xtra West*, *Angles*, and *The Loop*.

Several newspapers represent different ethnic groups; the biggest Chinese newspaper is the *Sing Tao* . Other ethnic newspapers include *L'Eco d'Italia Marco Polo News*, *Kanada Kurier*, *El Contact Directo*, and *Charhdi Kala Punjabi Weekly*, serving the Italian, German, Spanish, and Punjabi communities, respectively, and can usually be found at newspaper kiosks or in the neighborhood that supports a large segment of that population.

Vancouver Magazine is a sophisticated journal of city life with an emphasis on the arts, dining, and entertainment.

Where Vancouver is a slick, advertising driven magazine that will most likely show up in your hotel room.

Besides the aforementioned bookstores, a good source for magazines is the Magpie Magazine Gallery, 1319 Commercial Drive (☎ 604-253-6666).

Pharmacies

Shoppers Drug Mart has several locations throughout the Greater Vancouver Region. Call ☎ 800-363-1020 for store locations. There are three in the downtown district: inside the Denman Place Mall at 1020 Denman Street ☎ 604-681-3411, open until midnight; inside the Pacific Centre at 700 West Georgia Street ☎ 604-683-0358; and at 1125 Davie Street ☎ 604-669-2424, open 24 hours.

Police

Dial ☎ **911** for emergencies.

For all other calls, dial ☎ 604-717-3321.

Radio Stations

CKNW, 980 AM covers news, weather, and sports. The National Public Radio equivalent in Canada is the CBC (Canadian Broadcasting Corporation); FM 105.7, also known as CBC Radio 2, which plays many different music styles (including plenty of classical) and adds a healthy supply of news, interviews, and arts discussions. For Top 40, try CKZZ at FM 95.3.

Restrooms

You can find clean restrooms in the following places: hotel lobbies; museums; the Public Markets (Granville Island, Robson Street, and Lonsdale Quay); malls including the Pacific Centre at 700 West Georgia Street and the Bentall Shopping Centre at 595 Burrard Street (on the ground level); supermarkets such as Safeway and Capers in Kitsilano; and department stores such as The Bay and Eaton's on Granville Street (restrooms normally located on upper floors).

Safety

For the most part, Vancouver is much safer than its U.S. counterparts, such as Seattle. However, walking around at night in the following neighborhoods is not advised: the red-light district near Richards and Seymour Streets, between Drake and Nelson; the area between Gastown and Chinatown called East Hastings; and the neighborhood around and south of Pacific Central Station.

Public transportation is enthusiastically embraced by locals. You may witness occasional episodes of foul language or inappropriate behavior while using the system. Bus drivers have been trained to remove any person who is causing discomfort to passengers.

Do not leave anything of value in your car or you may be a victim of a smash-and-grab — very prevalent east of Gastown. You should also never leave valuables in your hotel room.

Smoking

Despite tight city anti-smoking laws, people continue to smoke — only not in public areas.

Bars seem to be the only place where you can light up without hassle, and hotels often have several floors reserved for non-smokers. Always check signs before you light up; Vancouver residents are quite sensitive about their right not to breathe smoke, and they won't hesitate to speak up about it.

Taxes

There is a 7% Provincial Sales Tax (PST) on everything except food, restaurant meals, or children's apparel. There is also a General Sales Tax (GST) of 7% levied by the federal government on everything but alcohol, which is subject to a 10% tax. Hotels charge an additional 10% lodging tax. The GST may be refunded to you if you fill out the paper work properly and submit your original receipts; however, you won't be refunded on any purchases concerning car rentals, parking, restaurant meals, tobacco, or alcohol, and you must spend a certain minimum amount abroad in order to collect the refund. You can pick up a tax refund application from your hotel or the Travel InfoCentres.

Taxis

Taxis line up for fares at downtown hotels. You can also call a taxi company directly and have a ride within 5 to 10 minutes, but may have to wait longer when it's raining. Options include: Black Top & Checker Cabs (☎ 800-494-1111 or 604-731-1111) or Vancouver Taxi (☎ 800-871-8294 or 604-255-5111), which has wheelchair-accessible cabs.

Telephone

Pay phones are usually located in glass telephone booths in grocery stores, hotel lobbies, or on the street. To call, insert C25¢ in the slot, wait for a dial tone, and dial your local number. Most phones also take pre-paid phone cards that can be purchased at postal outlets, pharmacies, and even tourist information offices. Local phone calls made from the phone in your hotel room can cost up to $1 or more *per call,* so check with your hotel on their policy. Call AT&T (☎ 800-575-2222, Sprint (☎ 800-877-8000), or MCI (☎ 800-950-1022) for operator assistance.

Time Zone

Vancouver is in the Pacific time zone, the same one as Los Angeles and Seattle. Daylight saving time (one hour ahead) is observed from April to October.

Transit Information

Call ☎ 604-521-0400 for schedule and other information.

Weather Updates

For weather, call Talking Yellow Pages (☎ 604-299-9000) and punch extension #3501.

Or dial ☎ 604-664-9010 or ☎ 604-664-9032 for weather updates from another service.

For ski reports, dial ☎ 604-687-7507 for Whistler/Blackcomb or ☎ 604-419-7669 for Cypress Mountain ski area.

On the Internet, the Web sites www.cnn.com, www.weather.com and www.weatheroffice.com provide free Vancouver forecasts.

Fast Facts: Victoria

AAA

The British Columbia affiliate, BCAA, has an office at 1075 Pandora Street (☎ 250-389-6700) open Monday–Saturday, 9 a.m.–5 p.m. Members of AAA can pick up maps, tour books, and traveler's checks at no charge; they can also make travel arrangements here or by calling ☎ 250-382-1221. The emergency road service telephone number is ☎ 800-222-4357.

American Express

The American Express office, 1213 Douglas Street (☎ 250-385-8731) is open Monday–Friday, 8:30 a.m.–5:30 p.m., Saturdays 10 a.m.–4 p.m. AMEX cardholders may cash traveler's checks and pick up mail (envelopes only); they also have a travel agency here. For lost or stolen credit cards, call ☎ 800-668-2639. For lost or stolen traveler's checks, call ☎ 800-221-7282.

Area Code

The area code for Victoria, Vancouver Island, and the Gulf Islands is **250.**

ATMs

You can find ATM services provided by major banks in the heart of downtown and throughout the suburban areas. They're most common along Douglas and Yates Streets, including those inside Royal Bank, 1079 Douglas (☎ 250-356-4500); Scotia Bank, 702 Yates (☎ 250-953-5400); Bank of Montréal, 1225 Douglas (☎ 250-389-2400); and Toronto Dominion, 1080 Douglas (☎ 250-356-4018).

Baby-sitters

Most hotels either have someone on staff who looks after children, or can make arrangements to care for your child — just be certain to advise them of your child's special needs well in advance. If you're staying somewhere that doesn't happen to provide this service, try one of the following child sitting services: Island Nannies (☎ 250-655-8831) or Wee Watch Private Home Daycare (☎ 250-382-5437). Little Bear Baby Equipment & Accessories (☎ 250-598-1309) rents items like car seats and cribs and delivers them to your hotel, though many hotels may have these items on hand free of charge — ask first.

Camera Repair

Lens & Shutter, 615 Fort Street (☎ 250-383-7443), provides one-hour film processing, repairs, and supplies. As does Broad Street Camera & Repairs, 1309 Broad Street (☎ 250-384-5510 or 250-384-5480).

Convention Center

The Victoria Conference Center, 720 Douglas Street (☎ 250-361-1000), is attached to The Empress hotel.

Credit Cards

For lost or stolen cards, contact the following: Visa (☎ 800-847-2911), MasterCard (☎ 800-307-7309), or American Express (☎ 800-668-2639).

Customs

Canada Customs & Revenue (☎ 800-461-9999 or 250-363-3531) is located at 816 Government Street; the closest U.S. Customs office (☎ 604-278-1825) is located at Vancouver International Airport.

Currency Exchanges

The following exchanges are in Victoria: American Express, 1213 Douglas (☎ 250-385-8731); Calforex, 724 Douglas Street (☎ 250-384-6631); Custom House Currency Exchange ☎ 250-389-6007, with locations at 815 Wharf Street, Bastion Square, Eaton Centre, and the airport, among others;

Money Mart, 1720 Douglas Street (☎ 250-386-3535), which charges high commissions; and Thomas Cook, 1001 Douglas Street, Suite G-3 (☎ 250-385-0088).

Dentists

Dentists Emergency Referral Service, 1964 Fort Street (☎ 250-595-3377), recommends emergency on-call help.

Another option is Cresta Dental Care, 3170 Tillicum Road (☎ 250-384-7711), in the Tillicum Mall (follow Douglas Street 2.5 miles north away from town and turn left on Tillicum) provides walk-in service Monday–Friday, 8 a.m.–9 p.m., Saturday 9 a.m.–5 p.m. and Sundays 11 a.m.–5 p.m.

Doctors

All major hotels should either have a doctor on call, or be able to refer you to one. Medical clinics include:

James Bay Medical Treatment Centre, 230 Menzies Street (☎ 250-388-9934), open Monday–Friday 9 a.m.–6 p.m., Saturdays and holidays 10 a.m.–4 p.m.

Mayfair Walk-in Clinic, 3147 Douglas Street (☎ 250-383-9898), open Monday–Friday 9 a.m.–5 p.m.

Electricity

Canada's electrical outlets put out 110 volts AC (60Hz), same as those in the United States.

Embassies and Consulates

Embassies and consulates are located in Vancouver. See "Fast Facts: Vancouver," earlier in the chapter.

Emergencies

Dial ☎ 911 for all emergencies including fire, police, and ambulance.

For questions about possible poisons, dial ☎ 800-567-8911.

Hospitals

The closest hospitals to downtown are Royal Jubilee Hospital, 1900 Fort Street (☎ 250-370-8000), 2 miles east of downtown, almost in Oak Bay; and Victoria General Hospital, 1 Hospital Way (☎ 250-727-4212), follow Douglas Street north out of town until it becomes Highway 1 (the hospital exit is about 3 miles from downtown).

Hotlines

The following hotlines are available in Victoria:

Crime Stoppers (☎ 250-386-8477).

Emotional Crisis Center (☎ 250-386-6323).

Help Line for Children (☎ 250-310-1234).

Poison Control Center (☎ 800-567-8911).

Road conditions in B.C. (☎ (250)380-4997).

Royal Canadian Mounted Police (☎ 250-595-9211).

Sexual Assault center (☎ 250-838-3232).

SPCA (animals) (☎ 250-385-6521).

See also "Emergencies" earlier in this section.

Information

The Travel InfoCentre, 812 Wharf Street (☎ 250-953-2033), near The Empress hotel, is the main information office, open Monday–Friday 9 a.m.–5 p.m. A tourist office is also near the ferry terminal in Swartz Bay on Patricia Bay Highway.

Internet Access

The Greater Victoria Public Library, 735 Broughton Street (☎ 250-382-7241), provides 11 Internet terminals; you have to purchase a visitor's card for $5 which gets you two half-hour Internet sessions, and you receive $2 back when you turn the card in. The library is open Monday, Wednesday, Friday, and Saturday 9 a.m.–6 p.m. and Tuesday and Thursday 9 a.m.–9 p.m.

Web cruising and other business services can also be done at the following locations: Cyber Station of Victoria, 1113 Blanshard (☎ 250-386-4687), on the corner of Fort Street; J&L Copy Plus, 777 Fort Street (☎ 800-811-0333 or 250-386-3333); and Mocambo Coffee, 1028 Blanshard (☎ 250-384-4468).

Liquor Laws

You must be 19 years old to legally drink in British Columbia. See "Fast Facts: Vancouver," earlier in this chapter, for complete information.

Mail

Stamps for mailing letters within Canada cost C46¢, letters to the United States cost C55¢ and letters overseas cost C95¢.

The central post office is located at 714 Yates Street (☎ 250-953-1352); a smaller branch is located at 1625 Fort Street (☎ 250-595-2552).

A postal desk is also located at Shopper's Drug Mart, 1222 Douglas Street (☎ 250-381-4321), as well at other suburban locations; call ☎ 800-363-1020 for store locations. Many other postal outlets are listed in the Yellow Pages under the heading "Postal Services." Also ask at your hotel desk if they provide stamps or mailing services.

Maps

Maps of the city are available for free from the Travel InfoCentre (see "Information," earlier in this section). Maps are also in the beginning sections of the Yellow Pages as well as in the free visitor's guides you find in your hotel room. Bookstores stocking maps include Chapters, 1212 Douglas Street (☎ 250-380-9009), and Munro's Books, 1108 Government Street (☎ 888- 243-2464 or 250-382-2464).

Newspapers/Magazines

For Victoria's daily news, check out the *Times Colonist.* For arts and entertainment, the alternative newspaper, *Monday Magazine,* comes out on Thursdays and can be found around town at the Travel InfoCentre, grocery stores, restaurants, and elsewhere. *The Globe and Mail* or *The National Post* keep you in the loop for Canadian and world coverage as well. Some hotels include delivery of a daily newspaper in the room rate. You can purchase newspapers and magazines at any grocery or convenience store, pharmacy, or gas station.

Pharmacies

McGill & Orme, 649 Fort Street (☎ 250-384-1195), corner of Broad, is open Monday–Saturday 9 a.m.–6 p.m., Sunday noon to 4 p.m.

Shopper's Drug Mart is ubiquitous; one handy location is at 1222 Douglas Street (☎ 250-381-4321) open Monday–Friday 7 a.m.–8 p.m., Saturday 9 a.m.–7 p.m., and Sunday 9 a.m.–6 p.m.

Police

Dial ☎ **911** for emergencies.

For all other calls, dial the Victoria City Police at ☎ 250-995-7654.

Radio Stations

The National Public Radio equivalent in Canada is the CBC (Canadian Broadcasting Corporation) and can be found at 90.5 FM for news, arts, and weather. CFAX, another news and sports source, is found at 1070 AM. For alternative music programming, tune in to CFUV, the University of Victoria's radio station at 102.0 FM.

Rest Rooms

Hotel lobbies offer reliable rest rooms, as does the Greater Victoria Public Library, 735 Broughton Street (☎ 250-382-7241), and bars, museums, restaurants, and service stations in town.

Safety

There's very little crime in Victoria of any sort — the occasional car break-in is about the worst of it. Of course, take the same care you would in any city: Avoid uncrowded and unlit areas at night and do not leave valuables in your car.

Smoking

Despite tight anti-smoking laws, people in Victoria continue to smoke — only not in public areas. Bars seem to be the only place where you can light up without hassle, and hotels often have several floors reserved for non-smokers. Always check signs before you light up.

Taxes

For complete tax information, see "Fast Facts: Vancouver."

Taxis

Call ahead for taxis as you can't often find them cruising the streets. Popular companies include: Blue Bird Cabs (☎ 800-665-7055 or 250-382-1111) and Empress Taxi (☎ 800-808-6881 or 250-381-2222), which has some wheelchair-accessible cars.

Telephone

See "Fast Facts: Vancouver," for complete information.

Time Zone

Victoria is in the Pacific time zone, the same one as Los Angeles and Seattle. Daylight saving time (one hour ahead) is observed from April to October.

Transit Information

Call the BC Transit Bus Line (☎ 250-382-6161 or TTY 250-995-5622) for schedule information. To arrange transportation for wheelchair users or senior citizens, call "handyDART" (☎ 250-727-7811) two days in advance; they can transport regular wheelchairs but not motorized scooters. Service is provided within Victoria and to some outlying communities.

Weather

For general weather reports, call ☎ 250-953-9000 and listen to the menu options for the city you want; Victoria is extension #3502. For marine conditions, call ☎ 250-656-7515. You can also choose to pay for personal weather forecasts provided by Environment Canada. The charge is C$2.99 per minute at ☎ 900-565-5555.

On the Internet, the Web sites www.cnn.com, www.weather.com and www.weatheroffice.com provide free Victoria forecasts.

Toll-Free Numbers and Web Sites

Major carriers flying into Vancouver International Airport

Air Canada
☎ 800-661-3936
www.aircanada.com

Air New Zealand
☎ 800-262-1234
www.airnz.com

Alaska Airlines
☎ 800-252-7522
www.alaskaair.com

American Airlines
☎ 800-433-7300
www.aa.com

British Airways
☎ 800-247-9297
www.british-airways.com

Canada3000
☎ 1-877-359-2263
www.canada3000.com

Cathay Pacific
☎ 800-233-2742
www.cathay-pacific.com

Continental
☎ 800-231-0856
www.continental.com

Japan Air Lines
☎ 800-525-3663

KLM/Northwest
☎ 800-447-4747
www.nwa.com

Korean Air
☎ 800-438-5000

Lufthansa
☎ 800-645-3880
www.lufthansa.com

Qantas
☎ 800-227-4500
www.qantas.com

Singapore Airlines
☎ 800-742-3333

TWA
☎ 800-892-4141
www.twa.com

United
☎ 800-241-6522
www.ual.com

Major carriers flying into Victoria International Airport

Air Canada B.C. Connector
☎ 800-663-3721 or 250-360-9074
www.aircanada.com

Air New Zealand
☎ 800-262-1234
www.airnz.com

British Airways
☎ 800-247-9297
www.british-airways.com

Canada3000
☎ 1-877-359-2263 or 416-679-3590
www.canada3000.com.

Delta
☎ 800-221-1212
www.delta-air.com

Qantas
☎ 800-227-4500
www.qantas.com

Reno Air
☎ 800-736-6147
www.renoair.com

Car rental agencies

Alamo
☎ 800-327-9633
www.goalamo.com

Avis
☎ 800-831-2874
☎ 800-TRY-AVIS in Canada
www.avis.com

Budget
☎ 800-527-0700
www.budgetrentacar.com

Discount
☎ 800-263-2355
www.discountcar.com

Dollar
☎ 800-800-4000
www.dollar.com

Enterprise
☎ 800-325-8007
www.enterprise.com

Hertz
☎ 800-654-3131
www.hertz.com

Lo Cost Rent A Car
☎ 800-986-1266
www.locost.com

National
☎ 800-CAR-RENT
www.nationalcar.com

Rent-A-Wreck
☎ 800-535-1391
rent-a-wreck.com

Thrifty
☎ 800-847-4389
www.thrifty.com

Major hotel and motel chains

Best Western International
☎ 800-528-1234
www.bestwestern.com

Clarion Hotels
☎ 800-CLARION
www.hotelchoice.com

Comfort Inns
☎ 800-228-5150
www.hotelchoice.com

Days Inn
☎ 800-325-2525
www.daysinn.com

Fairfield Inn by Marriott
☎ 800-228-2800
www.fairfieldinn.com

Hampton Inn
☎ 800-HAMPTON
www.hampton-inn.com

Hilton Hotels
☎ 800-HILTONS
www.hilton.com

Holiday Inn
☎ 800-HOLIDAY
www.basshotels.com

Howard Johnson
☎ 800-654-2000
www.hojo.com

Hyatt Hotels & Resorts
☎ 800-228-9000
www.hyatt.com

ITT Sheraton
☎ 800-325-3535
www.sheraton.com

Quality Inns
☎ 800-228-5151
www.hotelchoice.com

Radisson Hotels International
☎ 800-333-3333
www.radisson.com

Ramada Inns
☎ 800-2-RAMADA
www.ramada.com

Residence Inn by Marriott
☎ 800-331-3131
www.residenceinn.com

Super 8 Motels
☎ 800-800-8000
www.super8motels.com

Travelodge
☎ 800-255-3050
www.travelodge.com

Wyndham Hotels and Resorts
☎ 800-822-4200
www.wyndham.com

Where to Get More Information

I like to think that you'll find most of what you need between the covers of this book, but if you're craving more, that's okay by me. To get more information about Vancouver and Victoria, contacting the respective tourism offices, all of which are exceptionally helpful, usually works best. Here's the contact info:

Greater Vancouver Convention and Visitors Bureau

200 Burrard St. #210
Vancouver, BC V6C 3L6
☎ 604-682-2222; Fax: 604-682-1717

Tourism Association of Vancouver Island

45 Bastion Square #302
Victoria, BC V8W 1J1
☎ 250-382-3551

Tourism British Columbia

Box 9830 Stn. Prov. Government
Victoria, BC VW8 9W5
☎ 800-663-6000

Tourism Victoria

31 Bastion Square, 4th Floor
Victoria, BC V8W 1J1
☎ 250-414-6999; Fax: 250-361-9733

Vancouver Tourist InfoCentre

Plaza Level, 200 Burrard St.
Vancouver, BC V6C 3L6
☎ 604-682-6839

Victoria Visitor InfoCentre

812 Wharf Street
Victoria, BC V8W 1T3
☎ 800-663-3883 or 250-953-2033;
Fax: 250-382-6539

If you're Web-wise, you can explore the following Internet sites while planning your trip:

- ✔ www.hellobc.com (BC Tourism)
- ✔ www.tourismvancouver.com (Tourism Vancouver)
- ✔ www.city.vancouver.bc.ca (official Vancouver city page)
- ✔ www.tourismvictoria.com (Tourism Victoria)
- ✔ www.city.victoria.bc.ca (official Victoria city page)
- ✔ www.travel.victoria.bc.ca (travel listings)
- ✔ www.gov.bc.ca (BC Government information)
- ✔ www.theweathernetwork.com (Canadian weather information)
- ✔ www.crd.bc.ca (provincial parks office)
- ✔ www.gulfislands.com (Gulf Islands tourism)
- ✔ www.tourismwhistler.com (Whistler tourism)

One book worth checking out is *Frommer's Vancouver & Victoria* by Shawn Blore, an easy-to-use guide; it provides good listings of nightlife, accommodations, and dining choices for the two cities. For additional city information, try clicking onto the following Web sites:

- ✔ **CitySearch** (www.CitySearch.com) offers event listings for Vancouver through a parternship with local content provider www.vancouverplus.ca.
- ✔ **Digital City** (www.digitalcity.com), run by America Online, is a somewhat fluffy but still useful service that can get you oriented in Vancouver and Victoria.

✔ **The B.C. Yellow Pages** (www.bcyellowpages.com/cityscene) lists restaurants, nightclubs, city events, shops, and sports.

✔ **Where Vancouver** (www.wheremags.com), the magazine voted most likely to end up in your hotel room, lists rather sanitized but useful city information.

Several of the local newspapers also maintain free Web sites where you can read news and get some events listings. These include

✔ **www.vancouversun.com** (*Vancouver Sun,* a daily, city newspaper)

✔ **www.vancouverprovince.com** (*Vancouver Province,* a daily, city newspaper)

✔ **www.straight.com** (*Georgia Straight,* weekly Vancouver newspaper)

✔ **www.monday.com** (*Monday Magazine,* weekly Victoria newspaper)

Finally, if you need transit information before you leave home, surf over to these coordinates:

✔ **www.translink.bc.ca** (Vancouver transit)

✔ **www.transitbc.com** (Victoria transit)

✔ **www.bcferries.bc.ca** (all ferries)

✔ **www.yvr.ca** (Vancouver International Airport)

✔ **www.cyyj.ca** (Victoria International Airport)

✔ **www.viarail.ca** (Canadian national train network)

✔ **www.greyhound.ca** (Canadian arm of Greyhound bus service)

Making Dollars and Sense of It

Expense	Amount
Airfare	
Car Rental	
Lodging	
Parking	
Breakfast	
Lunch	
Dinner	
Babysitting	
Attractions	
Transportation	
Souvenirs	
Tips	
Grand Total	

Notes

Fare Game: Choosing an Airline

Travel Agency:_____ Phone:_____

Agent's Name:_____ Quoted Fare:_____

Departure Schedule & Flight Information

Airline:_____ Airport:_____

Flight #:_____ Date:_____ Time:_____ a.m./p.m.

Arrives in:_____ Time:_____ a.m./p.m.

Connecting Flight (if any)

Amount of time between flights:_____ hours/mins

Airline:_____ Airport:_____

Flight #:_____ Date:_____ Time:_____ a.m./p.m.

Arrives in:_____ Time:_____ a.m./p.m.

Return Trip Schedule & Flight Information

Airline:_____ Airport:_____

Flight #:_____ Date:_____ Time:_____ a.m./p.m.

Arrives in:_____ Time:_____ a.m./p.m.

Connecting Flight (if any)

Amount of time between flights:_____ hours/mins

Airline:_____ Airport:_____

Flight #:_____ Date:_____ Time:_____ a.m./p.m.

Arrives in:_____ Time:_____ a.m./p.m.

Notes

Sweet Dreams: Choosing Your Hotel

Enter the hotels where you'd prefer to stay based on location and price. Then use the
worksheet below to plan your itinerary.

Hotel	Location	Price per night

Menus & Venues

Enter the restaurants where you'd most like to dine. Then use the worksheet below to plan your itinerary.

Name	Address/Phone	Cuisine/Price

Places to Go, People to See, Things to Do

Enter the attractions you would most like to see. Then use the worksheet below to plan your itinerary.

Attractions	Amount of time you expect to spend there	Best day and time to go

Going "My" Way

Itinerary #1

- ☐ _____
- ☐ _____
- ☐ _____
- ☐ _____

Itinerary #2

- ☐ _____
- ☐ _____
- ☐ _____
- ☐ _____

Itinerary #3

- ☐ _____
- ☐ _____
- ☐ _____
- ☐ _____

Itinerary #4

- ☐ _____
- ☐ _____
- ☐ _____
- ☐ _____

Itinerary #5

- ☐ _____
- ☐ _____
- ☐ _____
- ☐ _____

Itinerary #6

- ☐ _____
- ☐ _____
- ☐ _____
- ☐ _____

Itinerary #7

- ☐ _____
- ☐ _____
- ☐ _____
- ☐ _____

Itinerary #8

- ☐ _____
- ☐ _____
- ☐ _____
- ☐ _____

Itinerary #9

- ☐ _____
- ☐ _____
- ☐ _____
- ☐ _____

Itinerary #10

- ☐ _____
- ☐ _____
- ☐ _____
- ☐ _____

Notes

Notes

Notes

Notes

Notes

Index

health insurance, 71–72
helicopters, 54, 224
Helijet, 54, 224
Henry Birk & Sons, 190
Heritage Tours, 280
Hermann's Jazz Club, 297
Hertz, 36, 225, 327
Highway 17, 224, 226
Highway 99, 224
hiking, 214, 306. *See also* walking tours
Hill's Indian Crafts, 289
Hill's Native Art, 11, 192
HM Customs & Excise, 71
hockey, 79
Holt Renfrew, 186
Homers, 208
Hong Kong Bank of Canada, 30
Horizon Air, 54
horse-drawn tours, 169, 280
Horseshoe Bay, 217, 219
Horticulture Centre of the Pacific, 277
hospitals, 318, 323
Hot Jazz Society, 201
hotels. *See* accommodations;
    Accommodations Index
House of Hewhiwus, 218
Howe Sound, 162, 179
Howe Sound Inn and Brewing
    Company, 217
Hudson's Bay Company ("The Bay"),
    11, 12, 185, 278, 287
Hush, 39

• I •

Ice House, 298
IMAX theaters, 161, 272, 277
immigration, 69–70. *See also* customs
Indian Arm, 171
Infinity Travel Concepts, 34
Inner Harbor
    accommodations, 61–62, 228,
        235–240, 243–246
    basic description of, 228
    nightlife, 300–301
    shopping, 288
    sightseeing, 269–272, 274–277
    restaurants, 253–254, 258–259, 262
InnSite, 67

insurance
    car rental, 74–75
    liability, 74–75
    medical, 71–72
    travel, 71–72
Interac, 30
International Jazz Fest, 297
International Travel Maps and
    Books, 190
International Wine Festival, 19
Internet. *See also* Web sites
    access at hotels, 319
    cafes, 319, 324
Intrepid Theatre Company, 302
Inuit Gallery, 192
Irish Heather, 204
Irish Linen Stores, 289
Island Nannies, 322

• J •

James Bay, 225, 323
    accommodations, 63, 228, 240,
        246, 299
    basic description of, 228
    sightseeing, 278
James Bay Bicycle Works, 229
James Bay Medical Treatment
    Centre, 323
James Bay Tearoom, 77, 281
James Bay Trading Company, 289
Japan Air Lines, 326
jazz
    festivals, 20, 297
    information hotline, 76, 201
    in Vancouver, 20, 76, 201–202
    in Victoria, 297
Jefferies & Co., 291
Jericho Beach, 154–155, 178
Jet Lounge, 298
jewelry, 193, 195, 293
Joe Fortes (club), 206
Joe's Café, 10, 144
Juice Zone, 143
Juicy Lucy, 144

• K •

Kabuki Kabs, 280
Kariya, Paul, 314
Karloff, Boris, 315

• Z •

Zulu Records, 194

• *Accommodations Index* •

• *Restaurant Index* •

Notes

Notes

FOR DUMMIES
BOOK REGISTRATION

Register This Book and Win!

We want to hear from you!

Visit **dummies.com** to register this book and tell us how you liked it!

✔ Get entered in our monthly prize giveaway.

✔ Give us feedback about this book — tell us what you like best, what you like least, or maybe what you'd like to ask the author and us to change!

✔ Let us know any other *For Dummies* topics that interest you.

Your feedback helps us determine what books to publish, tells us what coverage to add as we revise our books, and lets us know whether we're meeting your needs as a *For Dummies* reader. You're our most valuable resource, and what you have to say is important to us!

Not on the Web yet? It's easy to get started with *Dummies 101: The Internet For Windows 98* or *The Internet For Dummies* at local retailers everywhere.

Or let us know what you think by sending us a letter at the following address:

For Dummies Book Registration
Dummies Press
10475 Crosspoint Blvd.
Indianapolis, IN 46256

...FOR DUMMIES ™

BESTSELLING
BOOK SERIES